Exhibit Marketing

Exhibit Marketing

A Success Guide for Managers

Edward A. Chapman, Jr.

Second Edition

McGraw-Hill, Inc.

New York   San Francisco   Washington, D.C.   Auckland   Bogotá
Caracas   Lisbon   London   Madrid   Mexico City   Milan
Montreal   New Delhi   San Juan   Singapore

Library of Congress Cataloging-in-Publication Data

Chapman, Edward A.
    Exhibit marketing : a success guide for managers / Edward A.
Chapman, Jr. — 2nd ed.
       p.   cm.
    Includes index
    ISBN 0-07-011232-0
    1. Exhibitions. 2. Marketing. I. Title.
T396.C43   1995
659.1'52—dc20   95-23276
                                           CIP

First Edition published with the subtitle *A Survival Guide for Managers.*

1 2 3 4 5 6 7 8 9 0 BKP/BKP 9 0 0 9 8 7 6 5

ISBN 0-07-011232-0

*The sponsoring editor for this book was David Conti, the editing supervisor
was Peggy Lamb, and the production supervisor was Pamela A. Pelton. It was
set in Palatino by Ron Painter of McGraw-Hill's Professional Book Group
composition unit.*

Printed and bound by Quebecor-Book Press

This book is printed on recycled, acid-free paper containing a
minimum of 50% recycled de-inked fiber.

Contents

23. International Business Culture, Language, and Practices   299

Preface

Exhibiting is like an iceberg. You see just a small bit. When it comes to exhibiting, what people first think about are booths and signs. They are certainly visisble. But that's just the tip. Hidden below the surface is, or should be, a marketing process. Each booth participation is like starting, operating, and then closing a business.

The closest parallels we sense are managing a political campaign, making a movie, writing a book, or landing a plane on an aircraft carrier. I've done all these things, and they are the same. Win and you know it. Lose and you'd best figure out why! The point? Grade yourself. The fun and challenge of exhibiting is that you can know right away!

Our first edition, published in the '80s, was based on a premise. Exhibitors, small and large, often think of a booth as the end-and-be-all. Plop it in a hall and the buyers will cascade down the aisle with checkbooks in hand. Or at least you won't let competitors steal a march! Fine, but that does not happen just because you are there, rose-in-teeth. Our premise remains.

We certainly do not ignore booths, signs, and all the rest of the tactical issues. Even if that is the only kind of help you are looking for you have made a good investment in this book.

The Management Process

However, our goal is more than glitter, glitz, and cost of producing an exhibit. The booth is a stage. We dwell on the strategic and tactical steps to make that stage deliver more return to you. This does not mean more work—just smarter work.

This New Edition

Fundamental management does not change quickly. However, its applications are dynamic. Budgets seem to go nowhere but down, but demands go up. The pace of change increases—new products, uses, markets, and so on.

Some years back phone companies and other communications outfits postured that video conferencing, video tape, E-mail and interactive-electronic-everything, would result in less need for face-to-face meeting. I was both a believer and professional purveyor of the concept at the time. It was poppycock. We explain why we were wrong in this book.

The decline of exhibiting was premature. It grows. Added to that, technology has made the exhibit marketing management process more cost-effective. In addition, markets are expanding and whole new industries are emerging—new shows and a global focus. It's exciting!

The reason for exhibit growth is value. There can be true return. But you have to know how to deal with what is under the surface of that iceberg tip. Helping yourself to more value, with ease, is our mission.

Edward A. Chapman, Jr.
Naples, Florida USA

Acknowledgments

When you write a trade book it helps to have experience in the field. Even with that, however, book writing is not like unzipping your mind and letting what's tucked away up there find its way to a piece of paper. People have to help. Were I to list the names of everyone who taught me all of what is tucked away in this book we would run out of ink.

Our first edition included a long list. Many were associates and teachers when I was an exhibit manager at the "old" New York Telephone Company and the "new" AT&T. They still count for me, but we restrict outselves now to those directly related to the new edition, which is far more than just an update.

These contributors include show manager Connie Akin, Mike Bandy at IEA, international freight expert Stephen Barry, David Bowie at the U.S. Commerce Department, and consultant Ed Jones. Allied Van Line's Ed Laub, corporate events manager Mary Jo Mendell from Nielsen Market Research, show manager Mike Muldoon, and Baylor University's Jeff Tanner make the list. We also must thank people from other nations. Among them we express thanks to Sylvia Phua at Pico Art Industries in Singapore. One who did more than most was Zhao Weiping in The People's Republic of China. He is an economist and General Manager of the Exhibition Department at the China International Exhibition Centre Company in Beijing. His thinking has been invaluable.

Other personal and professional friends helped. Margit Weisgal, my own company associate, is one. Events and exhibit manager Tom Fitzgerald from the Amdahl Corporation is another. I've known David Sable and his family for over 20 years. He was a longtime advertising

VIP with Young & Rubicam and now a VIP with Genesis Direct. As always, David, thanks. Exhibit designer and builder Joan Carol was very special. Her company's sketches appear but more important is her insight. Thank you, Joan.

Saved for almost last—old friend, computer genius, and gentleman Mitch Fink. He is always there and thoughtful. Then there is the notable, powerful political thinker, Mary Ann Fish. This is my third book. Mary Ann has been involved, behind the scenes, in all three. 'Nuff said?

First edition readers who are friends will remember that *Acknowledgments* concluded with thanks to my father, a distinguished librarian and academic author. He read and commented on every word of that manuscript before it went to McGraw-Hill. He kept saying, "Keep your ears open and mouth closed." He died between editions and did not get a crack at this manuscript. But if you find the book of value he gets a chunk of credit. It is dedicated to him.

Exhibit Marketing

PART 1
The Quick Fix

1

The Show: What's in It for You

Making money—creating value. That is what exhibit marketing is about. Or what it should be about. But managers think of it mostly as cost, dollars for flag-waving or simply for keeping competitors at bay. An article in the *Harvard Business Review* voiced large-company CEO attitudes about exhibiting, best summarized as a costly but unavoidable evil.[1] What amazes us is that it's not all that hard to "make a buck" with the help of an exhibit! It need not be instant gratification. However, we must at least project and measure practical value in the future.

Frankly, though, because of the way many organizations approach exhibiting, the cost rather than value, idea is rational. It emerges because companies don't plan to earn on their investment in the first place.

The exhibition industry's not-for-profit research and educational arm, the Trade Show Bureau (TSB), studied how often exhibiting objectives are established in advance. Among large and midsize companies, only half bothered writing down goals, even on the back of an envelope. Among those that at least scribbled something, half were satisfied with loosey-goosey, image-burnishing, self-serving statements more attuned to internal desire than marketing reality. ("We must show our commitment to customers." "We must position the company on the cutting edge.") Of the companies in the study only one-quarter set practical show goals that could be measured later to check progress.[2] An excuse, we'll guess, is that many of these outfits participate at the same shows year after year on autopilot, exhibiting just because it's expected, a tradition. But that does not get them off the hook. Instead of just worrying about dollars tossed around on faith, they should manage the process so that it earns a return.

Just Starting Out? Stay Right Here

In case you are like me and never read a book preface, what follows is a replay of our preface explanation of how this book is organized:

Part 1, "The Quick Fix," is for those just getting started and facing deadlines for that first show. It summarizes many subjects explored in greater depth later.

Part 2, "Planning to Manage Your Program," is for those who have been doing the job for a while and want to improve. Part 2 is also a wake-up call for top management.

Part 3, "Creating and Managing an Exhibit," fixes on key subjects from time management and booth picking to staff training.

Part 4, "The International Scene," takes a good look at key issues we face in the ever-emerging opportunity to exhibit and market overseas.

Part 5, "The Industry and Management," provides perspective and information on the industry, from who does what to how to *attend* a trade show.

If this is your first booth, these first three chapters (Part 1) will help you calm nightmares and start you on the way toward process management that makes sense, as well as help you make dollars and cents. The rest of Part 1 is a reference on what to explore as you refine what you want to accomplish later. *More experienced people should glance, too, as a refresher.*

Find Yourself among First-Timers

You face one of several scenarios. What were you told?

- "Over the years you've worked your way up in the company, and you know everybody. Coordinating exhibits is a new way for you to grow."

- "Just coming out of college, a big job for you is to learn what's going on in the company—and exhibit management is a great way to gain that understanding."

- "With staff reduction a reality and your long experience in the company, running our exhibits will be a great way to cap your career."

- "Belt-tightening is a way of life these days, and all we are asking is that you add this exhibit job to the rest of your duties." (Do it or you are dead.)

- "We only do a few shows a year, and you can add the work to your schedule without much difficulty, and you get to travel a bit." (That is all? Yeah.)

They never told you the travel included weekends. Fellow managers think you live the glamorous life, but that is only because they do not spend time in redundant hotels or airport-clumping. Nobody knows the pressure of getting the booth up and ready in the middle of chaos. They know little of the joys of a $4 hot dog lunch we call "a tube steak" from the stand on the edge of the floor during setup. Most important, few realize that if you do the job right, the show does not end with the closing bell, when you pack up the booth, gasp, and head for home one more time.

Red Flag Cautions

Getting the booth itself planned, moved, set up, torn down, and shipped back home can seem daunting, an end in itself. Yet that is the least of what is needed. We forget that the booth is just a stage. Most of the value we create comes from how that platform is used. That is where we must spend the time and energy in planning and execution.

Exhibiting Close to Home

When you have to go on the road to another city, or nation, it is instinctive to do some advance planning. Somehow that urgency does not emerge when it's a local event. We make decisions too late and planning gets sloppy.

Retail Exhibiting

Lots of local retailers appear at consumer shows in their communities. These are special-interest events: home and garden events, as well as antique, boat, vehicle, and sports gear expositions. We wave a big "red flag" for these exhibitors.[3] There are three reasons for us to fly the flag:

- Retailers drop the ball on booth design. Perhaps because expos are short-lived affairs, retailers pay far less attention to appearance than they do at their home shops. Yet they will meet many new people who will judge them, in part, on appearance.

- Retailers tend not to understand or accept show rules—setup ground rules and daily operations regulations. The result can be anarchy, the Balkans all over again.
- Many retail salespeople do not understand the difference between selling at the store and selling from a booth—especially the need to learn from visitors.

Though retail shows aim at special interests, they are also like Saturday afternoon at the mall. The difference is that there is less commitment required to stop at a booth, in contrast to stepping into a store. There is a need for more talk to help dealers sort out the serious.

Quick Fix Contents

Part 1 of this book is for first-time exhibit managers. In the following two chapters, you will find summary instructions covering the most important subjects:

- *The booth and graphics.* We outline options and suggest ground rules for small booths and signs and address related physical questions.
- *The exhibitor kit.* We discuss the information packet, with order forms, provided by show managers to exhibitors. What's hot and what's not?
- *Budgeting.* We provide a short-form budget to estimate costs.
- *Preshow promotion.* Promoting your booth in advance can really help. We provide suggestions on what can be executed quickly and inexpensively.
- *Tasks list.* What to do and when. We cover it.

There is more included in the three chapters of "The Quick Fix," but these summaries should get you through that first show in a position to prosper.

Person-to-Person Selling

This part of the book summarizes coverage of selling techniques at the booths. However, this is the one place where we suggest more. Face-to-face booth meeting is what exhibiting is all about and where you will win or lose.[4] So, besides these first three chapters, we ask that you also go through Chapter 18, "Exhibit Floor Selling." Your exhibit stage can come alive when you know how to trade information with your visitors.

2

The Three-Hour Planning Process

It should take just three hours to plan your first exhibit, including a half hour to read and make notes from the chapters included in "The Quick Fix." *Less, if you have experience.* Then roll it out! You will do fine and learn a lot about how to get better in the future. Work hard, but enjoy it.

Writing the Plan

Your three hours of planning will not be accomplished in one lump. That is why it is a very good idea to write down what you want to do—what can be done now and what can be done later. Here is a list of the elements that should be in your written plan:

- *Products and services.* What do you offer your customers? Write a list in priority order of what is most important to you at this time. You may end up offering a visitor something else, but effective exhibits emphasize what is most important at the time.

- *Top prospects.* With a view toward your most important offering, write profiles of the type of prospect or customer most meaningful to you. Profiles could be made up according to a certain classification such as the company's size or geographic area. Try to be realistic. Most of us want to supply everything we sell to a world market! Guide your thoughts by what truly can be accomplished in a year or two.

- *Show analysis.* Take a solid look at the audience, and don't hesitate to ask questions of show management. The entire visitor group is not often for you. It is far more likely that just a portion of those attending comprise your true target. (Because of time constraints, it is unlikely that you can reach everyone anyway, even within your bull's-eye target market. Don't worry about that. Just do as much as you can do.)

- *Goals and objectives.* Write a mission statement for the show that combines what you want with the interests of your audience.

- *Booth Plan.* Focus your signs and anything you might mail to prospects in advance on the emphasis points that reflect the characteristics of your bull's-eye target. Your text should not tell all; instead, it should pose questions of interest that can be answered as a result of a booth visit.

- *Literature.* Assemble a small quantity of the booklets, brochures, or catalogs you will want to have available at the event. Don't bring too many. It is far better to get the names of those interested and mail the items to them after the show is over. (Booths are places for conversation, not dispensing things.)

- *Work forms.* You will need lead and possibly order forms. In addition, you will want some office supplies at the show. The booth is an "office" as well as a display center.

- *Staff and training.* Determine the team size and skills required to work at the booth. In addition, plan the training that will be needed to make your people comfortable and effective.

- *Promotions.* Make plans for any advance mailings or extra events at the show, such as VIP meetings, hospitality, participation in seminars, and development of news releases for trade magazines.

- *Logistics.* In addition to planning the booth itself, you will need to plan for transportation as well as services at the exposition itself. Most of these items can be found in the instructions provided by the show manager in the "exhibitor kit."

- *Budget.* Prepare a cost estimate that you can track as you go along.

- *Schedule.* Create a work schedule to alert you when implementation plans should start and finish. Items that take longer to complete should be started first.

- *Follow-up and evaluation.* Determine, in the overall advance plan, how you will follow up on show results, such as leads and orders or requests for literature. Importantly, as well, make decisions on how you will evaluate your success, at least from a work production viewpoint.

This quick fix part of this book includes summary information to aid you in completing each of the written plan elements. More extensive coverage is given to each in other parts of this book. This list may seem daunting, but it is not. We try to make each job easy and quick.

Unless you are starting in a full-time professional exhibit management role, you have other things to do. If you are a start-up full-time professional you will have several events to plan at once. In either case the most important element in the written plan is the *schedule*. A solid work-start and completion calendar will allow you to blend work steps for an individual show with other work.

Setting Strategic Goals and Tactical Objectives

This is your most notable task. A clear set of goals and objectives will make the rest of the process easier. Most exhibit planners work with other people in their organizations. If you can get everyone in your company to agree on precisely what is to be accomplished, there will be far less "hip shooting," which often leads to extra work, higher cost, and lower ultimate achievement.

Strategic Show Mission

A show mission statement is different from a company mission statement. A company mission statement tends to be very broad, internally oriented, and even fuzzy to some outsiders. A show mission should combine the apparent interests of your target audience with the products or services that you want to emphasize at the show. For instance, a generic company mission might read, "Deliver market-driven products supported by services that are of value to customers, shareowners, and employees alike." In contrast, a hypothetical show mission could read, "Introduce our latest products to potential customers in the Midwest who are looking for a cost-saving, high-quality alternative to what they are using today."

The implementation of the show mission can lead to interesting, practical approaches. For instance, even if your company is at a national event, a booth sign might read, "Learn about our latest cost-saving products and our new Chicago office." That copy signals product advantage for everyone and alerts Midwest prospects to explore something new in service that is tailored to them.

Tactical Objectives

There are all manner of reasonable objectives. Even those wishy-washy, image-burnishing statements such as "enhancing our position in the market" are okay. You can introduce a new product or service or open up a new territory. For most, however, primary goals will include writing orders or gathering leads that can lead to future sales. As you think, consider the following:

- Contacting your current customers for new orders
- Prospecting to create relationships with new potential customers
- Developing enhanced or increased awareness of products and the company as a whole within the entire audience attending an event
- Learning more, which is perhaps the most important goal, about the industry you are serving and the specific issues that are important for your customers and prospects.

Number Goals

Some of your objectives can be enhanced with, "How much?" That is true, at least for work production at the show. By creating a number goal, you add a lot of discipline to the process; moreover, everyone likes a goal they can shoot for against which they can measure themselves:

- How many of your current customers do you want to meet each day?
- How many new people do you want to meet each day?
- How many orders do you want to write each day?
- How many leads do you want to take each day?
- How many press releases do you want to give out to the trade press?
- How many seminars do you want to attend for learning reasons?
- How many seminars do you want to participate in or deliver?

Gathering Facts

To help create a mission statement and specific goals, there are several sources you can count on, as described below. You may not need to do all that we suggest in the following checklist, but some of these sources are certainly appropriate.

Show Prospectus

The sales literature covering the show can be a valuable tool. It will provide at least some information in a number of different respects:

- The size and nature of the overall audience anticipated at the event
- An outline of educational programs
- Exhibitors who already plan to participate

As you read, you may find deficiencies. For instance, the audience promised will be based on last year's registration and a hope for this year. (If the show moves to a new venue each year, you should also anticipate a larger audience portion coming from the region where the show takes place this year.) Importantly, it may be that you have not been provided with audience estimates broken down by subgroups. Even at the most highly targeted event, you will find that everyone is not for you. There will be, instead, a special target for you within that overall audience.

When you look at audience data from the past show, ask yourself some other questions, too. Are the figures from an outside audit, or are they self-generated? Do the numbers include a breakdown among buyer delegates, exhibitor personnel, and others such as trade press? Or are they all lumped together? Some consumer shows are satisfied with a turnstile count. If so, ask the show manager to estimate the number of children and repeat visitors.

Write your questions, and call the show manager. Most are quite cooperative, and they will give you all the extra information they can. One manager for a very large show management organization told us, "We don't publish all the data we have because so few seem interested." Regardless, you will be able to gauge the level of show management professionalism on the basis of what you can learn.

Psychographic Profiles

"The profile of the customer audience can be expanded by studying the value system of customers," says Baylor University's Jeff Tanner.[1] He explains this relatively new area in consumer terms: "Demographics used to be pretty much restricted to things like age, sex, income, race, family size, and so on. Now we are trying to add information on customer value systems. For instance, among wealthy people, are your customers 'old money or new money'? Are your customers station wagon rich or mink coat rich? By adding a psychographic profile to other demographics, marketers are able to fine-tune strategies."

Companies can also be profiled from a psychographic angle. For example, there are different kinds of corporate cultures. A Seventh Avenue clothing manufacturer's culture is different from that of an insurance agency. Nike is different from Bethlehem Steel. Tanner points out that businesses have value systems in part derived from company culture and history.

For instance, are your best customers defensive- or offensive-minded? Do they signal needs to protect what they've got? Or are they more offensive-minded, more inclined to take risks? You can position your product to reflect customer outlooks.

Tanner illustrates by comparing two ads from the same company selling 800-number telephone service. One featured reliability and quick repair. It would best appeal to defensive companies who fear losing something. Another 800 ad covered only features and costs. That appeals to the offensive-minded. Who are your best customers? Where do they fit? Add this data to your profile, and your strategy will be improved. For instance, why are you exhibiting? If your first thought is, "We have to be there because our competitors are there," you may be operating from fear and have a defensive or protective view. Those who sell products to your company can position them in that context.

Attendee and Exhibitor Lists

The organizer should be able to provide a list of those who were at the last show, including both exhibitors and attendees. Most often these lists are available in a label format that you can use for a preshow mailing. You may have to sort the names to select only the true targets. Besides last year's lists, many show management groups will provide early-registration names for the upcoming event—perhaps one month in advance.

Other Exhibitors and Competitors

Most exhibit managers, even those working for competitors, are willing to share insights on the audience. Just avoid what might be proprietary information. Ask what these folks think about the audience and the educational programs.

Internal Sources

Talk with your own people—your sales and technical staff who have had experience at the show or in the industry. You can even poll your own customers to see if they plan to attend. If you do that, ask them *why they plan to be there*, and try to set up a meeting. The why is most important. That will provide you with show planning guidance.

Creating Number Goals

The process used to set numerical work production objectives is easy. For instance, you can count and even name your current customers who will attend the show. Try to arrange to see these people during quiet times. One idea is to meet with them at breakfast, where you can relax and have a longer meeting—far more than is possible in the hub-bub of the booth.

Prospecting Goals

There are several work production objectives you can select. Pick anything you can count. For most of us it boils down to sales leads for future follow-up. There are two types of leads. One is little more than an inquiry. The other, because of what you have learned in conversation, requires very serious follow-up. You can set goals for both.

Setting a prospecting goal is simple because you are dealing only with time, space, and people:

- How many people will be on duty at the booth? That depends on space. For instance, if your space is 10 feet, you will have two or three on duty. For a 20-foot space, figure five.

- How many hours will you be open for business? The exhibitor information kit will tell you. For instance, it may be a three-day show, 6 hours a day. That's a total of 18 hours.

  Note: Some hours may offer but light traffic. Typically, the last afternoon of an out-of-town show offers less because attendees are on their way to an airport. If so, deduct a couple of hours from the calculation that follows.

- Based on an average, each person on duty will meet about 10 people in an active traffic hour at the booth, including visitors who are not really interested. (The range is from 7 to 15, depending on the degree of the technical complexity of the products and services you offer.)[2]

- You cannot count booth contacts accurately. However, studies allow us to estimate the number of leads you will garner from contacts.[3] For planning purposes, estimate that 20 percent of the number of contacts estimated will result in leads. These leads include simple inquiries as well as serious leads that require follow-up after the show.

If, as an example, you estimate 16 hours that are active, and two people on duty, you will meet about 320 people. Your work production goal would be 64 leads of one type or another.

We focus on personal prospecting because the primary economic value of an exhibit is in low-cost, person-to-person contact. Trade Show Bureau reports cite the cost to make a personal call in a prospect's office in the $300 range including salary and expense. At a booth—$100 less.[4]

Awareness Development

Your booth, signs, products, and people will be seen by far more people than you can talk to. Thus, the general appearance and message clarity are very important. There are other factors that blend into reaching awareness development goals:

- Preshow promotion, including direct mail and advertising, creates awareness.
- Literature and show giveaways produce the same effect. But we urge caution in what and how much you hand out since it is far better to take names and mail literature after the show. As a rule of thumb, use 5 percent of the anticipated audience as a maximum for the number of brochures you bring to the event.
- News releases can be distributed covering new products or enhancements. These can help build awareness after the exposition.
- Presenting seminars, though they cannot be obviously sales oriented, will create appreciation and thus enhance company reputation.

Establishing Learning Objectives

There are three places to look for from which you can learn at a show:

1. The most important learning will come from your customers and prospects. There is a tendency for us to think only about what we want these people to learn from us, rather than considering what we can learn from them.
2. Other valuable sources of information are the seminars. Exhibitors who ignore chances to attend seminars are losing a big opportunity. You can gain a far better sense of what's important in the industry, and you may even identify people to try to meet.

3. Your competitor's exhibits are also important sources of information. One reason for exhibiting is to blunt competition. However, it is not enough simply to note the names of your competitors who are exhibiting. Take advantage of the opportunity to observe what they are trying to emphasize. Write down the text of booth signs. (Photography is banned.)

Estimating Costs

In Chapter 7, we present information on how to create budgets for medium-sized and large exhibit operations. If, however, this is your first show, it is likely that your booth will be smaller, less complex. For that purpose we provide a simple budget form limited to eight lines as shown in Figure 2-1. What follows is an explanation for each item:

1. *Booth space rent.* This is your rent for booth space.

2. *Booth and graphic signs.* This is the actual cost of the materials and labor used in constructing the booth. You might want to revise this estimate after you investigate. We provide some guidance in Chapters 3 and 13.

3. *Transport of exhibit materials.* Moving your booth, product samples, and literature to the event site and back costs money, even if you drive your own car or simply check your containers with the airline.

4. *On-site services.* This line covers services and rentals at the show itself. At the very least you will require electrical service and some setup help. The service information kit supplied by the organizer

---

The Eight-Line Budget

Item	Estimate	Actual
1. Booth space rent	_____	_____
2. Booth and graphic signs	_____	_____
3. Transport of exhibit materials	_____	_____
4. On-site services	_____	_____
5. Preshow and at-show promotion	_____	_____
6. Customer hospitality	_____	_____
7. Staff expenses	_____	_____
8. Contingency (10 percent of above)	_____	_____
Total budget	_____	_____

Figure 2-1. This form is appropriate for small-booth operations. For more complex show participation, see Chapter 7, "Exhibit Budget and Company Costs," and related forms.

will help you create this estimate; from materials handling (called *drayage*) to booth cleaning and plant rental.

5. *Preshow and at-show promotion.* You probably will need to do some mailing or advertising to boost booth traffic, and you will need to have some giveaways or prize promotions at the booth.

6. *Customer hospitality.* This line can include such things as VIP entertainment, food and beverage services in a suite—even sports or theatrical tickets.

7. *Staff expenses.* For the most part these costs are limited to hotel, meal, and travel costs.

8. *Contingency.* Estimate all expenses and then add 10 percent for contingencies.

What to Do First

Some work items take more time than others to get done, so those should be started first. Among them are the following.

Booth and Signs

Even if your company already owns a booth, you have to get going as far in advance as you can. The booth must be checked to see if any refurbishing or new signs are needed.

Large companies keep an inventory of booths. Don't be lulled by this. Exhibiting is somewhat seasonal, and all of your properties may be booked well in advance.

If you do not have a booth, shopping for one can be time-consuming. You should get going on that right away. There is information on choices and where to go in Chapter 3.

A quality look is an absolute requirement. Your booth will be seen by many people who will create their own instant impressions about your company, products, and people.

Products and Literature Displays

Never assume that what you will need from inside the company is immediately available. Check on display samples, demonstrations, and literature right away. Make sure that you have what you need reserved, tucked away for the event.

War stories abound about exhibit managers' being assured that needed product samples and literature were readily available, only to find out just a few days before an event that the materials were not where they were supposed to be.

Staff Recruiting

It sounds easy to recruit staff, but that is not so, except in the smallest outfits. The sales or technical people you will need live busy lives. Most think that working at a company booth is not worth their time. The benefits are not necessarily direct or easily understood. You may have to spend some extra time to persuade them to come.

It is easy to recruit salespeople to come if they will be seeing their own current customers. However, salespeople will need to be persuaded to prospect as a team and to sell to those that others may serve.

Preshow Promotion

What you want to tell visitors in advance has to be executed in advance:

- The single most important preshow promotion you have is free—the listing in the show program. Provide a business reason for visiting your booth.

- Show tickets, provided by promoters for many shows, must be sent out in advance to your customers and prospects.

- Letters must be sent and advertising prepared well in advance.

- Your own salespeople can help draw an audience from their contacts and customers. That effort, not often thought about, demands early action.

- There may be a need for a special brochure. Writing, design, art, and production take longer than most of us think. Get it going early.

Travel and Hotel

You can save much expense money by making travel and hotel arrangements well in advance. This is one reason for getting the staff signed up early in the game and making that list stick. Most shows offer special discounts for travel and hotels. Take advantage of that blessing unless you work for a big corporation with access to its own travel discounts.

The Exhibitor Kit

After you have signed up, the organizer will send you a loose-leaf binder containing show information. The industry calls these thick compendiums *exhibitor kits.* Added to lots of information sheets are actual order forms. Check the order forms early since some suppliers offer discounts for early orders. The most important parts of the kit are the listing of show regulations and the ordering forms.

Show Regulations

Read the rules for the show. Among other things you will learn the show hours, when you can move in, when you can move out, booth design rules, fire regulations, and insurance requirements as well as many other things that really are important. The objective of the organizers is a smooth, safe show that offers all participants an equal opportunity for success.

Drayage Service

This order form covers the scheduling and labor cost for moving materials within the hall and storing your unused crates or supplies during the event. Except for very small booths that you can literally carry in over your shoulder, the use of drayage service is a must. When you think about all the freight that must be moved in and out of a show hall, you will realize that professional service, and management, is vital to avoid chaos.

Setup Labor

Most large hotels and convention halls work with union agreements. Depending on where you are going, there will be different jurisdictions working in different areas. For instance, carpet layers are not carpenters. Order forms for all are in the kit so it is easy to figure out.

> *Note:* Some exhibitors gripe about using professional labor. "I can do this myself!" Maybe so, maybe not—but you should be concentrating on the marketing and sales preparation anyway. Money well spent we say, and, regardless, these are the rules, just as there are rules within your own company.

Electrical Service

The contractor installs electrical services and even plugs in your lights and appliances. Virtually any place you go, the use of professional electricians is a must, if for no other reasons than safety and hall insurance. You may say, "I can plug in a light." True, but how many on a circuit? And what about your exhibit neighbor? At the least, electricians are safety cops.

Insurance Certificate

Exposition managers require a certificate of insurance, prepared by your insurance agent. It will include coverage such as comprehensive general liability, personal injury liability, property damage liability, and worker's compensation. It may not seem so as you walk the floor during a show, but there are dangers, especially during setup and teardown. The show management group or sponsoring association will be shown as the certificate holder.

Imprinters

Increasingly, expos offer visitors and exhibitors one of several forms of automated registration service at booths. These include the use of credit-card–type "swipe" imprinters that produce a paper printout of the visitor's name and data. We do not think any of these systems provide all that is needed by an exhibitor. However, they are so pervasive that it becomes almost mandatory to sign up and pay for the one offered. (We cover problems and solutions in Chapter 17, "Exhibit Staff Recruiting, Training, and Management.")

Outside Setup Contractor

If you are just starting out working for a large corporation, you may have an arrangement for booth setup through an independent labor contractor, not the official show contractor. (See Chapter 16, "Exhibit Transportation and Setup at the Show.") If you use an outside contractor, you must submit a form which is in the exhibitor kit, well in advance. Your independent contractor draws from the same local labor pool as does the official show supplier. Your advice alerts the show's contractor to reduce its own labor call for the event.

Other Exhibitor Services

As you thumb through your exhibitor kit, you will see several other services that may help. Among them you should find:

- Telephone service and telephone instrument rental
- Computer, printer, and modem rental
- Audiovisual equipment rental and service
- Booth rental
- Booth carpet rental
- Custom sign making service
- Extra furniture rentals such as counters, tables, chairs, and stools.
- Plant and flower rentals
- Booth cleaning service
- Photography service
- Plumbing and high-pressure air service
- Rigging to hang materials from the ceiling or similar services
- Booth security in addition to that provided for the overall show

You will also see, in the kit, vendor payment expectations. There are times when advance payment or cash is needed. (Some vendors have found, to their surprise, that some exhibitors let small bills linger unpaid, long after the show.) You will also see that for many advance prepaid orders, the vendors will provide discounts. If you want more information, see Chapter 16.

Show Rules

We have already touched on this subject, but we return to it now because it is important to understand some whats and whys. If you are exhibiting for the first time with a small booth, it is unlikely that you will break rules. However, some fundamentals are important. In the USA the back-wall height for a small booth is 8 feet. Sidewalls are lower. The full 8-foot height can be extended toward the aisle only 3 feet. From there out to the aisle edge, the height limit is 4 feet. Keep in mind the reason for these restrictions: The objective is to allow visitors to see down the aisle as well as right into the booth they are in front of. If you do anything to obstruct that view, it is not polite to visitors or your exhibit neighbors. You will be asked to remove the obstacle.

The exhibitor kit section on show rules will include a chart, often supported with line drawings illustrating space use limitations. You will see that some larger booth spaces, islands, or end-aisle peninsula booth spaces are allowed higher structures. However, the intentions to provide visitors the chance to see several booths at once and to be fair to all exhibits prevail.

You will also see setup and teardown times cited. Please don't expect any favors! Continuing setup or changing your booth during show hours, for instance, is an annoyance to visitors and other exhibitors. (And it makes you look bad!) One rule at almost all shows is that you must stay open for business until the actual closing time each day. Many inexperienced exhibitors violate this one, especially on the last day when they figure most attendees have departed. It is unprofessional to start teardown early, and you can lose sales as well.[5]

What to Exhibit

In the section of this chapter devoted to writing a plan, we covered show mission statements. As you write a mission statement, what to exhibit will become obvious. The danger is that one can try to show too much!

- If you offer several different products, you may be tempted to show everything, even if the show audience is interested in only one or two lines.

- Manufacturers offering products for resale tend to display samples in much the same way that retailers mass products on shelves. That is not necessary unless you are also offering the display device to stores. It could be far more effective to diminish product display and substitute signs or demonstrations emphasizing business issues, such as inventory management or profit potential per square foot.

- Exhibitors offering services, technology, or machines to businesses like to focus on "features." What to exhibit for these companies, however, would be better aimed at *applications* of their specific offerings to those attending the show.

Preshow and At-Show Promotions

Promotional needs and types depend on the show, what you offer, and the relative importance of the event to your business. For instance, let's assume that you plan to exhibit at a summer meeting of the Maryland Bar Association, a smaller show with few attendees and exhibitors. The extra promotional needs are less than they would be at a trade show with hundreds of exhibitors and an audience size measured in thousands. An exception might be if your company is large and thought of as an "industry leader." If so, you might do something extra even at the small events.

Traffic-building promotions are targeted to two groups of customers: current and prospective.

- Current customer promotions require at the very least an invitation to meet at the show. This invitation should be more than a courtesy gesture. It should cite business reasons to visit. Some companies poll their customers to see who is attending.[6]

- New-customer prospecting is, for most, the key objective of trade show participation. Visitors attend trade shows to see what is new to them, both products and companies. You should help them find you. There are several options open to do that job:

  1. News releases or advertising can be placed in industry publications in advance.
  2. You can use a direct-mail announcement to people and organizations on an industry list or on a preregistration list available from the show organizers.
  3. Promotions at the show can help. For instance, at a small show where all participants stay in the same hotel, you can arrange for invitations to be placed outside room doors.
  4. If your booth is small among many booths at a very large show, you can hire hosts or hostesses to pass out flyers outside the convention hall.
  5. Your listing in the show program is valuable since everyone reads it. Cite business reasons to visit your booth.

There are many other promotional methods. For more ideas, check Chapter 14, "Promotional Activity Before and During the Show."

Time-Line Chart

Earlier we pointed out that when you are putting together an exhibit, there are some things that have to be started at the outset. In addition to meeting show deadlines, the most pressing work is that which needs to be completed by others and that, therefore, cannot be accomplished overnight.

28-Day Time Line

Week 4

_____Send your program listing to the show. They are printing it tomorrow!

_____Prepare your fundamental plan and budget.

_____Make hotel, travel, and VIP hospitality arrangements.

_____Check the company booth and graphic signs. There will be problems.

_____Start recruiting booth staff people.

Week 3

_____Check on the availability of display products and literature.

_____If you need new signs or need exhibit touch-up, order it now.

_____Write and start production of invitations to the booth for customers and prospects.

_____Send staff member names to the show for badges. Revise travel reservations.

_____Fax service orders to on-site show suppliers.

Week 2

_____Complete new signs and exhibit repairs and ship.

_____Mail letters or invitations to customers and prospects.

_____Work out any special VIP hospitality details and costs.

_____Pull together and ship other materials, including literature.

_____Write news release and make copies for the show pressroom.

Week 1

_____Write thank-you follow-up letters to be used after the show.

_____Confirm receipt of orders for on-site show services.

_____Pack office supplies, lead forms, and show-order copies.

Figure 2-2. Time-line illustration for a small-booth operation for which there is little time—in this case, only four weeks—to prepare. This time line is useful when a late decision to participate with a small booth has been made. You can still do the job, but life gets compressed!

A time-line chart is your pathfinder in scheduling your work as well as that of others. If you share it with others you work with, your time-line chart will signal your coworkers when their work must be finished and, importantly, why, as they will be able to see how their work fits into the grand scheme. A sample time-line chart in Figure 2-2 illustrates a typical work-completion schedule.

Exhibit Measurement

How do you measure success? How far is up? We've already covered goal setting. The next step is figuring how close you have to come to meeting those goals. To do so, you can measure work production or, occasionally, dollar return.

Work Production Measurement

The actual work done at the exhibit forms the basis for this measurement system. You relate what you can count to dollar expenditures and create a "cost-per" index that you can use over time. You can measure any work item that can be counted on a regular basis, and then compared. For instance:

- Cost per lead obtained
- Cost per order written
- Cost per item of literature distributed
- Cost per news story printed

Value Measurement

Some outfits can measure dollar return against cost. For them there is an index we call the *expense-to-revenue ratio.* Dollar returns are calculated against exhibit cost to create an index that can be used, over time, to evaluate relative exhibits' performance. One value of using this process is that it avoids internal conflict. Salespeople resent implications that exhibits sell. They are correct. Exhibits don't sell. People sell. Exhibit results should be positioned as supportive.

Both indexes are detailed in Chapter 9, "Measuring Return on Investment." Short-form accomplishment planning is covered in the next chapter, "Operations Before, During, and After the Show." Read on, highlighter in hand.

What's Hot and Not for Exhibit Managers

Thus far we have been covering what we think is important. That is what you paid for when you bought the book. We would, however, like to let you know what other exhibit managers think, at least from the vantage point of their relationships with show management. It may help you sort out the planning issues according to their importance to you.

The Seminar Survey

The author and two well-regarded show managers led a seminar at an International Exhibitors' Association (IEA) convention.[7] The seminar objective was to explore exhibitor–show management relationships. The two show management experts were Connie Akin from the Produce Marketing Association[8] and Michael Muldoon of the Convention Management Group.[9] His company organizes trade shows for several associations.

At the seminar's end we asked volunteers to complete a questionnaire on the most important issues raised, or not raised, in the session. Of the 60-plus who attended, 15 were willing to participate. For those with marketing or advertising experience, the results are about equivalent to what one learns as a result of what is called a "focus group" research session. Conclusions point to major issues, but not really on what researchers call "a quantifiable basis." However, they can and do give you an idea about what's hot and not.

Seminar and Survey Issues. Some readers with marketing research background may be persnickety about our method. In short form, here is what we did. A list of 28 possible issues or concerns was provided to those who attended at the start of the seminar. At the end, when the survey was taken, the same list was provided in "check off format," with room for comments and additions. Respondents did not have to provide names. However, those that elected to make comments that could be quoted in the report and for publication were asked to provide their names and company affiliations.

That list of 28 issues, for those who care to explore, is presented as Figure 2-3. Even though there is no statistical validity, we have elected to show the percentage of those participating who selected each question.

The Results. We are now at the place where most readers want to be, after taking some of your precious time to protect ourselves from arrows that could be fired by some "experts."

What's Hot. Over 80 percent felt that breaking down the audience estimate by subgroup was very important. The subgroups of interest are "special interest," geographic area, and job title or responsibility.

> *Note:* Mike Muldoon pointed out that estimates are provided on the basis of past experience. He said, "At even the most stable show there can be a true audience change of 40 percent, year over year."

Seminar participant Lisa Sinicki from The Design Agency, an exhibit production company, commented on her questionnaire form: "Show management information must be taken with a grain of salt. A client

The 28-Issues Rating

		Percent
1.	Audience estimate by subgroup	86
2.	Show history and change potential	73
3.	Nature of the seminar program	47
4.	Press coverage	53
5.	Nature and content of attendance promotion program	53
6.	Promotion assistance for exhibitors	33
7.	Exhibitor participation in seminars	40
8.	Mailing list availability	47
9.	Setup and teardown time	13
10.	Loading docks—size, lighting, and so on	6
11.	Exhibitor kit quality and readability (*Note:* See page 18)	6
12.	Show floor meetings out of hours	0
13.	"Show rules" flexibility	0
14.	Drayage cost reduction	20
15.	Fire prevention regulations	0
16.	Show security	0
17.	Electrical and A/V control by the show	0
18.	Registration company–provided lead administration services	20
19.	Private off-site event coordination	33
20.	Final prereg list availability and timing	40
21.	Provision of exhibitor education (*Note:* See page 27)	6
22.	Seminar competition with the exposition in show hours	40
23.	Postevent research and exhibitor tie-in research	47
24.	Criteria for setting booth space rent prices	13
25.	How to influence show management on future directions	60
26.	Getting through "ad clutter" at shows	6
27.	Show versus exhibitor responsibility for results	33
28.	Relative value of national, regional, and local shows	20

Figure 2-3. The survey responses reported here are useful for overall direction. They reflect the views of managers at larger, experienced exhibiting companies. The list duplicates what respondents saw in the survey, including the order in which the issues or questions were presented. To some extent the order of questions may have impacted upon responses. However, major concerns or issues do surface.

decided on a show when told by the show that 10,000 attendees matched the exhibitor's market profile. Four weeks before the event the prereg list arrived and showed that only 600 matched the profile. Our client went ahead anyway and had one of its most successful shows ever." The figures presented by show management did not mean a lot.

We offer two points: First, expo managers do not have to blur or inflate figures. Second, as Sinicki points out, "Sometimes the registration questions asked distort the quality and accuracy of the answers."

Best of the Rest.   Read with your own grains of salt, but here is a summary of issues mentioned by over half of the respondents as important:

- *Show history.* How stable is the show? How much does the audience change year to year? What changes occur as it moves from city to city?
- *Exhibitor influence.* "How can I influence what happens at my important shows in the future?"
- *Promotion.* What is the nature *and content* of the show's audience promotion program? (Many expo executives provide information on the media used, few on what is said.)
- *Press.* To what extent will trade press representatives attend the show? What is being done to encourage that attendance?

Not in the Top Five. Only 5 of the 28 issues were cited by over half of our respondents. That does not mean that those below the line are not important. Here are three examples of issues not included in the top 5:

- *The show's seminar program.* Information about the nature and content of that program was cited as important by just under half of the respondents.
- *The exhibitor kit.* The quality and thoroughness of the exhibitor kit was rated as an important issue by only one volunteer. However, remember that the audience included those with solid experience. They read their kits.

    Note: Two comments about the kits emerged that seem very important. Connie Akin pointed out, "We provide good exhibitor kits, but that does not mean we can cover everything. A trade show manager must encourage exhibitors to call with their questions and concerns, to give us a chance to become partners in success." Seminar attendee T. Harrison, exhibit manager from Phillips Petroleum, offered a suggestion. It is that exhibitors "need a deadline and critical dates sheet." We find this to be true not only for experienced exhibitors but also for those facing the daunting task of exhibiting for the first time.

- *Exhibitor education.* Only 1 of our 15 respondents pointed out exhibitor education as an important area of concern. However, our respondents were people spending $2000 to $3000 to attend an IEA convention to get that education rather than relying on show managers to provide it. Our survey respondents were investing their money wisely since, for the most part, show managers arrange few, if any, coordinated long-range education programs for their exhibitors.

The Exhibit Manager–Expo
Executive Relationship

Seminar attendee J. P. Stevens III, from IBM's Microsystems Division, commented with his analysis of the association–exhibit manager relationship: "There are three categories. First is marketing and strategy. Second is the show/exhibitor relationship, working together for everyone's good. Third is working together on logistical issues." Stevens's comment is a good way to sign off on this chapter.

3

Operations Before, During, and After

With plan in hand you have a pretty fair notion of what has to be done. The aim of this chapter is to address implementation questions that may come up in the course of implementing the plan.

What to Do about a Booth

If you already own the exhibit you plan to use, jump over this section to "The Sign Guide." On the other hand, if you need to put your hands on a booth, you have many options, as we cover here.

Pipe and Drape

Show organizers will provide the basics in return for your space rent. For the most part in the USA, and to some extent in other parts of North America, this is called *pipe and drape*. The space rear is covered by a colored drape hung on a pipe system 8 feet high. Lower side rails, also covered with drape, extend out to the aisle. The color is standard, selected by the show. A draped table and a couple of chairs completes the package. There is a stenciled sign showing your company name and the space number. It is pinned to the back wall curtain. Bring signs, literature, or samples, and you are in business. You might want to rent carpeting.

Small booth spaces are outfitted differently in other countries. Most common is called the *shell scheme*. We mention it here because that system is being introduced gradually in the USA. In contrast to drape, the exhibition producer provides "hard" back and sidewalls. Typically, these are painted a flat white and include a thin signboard running along the aisle edge at the top of the space. You decorate the interior. If you are curious about what that might look like, Part 4, "The International Scene," includes a sketch that illustrates the shell scheme. In this example cited in Part 4, the shell was designed for small Canadian companies exhibiting in their own pavilion at an international exposition. The same concept works for small independent exhibitors along an aisle.

Most exhibitors prefer to do more, regardless of the system, because they know they are likely to be seen by many people who acquire their first impression from the visual appearance of the booth.

Booth Rental

A reasonable step up from pipe and drape is renting an exhibit structure. You will see that these are placed in front of the drape and allow you far more flexibility in display. These booths come with optional counters, display racks, furniture, and *headers*, the term used to describe signs at the top of the booth. There are several sources for rental booths.

The Show Decorator.   One source will be the show's own general contractor, often called the *decorating company*. Within the information packet provided by the expo, called the *exhibitor kit*, you will see a line of rental booths offered. Increasingly, decorating companies offer packets that include booth options such as carpet and electrical service in a package with booth and setup.

Exhibit Designers and Producers.   Virtually all of these companies offer rental programs as well as booths you can purchase. The cost will be somewhat higher, if for no other reason than that you have to pay for transporting the booth to the show. However, there is likely to be more flexibility in what you can obtain, and you are more assured of getting the quality you want.

Already-Manufactured Units

There are scores of manufactured exhibit units for sale. Almost universally, they are based on the use of patented framing systems covered with panels or fabric faces. These systems break down into two types of units: portable and near custom.

Portable Units.   These units are very light in weight and can be hand carried into most exhibit halls. There are two types: One is called a *tabletop unit,* and you can place it on the table provided with the minimum pipe and drape, show-provided decoration. The second type, more popular it seems, provides a full back wall, from floor to booth top. Optional in both situations are light fixtures.

Full-wall portable displays are offered with different features to suit basic exhibiting needs, depending on the type of product or service you sell.

If you are contemplating a tabletop unit, look for one that is fairly tall so that when it is placed on a table, it goes up to about the full 8-foot height. Purchase a couple of lights with the package. Even though it is somewhat more bulky to carry, the larger tabletop unit configurations enhance visual appearance.

Near-Custom Units.   Manufactured exhibits of this type remain relatively light in weight but are far more substantial. Most often they do require professional shipping and delivery to your space. Most of them come with optional counter systems strong enough to withstand the weight of product samples such as computer terminals. Exhibitors frequently purchase their own carpet with these booths, shipped to the show with the booth.

Joan Carol, of the Joan Carol Design & Exhibit Group, headquartered in Clinton, Maryland, is one of the USA's largest distributors of portable and near-custom units. She points out two values provided by exhibit designers and producers that can be important, especially for first-time exhibitors:

1. You will be led through a needs analysis, the same sort of process used to start custom projects for those big companies with the monster booths. It can be an enjoyable learning experience, and you will end up with a great small booth.

2. Part of the needs analysis will explore the future. Carol said, "Some hardware grows, some does not." You may not see any changes on the horizon. That is one situation. Or you might be in an expansion mode in the next few years, either in product mix or in the potential need for a larger booth. The answers will influence the recommendation as to which basic system to start with.

You will find there are a number of purchase options. For instance, some exhibitors are better served by a Velcro-compatible surface, others are better off with a high-tech laminate surface. In another context, here is an illustration. Assume that you plan exhibiting at three events. For two larger expos you need a floor standing unit. At the much smaller third show a tabletop display is sufficient. Knowing that, the designer will select a system that allows the table unit to be incorporated into the floor standing unit. Lift it off and presto!

Metric Measurements. A large number of the already-manufactured systems popular in the USA were created and patented first in Europe. They are based on the use of aluminum uprights and crossbars. Each was designed with special connectors, and some provide slots for graphic signs.

These systems were designed using the metric scale. That does not present a problem if you know and remember that. One booth we worked with, for instance, included slots for sign panels. We provided very exact measurements to our sign maker, but failed to cite slot depth. Our signs, done to English standards, were too thin. Touch it and our booth rattled in protest! (The emergency fix? Old matchbook covers and folded paper towels were stuffed into the slots in back. It was not pretty back there but we sounded a whole lot better up-front.)

An English system–metric conversion chart appears in Part 4, "The International Scene." You probably don't need it. Just alert your supplier to use the metric system—and cite the depth as well as height and width for signs!

Custom Exhibits

This is the top end. Booths are designed and fabricated from the ground up after a needs analysis is performed by a professional design team. They are unique, as you might assume, and designed to meet specific exhibitor requirements. They are also more costly, including custom-designed crates that are used for shipping and storage.

Over the years custom designers and builders have preferred wood as a frame material, covering it with all kinds of surface materials. However, they also use the metal extrusions found in already-manufactured exhibit systems as a frame. Regardless, unusual shapes and visual impressions emerge. Increasingly, local dealers for manufactured exhibit systems are moving into the custom arena, competing with traditional design and build teams.

The focus of this chapter is on what a first-time exhibitor, or a small company, might need. Most ground-up custom design is done for midsize and large companies with a big schedule. We delve more into those needs and some nontraditional approaches in Chapter 13, "Exhibit Design: Structure and Graphics."

Cost Guide

Rentals cost less than the rest. That is especially so when renting through the show organizer's decorating company on site. There are times when that is not wise. For instance, for somewhat more you can work with a local exhibit house and rent with an option to purchase later.

If you want to go ahead and purchase an already-manufactured unit, there is a wide range. For instance, a portable tabletop unit can cost from $500 to $1500. A floor-standing portable back wall type of unit can cost from $3000 to $5000 for a 10-foot-wide unit. The heavier, modular exhibit structures are more, depending on options, and cost from $4000 to $8000 covering 10 feet. Though there are all kinds of prices, depending on need, one rule of thumb is to plan on spending $70 per square foot of booth space filled with an already-manufactured, floor-standing booth. *Warning: These cost ranges do not include the cost of graphic signs.*[1] In Chapter 13, we explore costs for ground-up custom-designed and built exhibits.

Source Guide

A puzzle for first-timers: Where do I get one of these booths? It's not quite as easy as nipping over to K-Mart or Sears but pretty near! Check the classified or yellow pages section of your telephone directory! The section heading will be worded something like "Display Designers & Producers." Many first-timers do not discern the degree to which exhibiting has become part of business culture. All large and most middle-sized metro areas offer outfitters who are qualified.

There are, as well, exhibition industry source directories. Among them are the *Tradeshow Week Services Directory* and *Exhibitor Magazine's Directory of Exhibit Systems*. A third is the International Exhibitor Association's *Membership Directory and Product/Service Guide*. Another is *Exhibit Builder Magazine's Source Book Directory.*[2]

Decision Factors

There are two fundamental considerations that can lead you to making an appropriate choice. One is the rent or buy choice. The other is booth type.

Rent or Buy.   This is a relatively easy choice. It depends on how often you will be exhibiting and the importance of the event or events. Logically, if you are to participate in but one or two shows a year, renting makes sense. *The Rent or Buy Rule of Thumb: Renting costs one-third of the cost of purchase.* The least expensive rental is, of course, renting from the show decorator. You can also rent from an exhibit design and production company, often with an option to buy if the program expands.

There can be situations, however, that would inspire you to purchase your own booth even if there are only one or two shows in which it will be used. It may be that you sell business to business and that most orders are written at one or two industry events. Or you might be a retailer appearing at only one or two consumer shows a year. In either case the importance of your visual appearance cannot be overstated, and you risk less by planning and purchasing your own booth.

Booth Design Type.   Rent or buy, the already-manufactured structure you select should depend on what you are offering. Don't be hornswoggled by the first booth you see. Think about the products you sell and your purpose in exhibiting. There is exceptional diversity available.

- *Services or Floor-Standing Product.* If you offer services or require a backdrop for a floor-standing product display, you should focus on booth types that offer roomy areas for large graphics—perhaps less in counters. Figure 3.1 illustrates this type of booth. It was designed by the Dottinger Design Corporation, a long-time custom display producer.[3] Robert Dottinger says, "This design is based on using already-manufactured frames. It is an expandable concept, both outward and up (by adding a light weight roof frame). The key is providing a conversation area and using signs that invite that."

Another approach, in a 10-foot size, appears as Figure 3-2. It was designed by the Joan Carol Design & Exhibit Group (endnote 1 for this chapter). Joan Carol says, "This idea is more likely to emerge when there is a need to cut back from a large booth to a 10-foot space and an end-aisle position has been rented. The 'bridge' to aisle counter signals that. The round and flat backwall areas are for graphics." Regardless, an already-manufactured system was the design base.

- *Desktop Products.* If you offer products best displayed on a "desktop," you will find units that come with heavy counters for this purpose. Chapter 20's Figure 20-1 illustrates this type of booth. An unusual "high counter" is illustrated in Chapter 13. Many booths that also feature back-wall space for small-product display also come with substantial counter space. In all cases there is less room or emphasis on graphic signs than is the case for selling services.
- *Small-Product Display.* If you offer small products, perhaps to retailers for resale (or consumers at their shows), the most practical booth type would be one that offers a considerable amount of shelving, or *slot wall*, most likely on the back wall for product racking. Figure 3-3 illustrates this type of booth. It also shows an expansion capability for larger spaces.

Chapter 26 is for retailers exhibiting at consumer events. A frequently observed problem is that small exhibitors display on counters or

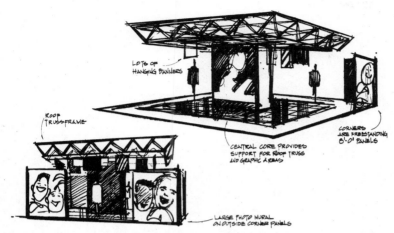

Figure 3-1. The design concept is aimed at inviting conversation, a design method most often used to offer services rather than products (that can be displayed or demonstrated). Illustrated is an expandable concept, from small booth to larger, including the capability to add height where that is permitted, using the roof frame. (*Sketch courtesy of Dottinger Design, Pompton Lakes, New Jersey.*)

tables near or on the aisle. That is not the best approach. Display should be inside or at the back of booths. A more inviting appearance is created, and there is no "wall" between visitors and those who staff the booths. Experts, worldwide, agree that the concept is more effective. In addition, the rules at most events prohibit extensive display at the aisle edge to prevent clogging.

Booth Weight.   As you explore manufactured units, you will be given information on weight, stability, and strength. In the true "portable" world, the booth type you can carry into a show hall all by yourself, low weight is emphasized. In this case remember what else you may have to transport to the show. If you have to bring several hundred pounds of equipment or product samples to the event, commercial transport and in-hall delivery will be required anyway. The fact that you can carry in the booth won't save enough to worry about.

Whatever product, situation, and budget, don't forget that a booth and the graphic signs you add form what is simply a stage. Products and people are the raison d'être of exhibiting.

The Sign Guide

Even if you already have a booth and it's in good shape, you have to pay attention to graphic signs. You may need new messages for your

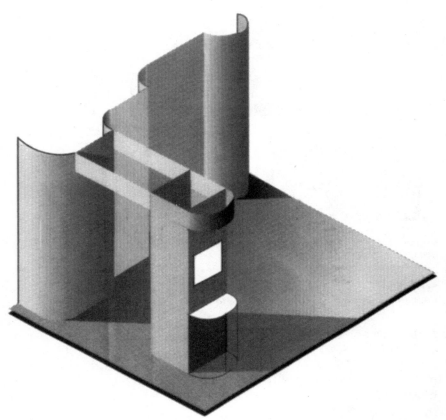

Figure 3-2. Another approach to offering services is a curved backwall, upon which graphic signs are applied. In this case a small aisle column and counter are added. (The bridge is small and optional.) This design was based on already manufactured frame parts from Nimlok, Niles, Illinois. (*Sketch was provided courtesy of the Joan Carol Design & Exhibit Group, Clinton, Maryland.*)

next show. Even if you want to retain the same message, it's wise to assure yourself that your signing is not battered looking.

Our point here is that you should consider the development of new signs. Exposition visitors are bombarded with signs, and all vie for attention. The less text the better. The objective is to encourage person-to-person contact.

Sign-Writing Rules of Thumb

Rule 1: Attract only potential buyers.   Be specific about who should stop at the booth and what can be learned. If you are too general, you will waste a lot of time talking to the wrong folks.

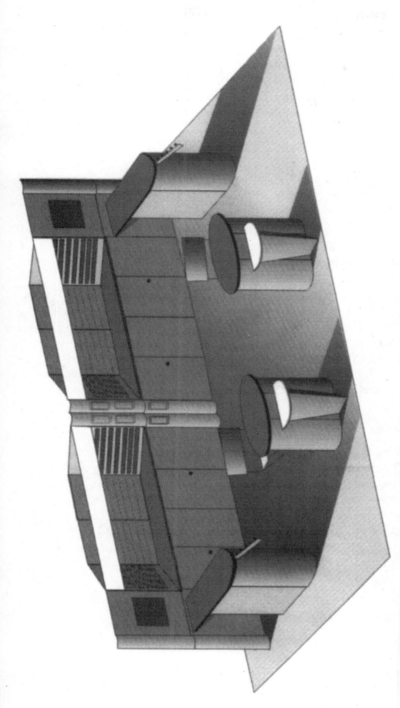

Figure 3-3. This illustrates both small-product display racking and a greater emphasis on counter areas. There is less room for signs. It also illustrates how 10-foot units can be placed side by side in larger booth spaces. As in Figure 3-2, the design was based on parts made by Nimlok, one of several manufacturers. (*Sketch courtesy of the Joan Carol Design & Exhibit Group.*)

37

Rule 2: Position the booth as a learning center.   Do not overwhelm visitors with product information splattered on signs. They are rarely read.

Rule 3: Think about audience interests.   You may be selling great fishing lures, soups, or computers, and these are part of your story. But remember that the *application* of that computer or inventory cost and management system could be just as important from a business visitor's viewpoint.

Rule 4: Signs at different heights work in different ways.   A large sign high in the booth is noticed from far away but not really "seen" close up. Close in, smaller signs, lower in the booth or on countertops are better.

Rule 5: Always cut copy.   After you write your first draft, put it aside for a while. Then go back to the draft, reread it, and try to cut the number of words in half! Professional writers follow this approach.

Rule 6: Avoid "internal" terms.   Copy such as "See our new Model 32B Can Opener" means little except to owners of the 32A. Better to cite the application saying, "See our new can opener with automatic contents removal." Try, as well, to avoid industry-speak. Acronyms and the like that you think are well understood may not be understood by others in the same way. In addition, there are always new people entering the market.

"Header" Copy

Many booths come with defined sign areas at the top, either along the back wall or along the aisle. In some cases they cover lights that can show through the sign and at the same time cast light down, perhaps on lower back-wall signs or on counter-displayed products.

Most exhibitors use these headline areas to "pop" the company name and logo. That's fine if your company name is well known and, by itself, will attract visitors. Often, however, the header should be used to signal a reason to stop at the booth: "Learn about the Latest in Antipollution Stack Scrubbers."

Artwork and Photographs

The same sort of rules of thumb that apply to text signs apply to artwork sketches, charts, or photographs. They should be audience relevant. There is not enough time to be decorative for the sake of decoration alone. The goal is getting the right visitors to stop. That's it.

Sign Costs

There are so many variables that it is virtually impossible to provide a short-space guide. Don't forget, however, that even if you purchase an already-manufactured booth, that your signs have to be designed and produced on a custom basis. A single large sign can cost several hundred dollars, with the most expensive being those that fit in a back-lighted transparency box. There are, however, ways to save—and be more effective at the same time.

- Restrict graphics to what's really needed. Say it in simple fashion. The beauty of this is that it works better at the same time it saves dollars.
- Allow as much time as possible for production. There are a number of steps in the process, and you want to avoid overtime costs.
- Be sure of yourself before production. Postproduction changes, especially for small reasons, are very wasteful.

Audiovisuals

If it's at all possible, avoid using videotapes or films in small booths. There are two reasons: Most important is that the lighting and sound levels in exhibition halls are too high. The second is that most audiovisual productions are not produced primarily for exhibit use. They are too long, considering the distractions. Presentations of this type should be saved for room environments where sound, light, and time can be controlled to a far greater degree.

What to Take to the Show

Your booth is packed, sales team organized, and customers alerted. However, your booth is more than a display center. It is also a branch office that you build, run, and remove over a short time.

Office and Sales Supplies

Whatever you use to do business in your office will be used at the booth. You will think to take the obvious—order and lead forms, literature, and business cards. (Take more cards than you think you will need, less literature. You can send that later.)

There are some items that do not pop to mind as readily. For instance, you should take copies of show service orders. Another—traveler's checks to pay for emergency floor purchases. Credit cards may be fine in most cases, but don't take the chance. You should also take some office supplies—stationery, envelopes, stamps, paper clips, pens, notepaper, and clipboards. Some of these items are readily available in stationery or office supply stores. However, many times you will be setting up on weekends in tight time intervals. Running around a strange town to find office supplies takes a lot of time you won't want to spend in that way.

Figure 3-4 is a relatively complete checklist of the items you should pack up in small quantities and take with you to the event.

Booth Supplies

A packing list must be prepared that includes booth panels, lights, spare light bulbs, signs, counters, literature, and display products. If you plan to ship more than one crate, you can avoid setup confusion by making sure that your packing list identifies what items are in each.

Most of the time you will be exhibiting in a convention hall or large hotel. Professional help will be available to help you set up. However, there can be times when you will exhibit at very small events held in small hotels or suburban conference centers where no help is provided. We remember one situation—speaking at a Rotary Club luncheon held in a restaurant but needing a small booth display to help get the points across. In those cases you may be on your own.

Tool Kit.   For those do-it-yourself situations, a cruise through your basement or garage, or maybe that tool drawer in the kitchen, can be lifesaving. Make up a tool kit to take along:

- Some portable booths require a special tool to lock pieces together. Bring two of them because if you lose one, you will be out of luck. Others require custom fixtures. Bring extras.
- Hammer and nail selection
- Screwdriver set and screw assortment
- Pliers and a wire cutter
- Knife and scissors
- Industrial tape (especially Velcro tape and dots, and double-sided adhesive tape)
- Twenty-five-foot tape measure
- Indelible marking pen
- Touch-up paint in booth colors
- Twenty-five-foot, industrial-quality electric extension cord with a commercial "four-way" outlet box

Exhibit Office and Sales Supplies

- Sales lead and order forms
- Office letterhead, notepaper, and no. 10 envelopes, plus a supply of stamps
- A few 9 by 12 envelopes
- Folders for temporary files, plus peel-off labels
- Inexpensive hand-held staplers (several) plus staples and staple remover
- Paper clips and cellophane tape plus some rubber bands
- Ballpoint pens (several) and indelible marking pens
- Scissors
- Calendar
- Leather-bound appointment book to formalize appointments at the booth
- Leather-bound guest book for VIP sign-in if there is a hospitality suite
- Extra business cards
- Traveler's checks to pay for on-site purchases
- Preaddressed shipping labels to use for outbound shipments at the show's end
- Small medical kit and foot-care supplies, including powder, cream, and soak
- 100-watt light bulbs to replace lower-wattage bulbs in your hotel room
- Flashlight

Determine, in advance, the availability and hours open of the closest business center. If you carry a portable computer, pack the cable that links it to a printer.

Figure 3-4. This is a checklist of office supplies, company forms, and other items to take to the show.

In addition to office supplies, there are specific show-related items:

- Bills of lading for all items shipped to the show by commercial transport
- Copies of advance orders for services or rentals on site
- The show's exhibitor kit
- Hotel reservations and car rental list with confirmation numbers noted
- Staff and vendor names with home telephone numbers
- Travel tickets
- Copies of press releases to be distributed
- Literature samples
- Name badges if provided in advance by the event manager
- Sales training meeting agenda and supplies of handouts
- Show tickets left over, if provided by the show in advance for customers

Figure 3-4. (*Continued*) This is a checklist of office supplies, company forms, and other items to take to the show.

- Plastic sheeting to cover the carpet during setup
- Wooden shims for leveling
- Cleaning cloths, spray cleaner, and a portable vacuum cleaner
- Small fire extinguisher and a selection of medical supplies, just in case

Booth Transportation

It can be just as exasperating moving your booth across town as across the nation. However, if you plan the move and allow enough time, there should be few problems. There are three methods:

1. *Ship to the decorator.* You can advance ship to the show's general contractor. Your booth will be stored in that company's warehouse and transported to the hall and delivered to your space.
2. *Ship to the show floor.* Your booth can be shipped directly to the loading dock at the hall and then delivered to your space. If you elect this method, you or your hauler should check with the general contractor to determine the best time of arrival. To avoid aisle

congestion, most large and midsized shows "target" move-in times. Booth spaces the farthest away from the loading dock are brought in first. (Don't miss your allotted time—if you do, you may end up waiting until the very end.)

3. *Lug-a-booth.* The ground rule, virtually everywhere, is that you are allowed to carry your booth into the hall without the aid of any equipment, such as a dolly. We don't suggest doing this. It is worth the extra money for professional help. Focus on marketing—not the booth.

Chapter 16, "Exhibit Transportation and Setup at the Show," expands on what we present here. Cost is a concern. You will see that over-the-road and air carriers calculate prices using a formula that is customarily based on the space your materials take up. You will pay a second transport bill, the cost of moving materials in the hall itself. Because space-taking is not as important, these prices are calculated on a pure weight basis, price per 100 pounds, for instance. The term used to describe these services in the hall itself is *drayage.*

Saving Time and Money

What follows are some guidelines on how to reduce cost and stress. The stress comes from not having what you've shipped show up on time.

- *Concentrate.* Place items into as few crates or boxes as possible. Haulers and drayage companies charge minimums! In addition, the fewer the containers, the less likely it is that items are misplaced. (Exhibit managers have spent hours wandering around convention halls looking for small boxes that may have been dropped off at the wrong booth space. If you spot somebody else's box in your booth space, let that person know. You will have created an instant friend.)

- *Labels.* Provide lots of easy-reading mailing labels. Include the hall address, name of the show, your company name, and especially your booth space number and a back-home phone number. Tape one label on top and at least two others on either side. Though it takes extra time, hand print these labels on large sheets using a felt-tip marker. Doing this makes it far easier for workers operating in the crunch of show hall setup to read where you are. Number your crates or boxes on the labels; "1 of 3, 2 of 3, 3 of 3." That allows you to take a fast inventory.

- *Special handling.* If you are shipping delicate objects, you will pack things quite well. But, in addition, ask for some special services by your hauler. For instance, an airfreight shipment may be handled up to 10 times from pickup to delivery.

- *Hall route.* If you go the lug-a-booth route, ask in advance where you can enter the hall. It is unlikely that the loading dock would be permitted, what with all else going on there. In addition, there may be some restrictions on the use of elevators or, more frequently, the escalator. We observed an exhibitor carrying a booth up an escalator. A slip, and they both tumbled.

- *Empty crates and repacking.* During the show your empty crates and boxes will be stored for you by the contractor. You will be given "empty-crate" stickers. Fill them out using a marker pen, with a big space-number ID, and the boxes will be taken away and delivered back to you after the close of the event. There are two things to remember: One is that cardboard boxes should be stored inside more substantial crates. (If you do not have heavy crates, ask an exhibit neighbor who does if you can put your cardboard boxes inside for storage.) Second is to retain your protective materials—bubble wrap or whatever. You will use them again outbound and won't have a chance to buy new. (Sheets of plastic bubbles are easier to handle than "popcorn," those loose white balls.)

Setup at the Show

Expositions are not easy to put together at the site. Scores, even hundreds, of exhibitors arrive at about the same time. Added to that, the show itself must be "dressed." And all of this takes place in meager time. If you are walking into this environment for the first time, brace yourself for what might appear to be chaos. It always comes together, frazzled nerves notwithstanding, but you can help yourself by having a grasp of what to do and where to go to get help.

Show Contacts at the Arena

When you arrive at that unfamiliar convention hall, you have three prime places to go for help:

1. *Service desk area.* Located adjacent to the exhibit floor, this office area will include service counters for each of the contractors serving the show, from carpet to chrysanthemums, audiovisual to security. If you have placed orders with some of these contractors in advance, they should have a copy. (Bring your own copy to help in case there has been a filing error.) In addition, you may have new items that

have emerged. New orders can be created, or old ones revised. You can work with the service desk people to schedule the work at the appropriate time. They are almost always helpful. For instance, if you are renting plants, the service supervisor will suggest delivery shortly before show opening, after other setup work is complete.

2. *Exhibitor registration.* This counter is always in the lobby outside the exhibit area. It is your first stop on the way in. This is where you pick up your badge, program, and assorted information. If you arrive early and that desk is not yet open, you may have to secure a work pass to get onto the show floor.

3. *Show office.* This office should be located near the registration area off the lobby. This is the place to go if you have any real problems. At larger events show management representatives, often called *floor captains,* are constantly on the show floor looking for problems or helping people out. It can be a very good idea to introduce yourself to one of these people, especially if this is your first exhibit. You are a customer!

Exhibitor Kit Contracts

Earlier we pointed out that you should bring copies of service order contracts sent in advance. You should bring the kit itself to the show as well. It can be useful as a reference manual on show rules and other things.

Booth Setup Sequence

There is a logical sequence to follow. You can plan the work in smooth fashion and know when to ask for various services to be performed. Here is the list:

- *Check your space.* Find out where you are, and look for any surprises. For instance, there could be a post or electrical service box in your space that did not show up on the floor plan. Also, see if your exhibit materials have been delivered, and if so, check your inventory.

- *Have carpet and electrical work done.* The first step is laying carpet and covering it with plastic sheets to keep things clean during setup. An exception: If you will require electric service out away from the back wall, have the electrical cable run first, then the carpet.

- *Erect the booth, making electrical connections later.*

- *Place the signs and products.*

- *Prepare storage crates.* The drayage people will have provided you empty-crate labels. Fill them out with a marker pen, showing the space number in large numerals, and affix them to at least two sides

of each crate. The contractor will come by and take them away for
storage during the show.

- *Touch up any scratches and clean.* Then cut away the plastic sheet
  around the structure.
- *Unpack and store literature and office supplies.*
- *Have any plants or flowers you ordered delivered and placed.*
- *Have carpet vacuumed.* Shows typically provide a just-before-open-
  ing carpet vacuuming service. If not, you can order it.

Exhibit setup and transportation are covered in more detail in
Chapter 16. Here is, however, a suggestion: If this is your first show
and you are doing anything at all complex, hire professional management to help. An exhibit house or independent labor contractor or
even a show decorator can provide this. It will cost some extra, but it
can be worth it.

Operations

If an expo is scheduled for an afternoon opening, there is a temptation
to delay your arrival until that morning. Those who do find themselves frantically trying to beat the setup deadline. The show opens,
and they are exhausted. They are not fresh and ready to meet
prospects. The first show day is an absolute waste. Getting set to go
becomes an end in itself, not the start of work.

Preshow Meeting

If you get set up early, you'll have time to do what should be done just
before opening. Even if your team is just two or three people, you
truly need to meet and remind each other about what you are about to
do, and how to do it. What follows is a meeting agenda:

- *Goals.* Define, again, your show mission, and establish the individual goals, using the methods cited in Chapter 2.
- *Products and services.* It sounds repetitive, but go over what you are
  offering—key selling features and especially the applications or
  uses of your products by buyers. If you are to demonstrate a product, save time just before the bell to practice.
- *Key customer list.* Compare and share the names of VIPs you expect
  to meet. Discuss exactly how you will handle each of these visitors.

- *Booth work schedule.* Agree on a sensible work schedule. Try to limit on-duty time to four hours a day. Provide breaks every two hours.
- *Selling methods.* Figure 3-5 is a list of hints covering the basics of methods used at booths. Photocopy this list, and go over it during the meeting.
- *Seminar coverage.* If there are seminars of special interest, agree on who will cover what and come back with reports or findings.
- *Competition analysis.* Agree on who will cover what competitor, observing to see and report.

This kind of meeting is best if it is combined with something social, perhaps a breakfast together, or if it's an early-day opening, dinner together the night before.

Selling Methods

The most important hint in our Figure 3-5 list is conducting discussions as dialogue presentations, trying to learn as much from the visitor as you hope he or she learns from you about products and services. Exhibits are far more than show-and-tell. We dwell on this and how to do it in Chapter 18. We urge you to read that over and add "how to" to your preshow meeting.

Current Customer and Prospecting Contacts

Separate, in your show operation, meeting new people from those you know already. You are in a better position to manage contacts with those you already know, so you can figure out in advance how to make sure you have time to meet new people as well.

- *Preshow appointments.* Talking with current customers can take a lot longer than greeting new potential customers. Try to schedule appointments with current people in advance for times when show floor traffic will be slow or even out of show hours. (Breakfast meetings are good.)
- Prospecting at the booth. These shorter contacts can be, long range, your future.

There are two reasons for us to suggest trying to set appointments with those you know in advance. First, there is an instinct to deal most

**Basic Hints on Sales
Prospecting at the Booth**

- Wear standard business dress and older, more comfortable shoes.
- Arrive at the booth 15 minutes early each day.
- Wear your name badge on the right so people catch your name.
- Speak slowly and clearly. Halls are noisy.
- Don't carry on extensive conversations with fellow staff members.
- Don't smoke, eat, or drink, even when invited to do so by a customer.
- Greet people at the edge of the aisle, not back in the booth.
- Don't sit down. Appear "ready to help."
- Never start a conversation with, "Can I help you?"
- Introduce yourself, and ask a leading question. (What do you do? Do you have any special purposes for attending the show?)
- Use the first moment to qualify. Then decide to go ahead or not.
- Describe what you are offering with tie-in to your prospect's interests in a very few moments—a summary.
- Ask about buying interest within five minutes. (Are you interested in this? Should we meet later back in your office? Do you think what we have fits with your needs?)
- If a prospect complains, move that person out of the booth to finish the conversation.
- Remain polite and professional, no hail-fellow-well-met approach. You must control the contact and know when to end it.
- Try to schedule appointments with current customers for times when the show floor is likely to be quiet. Save busy hours for prospecting.
- Do paperwork, leads, or orders, right away. Write clearly.
- Schedule a short after-hours meeting to clean things up for the day.
- Try to limit a day's work at the booth for prospecting to four hours. Save the rest for current customers and learning at seminars.

Figure 3-5. This is a list of basic booth contact performance hints that can be retyped or photocopied for use during training sessions. (For more information, see Chapter 18.) Note that a *qualified sales lead* is one you'd really like to follow up.)

with those we know. Second, short-range orders bring short-range benefits. However, a sense of balance is needed to keep your business growing.

Daily Operations

All too often, even after planning, the booth operation during the event takes on the aspect of a poorly run fire drill. People react to the moment, not to the plan. Essentials get lost. For instance, at the end of the day leads and orders have to be reviewed, often edited. But some booth staff workers who have to do this job accept early postday appointments to meet customers, not leaving time for reviewing leads, saying something like, "I'll remember what happened and will do it in the morning." Wrong on both counts. A short, scheduled, postday meeting helps. Review:

- Leads and orders written
- Notes on contacts and determine action
- Information to pass along on what was learned by attending seminars or by observing competitors

Postshow Operations

Getaway day is always frenzied. A sense of relief is combined with a desire to get home and lots of work. The same is true on that first day back in the office. The work pile has been building during the show.

Exhibit Teardown and Removal

Organize your departure in advance, during the show. The steps are the reverse of installation:

- *Dismantling.* Place orders for labor to help tear down and pack.
- *Rentals.* Confirm on pickup your delivery of rental items.
- *Transport.* Make outbound shipping arrangements.
- *Travel hint.* Many first-time exhibitors make their own outbound reservations with little regard for what is going to happen after the closing bell. Give yourself extra time, even the next day.

Added to last-day pressure, at many shows, is an exhibitor meeting where you can voice concerns and ideas for the next event. Often, at the same time, you will be given an opportunity to make preliminary space reservations for next year. Do that even if you change plans later.

The moment the closing bell rings, three things happen. First, a show contractor team starts rolling up the aisle carpet. Rolling in behind is another team, delivering empty crates to booths for packing. Third, shortly afterward, teams ordered arrive at booths to start teardown.

- Organize your materials by crate, with crate inventory in hand.
- Check display materials for scratches or damage, making notes.
- Place outbound shipping labels, prepared in advance, on each crate.

Never leave the hall before freight has been picked up and you have copies of shipping papers to use later if there is any slipup. (One of our favorite stories is about an exhibitor who did nothing at all about teardown—just walked out and went to the airport. At the end of work, in the night, casting a shadow from one security lamp 40 feet up, stood the lonely booth.)

Paperwork

The currency of exhibits are leads, orders, and seminar and competition notes. Exhibit professionals tell real horror stories about finding these papers packed away inside exhibit crates months after the last show! Don't let this happen to you. Take these papers away from the booth every day. Make sure they are all in your pocket instead of in some carton that gets loaded with the booth.

First Day Back Home

Even if you have been conscientious about returning calls during the show, there is a lot awaiting you when you get back to the office or store. Yet that first day must be, in part, an extension of your exposition experience:

- Leads and orders should start being processed.
- Competition and seminar notes must be typed and prepared for everyone to review.
- Costs have to be tabulated to date.
- Notes of exhibit damage have to be typed for future reference.
- If you took photographs of your booth, the film must be processed.
- A time should be set aside for you to think and write down your impressions.

Memories fade quickly. Work set aside because of what appears to be more important immediate needs ends up under a pile.

Where to Look for More Information

These first three chapters, "The Quick Fix," are intended as a start-up guide for those with little experience and as a review for those who are more experienced. These fundamentals will see you through and make you a success. However, there are more things you can do to assure profit. Pick what you want from our table of contents, but we immediately suggest:

- *Chapter 12, Managing Time.* We suggest time schedules, what to do and when, for different situations. Information there expands on the 28-day time sequence outlined in Chapter 2.
- *Chapter 16, Exhibit Transportation and Setup at the Show.* We realize that these concerns are of great interest to first-time exhibitors. What appears in this chapter is plenty, but you might feel even better after reading Chapter 16.
- *Chapter 18, Exhibit Floor Selling.* We ask that you do read this chapter, and in particular the how-to process that surrounds encouraging and managing dialogue at a booth.

When all is said and done, economical face-to-face contact is the raison d'être of exhibiting.

PART 2

Planning to Manage Your Program

4

Preparing an Annual Exhibit Plan

The three chapters in Part 1, "The Quick Fix," cover the essentials of exhibit marketing. Because of that, they are ideal for first-time exhibitors or more experienced folks who want to check what they do against a standard. Part 1 focused on what one should plan and do for an individual event. Part 2, starting here, aims at helping part-time or full-time exhibit managers plan their programs. The goal: improving results with less fuss and less time and money wasted.

Companies do a whole lot of autopilot exhibiting. They go back to one or several shows every year, mostly because they think that it's a must-do. What emerges is a blinders-on work procedure. One sales manager said, "I know what to do. I've been doing shows for 10 years." Wrong. That manager had exactly 1 year's experience, repeated 9 more times. The shows come and go, and that person is always in the middle of the same squeeze play.

There are other scenes. One is the fire-drill show. That results when somebody has a great idea about going into an event with a majestic-sounding name. Typically, this happens three or four weeks in advance—chaos. Another fire drill emerges when a new product is about to be launched and the company's big annual exhibit is changed six times in three weeks.

Then there is the "Let's expand our market" problem. The exhibit itself is fine but the company is fumbling. Here is an illustration. One particular Maryland-based firm was serving the mid-Atlantic area well, but it also had national aspirations. So it exhibited at industry events in Texas and California and was rewarded with great sales leads. Fine, except there was no sales and service operation in place to handle business from those states. Not one lead was followed up, as requested by prospects. When the outfit went back two years later, it had to dig out of a promise-not-kept reputation.

The Annual Exhibit Plan

Most outfits create annual exhibit plans. But people don't pay much attention to them. They are thought of as plans for spending money, not a strategy to make the long green. If there is a full-time exhibit manager or coordinator involved, that person often takes on the role of a cost manager and is not seen as a value manager. Most important, the exhibits are still thought about *one at a time,* not as part of a program.

In Part 1 we covered individual show mission statements and the need to define a clear set of audience-related objectives, some of which can be measured to provide guidance. The same is true for an annual exhibit plan. For the most part, even those companies that start the annual plan with a mission find themselves writing mush, a lot of good-sounding baloney. An exhibits mission should be practical, a clear statement of support to help reach company goals.

This chapter explains how to write an annual plan. The other chapters in Part 2, "Planning to Manage Your Program," cover process management methods used to support the plan. If you can adopt at least part of what is presented, you will be on the way to a changed corporate culture, a shifted perception of what shows can deliver to the company.

Exhibits in the Marketing Mix

A booth serves many roles: display, office, advertisement—in a sense, a stage for human activity from which support can be directed for sales and service people. However, an exhibit *program* must be part of something larger, far more strategic. When the annual plan is written, it has to explain exactly how the program relates to and supports essential sales goals and corporate strategies. For instance, the annual total marketing plan might require meeting specific product sales objectives. That reality should be reflected in the exhibit plan, which should include how the job will be done.

Marketing Communications

Added to relationships with corporate, marketing, and direct sales support strategies, exhibits are part of the marketing communications mix. The plan also should identify where exhibits fit in context with those programs.

Advertising.   Advertising is used to reach several goals. These can include everything from developing awareness to direct response. An ad plan should be written in parallel with the exhibit plan. For instance, if an advertising campaign is to be released at a specific time, the exhibit plan should specify how the exhibit program will dovetail. That could mean incorporating a key graphic approach, a theme, or special product display. In addition, advertising is often used to promote an exhibit, and this should be reflected in the ad program.

Sales Promotion.   Booklets, brochures, and other literature items will be planned. In addition, there will likely be a direct-mail program. The exhibit plan should reflect those plans, and sometimes it may have a substantial impact on those efforts. There are several areas to consider:

- In this book you will see that we suggest trying to reduce or restrict the distribution of fancy, expensive literature at shows. As an alternative, if "something" has to be available, we counsel preparing something simple and low cost, perhaps a fact sheet or flyer.

- Some companies serve several different industries, and trade shows may be more available in one industry than in another. This reality should lead to developing more tactical direct mail for the industries that cannot be reached with exhibits.

- Direct-mail programs should support exhibits and also products. We stress the importance of preshow promotion to help attract appropriate booth visitors. This support should be reflected in the total sales promotion program.

Media or Press.   Another chunk in a company's marketing communications program focuses on providing company or product information to press outlets. There are many ways in which a press program should relate to an exhibit program plan. For example:

- Business and even consumer press people attend shows to gather story information. A press plan should reflect what is going to happen with exhibits. This can run the gamut from a simple press release placed on the pickup table in the show's pressroom to a full-scale news conference announcing a new product. Some large shows even provide facilities for live and tape TV feeds.

- Press releases before events build booth traffic. This activity should become part of both the press and exhibit program plans for the year.

Special Events.   Many companies put together special events for VIP customers, shareowners, employees, or other groups. Often, these events require exhibit support. These activities can run from the annual corporate shareowners' meeting to sponsorship of cultural or sporting events. Some companies schedule internal management meetings before or after a key trade show because so many people gather anyway for the expo. These activities should be noted in the annual exhibit plan with as many specifics as possible.

The Synergism Medium

Writing a solid annual plan is not easy. What is fascinating about exhibiting is how so many different parts can come together. But pulling in those parts can does create problems in annual plan writing in all but the smallest of companies. Work groups or divisions—or whatever you call internal organizations—plan and work with blinders on toward group objectives. A budget management mentality propels this along with a "What's in it for me?" outlook.

An advertising theme going back a few years was "Spend it now or spend it later." The idea was that by spending a little now on the product advertised, you could save a lot more later on something else. In our case if you spend time and energy writing a solid, specific, and practical annual plan, you will save far more time and energy later. The agony option is operating the planning process *one show at a time,* working harder and longer—and often not getting the help required to get the most back on a dollar investment.

Exhibiting to Reach Sales Goals

We point out that several goals can be aimed at simultaneously, advertising, image, and marketing among them. But where booth operations can most easily be seen to provide a payoff is in support of direct sales activity. More on why later, but the number of sales calls needed to close a sales lead go down by three-quarters when the first contact is at a show, a big-time cost-of-sales saving.[1]

If direct sales support is one of your goals, put the hammer down on that in your plan. Outline what you will do, how it will be done, and how you can measure sales support without appearing to take credit for the ultimate sale. Don't forget that an exhibit does not sell...people sell. Chapter 9 presents two measurement methods that allow us to assess exhibit performance on its own.

Nonselling Exhibit Objectives

We have mentioned the less sales oriented objectives that you can cite in your plan: community, industry, and stockowner relationship improvement goals. Two specific goals come to mind from experience and observation: product evaluation and professional research.

Product Evaluation

Expositions can be ideal venues to explore the potential for new-product acceptance or to field suggestions for improvements on existing products.

- Major companies tuck product prototypes away in private rooms and invite key customers attending the show in for presentations and comment, after signing nondisclosure agreements. (It is important that these presentations do not become hidden sales approaches, for legal reasons.)

- Small outfits do the same, and sometimes right at the booth. A consumer home show manager in Vancouver, British Columbia, Canada, provided an illustration. A farm couple spent the winter designing a new wood carrier, an attractive rolling cart to carry logs in from the woodpile to the hearth. They wanted to offer the cart at a spring home show. The show manager pointed out that few would buy this product in the spring, but people might be willing to make suggestions. Those hints led to an improved design, which was introduced the following fall. The result: two years' worth of direct orders and several retail distributors signed on. The barn became a factory.

Professional Research.   Awareness and attitude research is costly and time-consuming. More and more companies, and especially those offering goods to fairly narrow business markets, find it very cost-effective to mount formal research programs within self-screened expo audiences. There are specialist companies that have emerged to do this, along with formal research on exhibit performance.[2]

Corporate Policy Impacts

An annual plan should point out how the exhibit operation will deal with corporate policies and practices influencing exhibiting operations.

Compensation System

The company's compensation plan can wield a heavy hand on your ability to recruit and manage an appropriate booth staff. The job is never easy but gets ugly if salespeople are paid mainly on a commission basis. Pure commission people do not like time away from their immediate paying customers. They may give short shrift to booth visitors not from their own territories. Some back out of booth duty in the interest of private meetings with their current customers. Special *team-building* training may be needed.[3]

Depending on your situation, this can be so important that it can influence show picking or emphasis. People are more important than booths when it comes to moneymaking. For instance, it can make sense to provide more company support at regional or local events if your company employs a pure commission staff or independent representatives. That is so even if it means reduced emphasis at traditional, large national shows.

Corporate Organization

Within small and midsize companies, exhibit responsibilities are concentrated, often as a part-time function for a sales or ad manager. At large outfits the corporate exhibit manager has to deal with and coordinate the efforts of large, semi-independent divisions or subsidiaries. The two major issues are always *who does what* and *who pays for what*.

For those in this position it is vital to bring the issues to the surface when writing an annual plan. Otherwise, it is inevitable that there will be time-consuming discussions and foot dragging all year. One approach is to suggest participation formulas on expenditures and create specific job lists, with the exhibit manager serving as a consultant.

Later in this book we look at the implications and opportunities for exhibit mangers created by the pattern of corporate downsizing that has affected us in the last few years. Reduced staffs can lead to reshaping the manager's job.

Convention Market Analysis

Annual plan writing time is ideal for taking a fresh look at the events where the company has participated before. In particular, those auto-pilot shows that become second nature deserve review. Events, and especially audiences, go through changes, just as companies do.

It is also a good time to look at new potentials. As industries continue to become more specialized, the need for increasingly specialized knowledge spawns new shows, perhaps smaller, offering appropriate learning and shopping opportunities. In some industries, insurance and banking for instance, there is increased emphasis on regional events. Industry segmentation has been influential as well. The emergence of cable TV, for instance, spawned a whole new series of television industry events.

Nontraditional Exhibiting

Lots of companies have expanded on the notion of participating at traditional trade or consumer events.

- Private, by-invitation-only educational and exhibit events are produced for VIP customers and prospects. Sometimes these are called *user group meetings*. Retailers, including the likes of auto or boat dealers, also produce local events for their customers and prospects.

- Companies have found that specialist manager customers within their target industry attend multiple-industry events aimed at their special areas. For instance, corporate computer managers and engineers often attend multiple-industry events in their specialties.

- Some industries do not have many or even any trade shows. For instance, there are few shows where you can reach manufacturers of rubber products, and especially tire manufacturers. If you want to reach these companies in a trade show environment, you might want to consider exhibiting where they exhibit. For instance, tire manufacturers exhibit at tire dealer events.

Types of Shows

You are used to the kind of show where you have exhibited in the past. You assume that everyone is familiar with your shows. With thousands of events taking place each year, that is unlikely. When you write your annual plan, it is a good idea to have a notion or two about what is out there.

Lead Writing Events.   These shows are typically those offering capital goods and services to other companies, especially those that are customized to a degree for end-user customers. Machinery and some computer events are illustrations. There are also events that involve purchase-for-resale that fit here. For instance, food manufacturers introduce point-of-sale marketing programs for retailers and chains, plus new products and packaging at their events. The same is true in other industries, including consumer fishing tackle manufacturers.

A third show type that fits in this group is one where the goal is encouraging influential people to recommend the use of company products. For instance, pharmaceutical companies *detail* physicians in large numbers at medical shows. Travel industry events offer hotels, cities, nations, and transport companies a chance to educate travel agents who might one day recommend their services. Specialty advertising and premium manufacturers exhibit to inform brokers who suggest items to clients.

Order Writing Events.   There are large groups of trade events at which final orders are written, instead of starting the purchase process with leads, though lead taking remains a part. Among these industries are fashion, furniture, gifts, hardware—down the alphabet to the early-year toy show in New York, which results in year-end holiday inventory in toy departments and stores.

Consumer Shows.   There are thousands of local events that act as both order writing and lead taking roles. Shows attracting local business buyers are among them, along with events aimed at those interested in antiques, autos, boats, gardening, home—down the alphabet to recreational vehicles, sports, and stamps. At many of these events one sees a combination of exhibitors, local independent outlets and national companies supporting their local dealers.

Special-Interest Groups.   There are, as well, exhibit opportunities at events produced for special audiences. Job fairs are among them, along with conventions for those interested in other specific problems or issues, such as events addressing the problems of the hearing impaired or the social and economic interests of minority groups, black or Hispanic, for instance. As an example, military organizations exhibit at job fairs for high school students. Telephone companies demonstrate equipment for the hearing impaired at those specialized events.

General Plan Coverage

An annual plan should touch on each aspect of interest. The plan's objective remains saving time, energy, and money as the year flows along, a tussle for large, complex organizations facing those *who does what* and *budget coverage* issues. In one lump, an annual plan should cover large national shows, regional and dealer support events, and nontraditional exhibiting.

Corporate reorganizations and downsizing have resulted in combining activities at midmanagement that once were treated separately. For instance, more managers find themselves supervising both exhibits and special events. These events sweep from the annual stockholders' meeting to internal sales and incentive gatherings to the VIP customer educational forums mentioned earlier. They must be part of the total plan as well.

Timing Implications.   The advantage of tying everything together in a lump at the year start is that you, and others, will see opportunities for cost savings and greater productivity. For instance:

- An annual sales or technical meeting can be linked to the company's largest trade show participation, leading into that event or perhaps following it. There are likely cost savings.

- The launch of a new product or advertising program can be reflected in or timed with a major trade event. Or, if you know that a competitor will be introducing something new at a given point, you can create a defensive show strategy for that period.

Budget Development

The budget section of your plan is easy or hard to write, depending on how you approach the exercise. The easy way is to take whatever was budgeted last year, update, and add a fudge factor that provides some running room when top management calls for the inevitable cut.

We suggest doing it the hard way. There are two reasons. First, you will learn a lot about the cost realities yourself. Second, you can defend the budget in detail because you know its implications.

The best but most time-consuming way is by using a building-block method, covered in Chapter 7. That is best for an experienced exhibit manager running an ongoing program. For part-timers or perhaps companies just embarking on an exhibit program, there are less precise short cuts, based on industry averages. These were mentioned in Chapter 3, and to save some back-and-forth, we touch upon them again in what follows.

Rule Exceptions

Before we introduce industry-average guidelines, there are some factors to float that may suggest revising the guidelines for your use. Averages are averages, and nobody is average.

- *Products.* The size, weight, and complexity of your products can influence budget allocations. For instance, if you must display or demonstrate large, floor-standing machines, costs will be above the average. The same is true for complex equipment that demands extra back-office space and expert technical help to operate. On the other hand, if you offer services that require only sign support, your cost will be lower than the average.

- *Booths.* Cost guides can depend on different factors. For instance, it may cost less to stock several 10-foot standard units that can be used in multiples than it would for one large custom designed exhibit. Second, budget guide averages include the amount of booth space rented. For instance, if you must show off a steam roller, it is likely that you will rent quite a large space. The backdrop booth cost, however, is likely to be less than the average for the space.

- *Corporate support.* There are times when exhibitors are divisions of or dealers for large parent companies that provide support, either on a co-op or promotional give-back basis. Often that includes the use of corporate booths, graphic signs, or demonstration and display product help. If this is you, decrease your cost estimate from the average.

- *Space cost.* There is wide divergence in the booth space rent charged by associations and show managers. For the most part this figure depends on what they are charged for renting the exhibition hall as a whole.

  Note: Rental can differ because of owner policy. Often, convention halls are built and administered by government authorities. A traditional approach was that the authority would operate its convention center to break even or even as a loss-leader. The payoff was attracting visitors to the area who would spend dollars in the local economy. Hall rental and perhaps a *hotel tax* on visitors covered costs. Increasingly, however, government itself faces financial problems and makes convention facilities support themselves. Prices go up.

The resulting cost range is substantial, from under $10 a square foot for booth space ($1000 for a 10 × 10) to well above $30 per square foot in the USA. The average is in the "low teens." The average per-square-foot booth space cost for the largest 200 trade shows in the USA is above $15 per square foot.[4] Take a quick look at the space costs for the program you are contemplating, and you can go above or below the average suggested.

Budget Rules of Thumb

With the preceding caveats in mind, there are some good ground rules that you can use to prepare a sensible budget, as follows.

Space Cost Method

Industry averages provide a good start-up guideline based on a relationship of space rent cost to other cost factors.

- *Including a Booth.* If part of your investment and out-of-pocket expense will include purchasing a booth, the averages signal that booth space rental should represent about 25 percent of the total *direct* cost. (That excludes the out-of-pocket expenses for people such as travel-related costs.) With exhibit schedule and planned space buys at each show in hand, add up the space costs for all, and multiply by 4 to come up with an estimated budget.[5]

- *If you have a booth.* If you already own a booth, your cost is lower, even if some touch-up or new signs are needed. Thus, the total cost relationship to space is lowered. We suggest multiplying space rental by 3 instead of 4 to create a broad gauge estimate.

People Costs

Even if the dollars do not come from the formal exhibit budget, it is a good idea to estimate the costs for those who will be at the booth. Travel, hotel, and food can add up. These are *indirect* costs, but they do come out of the company pocket.

- If your cost includes purchasing a booth, it is safe to add 35 percent to cover personnel out-of-pocket expense.

- If your cost does not include a booth purchase, add 50 percent to cover personnel costs.

An Illustration

Assume that your schedule involves a half dozen shows. Add up projected space costs for the group, and you total $9000. If you must buy a booth, multiply by 4, a total of $36,000 of direct cost. Then add 35 percent for personnel out-of-pocket, a rounded $13,000. The total budget for the year would be $49,000.

If you already own a booth, the total cost would be less for the same program. The $9000 in space rent costs would be multiplied by 3, a total of $27,000 in direct cost. Add 50 percent for personnel out-of-pocket expenses, a rounded $14,000. Estimate the total program cost at $41,000.

A thought: This guide provides direction for first-time exhibitors on whether to rent or purchase a booth. Put in an extra $8000 up front for a booth and with a six-show annual program, you will break even in the first year and reduce cost in the second.

Additional Budget-Building Information

When you write an annual plan, it can be unwise to provide heavy detail on budget parts since doing so invites questions you may not be prepared to answer at the level of detail required. However, for your purpose there is more information in Chapters 3, 7, and 13.

Budget Judgment

For some, it is hard to accept the cost of exhibiting. There are two reasons: First, there is a natural inclination to spend as little as possible to reach immediate goals. Second, many retain the notion that exhibits represent cost instead of value. Among our other objectives in writing this book, we aim to help you produce measurable value. We also advocate a long-term and strategic approach to exhibit marketing. It makes sense.

Building a Show List

For many, especially those businesses serving only one or two markets, the trade event opportunities are well known. The problem for these is less concern about *what* shows and far more about *how much to invest* in each. Some will be more important than others. We cover the methods used to fashion an objective analysis in Chapter 6. However, there are times when these companies want to enter what for them are new and unfamiliar markets.

Show finding is a more frequent problem for outfits offering products to businesses in many industries. The computer and communications companies fit that mold, as do training firms or those offering office furniture. Regardless, the time to search out shows is during annual plan writing. Otherwise, the ideas will come in over the transom, willy-nilly, all year. The plan becomes chaos.

Show Information Resources

There are several ways to approach the show finding exercise:

- There are several directories published.[6] A selection appears in our reference guide in Chapter 24. Some of these compendiums are fairly expensive. If you work with an exhibit house or exhibit consultant, you may find that they maintain a library.

- If you want to restrict exhibiting to one or two geographic areas, you can contact the Convention and Visitors Bureaus for lists and dates.

- Industry associations, your own or those serving your prospects, are likely to know about the events. If you are embarking in a new market and do not know what association to call, start by contacting the Washington, D.C.–based American Society of Association Executives or the International Association of Exposition Managers in Dallas.

- Industry publications are yet another information source for shows serving their fields. Their reporters typically attend the shows to gather information for upcoming issues. So, besides name and address information, you could probably gather a perspective. While you are talking with a trade press person, ask if you can be sent a sample or two of the publication. Articles cover issues of interest in that industry. Will your products help solve some problems?

- Some of your own salespeople could probably provide clues, or better yet they may be able to call up some of their key customers for some advice. For them it's a "free" sales call that helps build relationships.

With a list of names and addresses in hand, you then must contact each producer to see how much information they can add to what you have already learned. For instance, they should at least be able to provide you with audience breakdown information and a list of the seminars presented at the last event. Having a grasp of the educational program is like reading your prospects' industry magazine. You can look for signals about how your products and services may fit in.

Regional and Local Events

The first shows you will find out about are the big-time national or international hullabaloos that feature hoards of professional visitors and mobs of exhibitors. That's all wonderful, of course, but if you are just entering the market, it may be just as smart, and perhaps more productive, to look for regional or even local events serving that market. Before opening on Broadway, smart play producers run their shows out in their "hustings."

Regional shows allow you to concentrate in a geographic area that is appropriate for you, learning how you might do on the national scene. At regional events, 4 out of 10 visitors travel less than 50 miles to attend. At national shows it is far different. Over half travel more than 400 miles to be there.[7]

Beware of the First-Year Show

The sales literature and prospectus for any event presents an expectation. You are buying in on something that does not exist. That is true even for a large, national event that has been around since Noah walked down the plank. Even at those events there are audience changes each year, especially so if the shows move around. (Reversing the research cited just above, just under half of the professional visitors at a national event travel less than 400 miles to get there. Thus, a national event taking place in New York is likely to offer far more northeast visitors. The next year, when the show moves to Las Vegas, Seattle, San Francisco, Los Angeles, or San Diego, you will greet a West Coast crowd.)

There may be an audience change, but mature shows do have a track record that allows you to feel comfortable that there indeed will be at least some kind of an audience. First-year events are a different kettle of fish. These truly are a pure promise rather than a projection of reality. The event may appear ideal for your list, but it pays to do some extra homework before including it as part of your annual plan.

- Find out who is actually sponsoring the event. An old and respected association is one thing, a Johnny-Come-Lately or for-profit show producer could be something else.

- No matter who is producing the event, try to obtain some information on how it is funded. Credit-rating information on the sponsor can be part of that. It can take two or even three years for a trade show to become self-supporting.

- Detailed information on the show's attendance promotion program is essential. Who are they trying to reach? How are they doing this?

How many? What are they saying? How is this program funded? (If promotion program dollar support depends on early exhibit rent income, there is greater risk.)

- Is there an education program planned for those attending? For all events other than pure buying-for-resale shows, these educational programs are a big influence on attendance. What subjects will be covered? Who will present them?

- Have other companies already signed up to exhibit? Can the show organizer provide the names of the exhibit contact people so that you can call and compare viewpoints?

Vertical and Horizontal Shows

What follows is academic, but it may be of some value to full-time exhibit managers and coordinators just starting. You can probably figure out where your company stands or wants to go. Our pioneer exhibits marketing research company[8] developed a common measurement that is helpful in looking at show types and how we can adjust other research results. The figure the company uses is called the *AIF,* or the *audience interest factor.* The AIF is a percentage of visitors who stop to talk or gather literature from at least 20 percent of exhibitors at an event. Each show is different, of course, and many have not done the research that produces this figure. However, there are some broad categories, and you can fit your type of event into the mix. After we run through a summary of types, we will explain how this can help in planning.

Vertical Shows

These events are very narrowly targeted. This group can be divided into subgroups. One is a show that attracts very specific buyers. (There is a national meeting for operating room nurses that fits. Visitors are all operating room nurses, and the exhibitors are specialists in producing products used in those rooms.) The AIF, or percentage of visitors that visit at least 20 percent of the booths, is an amazing 57 percent.

The second type of vertical show is one that specialists within organizations from several industries attend. Many call these *cross-industry events.* We mentioned these before. Computer experts, for instance, attend data processing conferences. The AIF is lower, down to about 48 percent.

Horizontal Shows

This broad show category also breaks into two. First are events that attract a wide diversity of exhibitors but attract visitors from only one industry. For instance, the American Bankers Association and Offshore Technology Conference attract bank or oil industry executives. But many exhibitors present products used in many industries, a less targeted approach. The AIF is less—down to 39 percent.

The second horizontal show type is where both visitors and exhibitors come from several different industries. The Plant Engineering and Maintenance Show is an example. A local business products event fits as well. The percent of visitors going to at least 20 percent of the booths is lowest—about 35 percent.

Planning Implications of the Different Types of Shows

Thank you for reading the above. What may seem like academic gobbledegook can really help annual plan writers. Plug in three realities:

1. Very narrow interest shows that combine specialist vendors and buyers tend to be smaller events. These also tend be less sensitive to audience change, depending on show location each year.

2. Broad-scope national events attract larger audiences. There is a greater tendency, as well, for audiences to regionalize, depending on where they take place.

3. Regardless, your booth and staff size, combined with the total time a show is open, will determine how much work you can do at the event. (See Chapter 6 for how to calculate, in advance, work production.)

Here are some things to think about at annual planning time. Assume one of the shows on your list is narrowly focused but small. About 2000 visitors are anticipated. You can calculate that between 950 and 1150 visitors will be interested enough to want to stop and talk or pick up literature. On the other hand, assume that a "horizontal" event, larger, is on your list. It offers four times more audience size, or 8000 visitors. However, the AIFs are lower, so you can calculate that between 2800 and 3100 visitors will be interested enough to stop.

You really never know until you get there. But it is wise to do as much as possible to translate a guess into a calculated risk and do what you can to reduce that risk. For instance:

- Comparing the two events, which one offers more long-term potential, all objectives combined? That answer will influence your investment and staff size.

- To what degree is preshow promotion required? (See Chapter 14.) At larger events it is more difficult for buyers to find the companies they want to talk to, so more targeted preshow promotion is needed.

Consumer Shows

By now the eyes of some of our readers who exhibit at public or consumer shows may be glazed over because of our emphasis on vertical and horizontal business-to-business trade shows. That is wrong. The same kind of audience interest levels are found in their events. Clearly a stamp show attracts only stamp dealers and collectors. A home show attracts both visitors and exhibitors with a broad range of interests. So the AIF just has to be higher at a stamp event or antique show than at an auto, boat, or home expo.

There are, however, questions that consumer show exhibitors can raise with producers that will influence planning. For instance:

- What will it cost consumers to come in the door? Demand elasticity theory signals that the higher the price, the lower the attendance. A high ticket price means that you are left with a smaller but far more purchase-interested crowd.

- To what extent are tickets discounted or given away to help create a larger throng? (If that number is substantial, it may not be a problem except that you have to work hard at the booth sorting out the serious from the curious. Some events become as much family afternoons out as they are specialized shopping expeditions.)

- How and to what extent will the event be promoted? What is the advertising message? You can play that back in what you advertise and promote.

A pubic show promoter, just like a business-to-business show manager, has few revenue sources. For the most part these sources boil down to exhibit space rental income and admission fee income. That is reality. There is a clash. Show producers have responded to exhibitors who seem interested only in big numbers with promotion programs and ticket distribution policies that build the total traffic. These same exhibitors later complain that the show did not provide enough qualified buyers in the total audience. Our advice to exhibitors: You can't have it both ways.

The Annual Plan Document

Every company has its own format for preparing and presenting departmental plans. That is sensible because top managers, and sometimes outside board members, have to evaluate many of them, and this chore is far easier when the plans all follow a similar format.

There are, however, suggestions we can make that should blend, in one way or another, with your company's approach. Typically, these papers start with a summary sheet that compresses everything—strategic, tactical, costs, and returns. The summary is followed by a tight but expansive explanation for those who wish to read it. Included are the following:

- *Company objectives.* Corporate, marketing, sales, and service goals must be restated. You must summarize these to assure top management readers that your plan was prepared with knowledge of what they know already. This first section of the annual plan should conclude with a short, practical mission statement for exhibits and events. Check the "Exhibiting to Reach Sales Goals" and "Nonselling Exhibit Objectives" sections of this chapter for some hints on what can be included. Regardless of what you select, however, position exhibiting and events management as cost-effective support, not an end. People sell. Exhibits help. Advertising builds awareness. Exhibits help.

- *Exhibits and events objectives.* This section should point out particulars on how your activities support corporate and other work group goals. Because what you do involves other departments, those relationships must surface in summary form. For example, you could mention the exhibit tie-in with a new advertising theme. Another could be recognition of the need to support a new-product launch or specialized sales program. A third might acknowledge support relationships with corporate or field work groups.

- *Costs and returns.* In more fulsome fashion, you should outline what the company will spend and what it should expect in return as a result of accepting the plan. This becomes your promise to management.

- *Addenda.* The plan should be supported by specific answers to anticipated questions. Two are most important:

  1. *The show list.* The participation list should be presented in a calendar format. Blended into the calendar should be major company events the exhibits program will support. If there are different levels of exhibiting, at national, regional, and local levels, for instance, they all should appear. For a sample, see Figure 4-1.

**Sample Exhibits or Events
Calendar**

January

New advertising campaign starts in national media.

- National XYZ show takes place using new theme.
- Regional XYZ show takes place using new theme.

February

Local dealer co-op advertising and direct-mail programs start.

- Two local support shows.
- VIP customer symposium to get comments on new product.

March

- National ABC show.
- 2 regional shows.
- 3 local support shows.

April

Launch new product at DEF show.
Related special advertising and promotion.

- National DEF show product launch.
- Annual stockholders' meeting features new product.

May

Start new-product advertising at local level.

- 3 local support shows.
- Regional GHI show.

Figure 4-1. For annual plan presentation purposes, an exhibit calendar should be blended with related marketing communications programs and major activities that are supported by marketing communications and events work.

June

Start lead gathering for fall sales push.

- National JKL show and related new-product awareness research.
- Regional MNO show.
- 2 local support shows.

July
- No shows.

August

Annual sales conference.

- National PQR show is location for the lead-in sales conference.

September

Fall sales push kickoff with direct-mail and exhibit support.

- 2 regional PQR shows.
- 3 local support shows.

October
- National STU show with second wave of product awareness research.
- 2 local support shows.

November
- 3 local support shows.

December

Annual sales seminar and awards weekend.

- No shows.

Summary.   6 national, 7 regional, and 18 local shows and 4 special events

Figure 4-1. For annual plan presentation purposes, an exhibit calendar should be blended with related marketing communications programs and major activities that are supported by marketing communications and events work. (*Continued*)

2. *Who pays what.* This expansion of the "Costs and Returns" section can address funding sources as they relate to various aspects of the program. For instance, if you provide different levels of support for various show types—national, regional, and local, for instance—this fact should be spelled out. If other departments make budget contributions to the corporate exhibit allotment, perhaps on a fair-share percentage basis, this fact must be cited so that each knows what it must budget.

   It is rare that an exhibit or events budget covers all costs related to participation. For instance, it is likely that another department provides demonstration or display product support. In addition, out-of-pocket costs for those who staff the booths probably are paid by each individual's office. Added to these may be the costs for providing literature or show advertising. It is appropriate to acknowledge these off-budget contributions and where possible to estimate the amount. For instance, you may be able to estimate total out-of-pocket travel costs based on a formula such as one presented in the "People Costs" section of this chapter.

3. *The value of time.* This is an optional addition to an annual plan document. If you feel it might be worthwhile in increasing understanding of the seriousness of an exhibit commitment, you can provide a cost estimate for the single largest cost related to exhibiting, and it is not in anyone's exhibit budget. This is value of the *time* devoted, especially by those in other work groups who staff and support exhibiting. We provide an estimating formula in Chapter 7 that shows you how to do this. You will be presented with figures that can create conflicting emotions. On the one hand, you may fear telling management how much it really costs the company as a whole to exhibit. Looking at the other side of that coin, you can be assured that corporate management will be more supportive of initiatives that ensure a payoff. Added to that, it is far more likely that managers in departments or groups that supply people for exhibit staffs will make their support judgments with more care. That can reduce the degree to which booth staffing is considered a marginal activity with people-shifting up to the last minute.

Planning Benefits

We are suggesting what, for many, may be a lot of extra work. Writing an annual plan is not and should not be an easy chore! There are benefits, however, for you and your company. We mentioned before that it can save you time and energy throughout the year by reducing back-and-forth discussions and departmental heel dragging. In addition, it is far more likely that you will end with a more cost-effective, results-oriented program. Consequently you will have elevated management perceptions of exhibiting and enhanced your own reputation.

There is one last benefit: At many large companies there is a tradition of current-year budget cutting. People in those outfits can almost predict when. The most popular months are April, August, and October. Managers with a solid plan in hand find it easier to manage that process. They can scale back to retain program balance. They can avoid a more petulant approach, chopping whole events out of an upcoming schedule, or begging for money from other departments going through their own cost reduction agonies.

5
Creating Exhibit Goals

Working Smarter, Not Harder

Business argot floats over and around us. The buzz words change all the time. Back in the exuberant eighties, one of the hot terms was *synergism*. That umbrella word was used to describe or defend corporate acquisition tendencies. In marketing communications, the term meant the ways in which media and messages were coordinated to provide a collective force. Ad agencies, pitching business, liked it as a justification for gathering in all sorts of marketing communications work splattered about in competing shops.

As harsher economic realities of the nineties emerged, newer terms became fashionable. Among them were *downsizing, process reengineering, consolidation, outsourcing,* and *total quality management,* or TQM. As you read, yet newer term-umbrellas are emerging to summarize or sugarcoat.

The nineties' pink-slip gobbledygook words boil down to working smarter, not harder. Most good managers have always put in more than the ideal 35- or 40-hour week. But smart-work has been late blooming in the exhibit management field. As pointed out in Chapters 3 and 4, many companies spend all kinds of money exhibiting without a truly firm grasp on why and what they want to accomplish. That's not smart. Everyone has a vague idea, but smart managers want a lot more!

Even though booth marketing has grown markedly over the last 15 years, management has retained its notion of exhibits as representing more a *necessary but evil cost* than an opportunity for *value*. (In some respects business people of 700 years ago, setting up tents at the fairs along Marco Polo's Silk Route between Europe and Asia, were working smarter because they defined value goals.) This chapter's purpose is to provide methods we can use to rekindle the value concept. This chapter, and in fact the entire book, aims at the application of total quality management (TQM) rationale in harvesting exhibit value.

The Mission Statement

Large companies work with mission statements to guide large numbers of people. They also drive a corporate stake in the ground that establishes, for customers and prospects, a "position." Company themes emerge. The U.S. Postal Service's "We Deliver" has been one of them, a two-word mission statement summary reflecting a service focus.

Show-related mission statements are more tightly written than one for a company. The idea is for internal managers to grasp how exhibiting as a whole fits in the company. This type of mission statement would be one to cite in an annual plan (see Chapter 4). More specific mission statements are written for individual shows.

Annual Plan Statements

There are a number of different goals possible, and selecting the best goal depends on the company or situation. Those goals that apply to you can emerge in a clearly value oriented exhibiting mission statement. (To make photocopying easier, the list below also appears as Figure 5-2 at the chapter's end, entitled "The Top 19: Exhibit Objectives Starter List.")

Exhibiting Objectives.   Start by selecting one or more of the value objectives that follow:

- Gather leads for sales follow-up.
- Write orders from old and new customers.
- Collect names for the company database.
- Distribute literature to inform and develop awareness.
- Illustrate company commitment to the industry.
- Support dealers, distributors, or outlets.
- Introduce new products, applications, or co-op marketing programs.
- Generate press coverage of company initiatives.

- Enhance image by giving nonsales seminars and demonstrations.
- Enter new markets.
- Explain how company products and services are applied.
- Prevent competition from gaining an advantage.
- Evaluate what the competition is doing.
- Learn about the issues of concern to the customer industry.
- Find out why customers buy from their viewpoint, not just "applications."
- Entertain VIP customers.
- Conduct research among current and potential customers.
- Educate and motivate employees and dealers.
- Sell to small and midsize prospects you can't afford to call on.

These 19 goals, plus others that may occur to you, are all value related. Those that apply to you can be blended into a value-oriented mission statement for an overall show program. The list is repeated for easy photocopying as Figure 5-2.

The statement should also include reference to cost-effectiveness. In that correlation make it clear that low-cost, person-to-person contact is the basis for cost saving. Research has validated that premise (see Chapter 3). As purely an "advertising" or "industry relations" medium, exhibits are expensive. The true economic value in exhibiting is the opportunity for low-cost, face-to-face contact with key buyers and prospects.

The Impact of Downsizing. We point out, in particular, a recent reality. Companies have been forced to reduce their sales and marketing staffs. For the most part that has meant giving up personal contact with smaller- or medium-sized customers. (Good news for smaller competitors.) However, outfits facing that can use participation at industry events to maintain and even develop small-customer relationships at low cost. However, that must be identified as a serious show goal by top management. It will change the way they exhibit at least to some degree and also affect the ways in which exhibit contacts are followed up after events.

Show Statements

An overall plan statement is completely selfish: *What we want out of exhibiting.* That is not the case when it comes to writing a mission for an individual show. Working smart translates to combining what you want with the audience and its interests.

The statement's value is that it helps you, and everyone else involved, aim at the same thing. With a clear statement in hand, it is easy to write sign copy or decide on booth design. Sales, technical, and advertising people will see their roles more clearly. There will be less confusion in planning and more focused work at the event.

Outside Information.   You know what *you* want. To position that in context with what the audience wants, you have to do some homework. Blinders-on inside thinking can create bad assumptions. For instance, "They are interested in our product features!" That may be the case. But why? A features focus may not give you the real *why-buy* answer. For instance, from a customer perspective, the why-buy might involve one or more other issues:

- *Applications* of features to solve specific problems
- Inventory management tools that control costs
- Servicing abilities
- Delivery schedules
- Product resale profit potentials in specific terms
- Financial arrangements
- Packaging implications
- Co-op marketing programs
- Advertising support

Information Sources.   Because you and yours are "in the business," there is a penchant to think you already know these things. However, it is likely that thoughts are prejudiced by your own motives. Explore a bit, and you may refine that thinking or discover ways to better reflect customer interests:

- Read articles in the trade periodicals serving your customers. The articles will highlight issues of current concern from a customer viewpoint.
- If your event is operating a symposium with the exposition, read that program. The seminars reflect audience interests just as does the industry trade press.
- Talk to your salespeople. See what they can tell you about why customers buy.
- Consider some calls to customers with a list of possible issues in hand, and ask them to rank their reasons for purchasing your products or services.

To illustrate, a show statement might read, "Offer our line of high-quality pineapples in context with improved delivery schedules and our new point-of-purchase product displays." Another: "Position our automatic stack scrubber as a cost-effective solution to meeting new gas emission standards, tied to our ability to service and maintain our machines on a zero-defects basis."

We suggested a mission statement to a greeting card manufacturer going through a midnineties' business process reengineering. That process, among other things, meant pink slips for a number of salespeople. In effect, that statement read, "While maintaining relationships and introducing new products to major buyers, we focus most on the opportunity to maintain and develop relationships with smaller and midrange customers and prospects." We do not mention the company's name because it did not accept our suggestion at the time. We do not know all the reasons why. But it may have been that there was no work process in place to cover what its shows would generate. It may be, as you read this, that they have adopted the approach.

Regardless, by following the approach outlined you can end up with a booth and selling plan that is simple and effective. Here are a couple of examples:

Hill Refrigeration was introducing a new line of fresh produce display cases to be used in supermarkets that were very fancy and feature-rich—even cool mist floating up through the vegetables on the demonstration model at the Food Marketing Institute show in Chicago. However, Hill resisted the temptation to tell it all with signs, videos, and whatnot. Instead, they invited buyers with one simple sign, a cool answer to a hot topic in the supermarket industry: "Save 25 percent in energy costs with our new line."

Another, much smaller company at the same show did as well, even with what amounted to a homemade sign and 250 simple letters to key equipment buyers among the show's multithousand person audience. Tote-Cart, from Rockford, Illinois, became sensitive to increased concern over equipment breakage. It designed, built, and then asked visitors to see "The World's Strongest Shopping Cart." No features—wire thickness, wheel size, and all the rest. It did not even bring the rest of its lines of carts to the show. The prospects they wanted to see did, indeed, visit. Thousands of others walked by, not cluttering the space and wasting anybody's time; their own or that of the Tote-Cart team.

Another company, at another show, had a clearly defined mission that was reflected on its booth sign. That sign read, "See How You Can Produce Plastic ID Cards at Low Cost In-House on a Laser Printer." Those who had a need stopped. Others did not. Another: At a boat show we saw a sign: "Safe Boats for Young Families." Guess who stopped and who did not.

A well-known New York advertising writer penned what became a famous advertising line that traced back to a very clear objective. That line, for an automobile account, went something like, "The Loudest Thing You Hear Is the Ticking of the Electric Clock." The word around town was that this person did even better when trying to sell land he owned in Pennsylvania. Handwritten, photocopied, and placed on employee bulletin boards in ad agency bathrooms, the message was, "Good Amish Farmland for Sale. Call Extension 1234." He sold.

Clear objectives lead to an unconfused message.

Questions for Exposition Managers

A seminar was conducted at an annual meeting of the International Exhibitors Association.[1] A list of 28 questions that can be asked of show managers emerged. Some relate to tactical, implementation issues. Others are more strategic in nature and can aid in setting objectives for participation in a show or in developing plans to reach objectives. The list appears as Figure 5-1.

Focus Group Study.   At the end of the session a volunteer study was conducted. Of the 60-plus who attended, 15 were willing to share their views. Those opinions are summarized here. The perspectives are useful as an overall guide, much like focus group discussion results are of value in helping to set overall direction, or avoiding horrendous mistakes.

What's Hot?   Well over 80 percent of the volunteers felt that breaking down the audience estimate by subgroup was very important. There was recognition that even at tightly targeted events, the entire audience was not necessarily of interest to an individual exhibitor. The subgroups of interest are special interest, geographic, and job title or responsibility. The data could be very helpful in setting goals and determining budget allocations.

Seminar leader Mike Muldoon, a show manager, added that expo managers must be certain to explain that estimates are provided on the basis of past experience. He said, "At even the most stable show there can be a true audience change of 40 percent, year over year. In addition, audience interests change more than many realize because of the dynamics of the industry represented at the show."

Participant Lisa Sinicki from The Design Agency, an exhibit company, commented as well: "Show management information must be taken with a grain of salt. A client decided on a show when told by the show that 10,000 attendees matched the exhibitor's market profile. Four weeks before the event the prereg list arrived and showed that

Show Management Issues and Questions from the Seminar

1. How is the total audience estimate broken down by subgroup? That can include area of special interest, geographic representation, or job title or responsibility.

2. What is the show's history? How stable has been the audience? How does it differ as the show moves from city to city? In the case of a first-year show, who is backing the event, and how much financial support for the show is being provided?

3. What is the nature of the seminar program run in conjunction with the event? How were seminar subject and speaker selection decisions made? Why is this important?

4. How much trade and general press coverage can be anticipated? What arrangements have been made to recruit and serve the press?

5. What is the nature and content of the show's attendance promotion program? Where is it running and what does it say?

6. What kind of promotional assistance is provided to exhibitors who want to get involved with their own preshow promo programs? And why should they do it?

7. To what extent can an exhibitor participate in the seminar programs, and what are the ground rules for participation?

8. Are mailing lists provided by the show producer, either early current-year registration or prior year? Can lists be provided in computer-readable form or just labels? Can subgroups be selected, by title, job function, or geographic representation?

9. How much setup and teardown time has been provided for in the hall rental agreement? How much of this time includes "overtime" labor hours?

10. What are the loading docks like in the facility? What are the truck size limits, and what is the lighting like on the docks? Is the show targeted?

Figure 5-1. The seminar audience, made up mostly of corporate exhibit managers, felt that strategic issues and answers that provide goal-setting direction are most important.

11. What are the most important sections in a show's exhibitor kit? What is mandatory and what is optional? To what extent can "independent" contractors be brought in? What are the ground rules?

12. To what extent can the show floor be opened before or after the show day for a private event, a press briefing at the booth, or a VIP group visit? And what are the ground rules and costs for this?

13. To what extent can show rules be shifted? For instance, for hanging banners, extra booth height, or perhaps an indoor flying blimp?

14. How can we reduce drayage cost? Related to that, what are the current rules in big halls regarding bringing in your own materials?

15. What is the latest in fire prevention regulations as they relate to the use of materials, one- and two-story booths, and so on?

16. What should we look for in context with show-provided security? Where should we step in and pay for more? What should that cost, and who should provide it?

17. Why is electrical-audiovisual service so tightly controlled by the show?

18. What is all this about postshow lead service from registration companies? What do they provide, and what makes sense?

19. If we want to run a private event, either for customers or even to have our own sales conference, when should it be scheduled, and are there any problems with the idea?

20. When will the final registration list be completed, and when can we get a copy?

21. To what extent are exhibitor educational aids provided to help us do better?

22. To what extent do educational, "general sessions," or other activities compete with activities on the show floor? Are there events that stimulate staying on the floor?

23. Will the show provide postevent research on visitor actions, and can exhibitors get their own studies as part of the process?

Figure 5-1. (*Continued*) The seminar audience, made up mostly of corporate exhibit managers, felt that strategic issues and answers that provide goal-setting direction are most important.

> 24. What gets involved with setting booth space rent prices on the floor? In a similar context, what are the considerations in setting prices for show services?
>
> 25. If I want to influence what happens in the future at my most important shows, what is the best approach to doing so in an effective way?
>
> 26. What is your feeling about "ad clutter" at shows—not just booths but preshow and at-show promotions that are aimed at delegates? What's the best way to get through?
>
> 27. To what extent is the show responsible for results?
>
> 28. How do I figure out whether the big national shows or the regional and local events are best for me?

Figure 5-1. (*Continued*) The seminar audience, made up mostly of corporate exhibit managers, felt that strategic issues and answers that provide goal-setting direction are most important.

only 600 matched the profile. Our client went ahead anyway and had one of its most successful shows ever." The figures presented by show management did not mean a lot.

There are two points to make note of: First is that expo managers do not have to blur or inflate figures. Second, as Sinicki points out, "Sometimes the registration questions asked distort the quality and accuracy of the answers."

Best of the Rest. Here is a summary of issues over half of the respondents felt important:

1. *Show history.* How stable is the show, and how much does the audience change year over year? What changes as it moves from city to city?

2. *Exhibitor influence.* "How can I influence what happens at my important shows in the future?"

3. *Promotion.* What is the nature *and content* of the show's audience promotion program? (Many expo executives provide information on the media used, few on what is said.)

4. *Press.* To what extent will trade press representatives attend the show? What is being done to encourage that attendance?

Show Manager Relationships. In one way or another, all these issues and answers can have an impact on fundamental planning. Seminar leader Connie Akin, a show manager, said, "We have to encourage exhibitors to call with their questions and concerns, to give us a chance to become partners in success." We agree. We asked a show manager, not at the seminar, why their event did not publish data in detailed form. The reply was, "Our show is one of the largest in the world and we have plenty of data. However, *so few ask for it* that it does not make sense to publish. We wait for phone calls and then send an abstract."

Seminar attendee J. P. Stevens III, from IBM's Microsystems Division, commented with an analysis of the association–exhibit manager relationship: "There are three categories. (In order) First is marketing and strategy. Second is the show-exhibitor relationship, working together for everyone's good. Third is working together on logistical issues."

The Top 19: Exhibit Objectives Starter List

- Gather leads for sales follow-up.
- Write orders from old and new customers.
- Collect names for the company database.
- Distribute literature to inform and develop awareness.
- Illustrate company commitment to the industry.
- Support dealers, distributors, or outlets.
- Introduce new products, applications, or co-op marketing programs.
- Generate press coverage of company initiatives.
- Enhance image by presenting nonsales seminars and demonstrations.
- Enter new markets.
- Explain how company products and services are applied.
- Prevent competition from gaining an advantage.
- Evaluate what the competition is doing.
- Learn about the issues of concern to the customer industry.
- Find out why customers buy from their viewpoint, not just "applications."
- Entertain VIP customers.
- Conduct research among current and potential customers.
- Educate and motivate employees and dealers.
- Sell to small and midsize prospects or customers you can't afford to call on.

Figure 5-2. Edit or add to this starter list of goals to help clarify and direct exhibiting.

6

Time, Productivity, and Space

Now add in the numbers. Many companies, even those as good as Hill or Tote-Cart (see Chapter 5), don't go much further than a well-written, specific show mission. Only about one-quarter of those surveyed in the research we covered in Chapter 2 take that next step—setting some number objectives to go along with the statement.

The chief value in taking this last step lies in encouraging people to pack their business hats in the suitcase when zipping off to the annual show. Most of us respond well to number goals. They make us more comfortable doing our jobs.

Exhibit team members tend to fall into one of several groups. One group just hates it, feeling that time is being wasted. A second visualizes a "holiday on the company." Whoopee! A third's hidden objective is making contacts with that next job in mind.

Then there are those who want to attend seminars for personal learning purposes. And, of course, many simply want to schmooze with their current customers—cementing relationships and perhaps writing some orders. Regardless of personal objectives and attitudes, booth team members will respond well if given some specific numbers to shoot for. People enjoy tracking their own progress.

There is another value that is just as important: To the extent that you can assign number objectives, you will be able to measure progress later. We dwell on these easy-to-use measurements in Chapter 10, but you will end up with some *objective* as well as subjective ways to evaluate exhibits side by side. That is impossible unless you pick out one or two places to assign number goals up front.

Going back to our list of objectives, *numbers are not everything.* However, they do build team comfort and at the same time can provide a method of measuring shows (not people) later on a consistent, unbiased basis.

Number Objectives

We poked around trying to find out why so few set at least some number goals. Answers included the following: "If I set a number goal and don't make it, the boss will be unhappy." "If our goals are too low, everybody will relax when victory is in sight." "If our goals are too high, team members will do anything to reach them; garbage leads." "Nobody is going to believe the numbers anyway." The real answer is that many do not know how to set realistic numerical exhibiting objectives. It only takes 10 minutes with a calculator.

Number Goal Categories

We group exhibiting goals into four categories to show where numbers fit:

1. Current customer contacts for order writing and competition defense

2. Awareness development and image enhancement

3. Learning

4. Prospecting

Current Customer Contacts.   You or your sales team members know these people. Write their names down and count them up. You can track progress in making these contacts at the show. In some cases it may be possible to write in a specific dollar goal for each customer. Add those up for a show goal.

There are other values. For instance, with the names pulled together, you might see that there is not enough time to see all of them during the day. You might then plan to meet at least some off site, after or before hours. Another value is that a list can be posted at the booth along with the booth staff schedule. If a VIP shows up when the appropriate contact is not there, an appointment can be made for a return visit. See Chapters 15 and 18 (on off-site events and exhibit selling) for more.

Awareness Development and Image Enhancement. There are several activities that lend themselves to number goals:

- Number of brochures, samples, or giveaways to be distributed (We discourage this practice, saying, "Take names and send later." But many will do it anyway.)
- Attendance at a "booth show" or professional presentation
- Reporters to meet and trade releases to distribute (Large companies count stories or column inches that appear, plus "mentions" in articles or on radio or TV.)
- Seminars to present and anticipated audience
- Professional research to create awareness and attitude benchmarks, or to check progress against benchmarks already established

Learning. There are four ways to learn at a convention and many companies fall down on them. Some lend themselves to setting number goals. One is finding out what competition is doing. Second is learning more about industry issues and answers by attending seminars. Third is learning about product applications and features through a research program at the booth. Fourth would be outside professional research to evaluate exhibit effectiveness.

- Count and list your competitors in advance. Plan to visit each of the booths and write a report.
- Select seminars of particular interest in advance. Attend and write a report on each.
- Conduct booth research on product features, applications, and potential acceptance. Some companies, working on upcoming new products, invite customers and prospects to private briefings and provide an opportunity for suggestions.
- Awareness of the company and its products and sales performance can be evaluated with outside professional research.

Prospecting. One place where exhibiting value shines brightly is the opportunity for face-to-face prospecting and qualification. Prospecting breaks down between brand-new customers altogether and new people within current customer organizations. There are three places for number goals:

1. Booth contacts
2. Names trapped for mailing lists
3. Leads for personal follow-up after the show

Exporting Your Business
Approach to the Show

All too often goal-directed managers lose sight of that need when they plan a booth program. Combining show-related mission statements and numerical goals helps you, and all of those around you, to keep those business hats firmly planted. The greatest value for all is that exhibits start to be thought about in value terms, instead of just a costly "stand up and salute" exercise.

Some of the items listed in our four groups of countables reflect what may be only occasional activities. Others mirror actions you take at every show. These are the goals you want to consider later in creating a technical measurement system.

How to Create the Numbers

Having picked out what you want to count, how do you make the estimates? What follows is a procedure to avoid outright guessing or a wide-eyed dream. It is not perfect, but it is practical and easy. A moment with that calculator and, presto, goals!

There are only four factors to deal with—audience, time, space, and your team size. The process reflects the amount of work one person can do in an hour. It factors in the total number of hours you will be open from first-day ribbon cutting to the final closing bell.

The procedure can work, with adaptation, for about anything you can count. We focus here on prospecting. There are two reasons. First, prospecting is considered, by many, a key exhibit value.[1] Second, there is a body of research that backs up the base figures you will see.

The numbers that emerge on your calculator screen will not be "stretch" objectives. Instead, they reflect reality as identified in research among the bad, good, and indifferent. We presented a seminar for exhibitors at the Promotional Products Association International show. One leaped up and challenged the process. About 20 minutes later this same man stood again and apologized. He had "run our math" based on what he remembered about his performance at a past show. We were 5 percent off, on the low side.

The Sublime

In the best of all possible worlds you should evaluate your audience, estimating the number of people (and space) you would need to achieve 100 percent market penetration. With audience total in hand, you could do the following:

- Divide the audience total by the number of show hours. "People to meet per hour" is the result.

- Divide that by an estimate as to how many visitors an individual booth staff member can meet in an hour. That tells you the team size.

- Estimate the space needed for one booth staff member and one or two visitors. Multiply by the team size and you will know how much space to rent.

We do not detail the exercise here. It is far more likely that you face limits on team size, space, and cost, regardless of audience size. (We cover the specifics in this chapter's segment addressing that.) If you have extra time one day and would like an academic exercise, you might try this approach just to see how things turn out. For many companies, even at midsize shows, the results might amaze—space bigger than a basketball court staffed by platoons!

Audience Analysis.   Regardless of the method you use, it makes solid sense to evaluate your audience, both from size and interest viewpoints.

Chapter 2 readers know that even at the most narrow interest trade event, such as a convention for operating room nurses, there is no exhibitor who sees everyone. This reality is perhaps easier to see in the makeup of a narrow-interest consumer show. There are shows for stamp collectors. One might assume that dealers want to meet everyone. However, a dealer and segment of the audience might share an interest only in European stamps.

To find your target within the target, you will have to read the information provided by the expo manager and even talk to that person. Most provide an estimated audience based on past history. Some publish a very thorough breakdown from outside, independent research. (That includes large consumer shows.) Many do not. One show manager said, "We have data but so few seem interested that we don't publish." Small events simply can't afford extensive outside research.

Call. Even if data are not available, virtually all producers are willing to provide educated guesses. When you are reading or asking questions, here are some possible deductions from the total audience expected that you can evaluate:

- In the total count are exhibitors included? If so, how many? Deduct them unless one of your objectives is to meet with and sell to the other exhibitors.

- To what extent are trade press representatives included? The group may be its own target market, but it can be eliminated when it comes to prospect goal setting.

- Are delegate spouses included? If your customers include wife-husband partnerships, keep the number. If not, deduct it.

- Are seminar speakers or students included? You can deduct these numbers for prospecting purposes.

Add up all these deductions from the estimate, and then ask more questions that can result in even more refinement:

- To what extent are your specific business segments represented—type, title, whatever? The rest can be eliminated.

- Is there a geographic implication? Even national events change audience makeup a great deal as they shift from area to area, coast to coast. The audience will be dominated by visitors closer to the show. If that counts for you, in terms of sales and service coverage, make a deduction.

- Is the estimate based on turnstile counts? At some events each individual visit to a show floor is counted. If so, use judgment and make a deduction for repeats.[2]

Reduce the total audience estimate by your deductions. What emerges is a number that represents the total number of contacts you would want to make to reach your 100 percent. This is valuable information, even though there is probably little chance for you to greet all of them.

An Alternative and Easier Method.   For those overwhelmed by time problems or those underwhelmed by an expo manager who seems to know less than you might like, there is an industry standard that can provide less accurate but usable information.

In Part 1, "The Quick Fix," we summarized research sponsored by the Trade Show Bureau, much of it done by Exhibit Surveys, Incorporated, the industry research pioneer. The lowest figure we found—and the one influencing our projection— was that *the average percent audience interest in a single product is 16 percent of the total.* (That figure is for one show type, a "horizontal" event attracting diverse customers and exhibitors. If your event is quite narrow, the percentage is higher. However, we like to be conservative.)

Thus, you can try calculating 16 percent of the total audience estimate, ignoring deductions. See Figure 6-1 for an audience analysis work form.

Audience Analysis

Total estimated audience   _____
Less deductions:
    Other exhibitors   _____
    Press   _____
    Students   _____
    Spouses   _____
    Other (regional, title, subgroup)   _____
        Total deductions   _____
    Total audience less deductions (target audience) _____

Alternate Method

Total estimated audience   _____
Percent interest in a product line (low average) _____ × 0.16
    Total audience less deductions (target audience)

Figure 6-1. Planning form: Audience analysis for goal setting.

The Waste Factor Adjustment.   Research for a private company points out that one-quarter of its booth visitors wander in for no advantageous reason. They are curious or looking for directions to restrooms. It is smart to plan on that in advance. These people will emerge, and we need to be polite, but dealing with the problem has an effect on goal setting.

For instance, assume you really do want to rent the space and bring enough people to reach 100 percent. You would have to add one-third to your target audience (the same as one-quarter if it is a deduction from what can be accomplished with a given number of people in a space already determined). To illustrate, if your target audience size to reach 100 percent is 1600, you would have to rent sufficient space and bring enough people to talk with 2100 delegates during the show.

The Space and Team Reality

Seldom can we start from ground zero and doing what we want without cost and other boundaries. Mostly we start with the space already rented and little option to change. Even if your space allocation has already been contracted, it could be good to know what would be needed to reach 100 percent of total potential. It might help with next year's budget. However, it is more practical now to get a grasp on *what you can do with what you've got!* That is what we address now.

Time, Space, People, and Productivity

This chapter's readers know the essential components of exhibit goal setting. Let's now look at how they can be used in your goal setting for booth prospecting when the space and team size are facts of life.

Time Impact

An aggressive sales manager might say, "We want to write $XYZ in orders at the show." Is that realistic? How long does it take to negotiate and write an order? Another might say, "We want to get 150 new customer prospects." Is that realistic? Another: "We need to educate everyone on the new-product line." Is that realistic? The authentic answer starts with the time that is available.

There are a couple of approaches to calculating time, but our favorite is one we've used as an exhibit manager. It is based on *the number of hours the event is open when traffic is moderate or heavy*. Start by adding up all the hours a show will be open, from ribbon cutting on the first day to the final closing bell. Then eliminate the number of hours you feel traffic may be light.

Slack-Hour Analysis. If you have personal experience at an event, you already know if and when and how many hours may be light. If not, call the show's manager and ask. Or perhaps another exhibitor. Explain your purpose and for the most part show managers will provide a calculated guess based on experience. *They are delighted when an exhibit manager wants to create solid goals. They hear from "complainers" all the time who blame the show for poor results without trying to do the right job for themselves.* During discussions be alert to slack-hour potential in the following situations:

- At an out-of-town event visitors may have booked flights out at the last day end. As they realize what is involved with getting to the airport, they may leave early.

- Very large shows in major cities may suffer at the end of every day. For instance, a major event in Chicago might result in buyers standing in lines for show-sponsored busses or taxi service. They leave the floor early.

- Do seminars take place during the same hours the expo floor is open? You might see low traffic then, especially during "supersessions" presented by VIPs.

- One "do not deduct": Some show managers serve luncheon to delegates on the show floor or sponsor late-day cocktail receptions there.

Waste Factor Analysis

Audience based on reaching 100 percent of target
(See Figure 6-1.) _____
Amount of "wasted" traffic   × 1.33
    Audience total to reach _____

Note: If space and team sizes at the booth are known, calculate the total audience you will reach based on team size, contacts per hour, and the number of hours. Then reduce that number by 25 percent to see how many true potential customers you will meet.

Figure 6-2. Planning form: Waste factor projection.

Even if booth visits are casual or if the luncheon is followed immediately by seminars, keep these hours in your active-hour count.

Subtract your deductions from total show hours. You have a key base figure! See Figure 6-2 for a work form covering calculation of the waste factor.

How Hard We Work

The second key is work production per hour for an individual, and in this case that translates to the number of people a booth staffer will meet in an active hour. Studies show that the range is between 7 and 15 in an hour, some visitors alone, others in groups of 2 or 3. Much of the difference traces to the amount of technical discussion. For instance, at a high-tech medical or engineering event, it will be closer to 7.

We suggest starting with a base figure of 10 contacts an hour per person on duty. If, after using this base figure for a few shows, you see work production results running consistently higher or lower than your estimated goal, the contacts-per-hour base figure should be revised to reflect your reality. (A reminder: Our production goal is set to provide a business-as-usual comfort zone. It is not to push people. Improvements arise out of the increased quality of contacts that result.)

Now we have two of our three parts—hours and work production.

Space and Team Size

On the average a single booth team member will use about 50 square feet of space to conduct a semiprivate discussion with one or two visitors as long as everyone is standing up. That's about the size of an extra-large desktop, squared. Anything less than that makes people feel squeezed.

Add to that an average of just over another 10 square feet for "display properties," counter, backwall, product display, and potted palms. This is an average. If you are displaying a car, big-league machine tool, or an elephant, add more for display support.

Here are three illustrations based on our rules of thumb:

1. In a booth space that is 10 by 10 feet (or 8 feet deep by 10 feet wide), you will probably squeeze in two booth staff people and spill conversations out into the aisle, even though that is against the rules.

2. In a 10 × 20 foot, the average space size at large shows in the USA, you will probably squeeze in five booth team members.

3. Assuming a 20- by 30-foot "island" space, 600 square feet, you will end up with 9 or 10 work stations, with one staff member on duty at each. (Unless, of course, you are selling helicopters or boats and plop one in the middle.)

People produce. Booths are there to support them. But the space you have limits the team size and thus the work that can be done. Therefore, the relationship between team size on duty and space is important.

Regardless, there are only four factors to consider when developing an estimate for work production, in this case a lead goal. We're up to three: time, production, and team size, three-quarters to home! The fourth factor is the contact objective.

Contact Objective. All you have to do is multiply active hours by team size. Here is an illustration:

Assume you have a 10- by 20-foot space and will have five people on duty. Assume, as well, that there are three show days, 6 hours a day. However, you elect to remove 3 hours as "slack," producing a total of 15 moderately active hours.

- Multiply 15 hours by 10 contacts per hour for an individual. Result: 150.

- Multiply the team size, five on duty, by 150. Result: 750 contacts at the booth during the show.

A contact goal sounds great. But it won't work because you cannot track it without spending money on postshow research every time out. You will be unable to count them yourself as you go along. We made the effort but failed to keep track of the many short contacts that take place, part of the total. But computing your own contact goal, never published, provides a ballpark figure that you can use to establish objectives you *can* count.

The last shoe in creating a prospecting goal comes next. These you *can* count and keep track of, show by show. They lead to an apples-to-apples evaluation.

Conversion to Leads.   The private company study work that helped us develop the waste factor adjustment also allowed us to create what we call a 10-contact breakdown:

10-contact breakdown	
Those not at all interested	2
Interested but not buyers	4
Leads but not serious	2
Serious leads for fast payoff	2

This produces the *20 Percent Rule:* Roughly 2 out of 10 booth contacts will result in a request for short-term personal follow-up after the show. In many cases that can amount to a telephone conference but in others a personal visit. Two more booth contacts will require mailing-list addition for literature plus future potential.

The eye opener is that the percentage is so high. Remember, however, that show visitors are at least generally interested in the products or they would not have made the effort, or spent the money, to attend.

Here is how the *10-contact breakdown* gets us to where we want to go—an objective we can live with and track from show to show:

- Start with the contact objective. In our illustration above it was 750 contacts.

- Use 20 percent, 150, as the lead objective for fast, personal follow-up.

- Add another 20 percent, another 150, for mailing-list additions.

For our sample show, an 18-hour event with five people working at the booth, there should be a total of 300 leads.

No Cards in the Bowl.   Some experienced professionals, reading this, may think to themselves, "I've done a whole lot better than *that!* Both contacts and leads." That may be true. However, the prospecting goals we propose deal only with leads that have been personally qualified by the booth folks in advance of name taking.

A five-person team, working for three days, can surely capture over a thousand business cards![3] But what do those cards require? More work to sort out wheat from chaff. (And we will tell you about cost-effective ways to take that second step in Chapter 24, "Who Does What.") But for most outfits the economic advantage of a show is diminished by not taking full advantage of the chance to qualify and learn from prospects. Exhibiting accelerates qualified sales lead development as much as seven times compared to reaching prospects through normal field sales methods.[4]

Conversion to Sales

Sharpen your pencil again or reach back in the drawer for your calculator. It won't take long to set a sales goal from leads, and the process is of great value. One of the least understood of exhibiting's values is the ease and low cost of closing sales that start with a qualified booth lead.

Close Ratio and Cost to Close

Over one-half, 54 percent, of the qualified leads taken at a trade show are closed without the need for a personal visit later. And this includes big-ticket capital equipment. Selling costs are reduced by about 70 percent when the first contact is at a booth. Using traditional field sales methods, the average number of calls required to close is 4.3. The booth lead average is 0.8.[5] There are three reasons that these results are produced: time compression, audience agenda, and comparison shopping.

Time Compression. Everyone is already together, buyers and sellers alike. There is no linger time in reception rooms. No time spent tracing through office buildings or fighting street traffic. No telephone tag to set up appointments.

Audience Agenda. In the good old days you could hear things like, "We've got to go to this year's convention to see good old Bubba again—out on the diving board, revving up his Harley." Those palmy days are certainly long gone. Simply *attending* an out-of-town event can cost upward of $2000 or even more and a week of the visitor's life. It may appear that show visitors are relaxed, mainly having a good time, seeing old friends. That visual impression masks reality. Over three-quarters of today's show visitors arrive with a specific agenda in hand.[6]

Here is case in point. Our seat mate on a flight was a supervising nurse at a hospital in Jackson, Mississippi. She had been attending a medical convention. Exhibitors did not know that she had two very specific missions. The hospital was preparing to purchase a multi-million-dollar machine. Her job was to winnow down a list of 16 potential suppliers to 3 who would be invited to bid. Her second objective was to attend three seminars that covered applications related to the use of this technology. The purchase was made from one of companies she recommended.

Comparison Shopping.   The hospital story leads us to the last factor that lowers sales costs. Responsible buyers, consumer or business, are faced with the need to compare competing products and services. In today's world that can be difficult and time-consuming. For instance, we purchased a new computer system and software without being able to attend a show. Five bids were solicited through mail, telephone, fax, and personal contact. It took many hours over three weeks, and we were spending under $5000! Shows lower selling costs. But the reason for that is that they *reduce the time, confusion, and thus the hidden cost of purchasing.* Buyers can see competing products side by side and do so in a day! Had we been able to comparison shop for our computer system at a show, we would have asked for only two proposals.

Lead Dollar Value: The 50 Percent Rule

Earlier in this chapter we introduced the "10-contact breakdown." Knowledgeable sales managers probably found that research and its result no great surprise. It roughly mirrors general experience. For every 10 prospects, it is likely that only 1 sale will be made. The beauty of booth selling is time compression. You win, or lose, far more quickly. Either way, you lower selling cost.

By the time you get down to those last two leads for personal follow-up, the comparison shopping has been done. Many facts have been gathered from the purchaser's perspective. That leads to our *50 percent rule.* From a goal-setting aim, it is reasonable to assume that you should be able to convert one of each serious, qualified two leads to a sale within your normal cycle.

You may be thinking, "We sell big systems. They are all semicustom and take lots of time to specify, sell, and deliver. And final pricing may be way off from where we started. This won't work for us." Not true. Even if it takes two years from start to finish, you can project results.

Avoid Visions of Grand Things.   Time and again we have heard sales managers say, "If we get that one big sale out of a show, it pays for itself and more." One small fishing tackle manufacturer said, "If we can sign up a K-Mart or Sears sporting goods contract, we're made." That is not management or even a calculated risk. (And it is unlikely that this tackle company could gear up fast enough to meet the inventory requirements imposed by major chains without giving up other outlets.) Other managers say, "If we get a customer, we keep that customer for years. The short-term results don't count." Yes they do count, at least from a show measurement perspective.

Practical Management. What do you know? You probably know the average revenue value of that first sale to a new customer. Use that number to create an objective for lead conversion revenue. Multiply your lead goal by your average first-sale revenue figure and *cut it in half*. Why? Because you will sell to only one out of every two qualified leads. A conservative management figure emerges that is good for goal setting.

You may or may not be able to track dollar results later. Even if not, a dollar goal for leads, as well as orders at the event, can help. It will modify what you spend, up or down, on the basis of assumed value. Value is the name of the game.

See Figure 6-3 for a planning form you can use for prospecting goal setting.

Prospecting Objectives

Square feet of exhibit space	
Divided by	÷ 60
Number of work stations (room for one staff member and display)	
Total open hours for the event	
Less slack traffic hours	
Active hours	
Staff members on duty (work station number)	
Times contacts per person per hour	× 10
Total contacts per hour	
Times active hours	
Total show contacts	
Total show contacts	
Times	× 0.20
Leads for personal follow-up	
Total show contacts	
Times	× 0.20
Leads for mailing list	
Leads for personal follow-up	
Times percent conversion to sales	× 0.50
Sales within the cycle	
Average value of first sale ($)	
Times sales within the cycle	
Ultimate dollar objective	

Figure 6-3. Planning form: Prospecting and sales goals.

Exhibit Objective Trade-Offs

We focus on prospecting because so many exhibitors consider it to be their main goal. And we show how to set goals for order writing. We must point out, however, that it is unlikely you will be able to afford enough space, or bring enough people, to reach your full potential audience on a person-to-person basis at most events.

Order writing and prospecting may not be your only goals. Chapter 5's "starter list" of objectives lists 17 more, and you may have added to that. For instance, your company may feel it very important to create awareness and enhance its image across a broad spectrum of show visitors, whether they are prospects or not.

One solution is to do a trade-off. Sacrifice some lead taking or order writing booth space. Use it to present a show. At one expo we had a 30-foot wide space. We allocated 7 feet to present an interesting demonstration. It did help attract people who became leads, but its main purpose was creating broader awareness.

Our underlying suggestion is to adopt an analytical approach to planning and executing an exhibit program. When you do something, know why, what you are doing it for, and how much you can expect to realize from it. The process we have outlined is not perfect. With some experience you will want to adjust it based on your own realities. What counts is the concept.

7

The Show Budget and True Company Cost

It is a bit of a blessing that exhibit costs have gone up virtually 500 percent in the last two decades. Spending money in foolish fashion has never been a good idea. There was more than a little of that kind of squandering in "the good old days." Now, of course, the raw cost of doing the job widens eyes. It translates into more management attention and a true need to obtain value in return for investment. That is a plus for all involved.

Many exhibit coordinators were and sometimes still are deemed to be tactical cost specialists, not strategic value managers. Much of this book aims to help shift that perception. However, creating and running a budget remains part of the task.

In Part 1, "The Quick Fix," there is a short-form budget format. It is sufficient for a small booth at one show. If you are doing several exhibits a year or are involved with one of the center hall megabooth spectaculars, you need a whole lot more. That's what we present here.

Keep in mind that a budget must be more than a form upon which one writes figures—before and after. There are lots of managers who mindlessly write numbers, because they have to, but never use the document for planning purposes. Grand totals are enough. When somebody says, "Cut back by 25 percent," they do it across the board or "cut out the dinners" or whatever. Or when a total program budget is slashed, they simply start chopping shows off the schedule. (That is the sort of thing one hears when a government budget is cut: "We'll have to drop the *Xyz* project.")

Nonsense. A solid manager looks within a total budget to see where reductions are possible while retaining essential value, or even amplifying it. As you look over the detailed budget format we present, edit. Keep or add items you know you can use to manipulate work to produce better results. Get rid of items that, for you, would become mindless scribbling.

Total Company Cost: More Than the Exhibit Budget

Exhibit budgets tend to be documents that isolate costs for which the exhibit manager is held accountable; booth, graphics, freight, setup, and specific show costs such as space. Sometimes even specific exhibit costs are hidden away in vague budgets in another department.[1] What follows is a list of exhibit costs most often absorbed in other departments. A responsible manager includes these, *even if they are only estimates*, in a Show Cost Summary, reflecting a company's overall show commitment.

Typical Costs Absorbed by Other Departments

Most often, show-related advertising and personnel costs are not part of the exhibit budget. There may be others. The idea is to estimate these. The value is gaining more management sensitivity and support.

- *Advertising* Ads in trade publications and show periodicals are often covered by expense in the ad department. Because trade shows are considered secondary, you might get short shrift. No new "creative." Trap costs, outline values, and give credit.

- *Literature.* We do not advocate distributing thousands of pounds of fancy brochures at shows. It is better to take names and send later. But the allocation of company brochures to show attendees should be estimated. (Figure no more than 5 percent of the total audience estimated for the show.) A share of the design, writing, and production cost should be allocated, even if that figure does not show up on a formal budget for exhibiting. (There are different figures, depending on who did the research. But it is safe to say that between 65 and 80 percent of the brochures, catalogs, and flyers passed out at booths or slipped under hotel room doors are never read by anybody. If you simply must pass something out, encourage development of a low-cost flyer that offers other materials for those interested.)

- *Direct mail.* This is another marketing communications cost that may not show up on the exhibit budget. It may be easier, however, to isolate show-related costs.

- *Samples.* Companies such as Sara Lee and Anhauser-Busch, Domino's Pizza and Coca-Cola, or Colgate-Palmolive provide product samples at their exhibits. What department pays? Try to estimate these costs alongside the formal exhibit budget. (If your team goes to a food show, look with some suspicion at any staff member's expense account claim for lunch!)

- *Giveaways.* Some small items, and even more expensive premiums, are provided to show visitors. However, that use may not be tracked as a cost for participation. In this case it is a good idea to try and estimate a "fair share."

- *Product and technical support.* Some bring major league machine tools, trucks, computers, and the like to show or demonstrate. Are the costs of that product, and the people who must install, service, and demonstrate it, in any way covered in the cost for exhibiting? On some kind of basis, from a company viewpoint, at least an estimate should be prepared. Here is an example: At the Paris Air Show what departments cover flying in the company's X plane and keeping it working through demonstrations? That cost should be recognized in the cost of exhibiting, even if not in the formal exhibit budget.

- *Staff costs.* It is not often that the exhibit manager's budget includes costs for travel and hotel and meal expense for those who work at the booth. Yet these are company costs related to show participation. Again, however, at least an estimate should be provided by the exhibit manager or coordinator.

- *Press contact.* Big companies have special departments to handle media relations. Shows are important to them. Most often they absorb the cost in their own budget. From a company perspective, that cost should be reflected in a show cost.

- *Special events.* There are all sorts of off-site events that may, or may not, be part of the exhibit budget. These range from hospitality suites to private demonstration events. Some outfits put on annual sales or technical meetings before or after their big shows.

- *Speaker support.* Nonselling technical or management seminars are often mounted at shows where the company is exhibiting. While not part of the exhibit budget, for the most part, the costs do come home. (We have seen some cases where a high-level speaker requires exhibit support, even if there is no immediate marketing purpose.) Either way, the company is best served when all costs are identified, at least on an estimated basis.

The Cost of Time

We give this extra attention. The biggest cost of all is people *time*. We don't know of anyone who calculates it. Salaried employees or commission salespeople have only so many hours to give in a day or week or year. Where is that time best spent, for the person and the company? Is it at a show or someplace else?

The Time Cost Formula.   In almost all situations this must be an estimate. What it amounts to is a combination of three elements:

1. An estimate of average yearly take-home pay for those who will be working at the show.
2. An estimate of the value of benefits and office backup expense for these people. From what we have read, that amounts to about 40 percent of the actual paycheck.
3. The number of workdays that will be required, all people combined. For instance, you may have a three-day out-of-town show. Add travel and training, and each booth staff person will have spent the equivalent of five days in the interest of the show.

Time Cost Illustration.   Assume, for purposes of this illustration, the following:

- The average compensation for those involved is $50,000 a year.
- Benefits and office backup cost equates to 40 percent on top.
- Thus, the value of a worker's time is $70,000 per year.[2]

Excluding 104 weekend days, holidays, vacation and sickness days, there are about 220 workdays a year. Divide 220 into $70,000. Time cost is approximately $320 a day per person.

How many "person days" are involved for a show? The exhibit manager spends a lot of them, up-front and after. We ignore that for the illustration. Assumption:

- You have a 20-foot booth, and there will be five people on duty.
- There are three show days, but that equates to five, counting travel.

The result is 25 person days. At $320 each, that is $8000 in *time alone.* Then, of course, there are all the out-of-pocket expenses. Few individual budget lines rival spilling $8000 in time for a three-day, 20-footer. Managers carp about space and drayage and so on. Good. But the big numbers cover time.

Why do we surface "off-budget" costs? First, responsible managers should point out that cost is more than an exhibit budget. Second, management support will increase with the realization that more is involved than might have been anticipated. Ultimately, *value* has to be considered more and more.

Department or Division Support

Within many midsize and large companies, exhibit managers find themselves wandering down hallways with tin cup in hand, begging money from somebody else's budget. That happens typically after April, August, or October thundercloud pronouncements by corporate chieftains: "Now hear this! Everyone cut budget 10 percent."

Here's the rub. When budget allocations supporting shows are spread around, and that is normal, departmental exhibit allocations are relatively small. They even may be covered in some sort of contingency or miscellaneous line. What is the first to go when "Now hear this!" is bull-horned down from the corporate mountaintop? You guessed it.

Avoiding the Tin Cup. Exhibiting is a microcosm of the company's entire marketing process. Exhibit managers are running what amounts to a small business sponsored by a bigger one—with elements blended! That's what ultimately attracts people to the profession. (Fancy travel and hotels get old after the first year. During one six-month period this former corporate exhibit manager had exactly five days at home on weekends; those for Easter and Memorial Day. It is not for long a glamorous life. The best deal: taking home designer soap samples lifted from hotel bathrooms.)

The *balance* of exhibit-related activities required to gain maximum return is delicate. Preshow promotion is part of it. So is literature, up to a point. Exhibit design and graphics are a part. VIP meetings, press contacts, and participating in and presenting seminars play a role. Staff recruiting, training, and supervision as well. So does postevent followup. An exhibit manager's role compels keeping things in some kind of equilibrium to gather maximum return.

That is why the tin cup is often related to securing a department's support for a single event. By identifying, up-front, both in the annual plan (Chapter 4) and for specific shows, the needs from other departments, there is greater likelihood that the exhibit allocation won't be cut mindlessly.

"Selling" Corporate Partners. From AT&T to D&B to GE, GM, IBM to McGraw-Hill, and we could keep the alphabet running down to XYZ, there are corporate exhibit groups selling exhibit services to divisions and smaller organizations that are part of the family. Corporate may provide the basics—booth, signs, administration. The rest comes out of the back pockets of subsidiaries or divisions.

For corporate exhibit managers facing this, the most compelling reason to surface all costs potentials is to let divisions and owned companies know what they are in for. Those outfits should do the job right so that they gain the most return on investment. The corporate exhibit manager becomes a consultant or brings one in to sort things out.

The Big Show.   There is one last situation. It, too, is for the megacompany. There are some shows at which all departments participate. Each makes a contribution. There are skirmishes about how much represents a fair share and where a division's products will be placed, as well as "extras" including such things as joint preshow promotion and VIP entertainment.

In Chapter 5 we cover audience analysis. Most big shows can provide audience breakdown estimates by product interest. Those percentages can be used to split booth space and allocate a fair share of core costs.

As for the rest, costs absorbed in other departments anyway, providing an up-front estimate reduces internal warfare and produces better results for all.

The Core Budget and Show Costs

Budget management can get in the way of creating a situation where *value* is a greater management judgment than raw cost. There are two big ones, and we address them now.

Space Rent Cost

At most events this year's exhibitors are encouraged to sign up for next year's space during or right after the show. The producer offers incentives, mainly based on picking a specific location in a priority order. Few companies fail to respond if they know that they will be there next year regardless of current-year results.

These space reservations are confirmed with the advance payment for at least a part of the rental shortly after the current event. Corporate exhibitors running a budget are faced with a darned if you do, darned if you don't situation. To protect next year's program dollars will have to be spent from an already tight current budget. And what is worse, for those who want to measure productivity against cost, it is not fair to measure this year with a portion of next year's cost included. In fact, a muddy-water picture can emerge.

Booth Design and Construction

There will always be booth changes and graphics that shift from show to show. They are easy to track and allocate. However, there are those times when a whole new booth must be designed and constructed. The new booth will actually be used, with modifications, for several appearances. It is not fair to allocate all of its cost to the first show.

When you have a new booth or system designed and constructed, estimate the number of shows at which it will be used. You may not know for sure, but make an educated guess. Be fair to each show.

Most times a new booth will involve some kind of superstructure, plus a number of related work stations. That complicates making estimates. Some exhibitions will require using the entire package. Others just parts. Do the best you can. Very few will have the expertise to challenge a reasonable judgment.

Budget Versus Show Cost

The solution is a change in bookkeeping. From a corporate balance sheet viewpoint, the year the dollars are spent count. However, from a management judgment viewpoint, a show allocation is far more sensible.

Two Sets of Books

It sounds illegal and confusing. That is not so. The records kept by a company for financial and tax reasons do not always help process managers.

Budget Planning Form. At the conclusion of this chapter, you will see a budget planning form (Figure 7-1). It is more complex than the form supplied in Part 1, which is intended for smaller, first-time exhibitors. There are many more cost lines, and it breaks down expense groups into their components. Edit the horizontal rows to pick out what makes the best sense for you.

The form in Figure 7-1 also provides three columns. One is for expense from the exhibit budget itself. The second is an estimate of exhibit cost from other budgets (or, importantly, the show allocation that is appropriate from your budget under the circumstances). The last combines the two into a company cost projection for a show—regardless of budget.

After a show you will be making a *fourth* column to trap the actual costs of your exhibit. You can set up this kind of a budget management system on virtually any PC spreadsheet software program. (Chapter 11, covering small-computer management applications, provides more detail.) You may throw up your hands with a feeling that this is too complex. It is not. Get into it. It's easy.

Exhibit Cost Categories

Most companies keep an expense track record. However, if you are just starting out, it can help to see where averages stand. Ongoing studies are produced by responsible exhibit industry associations and in the publications cited frequently in the endnotes in this book. There are slight differences in the figures presented, often because of different samples. There are slight variations, year over year.

We elect to summarize. If you are preparing a big show budget or an annual plan, the following percentages will put you in a reasonable and defendable position. The budget categories below are those most frequently part of the exhibit manager's budget:

Space Rental Cost.   For the most part this represents about 20 percent of exhibiting cost. Multiply your space rent for a single show by 5 (or better, by what you plan to spend on space rent year-long, all shows together) and you will be in the ballpark for a program budget.

Exhibit Design and Construction.   The data is good. Figure about another 20 percent of cost. However, those contributing information come from a broad spectrum. Will you build a new booth this year, or just provide new graphics and maintenance?

Refurbishing and Changes.   On the average one can figure about 12 percent for an annual program. If you are not sponsoring a brand new booth this year, that percent will be higher.

Show Services.   Roughly 20 percent of your cost will be paid for show services. These include in-hall handling (drayage and local storage), setup, and all sorts of other services and rentals.

Transport.   Shipping booth properties from home to show and return is less—about 13 percent on the average. However, please think about this. If you are transporting a large machine tool as well as a booth, it is best to allocate more.

Special Personnel and Promotional (Specialty Advertising) Products. This can include the cost for hosts, hostesses, giveaways, and the like. Figure 7 percent. That could be more or less, depending on your goals and what you do.

The Rest. If you are one who keeps track of figures as you go along, you know we have covered about 92 percent of traditional exhibit budget costs, with some plus and minus along the way. Let's call the other 8 percent a *contingency*. Wags say, "That's close enough for government work." It is also close enough for a book that will be used by many who face different circumstances.

Out-of-Pocket Expenses for People

Having reached 100 percent, one way or another, we must add more. Put about 35 percent on top to cover the out-of-pocket expenses for people who will work at the event, no matter what budget it comes from. The 35 percent does not include the cost and thus value of their time.

Budget Planning Form

Budget item	Exhibit budget	Another budget	Show allocation
1. Space			
A. Current year			
B. Deposit (next year)			

Note: Show allocation should include this year's rent including prior deposit.

2. Booth, graphics, display products			
A. Design/build/refurb.			
B. Graphic signs			

Note: Show allocation should include percent of total based on use potential.

C. Products/samples			
3. Promotions before the event			
A. Direct mail			
B. Advertising			
C. Press releases			
4. Promotion at the event			
A. Advertising			
B. Press releases			
C. Booth giveaways			
D. Literature			
E. Booth shows			
5. Off-site activities			
A. Hospitality			
B. Training			
C. Special events			
6. Transport			
A. Exhibit properties			
B. Personnel			
C. Hotel food			
7. Show services			
A. Drayage			
B. Setup/teardown			
C. Electricity			
D. Telephone			
E. Plumbing			
F. High-pressure air			
G. Rigging			
H. Audiovisual			
I. Floral			
J. Carpet			
K. Security			

Figure 7-1. Show budget form.

Budget item	Exhibit budget	Another budget	Show allocation
L. Photography			
M. Registration device			
N. Booth cleaning			
8. Staff time value			
9. Research			
A. Professional			
B. Informal			
10. Follow-up			
A. Lead administration			
B. Telemarketing			
Total			
11. Contingency			
Total			

Form Modification.   It is unlikely that you will use this form as presented. For instance, you may never need plumbing, rigging, or high-pressure air. On the other hand, you may find it of value to add something like "refrigerated storage" or break down some items into greater detail. For some, it may be of value to separate transport of exhibit properties into truck, sea, and air. And so on. The form lends itself to a PC spreadsheet application (see Chapter 11). The goal is a budget you can manage by making changes.

Columns 4, 5, and 6.   This form is for budget building. Three more columns are required to track *actual* costs. Of particular interest to exhibit managers will be column 4. That is where the manager's own actual costs would be placed. Those absorbed in other groups, and thus the show allocation, may never be accurate because you won't see those bills. However, show cost allocation remains a good tool for future planning and management information.

Figure 7-1. (*Continued*) Show budget form.

8
What to Do After the Show

Midnight. High in the ceiling burned one security lamp. It cast thin shadows from roof girders onto the broom-clean floor. The show had closed at 2 P.M. Aisle carpet, booths, and everything else was gone by 10—except for one booth, a lone sentinel near the edge of the floor, a few empty crates next to it casting their own shadows.

The next morning a couple of workers from the decorating company came back, packed the booth, product samples, literature, and sales leads in the crates and hauled them off to storage. Their supervisor made a phone call.

The 20-foot booth belonged to a very large company. Its exhibit coordinator had supervised booth setup. She then went home, giving the sales manager in charge the order forms for move out, filled in, to be delivered to the show service desks. It never happened.

On top of that the sales manager and a team of four were so happy just to get things over with that they walked out of the hall, early, to catch planes. Booth lights were on, computer terminals humming, sales leads scattered about in counter drawers.

You say that can't happen? Talk to any show decorating executive, and your ears will burn with stories like this one—which indeed did happen. Then talk with any experienced account executive with an exhibit production company. Time and again, they report that when booth parts are pulled from storage to check and touch up for the next show, they find sales leads from the last one, three months back, in a carton tucked inside a counter. (One told us about seeing *signed orders*, as well as leads, in that carton!)

This is not logical, but it happens anyway: In our experience the larger the company, the more likely it is that in the course of show wrap-up, important details will be completely overlooked. In contrast, small companies, with exhibit costs coming out of the back pocket of the owner, often do much better at shows. They at least take home the leads and try to do something with them!

Divided They Fall

This big-company problem has been around a long time. Organizations are complex. The exhibit coordinator or manager is off in a corner, tied to authority and responsibility for what amounts to logistics management alone. Often the salespeople at a booth are not dealing with their own personal customers. Technical support people just want to do their jobs. There is no true ship captain.

The Exhibit Group Profit Center

You would think that an old-time problem would have dissipated by now, what with the increased need to deliver measurable return on investment. That is not the case. As part of downsizing, business process reengineering, TQM or whatever it is called, more and more big companies require that the exhibit group sell its services internally to groups.

On the surface that sounds like a good idea. Divisions, or subsidiaries, that stand to gain should pay the freight. Sometimes it works. Often it does not.

Division Ego.   Those in charge of divisions, work groups, or subsidiaries are measured on their contributions to bottom-line performance. These leaders tend to say, "If that's the way I'm measured and paid, then I will make the choice as to where, how, and what to spend to get there." Unfortunately, many of these people don't have a clear understanding of how exhibiting can benefit them most or of the work process required to achieve the benefits. (We hope many of these people are among our readers.)

Exhibit Departments' Limitations.   With the establishment of internal profit centers, exhibit departments in big companies must often compete with outside exhibit sources perfectly willing to serve divisions directly. That presents four problems:

1. An inside group must mark up services to cover costs of administration. The same is true for an exhibit house. Even though the

inside group works hard to become its own general contractor, there are times when it simply has to use outside administration. Thus, there can be some extra cost that covers some double-dip administrative costs.

2. Many inside groups would like to sell services such as training or lead follow-up and administration to groups. However, each wants that its own way. Some don't want anything at all. "We'll do it ourselves, thank you!" That lack of consistency leads to extra cost for those who do participate in a corporate-sponsored program.

3. A third but perhaps less persuasive problem emerges. When divisions or work groups run their own programs, there is less concern for corporate graphics and the use of companywide advertising strategies in context with exhibiting. (We dealt with one division that wanted its own internal logo used everywhere, a counterproductive idea.)

4. One complex company serving the oil industry ended up with five division booths at the Offshore Technology Conference. The chief executive officer from a big customer company showed up at one of the booths, looking for the vice president serving him. Booth staff people had never heard of this person. He was at the wrong booth. What is worse is that division people at this large show did not know other divisions were there and could not refer the visitor.

Many corporate profit groups are even more limited than before. Because they compete for business, they provide the booth, graphics, transport, on-site service, and that's about it. They have difficulty selling semiautonomous divisions' other services, including centralized lead administration, literature mailing, or telemarketing. They battle two related mindsets. One we mentioned before goes, "We know how to handle this. I've had 10 years' experience at shows." (Perhaps, but it may be just 1 year's experience, repeated nine more times.) We are, obviously, critical but sympathetic.

The other problem is more subtle. It reflects what experts call the "first stage of learning": *Those who do not know they do not know and thus do not elect to learn.* Even now, exhibit marketing is a late-blooming flower in terms of knowing how it must be done to gain maximum return.

Lead and Order Administration

We went to a trade show to do some specific shopping. It was the International Exhibitors Association's annual event, and we were looking for portable booths. On the last afternoon of the show, after exploring all the alternatives presented, we gave sales leads to three companies that supplied the type of booth design that met our needs.

Two of the three made contact the following week. We gave each a set of specifications along with a formal request for proposal. As things turned out, we did business with both of them. The third company called two and one-half months later. We were sorry, but the deal had been done.

Immediacy Counts

Studies by different organizations over time signal that the ideal time range for lead follow-up is between one and two weeks. There are two essential reasons for greater sales success stemming from fast follow-up:

- Both the buyer and seller have fresh memories about what was discussed at the booth. It becomes easy to continue the process, instead of starting over almost from scratch. Good note taking by the seller at the booth helps, too. It is especially important in situations where the person following up was not the person who took the lead.

- We have pointed out that purchase decisions are often made less on the basis of the product itself and more on the basis of the service and interest expressed by the seller. That is especially so in situations in which fairly similar products are being offered by competitors.

Gaining Extra Time.   Large companies with complex organizations sometimes find it difficult to manage the lead distribution process so that quick follow-up is possible on a consistent basis. There are, however, methods used to gain some extra time.

- Handwritten notes mailed to VIP leads right from the show can be very effective. The note often arrives in the prospect's office before that person gets home. They also illustrate a personal interest by the lead taker and the company.

In our office supplies checklist, see Chapter 3, we suggest bringing office stationery and stamps to the shows for this purpose. There are times, however, when it can be even more effective to write using notepaper provided by hotels in room desks. Just bring the stamps. But buy commemorative stamps, the same price but a bit special.

You might say to yourself, "This is a good idea, but we'll never have the time to do it in the real world." Notes can be handwritten and signed in advance. Just remember to keep the same pen in the folder. That way the date, the "Dear Ms. Jones," and envelope addressing are all that remains, and they will look the same. Preliminary writing can be done well in advance or during a preshow training session. The note does not have to be long. The sample below runs 52 words:

> *Dear Ms. Jones,*
>
> *It was a pleasure meeting you at our booth. I learned a lot and hope you did too. As promised, we will be in touch shortly. In case of a slipup, or if you want to call me, I've enclosed another business card. Again, thank you!*
>
> *Sincerely yours,*
>
> *Signature*

We remind people again about thank-you notes at the end of our show floor sales training coverage in Chapter 18.

- Formal corporate communications can be used as well. Some companies use both informal notes and corporate letters. The text is similar but a bit longer and more formal at the corporate level. A.C. Nielsen (of TV ratings fame, but they do a whole lot more) uses the approach. Itself part of the Dun & Bradstreet family of companies, there are several Nielsen divisions. It may take an extra few days to get leads onto the proper desk. Here is how they gain those precious days: Leads are put into a personal computer during the show and automatically sorted by the division responsible for follow-up. At the show's end the names are merged with a standard text letter. Each division president's signature has been scanned into the computer. Each prospect gets an immediate letter of thanks that includes the telephone number of the Nielsen VIP and that has been signed by that person.

This is not difficult or expensive. We cover how A.C. Nielsen uses personal computer technology in many ways to help manage events in Chapter 11.

Lead Feedback. Exhibit managers carp that they send leads out and never hear back on what happened. That is especially so when leads are sent to outside dealers. To gain perspective, sit in the chair of a busy salesperson. Each day is filled with work of one sort or another, much of it time-sensitive and demanding. Leads, regardless of the source, tend to find their way to the outer left-hand edge of the desk or in the to-do tray for coverage on a light day.

- Perceived lead quality is part of the problem. Show leads are far different than those that might emerge from, for instance, trade advertising. The lead giver has made a greater effort and spent more money to give the lead than it takes to read a magazine and circle a bingo card. In addition, the lead giver has been screened at the booth!

- Unfortunately, many leads sent to field offices contain very little of the information gathered at the booth that indicates the seriousness of the contact. Some do include a check-off on what product seems to be of interest. Sometimes one sees a note, "This is hot!" Or maybe not. A short explanation of *why* is needed. You have to "sell the salesperson" that making a special effort is worthwhile. We present an exhibit lead card concept in Chapter 17. You will see that the most important part of that card is "remarks." This is where the story can be told that gets the lead off that left-hand-corner slush pile.

- Exhibit leads sent out are generally accompanied by a request for feedback. Make it easy. *Restrain your information request to what you need to know to run a better program.* Exhibits support. They are not the boss. For instance, you might ask for a lead grade: high, medium, low, or no. Assuming high or medium, you might then ask for a guess as to revenue potential within a year. The response form should include an area for comments. The response device should explain why the feedback is important and not imply that the exhibit is trying to take credit for sales.

Less-Qualified Leads or Long-Range Prospects

Half the leads you gather will not require immediate personal follow-up. If you have been doing that name-gathering-fish-bowl-business-card sort of thing, an even higher percent of the names trapped fall into this less important category. The "leads" or names are not really any more qualified than trade magazine ad "bingo card" responses.[1] Some may have dropped off a business card, others may have asked for literature. Either way, you do not know enough.

However, in order to get a lead at a trade show, some kind of person-to-person contact was established at substantial exhibit cost. The visitors spent money to come to the show. Don't ignore them.

Literature Mailing

For the most part those who were not as interested in immediate action at the booth but requested literature probably provided some information about themselves. That should be noted in your database as well as the request for a brochure or catalog.

Some companies have several different pieces. If the specific item was not cited on the lead card, the best immediate response might be a letter listing all. The appropriate items are checked off and the letter sent back in a response envelope. Some may not be returned, an indication of low interest.

Response Enclosures.   Most companies take the trouble to enclose at least a short note with the item. That note should remind the recipient of the booth meeting and the request, now honored. These letters typically provide a telephone number to call for more information or an address. We suggest that a questionnaire be included, perhaps a short survey. That allows an easy way for the prospect to continue the dialogue, and you might learn something, too.

Mail Timing.   Just as with personal follow-up leads, time is of the essence. The quicker the piece arrives, the better the service impression made on the prospect. The mailing process is quite important in that regard. For instance:

- Unless you are scanning names into the computer, you can assume that it will take about five minutes a name for key entry into a computer. (That may seem slow, but it is about right, including the time needed for review and editing, coffee breaks, and other interruptions.) If you have 100 names, figure over eight hours of heads-down work. If at all possible, the work should start at the show itself. Wait until you get home, and several days of delay can ensue.

- Some companies distribute show leads to the field, even for literature fulfillment. We don't suggest it. That process should be centralized with a report sent to field offices citing the appropriate names and what was sent. That will help expedite things.

- Other companies do provide a central fulfillment service, either in-house or through an outside company. Even in those cases, however, there are problems to solve. Most of these organizations are getting their input from several sources. For instance, they may be responding to coupons sent in, or bingo card ad responses. In addition, they will be handling outbound direct-mail functions for the company. For the most part those requests are not particularly time sensitive. (Bingo card requests come in well after the ads are run anyway. Another week or so does not hurt.) Supervisors should be alerted to the special nature of exhibit-generated requests for information, giving this work very high priority.

Software Compatibility.   It is our conviction that the people who run the exhibits must also key enter the leads. *If you can do only one "extra" beyond providing the booth and graphics, this is it!* If any other work group in the company does this work for you, it will take a back seat to other, ongoing, responsibilities. From a sales viewpoint, the lost time problem can be staggering.

In Chapter 11 we cover computer-based exhibit management tools. We point out that the computer system and software used by the events and exhibits manager should be compatible with what is used in other work groups. Handling literature fulfillment is an ideal illustration. If you hand over a seamless diskette for processing, things will go faster. The more you help others help you, the better the ultimate result.

Postshow Qualification

Splattered about in this book you will note our plea that exhibitors do a better job of gathering and trapping information at their events. The supreme value of exhibiting is seen in the paper currency that it produces. For some readers we are preaching to the faithful. However, even among those there are many who are unable to convince others in their outfits of the need to work hardest at this.

It may be a tough internal sale, but there is too much advantage gained by show participation to toss away, whatever the at-show procedure. To an extent, those who attend an event and give you some kind of lead are self-qualified. The issue becomes how and to what extent? One method to learn more is the questionnaire idea above.

Telemarketing.   One of the least expensive methods used is making phone calls and asking questions. Telemarketing is used for a number of purposes. Few of us enjoy those phone calls at home (often during the dinner hour) soliciting donations, offering financial services or home improvements, but the method can work well in postshow prospect qualification. That is true in spite of the telephone-tag we play so often during the business day. Instead of a "sales pitch," work with your vendor on a script focused on asking questions.

In many or most metropolitan areas, telemarketing companies can be found in the classified telephone directory. However, many may not fully understand exhibiting. Exhibit industry publications list companies that do understand, or at least want to understand, the situation.[2] Special training is needed for those making the calls. The company may not be local. That should not pose a problem.

The Paper Products List

- Sales leads for personal follow-up
- Interested prospects for literature only
- Orders
- Reports on seminars of particular interest
- Audiotapes for seminars of particular interest
- Copies of industry periodicals distributed at the event
- Reports on competitor exhibits
- Copies of competition literature
- Copies of competition advertising in show publications
- Exhibit evaluation report by staff members
- Copies of news releases distributed at the show by you and your competitors.

Figure 8-1. The value of exhibiting is represented in its paper products. Different work groups inside the company may have greater interest in one or two.

The Paper Products List

Figure 8-1 is a list of the paper products that can be produced as a result of exhibiting. This is the currency of value that is so important. Exhibits can and do serve different corporate constituencies. As you serve each one of them, the value of exhibiting bubbles up to the top. You won't have to "sell" the medium to top management. Others will become your surrogates.

For most, running exhibits is an infrequent chore—they do it perhaps only three or four times a year. The work is blended in with a lot of other responsibilities. You must ask yourself, "What kind of process can I put in place that produces what we need without working myself to death on this one job?" To figure that out, work backward. That is why we offer the Paper Products List. Your own list should reflect what you want to accomplish. It will help you set goals, clarify mission, and reduce wheelspin.

Measuring Return on Investment

Big-time middle managers ask tough questions; but not as a challenge. "What's our ROI on this?" "What will be the bottom-line results on that program?" We pause and then ask, "What do you mean by 'Return on Investment' or 'Bottom Line'?"

Those terms were created as financial calculation descriptions. They are business shorthand for: Are we making money? If so, how much? The use of the terms led to something else as well: a way of thinking about the finances of individual operations in a company that do not necessarily show up on a balance sheet or income statement.

"Functional Measurement"

Did we just make up a new term when writing "Functional Measurement" as a heading? Perhaps not. However, it does describe a reality that has been around a long time. As organizations grew—business, government, military, social—managers needed shorthand, apples-to-apples, ways of evaluating contributions by individual work processes.

Functional Measurement Illustrations

There are thousands of them. Auto manufacturers, for example, track the cost of manufacturing. They can tell you, down to a penny, the cost for each car's construction. Manufacturing cost per unit is an important guide. There are many others. For instance, cost per labor unit is used to manage a single work process.

Service industries also employ internal ROI measurements to aid managers in doing their jobs. The telephone companies, historically, have led the way in that regard. They pioneered the use of index measurements that included "rolling averages." Results for three months are averaged in an index. After month four results are in, the first month is eliminated. That creates a trend line. It diminishes big ups and downs so managers can take a longer view of what they are doing and improve.

Quality, as well as work production, is addressed with functional measurements. "Inspection rejections per 100 units." "Customer complaints per 100." "Calls not answered within 10 seconds." "Phone directory errors per 1000." We can fill this page.

Selling is managed using index measurements—and related incentives. A raw commission percent is no longer enough. Does business generated reflect orders from old customers or new? New products or old—some squeezing company warehouses and reflecting imbedded costs? More and more, sales rewards are based on an index-based point system. It rewards those who sell what and who the company needs sold the most. A common measure used: product & service (P&S) points.

Marketing Communications Measurements

Advertising professionals don't take ultimate credit (or blame) for bottom-line performance, though what they produce is often absolutely critical to that measure. For instance, the emergence of many consumer brands can be traced to sophisticated advertising and creative media plans. The same is true for business-to-business products. Advertising's job is to make a new product old, fast. Or an old product new, fast.

The measurements most used are like those employed by managers supervising specific work functions inside their client organizations—quantitative and qualitative. That is why "ratings" are so important—TV, radio, magazine, newspaper, outdoor, and others. Terms such as reach and frequency (R&F) and cost per thousand (CPM) emerge. The numbers are used by media planners to figure out the best balance of advertising expense to gain the most penetration for their advertisers.[1]

Quality measurements are based on research. Ad themes are measured on the basis of test market programs. More frequently, potential creative impact is measured using what are called focus group interviews among targeted customer groups.

Interestingly, we have rarely seen focus groups used to test exhibiting's creative themes. Considering the money spent, we recommend the process. Focus group studies are not perfect, but they can wave red flags or signal a go. The results can reduce the degree to which a single management opinion drives creative decision making. "The boss likes golf. That's why the putting green is in the booth."[2]

Exhibit Measurements

There are two issues: One is making sure that top management supports exhibiting. There are a number of value measurements that lend themselves to that purpose. We cover many them in Chapter 9. Here we aim at measurements to help you do the job better as a professional, without spending long hours putting things together.

What we propose are index measurements, just like those that help managers run other individual business functions. They aid in planning and administration. They allow managers to adjust and improve as they go along.

We do not think it necessary to get into the sophistication of "a rolling-average index" to spot trends, as is the case in the telephone industry. The volumes are too small in exhibiting to warrant that. What is important is the search for an anomaly, figures that don't match with prior experience. For instance, let's say that your exhibits have been running along in a range of a 4.6 to 5.0 index level. Then a show delivers a 6.3 index! That's when you should look at *why*. The reasons can impact on all future planning.

What to Count

Any measurement system like this depends on consistency. Garbage in, garbage out. What are the things you do, show after show, that can be counted in reliable fashion? What follows is a short list, but you may have others to add:

- Number of personal follow-up leads
- Number of orders
- Number of literature requests
- Number of samples and/or literature distributed at the booth
- Number of revenue dollars from orders at the booth or those estimated for the future

As we said in Chapter 9, don't try to count booth contacts. Without outside research at every show, you won't be able to do it! Pick one or two items that you *can* count and that are appropriate for all your events. At least in these one or two areas you will have comparative statistics that can lead to thinking things through. (Even if the "math" is bad for one show, there may be compelling reasons to keep things as they are. But at least you will know that, and you can make management points by citing the differences.)

Dollar Masking.   What if you produce a figure for a show such as $720 per contact! That's about 10 times higher than reality. (And we should not try to count contacts ourselves anyway!) If something like that happens, you will be on the short list for a visit to the cardiovascular unit at your local hospital. Your boss will get there first. In a similar context, what if your revenue number is less than exhibit expense? Same thing. Do not panic. Exhibits work and have worked for well over a millennium. There are two places where we can make suggestions:

1. Evaluate what you are counting and how that count is created. Look, as well, at the costs that are allocated against these results.
2. Avoid *expressing* index results in pure dollar terms, such as "cost per lead" or "revenue per dollar of expense." You may understand all the subtleties and the use of the index. Others will not. They will take you literally.

The goal is not justification of the use of the medium. That's a given. *The purpose of an index measure is to provide the manager with signals. The raw numbers mean little.* The measurement game is played so that you can express some objective suggestions for the future versus playing the same old game, year after year.

Work Production Measurements

Most exhibitors must be satisfied with work accomplishment at an event. There is no realistic way to relate the work to actual sales revenue, even with an index system. The work item measured can be related to exhibit cost or time.

For instance, an index can be based on "cost per lead," "cost per inquiry," "cost per sample distributed," and the list goes on. Or that could be "lead per hour" and so on. It simply *does not matter* what you pick out, as long as it is consistent, show to show. In spite of what we suggest, if you want to count business cards in fish bowls, that is fine. Just do it all the time, and relate the number to something. You start comparing apples.

Illustration with Cost as the Denominator.   Suppose you decide to track "leads for personal follow-up" because you try for those at every event. Let's say that you spent $10,000 and obtained 50 leads for personal follow-up. That's a cost of $200 per lead! (That, by the way, is not at all expensive when you consider the close ratio for qualified trade show leads.)

Expression: Instead of raw dollars, express the result as 2.0 to 10. (Divide 10,000 by 50.) That avoids the necessity of explaining the exhibit function time and time again to those who don't care. It is even better to express the result as *2.0*. Period.

The next show emerges. You spend $11,600 and gather 53 leads for personal follow-up. The show rating comes out at 2.19—somewhat higher than our first but similar. The third show comes along. You spend $15,000 and obtain 64 similar leads. That produces a higher figure—an index of 2.34 for the event, but reasonable enough. The fourth exhibit costs $9500 and produces 61 leads. The result: an index of 1.56!

Now is the moment. Don't blame the other shows or thank this one. There can be outside factors, but a good manager gets very curious when numbers are out of line. In the case of this index, we are playing golf—the lower the better. When results are running 2-plus, and now we have a 1½, or 25 percent lower. What did that?

Solid managers take a long look. What was different in planning and execution for the fourth show that produced the remarkable result? The choice is yours.

Illustration without Cost As the Denominator. We have pointed out that indexes are typically created by comparing what is counted to cost, time, or some other common denominator.

Another approach, avoiding cost, is "leads per hour per square foot of exhibit space." If you had a 10 × 20 space open for 15 total show hours and generated 130 leads, the index number would be 103. The actual calculation: 200 square feet divided by 130 sales leads divided by 15 hours equals 0.1025.

The results work in the same way that an index based on cost as a common denominator operates. Track the index results for several events, and you should find yourself in a number range. Then watch for trends or a fluctuation. You will start to explore the reasons and improve future planning.

Dollar Return Measurements

Many companies can employ revenue return measurements. The method we use is called the expense-to-revenue ratio (*E*-to-*R*). It is a simple tool, around a long time.

If you spend $10,000 to obtain revenue of $20,000, the *E*-to-*R* is 1:2. The left side of the ratio, expense, is always expressed as 1. The right side is the revenue relationship. *Enter the revenue figure on your calcula-*

tor. Then divide it by the expense. The answer is the right side of the ratio, the revenue relationship to 1.

For example, if exhibit expense were $11,500 and the revenue $26,000, you would divide 26,000 by 11,500. The answer is 2.26. The *E*-to-*R* ratio is expressed 1:2.26.

This is not a bottom-line measure that shows up on a balance sheet. It is a manager's tool. *E*-to-*R* does not always reflect all costs and all revenues. However, if you are consistent in the types of expense counted and consistent in the way revenue is reported, the *E*-to-*R* ratio can become a powerful management tool.

It is used in the same way cost-based work production indexes are employed, though in this case higher numbers are better. Here is how it might work: Our first show produces an *E*-to-*R* of 1:2.26. Our second: 1:2.23. Our third: 1:2.28. Then comes the fourth show, and it produces an *E*-to-*R* of 1:3.65—way higher than before! You would try and figure out why. The answer could improve planning for all events.

Order Writing Shows.　There are many companies that write orders at their booths. Manufacturers selling to retailers at gift shows are among them. Retailers selling at consumer events form another large group. The *E*-to-*R* ratio is a perfect way to compare performances.

Many of these companies also generate leads for follow-up at the same shows. That is okay. We present a method below for estimating lead revenue. However, even if that method cannot be used, you can still use the *E*-to-*R* on orders written as a benchmark that encourages improved planning.

Some managers like to play with figures. It is possible to create *three* *E*-to-*R* ratios for each event: *E*-to-*R* for orders, *E*-to-*R* for leads, and *E*-to-*R* for leads and orders combined. For instance, our first show generated a 1:2.26 for orders, based on a cost of $11,500 and orders written of $26,000. What if leads were taken as well and the value estimate for the leads was $8000. Dividing 8000 by 11,500 provides an *E*-to-*R* ratio of 1:0.69 for leads. The third index combines the two: $26,000 plus $8000 is $34,000, divided by $11,500. The result is a total *E*-to-*R* of 1:2.96.

Taking the extra step gives managers more information. When the total *E*-to-*R* shifts dramatically, they can look beneath it and see where the change came from, leads or orders. Then explore the reasons why it changes.

Dollar Return Measurements at Lead Taking Shows

The *E*-to-*R* ratio works perfectly well in lead taking situations, just as it does for those who write orders at the booth as a primary task. You might ask, "Where do I get accurate revenue information?" The answer: You don't need it.

The Consistency Requirement. Many corporate exhibit managers become frustrated when they send leads out to the field and get evaluations back on only 25 or 30 percent of them. That is because they want the information to help justify use of the medium as a whole. They figure that the bigger the dollars, the more top management will support exhibiting. Maybe yes, but more often it does not matter. Reports generated by the self-interested are not as powerful as hearing from others that the exhibit program has paid off for them. Of greater value is using what reports do come in to build the E-to-R ratio index so future planning can be improved.

Some argue that when you do not hear back on all the leads, there is a lack of consistency. That is wrong. *If you are consistently inconsistent,* the resulting index numbers are, in fact, dependable. The only thing to keep in mind is that when the reporting procedure is in place, you don't mess with it all the time. Do not suddenly go on a tear to get more results back from one particular show's leads! The results from that show won't be apples to apples compared to others.

Lead Evaluations. Repeating what we said earlier in this book, restrain lead feedback requests to the essential. Grade the lead: High, Medium, Low, and No. In the event that the follow-up person grades the lead High or Medium, ask for a revenue potential within the normal selling cycle without implying that the exhibit group will hold the contact person's foot to the fire if things change. They will change. Some reports will "smoke you high," some will "smoke you low." The reports will be consistently inconsistent. They are good for index building because of that.

Worry less about justifying the use of the medium. Worry more about how you can improve the process for your company.

10
A Management Planning Illustration

In Chapters 4 through 9 we have traced exhibit planning. We covered developing an annual plan; creating a mission statement, exhibit goals, and budgets; and following up with postshow action and evaluation. Here we pull it all together in one hypothetical case history, a summary of Part 2, as a whole.

As you read, you will see several "figures," charts that isolate the numbers that emerge as we tell our tale. At the end of the chapter we will pull all these numbers together onto one chart, Figure 10-5. You may want to type that chart into your PC database as a "blank master" and then make copies for each event to fill in as you go along.

The Ding Company at the Bellringer Show

The Ding Company makes bell ringers for consumer and commercial markets. The product lines extend from front door buzzers and security alert bells and siren ringers to automated systems that play songs on carillon bells atop spires or steeples. Ding will be at the Bellringer Show to offer consumer products to dealers: expensive computer-driven bell-song-playing systems to civic and religious institutions.

Show Analysis

Though diverse in membership, the Bellringer Association is not large. It anticipates about 3000 visitors at the upcoming show. Because the show is fairly small, it does not have data available on the audience breakdown from past events.

Ding, however, knows the show. In addition, it gets verbal advice from show management. Ding also knows that while it is growing, it remains a regional supplier, able to sell and service only a portion of the country.

Show management points out that of the 3000 people who attend, 600 will be spouses, 300 will be other exhibitor personnel, and about 100 will be trade press, guests, and students. The buyer audience is really 2000. Ding estimates that 25 percent of the buyer audience is its target. It figures that 500 of the 2000 projected buyers are appropriate.

Ding took a proper approach, talking with the show manager and basing estimates on its own experience. However, readers of Part 2 will remember *the 16 percent rule.* Taking 16 percent of the audience promised at a fairly diversified show audience projected as interested in a single product line provides a conservative estimate. Had Ding used *the 16 percent rule,* its target audience would have been 480.

Even after the target audience for specific product interest is estimated, there is one more step. Roughly 45 percent of those who are interested are actually influential and in the market today. We round that off using *the 50 percent rule.* Of the 480 buyers from the region that Ding serves, about 240 offer important short-term potential.

The Ding story is told thus far, in summary form, in Figure 10-1. If you are mathematically oriented, you will have spotted a shortcut. Figure 8 percent of the total audience estimate. You will come up with those both interested and influential. Using a 3000 base, that is 240! Ding should focus on reaching as many of the 240 as possible.

The Waste Factor

To reach its full potential, the Ding Company must sort out the top 240 from an audience of 480 of interested visitors. And that's not all. *Remember the waste factor?* We have to add one-third to cover people who just show up for curiosity's sake or to get directions to the restrooms. These are not long contacts, but we have to plan for them. That translates to having a booth size and staff team capable of talking with about 640 people during the course of the show.

Time, Productivity, and Space

In summary, here is how these formulas work out for Ding at the Bellringer Show.

Exhibit Planning Summary

Show Analysis

1. Name	Bellringer Show	
2. Total audience estimate	3000	
3. Deductions		
Exhibitor personnel		300
Spouses		600
Others		100
4. Net buyer audience	2000	
5. Percent target	25	
6. Target audience	500	

The 16 Percent Rule Alternate

7. Total audience estimate	3000
8. Target audience	480

The 50 Percent Rule

9. Target audience	480
10. Both interested and influential	240

Figure 10-1. This summarizes information and estimates on the expo audience. Of the total of 3000 anticipated, a conservative 480 will have interest in the products, and, of those, 240 will also be influential in short-term purchasing.

Time.   The show will be open for three days, 6 hours a day, a total of 18 hours. However, 3 of these hours will provide but light traffic. Our "active hours" are 15.

Productivity.   We estimate that each booth staff person on duty will talk with 10 people in an active hour; some visitors alone, others in groups—including giving restroom directions. If there are 15 active hours and the need is to meet 640 people, the team must speak with just over 40 people per active hour at the booth. The team on duty should be four people.

Space.   The good old Ding Company does not bring carillon bells to its exhibits! Just the control devices and samples of its lines of consumer products. The booth design is restricted to desktop product demonstration and retail racking, plus signs.

Using our space guide, we can estimate that each staff person on duty requires some booth space for conversation with one, two, and sometimes three people, with a degree of exhibit backdrop, table, and display allocated. That rounds off to 65 square feet in four work stations. Four people would need 260 square feet of space—a booth space 10 feet in depth by 26 feet long.

Unfortunately, booth space is rented in 10-foot increments (3 m overseas), mostly 10 feet in depth, but sometimes 8. (Ignore the 8 for this purpose.) Ideally, you would rent a 30-foot-long booth space, and perhaps add a fifth team member. You would reach 100 percent of the target market and more!

Reality Goal Setting for Leads and Orders

The Ding Company is not a corporate monolith that can wait five years for returns. And it, like most others, booked space a year ago for the upcoming event. Regardless of show potential, it has to be satisfied with what it can do without spending all its resources in one place. Ding rented 20 feet, two booth spaces. It does plan to have four people on the booth staff plus the exhibits coordinator. The consideration is what can Ding do? Here is that reality. (It is reflected in Figure 10-2.)

Booth Contacts. Ding team members will talk with 10 per active hour—40 per hour for a four-person team. There will be 15 active hours. The Ding Company will speak with 600 people.

The Waste Factor. Add one-third when you are building up to needs, subtract one-quarter when you are faced with given limits in advance. The same thing. One-quarter of 600 is 150. Thus, the Ding team will talk with 450 people interested in its products. Of those, 225 will be both interested and influential in Ding's selling area on a short-term basis. It is somewhat less than the ideal of 240, but it is certainly acceptable.

The 10-Contact Rule. *The 10-contact rule* comes into play as another way to look at this. Of the total of 600 booth contacts predicted, here is the breakdown:

- People not at all interested: 2 out of 10   (120 for Ding's exhibit)

Exhibit Planning Summary

Lead Objective

11. Team size on duty   4
12. Contacts/hour/person   10
13. Contacts per hour   40
14. Active hours   15
15. Contacts estimate (40 × 15)   600
16. 20 percent personal follow-up leads   120
17. 20 percent mailing-list leads   120
18. Total leads   240

Order Objectives

19. Carillon Computer Ringing Systems: 3 (long range) $180,000
20. "25 New Songs" software: 10 (short range) $5000
21. Carillon Service Contracts: 5 (short range) $7500
22. Current dealer orders for consumer: 20 (short range) $220,000
23. New co-op display orders: 20 (short-range 60 units) $45,000
24. New consumer outlets: 60 (long range) $30,000
25. Short-range revenue goal: $277,500
26. Long-range revenue goal: $210,000
27. Total revenue objective: $487,500

Figure 10-2. This expands the Ding case to cover setting numerical goals for leads and orders.

- Interested but not buyers: 4 out of 10   (140 for Ding's exhibit)
- Buyers but not immediate: 2 out of 10   (120 for Ding's exhibit)
- Buyers with short-term buying interest: 2 out of 10   (120 for Ding's exhibit)

The last two categories produce 240, somewhat higher than the 225 we calculated above, but in the ballpark. The shorthand way of arriving at the same number is to use *the 20 percent rule*. After estimating booth contacts, use 20 percent of that figure for leads that require personal follow-up, and another 20 percent for mailing-list additions.

Lead Goal

Using one method, we came up with 225 leads. The other produces 240, the idealized total that Ding would feel represents 100 percent of its potential at the event—starting with its true target market of between 480 and 500 at the Bellringer Show.

This is far from a perfect science, but if you follow either one of the procedures, it is likely that your experience will not be any more than 5 percent off, assuming that each visitor is interviewed in advance of taking the lead. If all Ding wants to do is collect business cards in a fishbowl, the number of so-called leads will leap dramatically.

Readers will remember that a qualified leads estimate is based on contacts per hour. There is a range of between 7 and 15, depending on your product type. (You cannot count contacts accurately.) We suggest starting with 10 per hour per person during active hours. If, after two or three shows, you are running well above or below what we present here, adjust the 10 up or down to reflect your experience. *We are not trying to create "stretch" objectives but instead to quantify realities based on past experience and research studies cited earlier.*

Order Goal

There are few if any repeat orders for computer-driven devices that play songs on carillon bells atop spires or steeples. However, the company does offer service contracts. It also offers software updates that expand the number of songs that can be punched up!

The sales department reports that 20 prior carillon bell ringer clients plan to attend the meeting. Two goals are set for these old customers. First, product warranties have run out for 10 customers. The goal is to sell five service contracts. Second, all 20 should be interested in the software upgrade "25 New Bell Songs from Ding." With advance sales work done, the hope is for 10 orders at the show.

The consumer products group is another kettle of fish. There are 30 distributors or chain buyers planning to attend. They sell, at retail, door chimes and security alarms. The objective, with some prior sales work, is to write orders from 20 at the show. In addition, Ding has a new in-store display provided on a co-op basis. Goal: 20 as well.

Ding wants to focus on new-client development during show days at the booth. It has rented a small suite in the convention hotel for private client meetings in off hours and will invite these people there.

Revenue Conversion Objectives

Ding can make estimates though somewhat blurry. Better that than a blank sheet! Within the normal selling cycle, here is what is estimated:

Carillon Bell Ringer Systems.   The market is narrow. Though "everyone" will be at the Bellringer Show, not many will make the move to computerized bell ringing. Ding figures three sales in a two-year selling cycle. Revenue: $60,000 each for a total of $180,000.

New Consumer Product Distributors and Chains.   The market is much larger, but initial orders are smaller. Of the leads, estimate *for personal follow-up* (120) we apply *the 50 percent rule*. One-half will be converted into some kind of sale (60). The average startup sale has been $5000 of merchandise. The ultimate goal for the event becomes $30,000 in sales to new outlets.

Carillon Bell Service Contracts and Software Upgrades. Service contracts are priced at $1500 per year. Five orders equate to $7500. The new software ("25 New Songs") is priced at $500. If 10 orders are written: $5000. Total orders revenue objective for this line of business among old customers: $12,500.

Consumer Products Orders.   This is tough to predict. There are two chain operations (Ring-Mart and Melody Stores) that can explode the entire plant operation with just one order! However, the VP-level executives handling these accounts already know what to expect. The result is that from an objective-setting perspective, we use the average order from an old customer. That figure is $11,000. The 20 orders estimated: $220,000.

The second consumer products offering at the show will be Ding's new store display system offered on a co-op basis. The retailer share is $750 per unit. Excluding Ring-Mart and Melody Stores, there are 92 retail outlets reflected in the current client list of 30 customers. Assuming 20 orders, that equates to roughly 60 stores, or $45,000.

These objectives are summarized in Figure 10-2. You will see that our rose-color-glasses bell ringer illustration is aimed at providing $277,500 in short-term revenue for Ding, plus the potential of $210,000 in long term. Total goal: $487,500.

Exhibit Marketing Costs

Ding, like any other company, must spend money to earn it. Chapter 7 provides a lot of budget management information. Now we apply that to Ding's Bellringer Show program, regardless of what budget the dollars come from within the company.

Space at Bellringer is higher than the average. A 10 by 10 booth space costs $2000, $20 per square foot. Two spaces, 20 feet, were rented a year ago. Of the total $4000, half was paid as a deposit. The balance this year, plus a deposit for next year. Budget: $4000. Space rent is just the start and not the largest single-cost element.

Booth Cost.   Ding owns a modular booth system that can fill 40 linear feet. It paid $48,000 for the system two years ago and plans on using it for at least 10 events. That would be $4800 per show for use of the entire inventory. In this case 20 feet are needed. The "fair share," though not a current-year budget item, should be included in show cost. Value: $2400. Ding's manager, however, elects to ignore this appropriate allocation!

Figure 10-3 is the budget form from Chapter 7, filled out to reflect Ding estimates for the upcoming Bellringer Show. In summary, the exhibit budget allocation is $17,865. However, we estimate that even more, $21,800, will be allocated to the show by other departments and the company as a whole. The show cost estimate: $39,665.

The Ding exhibit coordinator had been instructed by the boss to keep exhibit budget costs under $20,000 and other company costs under $20,000. That is why the coordinator conveniently forgot to allocate $2400 of value in initial exhibit construction to the overall show cost, budget or not. With that tossed in, the show cost estimate would have come in at $41,265, well above the chieftain-mandated limit.

There are two other places where the coordinator could have "found" money to stay within constraints. One would have been in the 10 percent contingency. Eliminating that number, $3515, would have brought the estimate in at $39,750. The other place where the coordinator could find the money was in the estimate of *the value of time* expended by Ding employees at the show.

> *Note:* That value, $8000, was calculated on the basis of 25 person days; 3 show days for 5 people, plus a day of travel on either end. An average of $50,000 per year of compensation per person was used, increased by 20 percent to cover benefits and office backup, $70,000 per year. Dividing by 220 workdays a year, the value is just under $320 per workday. Not making reference to the $8000 allocation, the estimate would have been $35,265, well under the limit.

Of course, it would have been better for the exhibit coordinator to be completely honest. But figure-fudging is common, and we have to anticipate it. Regardless, the Ding coordinator is doing a good job.

Budget Planning Form

Budget item	Exhibit budget	Another budget	Show allocation
1. Space			
A. Current year	2,000	2,000	4,000
B. Deposit (next year)	2,000		
Note: Show allocation should include this year's rent including prior deposit.			
2. Booth, graphics, display products			
A. Design/build/refurb.	1,000		1,000
B. Graphic signs	1,500		1,500
Note: Show allocation should include percent of total based on use potential.			
C. Products/samples			
3. Promotions before the event			
A. Direct mail		1,000	1,000
B. Advertising		1,000	1,000
C. Press releases		500	500
4. Promotion at the event			
A. Advertising		2,000	2,000
B. Press releases			
C. Booth giveaways	500		500
D. Literature		1,000	1,000
E. Booth shows			
5. Off-site activities			
A. Hospitality	1,000		1,000
B. Training	500		500
C. Special events			
6. Transport			
A. Exhibit properties	3,000		3,000
B. Personnel		2,000	2,000
C. Hotel food		2,500	2,500
7. Show services			
A. Drayage	1,500		1,500
B. Setup/teardown	1,000		1,000
C. Electricity	400		400
D. Telephone	200		200
E. Plumbing			
F. High-pressure air			
G. Rigging			
H. Audiovisual			
I. Floral	150		150
J. Carpet			
K. Security			

Figure 10-3. This budget form was copied from Chapter 7. Additional columns can be added for actual. The point is that exhibit costs do reflect total corporate investment.

Budget item	Exhibit budget	Another budget	Show allocation
L. Photography			
M. Registration device	100		100
N. Booth cleaning	100		100
8. Staff time value		8,000	8,000
9. Research			
A. Professional			
B. Informal			
10. Follow-up			
A. Lead administration	200		200
B. Telemarketing			
Total	15,150	20,000	35,150
11. Contingency	1,715	1,800	3,515
Total	17,865	21,800	39,665

Figure 10-3. (*Continued*) This budget form was copied from Chapter 7. Additional columns can be added for actual. The point is that exhibit costs do reflect total corporate investment.

Many exhibit managers worry only about their own budgets, leaving the rest to others. In today's world, that is not enough. There is an old saying, "A budget is a way to go broke slowly." That is especially so when it reflects only about half of the true cost.

Early in this chapter we promised that each of the "figures" would be pulled together in a master chart at the end. Because the budget element is complex in itself, we present only the totals in our master chart (Figure 10-5).

Evaluating Results

In Chapter 9 we covered ways to measure return on investment. Now we apply that to the Ding case. Because the show has not taken place as yet, we will make an apple pie assumption—that the objectives set will be met on the head!

Using Results

As a reminder, these measurements are used to look for ways in which to improve future planning. They are not useful in convincing top managers that exhibiting is marvelous as a concept. There are other methods for doing that.

Functional Measurement Systems

These are work production measurements, similar to those for manufacturing or individual work functions: cost per item produced or cost
per labor unit. In exhibiting, we compare work produced that can be
counted, show after show, to the cost for each event.

Bellringer Show Work Production. Ding has some measurable
work production goals that can be counted with accuracy:

- There should be 240 leads, all combined.
- Look at orders: There should be 55 in all, for several product areas.

To create an index number, simply divide cost by the item measured.
In our Chapter 9 illustration there were 50 leads and $10,000 of exhibit
cost. The result was 2.0 to 10 (or 2.0). Here is how that would work for
Ding at Bellringer (Figure 10-4):

- $39,665 divided by 240 leads is $165.27 per lead. Mask the dollars. It
  is a 1.65 index.

Exhibit Planning Summary

Cost Summary Totals

Budget item	Exhibit budget	Another budget	Show allocation
27. Total	17,865	21,800	39,665

Results Index Summary (Functional Work Measurement)

28. Lead index: 1.65

29. Order index: 7.21

30. Total index: 2.34

Dollar Return Index Summary (Expense-to-Revenue Ratio)

31. Long-range *E*-to-*R*: 1:5.29

32. Short-range *E*-to-*R*: 1:7.00

33. Revenues combined *E*-to-*R*: 1:12.29.

Figure 10-4. This reflects Ding performance from both a cost and returns viewpoint, on an index basis.

- $39,665 divided by 55 orders is $721.18 per order. Mask dollars. It is a 7.21 index.
- $39,665 divided by 295 (leads and orders) is $234.46 per work item. Index 2.34.

These numbers, taken by themselves, are *absolutely meaningless*. The value to Ding's coordinator comes after three or four shows of measuring on a consistent basis. Assume that the first three shows produce functional measurement results in the same ballpark. Along comes show four, and the results are substantially lower. *With this kind of measurement, that's the name of the game: Drive the numbers lower.*

With this kind of show four result in hand, the Ding manager will take a close look at planning and try to figure out why. The answer can impact on all future planning.

Bellringer Dollar Return Measurements. Ding also has revenue objectives for short- and long-range return on investment:

- Carillon System long-range sales: $180,000
- New consumer product dealer long-range sales: $30,000
- Total long range: $210,000
- Carillon (25 songs software) short range: $5000
- Carillon service contacts short range: $7500
- Current consumer product short-range dealer orders: $220,000
- Co-op short-range display orders: $45,000
- Total short range: $277,500

The expense-to-revenue ratio index in Chapter 9 is calculated by *dividing the revenue item by expense.* In that chapter's illustration, we divided $20,000 in revenue by the $10,000 in expense. The *E*-to-*R* ratio was expressed as 1:2. Expense is always 1, and the revenue side is always a multiplier. For Ding at Bellringer:

- Long-range total ($210,000) divided by expense ($39,665) produces an *E*-to-*R* ratio index of 1:5.29 for long-range revenue.
- Short-range total ($277,500) divided by expense ($39,665) produces an *E*-to-*R* ratio index of 1:7.00 for short-range revenue.
- Revenues combined ($487,500) divided by expense ($39,665) produces an *E*-to-*R* ratio index of 1:12.29.

As before, these numbers, taken by themselves, *are absolutely meaningless*. The value to Ding's coordinator comes after three or four shows of measuring on a consistent basis. Assume that the first three shows produce *E-to-R* measurement results in the same ballpark. Along comes show four, and the results are substantially higher. *With this kind of measurement, that's the name of the game: drive the numbers higher.* Again, that will lead to thinking about future show planning.

Pie in the Sky?

The Ding story is, of course, idealized. It presents a rosy picture. It is, however, practical. If you can apply the work process outlined in Part 2, reflecting it in your work operation, there is no doubt that you will be able to ring the bell at your future shows.

Exhibit Planning Summary (All Combined)

Lead Objective

11. Team size on duty	4
12. Contacts/hour/person	10
13. Contacts per hour	40
14. Active hours	15
15. Contacts estimate (40 × 15)	600
16. 20 percent personal follow-up leads	120
17. 20 percent mailing-list leads	120
18. Total leads	240

Order Objectives

19. Carillon Computer Ringing Systems:
    3 (long range) $180,000

20. "25 New Songs" software:
    10 (short range) $5000

21. Carillon Service Contracts:
    5 (short range) $7500

Figure 10-5. This is the comprehensive Ding story at the Bellringer Show. You do not have to be as detailed. The goal is a guide to influence planning for an individual event or program.

22. Current dealer orders for consumer:
    20 (short-range) $220,000

23. New co-op display orders:
    20 (short-range 60 units) $45,000

24. New consumer outlets:
    60 (long range) $30,000

25. Short-range revenue goal: $277,500

26. Long-range revenue goal: $210,000

27. Total revenue objective: $487,500

Cost Summary Totals

Budget item	Exhibit budget	Another budget	Show allocation
28. Total	17,865	21,800	39,665

Results Index Summary (Functional Work Measurement Reflecting Cost)

29. Lead index: 1.65

30. Order index: 7.21

31. Total index: 2.34

Dollar Return Index Summary (Expense-to-Revenue Ratio Reflecting Cost)

32. Long-range *E-to-R:* 1:5.29

33. Short-range *E-to-R:* 1:7.00

34. Revenues combined *E-to-R:* 1:12.29.

Figure 10-5. (*Continued*) This is the comprehensive Ding story at the Bellringer Show. You do not have to be as detailed. The goal is a guide to influence planning for an individual event or program.

11
Computers and You

Tom Fitzgerald was sitting in his room at the North Sydney Gardens Hotel. The sun was coming up in the east over the Pacific. The coffee was steaming in his cup. He turned on his notebook computer. An orange screen glowed. The machine was plugged into the room phone line. It called his home office in Sunnyvale, California.

There was a message. Could he do a fast summary on year-to-date spending? Fitzgerald touched a half dozen keys on his electronic piano. The data was inside. A few manipulations and a quick review. The computer modem made music, and the report was on its way half way across the world. The coffee was still hot in Tom's cup on a fine Australian morning. He then read the Sydney newspaper.[1]

Another city, another person. It was 7:30 A.M. on a snowy cold January Monday in Northbrook, Illinois. Mary Jo Mendell was there, in her office, after flying back into Chicago's O'Hare Airport from a trade show over the weekend.

She pulled a computer disk out of her briefcase and slipped it into the office PC. Later that morning the outgoing mail was picked up. There were 87 letters in her outbox. All were signed by a division vice president, thanking show visitors from the last week for providing sales leads for that division's line of business. Mendell also had her coffee.[2]

Those who read this chapter's endnotes will note that both Fitzgerald and Mendell work for big outfits, the Amdahl Corporation and A.C. Nielsen, respectively. They also know both are full-time professionals in corporate exhibit management. Is that a signal that computer-aided exhibit management is only for corporate elephants? *No.*

Even the smallest companies use computers. The technology is becoming easier and easier to use—and far more affordable. The small-computer technology used in other parts of your business can help you make money on exhibiting, too.

Three Computer Chunks

Boil it down and computers that most of us use are providing only three functions: spreadsheets, word processing, and communications. In fact, most of the big computer software companies now offer their products in "suites" of related software that deliver these three functions, plus some bells and whistles.

Both Fitzgerald and Mendell put together their exhibit management programs using off-the-shelf programs you can get at the computer store in a strip mall! Fitzgerald, who is a do-it-yourself tinkerer anyway, modified the programs himself. Mendell said, "Not me. I took advantage of Nielsen friends who know far more than I do to help build my program." Either way, it works.

What are called *integrated programs* are also on the scene. They combine all the chunks and are refined to reflect specific industry needs. We are most familiar with them as we see their output in doctors' or dentists' offices. They are also broadly used in restaurants and other retail establishments. These industry-specific software programs tend to be more expensive than off-the-shelf programs. But they save a lot of work getting started. There are now corporate exhibit management packages. Plug in and go!

Regardless of your choice, it is wise to know a little about how these products work. A primer follows.

Spreadsheet Programs

Think about that green color grid paper you probably used at some point in school. There were columns across the top and rows down the side. Each sheet was a series of boxes you could add up going down or sideways.

That is what spreadsheet software replicates and improves upon. There are many brands. We cannot be too specific in a book because books are used a long time. The computer world is very dynamic! However, Microsoft, Lotus Development, and Novell are three large companies that offer spreadsheet programs.

Spreadsheet Program Advantages.   In contrast to cherished but old-fashioned grid paper, computer versions are fabulous. Perhaps the least of these is that "box size" (and number of boxes) is up to us. How many characters do you want to put in a column? Decide and it is yours. How many lines in a vertical row? Forever. How many columns and rows? Again, what you want.

> *An illustration:* You will find spreadsheet programs are used to store names. What if you have a need to store long names, such as "The Honorable Theresa and Mr. Richard Bellinghausen?" Set up the name column to absorb 52 characters in width. If letters go to cities such as "Research Triangle Park," allow 22 characters in that column. That is in another "row" and thus "box." Width can be different.

More important than box design is that mistakes are easy to fix. Make an error on the old-fashioned grid paper and you start over or use ugly whiteout paint to correct it. Use the computer, key in the revision, and it is there. If it is a new figure to be reflected in a total, the software will add or subtract for you, producing that new total.

Most important is manipulation. Pick your columns and rows. Pull them together and publish a report. That's what Tom Fitzgerald did in Sydney. He asked the computer to pull actual costs for the months thus far. Presto. An accurate report for his boss.

Merging is another manipulation. That's what Mary Jo Mendell did on that cold Monday morning near Chicago. The lead names came from her spreadsheet program. They joined with a standard letter in her word processing program. The 87 letters and envelopes were produced before mail pickup that morning.

Spreadsheet Applications

Exhibit and events managers find all sorts of ways that spreadsheet software can be employed to great advantage. Figure 11-1 presents a rather complete list edited from an article written by Edward Jones for *Exhibitor Times Magazine.* We pay special attention here to those most commonly used.

Budget Management. Both budgets and actual expenses can be entered and thus tracked. For instance, you could enter the budget lines on the forms we present in Chapters 3 or 8, plus any other categories that might interest you.

Here is how that might work. Each budget category might be assigned a column across the top of the grid. Down the side each show could be given three rows: budget, actual, and difference between budget and actual. The program can add across to provide you a total for a show. It can add down to provide a total by expense category.

Computer Management Functions

Major Tasks

- Annual and show-by-show strategies
- Show schedules—by division or product group if required
- Planning—by division or product group if required
- Forecasting (expenses, leads)
- Budgeting—by division or product group if required
- Task coordination and management—tick lists of jobs to do and when
- Properties management—inventory of properties, freight
- Information dissemination—especially repetitive-type communications
- Reporting and tracking
- Follow-up and measurements

Information Categories

- *Show information:* Show name, dates, location, sponsor, location including space number, exhibit size, dates and times for setup, teardown, show hours open.
- *Planning information:* Themes, products and services, booth visitors anticipated, number of leads.
- *Arrangements and coordination information:* Exhibitor kit arrival? Contracts? Deposits? Staff registrations? Hotel and room assignments? VIP travel? Exhibit properties used? Daily schedule of activities and work assignments? Insurance certificate?
- *Correspondence information:* Vendor and employee letters, thank-you letters, lead distribution cover letters.
- *Budget information:* Expense categories, anticipated and actual, division breakdowns, by show and by date and by category and by vendor.
- *Reporting information:* Show schedules, budgets, checklists, leads, sales, product interest projections.

Figure 11-1. This information was edited from an article that appeared in *Exhibitor Times Magazine* in 1994. It was written by Edward Jones, president of Executive Education & Management of Atlanta. EE&M provides consulting and exhibit lead administration services. It offers an integrated exhibit management computer program, "Show Business."

The software knows when you enter figures, or you can assign a date. At the same time you enter an "actual," for instance, this entry also can be stored by category in the month. That feature is what Fitzgerald used to produce his Sydney report on expenses to date while drinking a cup of coffee.

There are specialized programs serving consumers that are not general-purpose spreadsheets but do number crunching nonetheless. For instance, Mary Jo Mendell uses the Quicken brand from Intuit to spread costs for exhibits among divisions, to isolate expenses by category and by show. Programs of this type are used at home to manage bank accounts and reconcile checkbooks. Mendell "deposits" her budget at the start of the year. As each bill is processed with its codes, the amount is deducted from her Quicken total. The transactions are then automatically downloaded to the corporate accounting database. There are two advantages for Mendell:

1. At the end of each month corporate accounting sends overall expense reports to each group. Mendell reconciles this report against her own, private, Quicken-produced report. She finds errors, often coding mistakes by other departments that inadvertently find their way to her.

2. Corporate bookkeeping systems capture costs in large, somewhat amorphous chunks. For instance, there might be just one entry for "trade shows." It neither knows nor cares how many events took place in a given month. Mendell's private system allows her to answer management questions with accuracy and detail.

Properties Inventory and Freight Management.   Midsize and large companies often have several booths. A spreadsheet program is ideal for keeping track. Each crate of exhibit materials is identified with a number typed into its own column along the top of the grid. In addition to exhibit materials in crates, columns can be assigned to items that are not crated, such as a roll of carpet.

Rows down the side can be assigned as you want. Be as simple or exotic as you need, or have time to keep up to date. Here is a list to pick from or start you thinking:

- The name of the booth the crate is part of can help a lot.

- A list of the exact contents of the crate. Leave several rows for that.

- Where the crate is located can help if you store materials in more than one place.

- The dates the crate, or booth, will be in use might help some people.

- The date the booth was built (or last refurbished) might help some.

- The size measurements of the crate, and its cubic size, are of value to all.
- The weight of the crate is important for all.
- The show name and address and the booth number can be stored in this program as well.

When you plan a show, it may be that you will use all or only part of one booth, plus the rug. The computer program will publish a report on what materials you will need. Add the dates the materials will be in use. Plan another show and try to use the same materials during that time span and the computer will wave a red flag.

When you arrive at the convention hall, there is a charge for materials handling called *drayage*. The charge is based on weight. You can publish a special report listing what is being delivered that includes the weights. That will help ensure proper billing.

The same program can help you manage freight costs from your warehouse or exhibit shop to the show and back. For instance, pricing for crated materials is based on what is called *dimensional weight*. Not dead weight. (If you are shipping feathers, they still take up space in trucks or airplanes.) Publish a report that includes both the measurements and cubic sizes. Your hauler will appreciate that, and you will get an accurate bill.

An added plus emerges if you have stored the show name and address and booth number. The spreadsheet can be programmed to print out mailing labels, both outgoing and back to home, for each item.

Name Lists. There are lots of names, and spreadsheets are where we trap them. Booth staff members, hotel in-and-out name lists, leads—the list can go on. Each group can be in its own column with details on each row. The software can be directed to publish all sorts of reports as you need them.

It may seem as though there is a lot of work involved in entering data into a spreadsheet. That's true. However, it is going to be work that is done anyway, computer or not. The time savings appear in two ways. First, the information is easy to correct as changes appear over time. Second, the information can be assembled in different formats for different purposes with just a few keystrokes.

Mitchell A. Fink, a custom computer consultant and software designer in New York, makes a point that is important to remember. He said, "Do not oversell the notion that software ultimately reduces work time. That happens. However, the best value lies in quality assurance. Get it in once and get it in right. It will *stay* right, preventing all sorts of costly and time-consuming problems that emerge in situations where a mistake can emerge later on."[3]

Fink points out that we should mention "PIM, Personal Information Managers. Drift through your software store and you will find them." They can combine all sorts of features—name and address lists, follow-up dates, scheduling, and more. For many, one of these programs might be a good idea.

Specialized Spreadsheet Programs.   We have mentioned specialized accounting packages. They are based on spreadsheet technology. There are others. For instance, there are specialized programs for trapping names. These are offered, most often, for sales management purposes but can be applied to exhibiting. There are also inventory management programs. One that we have not as yet mentioned is time management. Time management programs, at their simplest, are calendars. There are, as well, more extensive project management programs that include all sorts of fancy features. For instance, they can flag when a specific work function should start so that it completes in time for the next phase to begin without undo cost.

Word Processing Programs

We've come a long way from the days when the hard-nosed newspaper reporter banged out stories on a manual typewriter with two stubby fingers. We've come a long way from the days of the electric typewriter with its built-in whiteout tape roll that allowed us to backspace and correct as we typed. (Our first book was typed that way, so it was not that many years ago—and it was agony compared to now.)

Today's personal computer software has become so sophisticated that we can even change typefaces and sizes by the word with a flick of the finger. And as for correction, it is done instantly without a bottle of whiteout in the desk drawer. The word processing programs have become more and more feature rich. This book was written using WordPerfect 6.0a for Windows, close to state of the art at this time. Even now there are so many bell-and-whistle features that the instruction manual runs 1000 pages and sits next to the computer. We will never learn it all! What amazes us is that if you are reading this two years after its publication, this technology will by then be old hat; yesterday's newspaper pounded out two-finger-style by a reporter with fedora-on-head and cigar-in-teeth.

Word Processing Features.   There are some fundamentals. Type once, manipulate and correct with ease, just as with the spreadsheet programs. Toss in a spell checker, grammar checker, thesaurus, and even a dictionary. Print out envelopes using the inside address on a letter. The list just goes on.

Spreadsheet applications and graphics additions have become part of the major word processing programs. They are not, today, as sophisticated as the stand-alone programs, but they are helpful. For instance, you can produce a simple newsletter now using a word processing program alone. For more sophisticated work, you still need special graphics programs.

The most important feature, and it has been around and becomes more sophisticated daily, is called *merging*. It is possible to store information in another program, such as a spreadsheet report, and pull it into the word processing program so that text can be built around it for an integrated product.

We mentioned that software programs now are offered in "suites." In part, at this writing, this is a marketing ploy by the big software (and hardware) companies. In effect: "Buy our product and we will toss in..." However, it is more than marketing. Software protocols are built in to make it easier for users to combine information from several suite programs into one document.

It takes little genius to see where these companies are going. We guess by the time you read this that big-time PC software players will have introduced single off-the-shelf programs that promise to *do it all, whatever you want, easily!* We wonder how thick the instruction manuals will become; how big the on-screen help menus?

Exhibit and Events Management Applications.   There are some obvious word processing applications for exhibit managers. Mary Jo Mendell merges lead names with standard letters that are all individually printed. Tom Fitzgerald and Mary Jo produce letters to staff members that give them all the information they need about the exhibit. Mendell actually produces a binder of preshow information for staff people and management using the technology and an in-house printing group. Figure 11-1 includes a list of word processing applications as well as spreadsheet uses, including:

- Letters and other documents for staff members
- Letters to exhibit sales lead givers
- Lead advisories, by work group, with cover letters and attachments
- Hotel advisories, by name, giving arrival and departure dates

Communications

Sales and exhibit managers spend time "on the road." Their portable computers are traveling companions. At home they deal with people who are all over the place! They need inexpensive, fast ways to move information. PC and communications network technologies do the job.

This is not a book about computers and software. Our goal in this chapter is to open eyes on how technology can serve exhibit and event managers. We dwell less on computer communications than the subject deserves because of that. Applications are what ultimately count, not where any computer sits or how fast it moves.

At the same time, we acknowledge two factors: Full-time exhibit professionals at big companies are road warriors. Over a year's time these people spend more time waiting around in airports than most of us spend on the highway, bus, or subway getting to work.

The second aspect is that exhibit management is never truly "centralized." Managers at companies large and small have to communicate with others who are not down the hall. Some of the people are inside the company. Others? Outsource suppliers.

The Road Warrior

Full-time or part-time, if exhibit management is part of what you do and you have a PC that goes along with you on the road, Tom Fitzgerald passes on some advice:

- Load everything on your portable that you have on the office PC. You never know what you might need.

- Software comes with security procedures. Employ those on the portable to prevent yourself from an inadvertent error when you transfer from your portable to office PC. Do not allow the home-base computer to be updated without review.

- Pack your own telephone cable with the portable. Most business hotels have room phones with a PC plug outlet in the back for computer terminals.

- Bring along, as well, a printer cable. Most business centers in hotels have the cables, but you never know—and you don't want to discover they don't have them just at the time you need a printout.

Communications Pathways.   Personal computers are provided with communications modems, or they can be added with ease and at little cost. These link you directly to other computers or to networks. The networks provide you with a mailbox number. Call your mailbox to check messages. They leap to your screen and can be stored and printed. Send a message to another subscriber? The same happens on the other end when that person checks in for messages.

Public Electronic Mail Networks.　There are a number of commercial services. You are assigned a mailbox number. Your computer modem calls your mailbox to see if there are messages or to send a message. You send a message. It can be to another mailbox or to a fax number. (In that case, of course, your message is played out in fax form.)

Calls to these services are made using 800 numbers. There is no charge for the call. Dun & Bradstreet has a service. So does AT&T and MCI. There is Procomm and OnLine America. After minimal setup charges, your monthly bills reflect how much is sent, rather than time. (For relatively short messages, a good rule of thumb is that the cost is about twice that of a U.S. Postal Service letter with the same number of pages inside.) The Internet system started as an electronic interchange network for use by scientific people, but seems to be emerging as the "hub of hubs."

You can send an E-mail message from your mailbox to a person who has a mailbox number address on another system. There are "gateway" numbers that you add to your recipient's address. For instance, we have an MCI Mailbox number. (It is 472-7402.) We send E-mail messages to both Tom Fitzgerald and Mitch Fink. Their mailboxes are on Internet itself. Tom's Internet E-mail address is tef00@amail.amdahl.com. For Mitch it is mfink@intercom.com. Those addresses are programmed into our computer, but the "gateway" number that connects MCI to Internet comes first, 376-5414.

Local Area Networks.　Briefly, if your work group is fairly large, say, at least five or six personal computers, it becomes economically viable to have one central machine in which your programs are stored. Your PC is now called a *work station*. Fink points out that these networks are best if they are "peer to peer." Apparently, things can get more complicated, and less user-friendly, if the marketing folks are in the same network with the engineering or research people.

Computer Scanners

Computer scanning has become a familiar part of our lives. In super-markets our purchases are passed over scanners at checkout counters that read the product and price codes and add up what we owe. They also feed information to the store's inventory management program. Portable scanners are also used in the aisles by those who stock shelves.

These are called *bar-code applications.* Even outgoing mail is now scanned and the recipient zip code bar-coded. The bar code is used to reduce the time it takes to sort mail. Large-scale mailers help by taking the first step themselves, adding the bar code for the recipient's zip code. (We are a very small mailer, and even we have that feature. Envelopes we produce on a single PC include the bar code, helping the Post Office save a step with its scanner-imprinters.)

Exhibiting Applications

Scanning applications are emerging in the exhibits management arena. They save time, enhance quality, and help build a better rate of return on investment.

Customer Letters.   A.C. Nielsen sends thank-you letters to show lead givers, signed by the vice president of the division responsible for the service that is of interest. In addition to merging the names and addresses with a standard letter, Mary Jo Mendell has scanned the signatures of each of these vice presidents into her PC! A signed letter emerges.

Lead Taking.   We pointed out before that one can assume that it will take five minutes per lead to key enter information into a database. Keying in 100 names, addresses, and other information represents over eight hours of work.

People ask, "Why can't we just scan the information into the computer?" Edward Jones, president of Executive Education & Management in Atlanta, says, "Up to a point you can. But the technology is not yet there to do the whole job easily." He makes two points that illustrate his concern:

1. Scanner technology reads printed documents easily—printed numbers, letters, or bar codes are no problem. For instance, Jones points out that scanners are now available that look like tiny fax machines. Slide a business card through and you have the data! He goes on to say, "You have accurate information, that's for sure. But people don't have their cards designed following the same format. You still have to rearrange the information in the home database."

2. The technology has been slower to emerge when it comes to reading handwriting. That can be very important when those important "remarks" must be trapped. Jones says, "Today's products are sophisticated, but each device must be programmed to recognize the handwriting of one person—and that may not include the handwriting this person uses when scribbling on the back of a lead form, standing up in a booth." Jones feels that it will take several

years for this technology to mature and be priced to make it a practical booth tool.

Automated Registration Programs. More and more shows use the services of registration companies that computer-capture names and addresses of just about anyone attending or exhibiting at an event. They provide visitors with what appears to be a credit card. Swipe the card through a device rented to exhibitors at booths and a printout emerges. In addition to the paper copy, at the show's end an exhibitor can purchase a computer disk with the information on it.

This technology is another excellent but interim step. There are some problems, part technology and part human:

- Many times delegate (or exhibitor) companies prepare advance registration advisories from a headquarters location. Typists do not know all the uses of the information they provide. They change the names but save time by keeping the address and phone number the same—even if those attending come from different locations. The result, from an exhibitor perspective, is that a lead from a division manager in California could be listed with a New York or Paris address and telephone number.

- There are many who register on site. Typically the lines are long. After filling out a form standing at some counter in the lobby and then waiting, if an error is made in typing the badge, very few will request a revision. "If it gets me in, that's all I need."

- Most software written for registration companies was not created with flexibility in mind. These programs are built on spreadsheets. For instance, they may not have allocated enough characters in the name line for a fancy title or long name. And, like a business card, the format followed does not necessarily match the format of your internal name and address file.

MACing or DOS: Purchasing
a New System

There are two computer operating systems. One, DOS, was designed to operate machines based on the IBM technology. The other system was created for Apple Computer's Mac series. Software has been created that works on each. Compatibility is on the march but is slow in coming. There are more IBM-type DOS-based machines. Thus, more software is around. The Macintosh series, however, pioneered graphics in computers.

Picking a Partner

Tom Fitzgerald points out that while industry standards and compatibility are emerging fast, it is still wise to select a machine and thus its operating system based on whom you deal with the most. "If everybody in the company uses IBM or a clone, and these are the people you work with the most, it is probably best to stick with DOS."

However, many exhibit managers communicate frequently with outside suppliers, and especially exhibit designers and producers. Because of an art focus, most of these outfits are part of the MAC camp. If most of your back-and-forth is with these folks, sit by the MAC campfire.

How Big the Machine

Whatever you are told, double it! Mitch Fink helped us select a new system in 1994. Ours came with over 500 MB (megabytes) of storage on the hard disk, 16 MB of random-access memory (RAM). For technical people familiar with the equipment of that time, this might seem very large for one writer who does not use the graphics capability. Fink says, "The new programs eat storage more and more, and they need extra RAM. That trend will continue as all the programs become more feature-rich. It does not cost a whole lot more to be bigger than you need today, so do it."

Integrated Exhibit Management Software Packages

Back to applications. You put together your exhibit and events management software using off-the-shelf programs, much like Mendell or Fitzgerald. You can call consultants like Fink or your own management information systems (MIS) department.

Most people, however, are not full-time pros who run a lot of shows. They can't afford the sweat equity and potential cost for creating perfect programs that match exactly their corporate needs. What they want is a program that can be installed that at least gives them half a loaf.

Integrated Program Features

Software like this, similar to what you find used in a doctor's office or hotel, has had much of the setup programming done for you when you install it. The spreadsheet and word processing features have been combined, and even the communications protocols, into one database. That makes combining information very easy.

Integrated programs for exhibit managers always include a budget package. Most will include an inventory management program. There will be a time management program or tickler list. You will likely find name-list capabilities, at least for staff and hotel lists.

Integrated Program Weaknesses

There are two basic problems with the integrated programs on the market as of this writing: With perhaps the exception of "Show Business,"[4] they were created by small companies without deep pockets or else pure obligation to the exhibit industry. Some of the program developers did not fully understand exhibiting, or they listened to only one or two consultants with narrow perspectives.

PART 3

Creating and Managing an Exhibit

12
Managing Time

Starting here, in Part 3, you are on your own. Part 1 summarized the entire exhibit management process. Its goal was to review the basics for part-time or full-time exhibit managers as well as to help first-timers get up and running at the first expo. Part 2 examined the management process, sometimes in excruciating detail. It is very important and easier than many think to manage the process with a mission and measurements.

From here on we explore specific subjects touched on in the first three chapters in greater detail and go on to cover some areas that were not appropriate there. We would be pleased if you read this book like a novel, front to back, devouring every page. However, you will not do that! You will pick out subjects that you feel are of greater value to you first.

We start with time management. If there is one exhibiting problem that everybody experiences the pressure of, time is it. Unlike many other corporate initiatives that can be delayed if an emergency arises, that show will open with you or without you. You do not want to end up with a sign in your booth space that says, "Compliments of a Friend."

The Montage Medium

Movies are shot out of sequence. For instance, if both the first and last scenes are to be set in the same location, they will be filmed at the same time. That is done to save production dollars and time. Film people compare the process to making a montage.

Exhibiting, in a different context, is also a montage medium. There are checkpoints along the way. Some jobs that have to be started out of sequence so that it all comes together properly at the end. Here is an illustration from another industry. When McGraw-Hill built a building in New York, the first contract went to the company constructing elevator cars! Those sturdy boxes were placed, in position, on the site before the steel risers to surround them grew toward the sky. They were too big to slip into place afterward without spending a small fortune.

We point out that many think of exhibiting only in context with "a booth." Part 2, however, should have persuaded many that the booth is a stage. That's all. However, there are few if any full-time exhibit managers who have not picked up the phone on a Monday morning and heard, "We've decided to go into the Easyshow a couple of weeks from now in Wynantskill, New York, and would like to get a company booth sent with just a couple of changes."

Gulp! A small-scale marketing and cost disaster is about to happen. If you do not know why, read, please, Part 2 of this book. This chapter is about *time*, and that phone call creates more time expenditure than anyone imagines. The callers, God bless them, think it's easy to get hold of a booth and slather up a sign. They think that's all there is to it. Everything else stops while you try to cobble together at least something.

Expanding the Time Envelope

Exhibit managers often think they need more time or people or money to do the job. More frequently it's an expansion *of the time envelope.* That means the same number of hours of work, perhaps, but spread out over a longer period.

The Vexation of Coordination.   Manage just one project and you will know that coordination is a major chore. Figure 12-1 lists the people and functions that can play a role. Even for the Easyshow in Wynantskill there will be telephone-tag, E-mail flying around, memos and lists and reports. There is little else one can do unless the time envelope is made larger.

Exhibiting Work Lumps

The opening bell may sound in just two weeks. Or it could be four months away. Regardless, much of the same kind of work must be done. There are three lumps, as follows:

Fundamental Planning

- Audience analysis and goal setting
- Display product needs

Coordination Points: People or Function

- Sales managers
- Technical managers
- Booth team members
- Advertising/sales promotion
- Exhibit house
- Graphics producer
- Freight hauler
- Travel agent
- Hotel
- Show or association manager
- Decorating company
- Decorating company subcontractors
- Others, depending on the situation

Figure 12-1. This basic list illustrates the coordination complexity involved with any exhibit.

- Booth and graphics needs
- Booth staff needs
- Technical support needs
- Pre- and at-show promotional programs
- Budget development

Execution Planning

- Travel and hotel reservations
- Show registration for people
- Creative execution—booth and graphics
- Shipping arrangements
- Exhibit hall on-site service orders
- At-show training and clerical support
- Budget revision

Postshow Planning

- Lead and order processing and follow-up
- Exhibit teardown and shipping
- Staff recognition
- Results evaluation
- Budget resolution

These simplified lists look neat and clean, and comfortably sequential. If only that were true, life would be simple. However, this is where the montage emerges. The job process is like making a "three-bean salad." From a job start and completion date basis, the "work lumps" get mixed together.

Examples of Out-of-Sequence Work

- An "execution" chore will be writing the words for the company listing in the show program. That may be due very early, during the fundamental planning period.
- The postshow lead and order handling process will have to be worked out far in advance of the event, if you don't have one now.
- Ordering mailing lists for a planned preshow promotion may have to be done early, long before the mailing itself is prepared.
- Graphic signs are very expensive to have made if left too late.

The rule of thumb for exhibit coordinators: *Think about what others will have to do, and the time it will take them (while doing other things as well), when asking for work.* Help those who help you. What results will be better and less costly for everyone.

The 16-Week Time Line

It is presumptive for us to pick, out of a clear blue sky, 16 weeks as an ideal time envelope for planning and executing an exhibit. If you are going to prepare a brand-new big-league booth, it takes more. If a few graphics changes are all that are needed, perhaps a bit less. We present a far shorter time envelope idea in Part 1, but that was for very small exhibits.

We picked 16 weeks based on personal experience with midsized exhibits and our need to keep other jobs going in parallel. In our busiest year as a corporate manager, we were responsible for 18 shows in 23 weeks, none less than a 30 footer and many larger. The 16-week period is not cut in stone. *What is cut in stone?* Some jobs have to be started sooner than others so that everything comes together at the end. In addition, fundamental decisions have to be made well in advance to help drive the process.

Weeks 16 and 15

- *Planning meeting.* Gather interested parties, and determine special show missions.
- *Audience analysis.* Look at past results and show manager input on anticipated audience segments.
- *Mission and goals.* Combine and create mission and goals with the audience in mind.
- *Exhibitor kit.* Read and write preliminary work schedule. Assign responsibilities.
- *Overall plan.* Prepare the plan including booth, preshow promo, and staff.
- *Off-site.* Determine needs for off-site operations, events, or hospitality.
- *Seminars.* Plan and "sell" company participation in nonsales seminars.
- *Rough budget.* Estimate costs, and compare estimates to annual program budget.

Weeks 14 and 13

- *Plan review.* Obtain plan approval, with comments and revisions.
- *Staff recruiting.* Start obtaining booth staff commitments, both sales and technical.
- *Budget final.* Tighten and gain approval for the final show budget.

Weeks 12 and 11

- *Booth plan.* Provide direction on structure and graphics needs.
- *Promotion.* Plan preshow promotion, show giveaways, and press package. Obtain mailing lists and make ad reservations.
- *Show program.* Provide listing information to show management.
- *Advisory package.* Start gathering information for staff information package.
- *Arrival/departure.* Plan when people come and go to reduce travel and hotel costs.

- *Training program.* Determine exact needs: what, when, where, and how.
- *Staff recruiting.* Check recruiting progress, and confirm the list of staff members who have agreed to attend the show.

Weeks 10 to 6

Regardless of the time envelope you select, there is a period in the middle when others are working on their part of the plan. There is less for the exhibit manager to do. There are, however, some things that should involve the manager:

- *Staff recruiting.* Finalize the list with a no-drop-outs rule.
- *Training.* Finalize plans for staff training programs.
- *Hotel.* Make preliminary hotel reservations with current room list.
- *Off-site.* Finalize arrangements for off-site events or hospitality.
- *Booth plan.* Check progress on booth changes and graphics.
- *Independent labor.* Inform the show if you intend to use a nonofficial contractor.
- *Promotion.* Check progress on literature, direct mail, and show give-aways.
- *Press.* Preshow releases should be sent to trade outlets. Check on this.
- *Budget review.* Confirm estimates with outside sources.

Weeks 5 and 4

- *Display products/literature.* Confirm delivery date to you for show shipment.
- *Promotion.* Review direct mail and lists for production, plus give-away delivery.
- *Press.* Check on development of at-show releases or press conferences.
- *Staff reservations.* Confirm, inside with people and outside with hotels and airlines.
- *Show service orders.* Make sure these have been sent.
- *Visitor information.* Obtain city information for the staff advisory package.

Weeks 3 and 2

- *Booth plan.* Approve or revise structure or graphics.

- *Shipping.* Finalize shipping list and start this process.
- *Advisory package.* Finalize, reprint, and send to all booth staff participants.
- *Training.* Confirm all aspects of planned training for staff people.
- *Promotion.* Ensure that mailings are being processed.
- *Press.* Make sure that releases are written and shipped.
- *Speaker support.* Make certain that seminar speaker materials are coming.

Week 1

- *Show papers.* Assemble to take with you to the site.
- *Office supplies.* Assemble to take with you to the site.
- *Money.* Get cash or travelers checks "just in case."
- *Arrival.* Check to make sure you arrive the day before you have to. (Others will ask you questions. You need time in advance to find the answers.)
- *Computer.* If you travel with a computer, check the batteries, cables, and disks.
- *Personal.* Personal health products, foot powder and so on, should be packed.
- *People lists.* Bring all lists complete with hotel, office, and home phone numbers.

At and After the Show

The time line leads up to the event. When you, the booth, and the rest of the team arrive, there are other time-related functions to cover. Among them:

- *Order confirmation.* Check with the decorating company's service desk to get things started for setup, on a schedule based on who does what first.
- *Credentials pickup.* You can pick up your own badge and materials in advance. You can, as well, pick up the badges for your booth team and have those waiting for them.
- *Staff meetings.* In addition to preshow training, it helps a lot to conduct daily staff meetings at the end of the show day. People compare notes and do better the next day.

- *Takedown and outbound freight.* Make these plans in advance.
- *Advance space reservation.* Make a preliminary space reservation for next year now.
- *Thank-you notes.* Write them in advance!
- *Order and lead forms.* Bring them home with you personally and send them on immediately—first day after getting back to the office.

If you have a computer software program you can build with, such as a spreadsheet or time management program, the headings proposed in our 16-week time line can be used to identify subjects and checkpoints.

13

Exhibit Design, Structure, and Graphics

Most exhibit managers—this writer included—can't draw a straight line without a ruler, much less design a booth. Where can we get help?

The Exhibit Manager's Responsibilities

The reality that we are neither designers nor architects does not get us off the hook. Exhibit managers must present designers with objectives and goals from both strategic and tactical viewpoints. We must then be able to interpret what they present in that context.

Design Instruction

We've heard exhibit managers say, "I don't know what I like until I see it." It is natural to say that, but it also betrays that they have not been trained to present design instruction in the first place. We dwell on the work process that makes it easy in Chapters 2, 4, and 5. However, in short form, what follows will get you through.

Strategic Considerations. What is the overall mission of exhibiting for your company? Is it lead gathering, order signing, audience education, press education, or a combination? What is the priority?

To what extent do objectives change, show to show? How frequently do product lines displayed differ? For instance, are you offering a service at one event, a line of manufactured products at another? Looking ahead, do you plan to offer brand-new products and services?

We pose these questions because there are fundamental design differences that depend on the overall situation. A booth design that emphasizes service selling differs from that offering floor-standing products. Desktop products are another story. Small retail items are also different.

Tactical Considerations.   Design is also impacted by the tactical. At one point in our exhibit management career, we were participating in over 600 USA domestic events a year. That's a far cry from a company that exhibits at 5 or 10 shows a year. Booth design and fabrication are vastly different.

To what extent do booths have to "troop" show to show rather than come back home? Are all the space sizes the same, or do they differ? How much product switching is needed, event to event? You get the idea. Give this information in advance to the designer, and what he or she offers you will be far closer to the target. The more detail the better.

Give designers copies of company ads and literature, theme lines, and logos. If your company has a style manual on how the company name is presented, provide it. A booth cannot look like an ad, but it can and should reflect the company's marketing communications culture.

Do Not Provide Design Ideas.   "Our products are used in offices, so our booth should look like an office." "Since our products are sold in stores…" "Our customers like to play golf, so we like to position our services in that context." Do you sell golf course grass seed? Office furniture? Store fixtures?

Most of us want to help too much. Resist the temptation to provide too much direction *on the design solution.* You are likely to get back what you ask for. It might not serve you as well as something else.

Pay for Design

One of the most frequent corporate mistakes is what exhibit builders call "speculative design." A vendor is asked for a no-charge competitive design. One of several vendors will be selected, or perhaps none. Sometimes these requests for proposal are not supported with adequate backup information, which leads to lots of back-and-forth in the preparation process.

Sit in the other chair. "Is this serious, or are these people giving lip service to a bidding policy, and will they stick to their old supplier in the end?" "Is our contact actually responsible for decision making or is he mostly a paper-gatherer?" "Do we present our strategy to the chieftains?"

Think of it from your viewpoint. Do you need a comfort zone from what has been done in the past? That is not unrealistic. In outfits going through lots of internal change, there can be things that change slowly. From a business culture, psychographic[1] view, are changes truly welcome? Let your outsiders know, and you will be better served.

You do better if you offer a fee for development, win or lose. Do that, and vendors will rightly feel that you are engaging in serious evaluation, not going through a corporate exercise. Designers can sense that they are the polite bidders who don't win. Your current supplier, for many reasons, will hold the gold. Do you get the best work from the other bidders? Not really. Lightning won't strike. They may say otherwise, but put yourself in their position.

The fee you pay, an honorarium, does not have to cover all costs. It is appropriate to feel that thinking can be at least partly speculative. However, out-of-pocket costs for presentation should be paid. Those can include the costs for slides or overheads, a model, computer graphics, meetings, travel, and so on. Part of your specification can include that costs for its proposal will be absorbed by the winning bidder. We do not suggest that. Keep it clean.

Exhibit House Design or Independent Designer? Arguments rage back and forth in the industry about the best course to take. Here are viewpoints expressed, pro and con, on both sides:

- *Pro.* An independent designer will not be influenced by the technology currently available in an exhibit house. The design will be more imaginative.

- *Con.* An independent designer will not be as cost conscious from a fabrication viewpoint. The design will be less practical.

- *Con.* If a design will be bid out to several exhibit builders for fabrication, the independent must prepare very detailed blueprints and specifications. There is extra cost for that.

- *Pro.* An exhibit house employed designer works closely with the production department in the company to make sure that what is recommended can be built.

- *Pro.* An exhibit house employed designer stays more closely involved after design approval. That reduces the detail required initially, leading to cost savings.

- *Pro or con.* An exhibit house produced design is actually more costly because of cost markups imposed that cover "free" design.

We don't take sides. However, we do cite an experience. It was a major project. The winning design was from an exhibit builder.[2] That company was commissioned to build a prototype series of units and create a very specific set of specifications that would be used by other builders bidding on fabrication of additional units.

Fabrication bidders were advised that specifications had to be followed exactly. However, custom exhibit houses are used to working on a single unit. Production managers take small liberties to make subtle improvements without informing anyone. Normally, one would never notice. However, in this case we spent several months on revisions to achieve a seamless look when units from several builders were combined.

The error was ours. For a job this large, fabrication bids should have been requested from long-run manufacturers of store displays—a different industry. Their in-plant layout and production process assures more consistency.

Common Problems

As you define your mission and goals, please keep in mind some common problems:

- Some very large, sophisticated companies do not support local managers with appropriate exhibits and graphics at small shows. Corporate VIPs don't visit these events. Just customers.

- Large corporate division managers, and their staffs, fall prey to tunnel vision. They look at what their assignment is, giving a backseat at times to what show visitors are looking for.

- Sales-trained managers first think about current customers. Many don't fully understand prospecting opportunities at expositions and how to take full advantage of them.

- Retailers at local shows are proud of their stores. Many reduce visual standards at these events because they last only a few days. They will be noticed by many who have never seen their stores.

- Many forget that their booths are with competitors at the same expo. Serious shoppers go to events to comparison shop. That is good if you are good; bad if you are less than good.

Questions to Ask Yourself

- Which is most important: lead taking, order writing, or audience education? Tell your designer.

- How many shows a year? Do you supply a key product in only one or two industries, or does what you produce fit as a secondary item in many industries?

- Are your products "big ticket" and customized to a degree? Or are they smaller ticket and sold to dealers in quantity? Make sure your designer knows.

- Are you a well-known, dominant supplier, or less so? There can be design differences.

Designer Responses

The essential design concept will be aimed at reaching goals in priority order. You will like what you see in almost all cases. When you must select between two or among more, the process will not be easy. You will learn more as a result, and the final product will be better.

The Dangers

An exhibit company account executive told us a war story we pass on as a warning. The client exhibit coordinator had gone through many of the steps we suggest. Three exhibit builders were selected to compete. All the designs were good but differed in many respects. Each one could be defended on the basis of how the firm interpreted the input.

A horror show emerged in the approval process. A group of executives were gathered who had not been involved with the design development process. Their vote would determine the winner. In addition, these executives knew little about exhibiting.

In order to save time, the three companies were not allowed to present their work. Instead, a less-than-relaxed exhibit coordinator was required to present all three. Again because of meeting constraints, there was little opportunity to outline goals and objectives—a three-minute summary and then on to a beauty contest.

Each of the three exhibit companies had been required to produce a model, no small expense. These were placed on a table, and the executives were asked to take a look, ask any questions, and then vote. The entire process took less than an hour. Then off to lunch. The executives learned little about exhibiting. Two of the three exhibit firms took a financial bath. The development work was on speculation.

Avoiding the Dangers.   There are several things one can do to avoid traps and encourage more sophisticated responses from top managers not involved with the exhibit process on a continuing basis.

- Make an effort to solicit input on what these people see as goals and objectives in advance.
- Write and distribute a short paper in advance of the "big" presentation. It can be just a page or two. It should outline the goals and objectives provided to each of the vendors.
- Ask top management for permission to let each vendor make its own case, even if it must be limited to a half-hour or even less.

Some readers may not have direct top management contacts. In those cases the between-level boss should be encouraged to adopt the practice. The final choice will be more productive.

Design Concept Responses

We will be more specific later, but here are some basic notions to tuck away as you evaluate some design responses:

- If your primary goal is prospecting, the design is likely to be very open and inviting. There will be little on the aisle edge to restrict flow into the booth.
- If order writing from current customers is the goal, the design will be more restrictive, more attuned to your need for a greater degree of private time. Traffic will be forced from one or two spots at the edge of the space.
- If your company is large and attracts curiosity seekers, there are a number of steps that designers take to reduce the chaff while encouraging the serious:
  - The entire booth area can be raised on a platform, perhaps 1 or 2 inches above the show floor. A subtle signal is sent. (The raised floor also makes it easier to run cables.)
  - Display stations are faced out, with demonstrations on the inside. Same result.
  - Greeting areas are emphasized, similar to the large-booth tradition outside the USA. Visitors go to the greeting area first, sign in, and then are escorted through the booth.

Color, Materials, and Lighting.   Designers often use color, materials, lighting, and so on to help the client toward his or her ulterior goals. Here are illustrations:

- Muted colors tend to be more inviting, less abrasive. Essentially these are what are called *earth tones.* Soft greens, blues, oranges, tans, and so on are in this family.

- Stark colors such as fire engine red, crisp black, strong blue, or bright yellow are seen more easily but tend to make the booth a less friendly place. (Often these harsher colors are used as accents to draw attention to something specific. The booth overall is treated in more gentle fashion.)

- Materials play a role. A smooth marble appearance, or steel-look, conveys power. These materials also can be intimidating. If you need to discourage curiosity seekers, this is one method you can use. Warm-side wood, carpet, or any roughed-up surface is less intimidating.

- Floor covering sends a message. An extra-thick carpet, with a double-thick pad, signals both that the company warmly welcomes visitors on the show floor and that it takes extra care of its customers. It also can hint of opulence and extra cost. Player's choice, and you are the player.

  Note: Floor coverings can also be used as pathfinders for visitors. For instance, in a large booth space, the floor could be a tile with the "path" in carpet.

- Booth lighting is more important than most people realize, from both attraction and selling viewpoints. Instead of boothwide flat lighting, more is accomplished using retail-industry methods. In both situations ceiling lights are flat (in stores or arenas), providing an even amount of light overall. Individual displays should feature peak-and-valley lighting. The eye is led to more important areas without ignoring the rest.

Custom Exhibits Designed from Already-Manufactured Systems

The custom exhibit tradition has been based on wood framing. The industry started as a spinoff from furniture making. Amazing results have been achieved. Units are beautiful and long-lasting. Depending on initial thinking, they can be quite flexible, show to show. However, they are relatively heavy, and most required custom-designed crates that in themselves are husky.

Already-Manufactured Systems

A more recent development has been exhibits built on aluminum extrusions. These units emerged as "portable" or "pop-up" displays for small booths. The units are strong but far lighter than their wood-based siblings and are less bulky.

On-site assembly is less cumbersome as well. Wood-frame units are put together with bolts and wing nuts. Graphic panel faces are hung in much the same fashion. The metal extrusions are made with patented slots and connectors built in, to make setting up at shows easier to do.

The last advantage is that these standard units come complete with packing crates, often made in a plastic-based materials far lighter than wood crates. Small units can be checked with luggage at airports or sent to shows via airfreight or overnight mail.

The Two-Industry Union

The "systems" end of the business has been restricted to providing custom graphics using an essential exhibit design shape that was fixed. The custom end has been wedded to shop equipment and crafts people focused on using wood as the unseen exhibit frame with great flexibility. One side said, "We take care of the big-time exhibits." The other said, "We make little exhibits look very good."

Things have come together. Old-line custom builders have had the time (financial and otherwise) to start cutting and bending metal instead of wood. The newer-wave portable and pop-up outfits have had the time (financial and otherwise) to move into custom exhibit design using their systems. The two sides will continue to compete with each other, all to your advantage.

The Marriott Story

We elect to illustrate custom design using already-manufactured frames with a situation faced by a dealer in the "already-manufactured" camp. It is a company that started 10 years ago offering small off-the-shelf exhibits with custom graphics. The company is the Joan Carol Design & Exhibit Group,[3] with its head office near Washington, D.C. The client was Marriott, with its head office in the same area. The job was far more complex than a simple portable, but at this stage the exhibit company was ready.

The Design Issues.   Most think of Marriott in context with hotels. That is the case, but life is never simple. Marriott is more than hotels. It also provides institutional food services to others, such as airlines. It also offers consumer products, including high-quality coffee.

One the one hand, Marriott needed a design that would help to market institutional food services, as well as its hotels to travel agents and tour packagers. On the other, it needed an exhibit to offer consumer products as part of the Marriott group.

First Uses.   The first use of the exhibit was in Seattle at a meeting where Marriott was seeking food service concessions from airport managers. Just over 48 hours after the close of that expo, the "same" exhibit opened in Cleveland at its annual shareowner meeting, displaying a broad range of company services and products.

There were a few truly custom units involved for each show, and, of course, the graphic signs were very different. The space sizes were different, too. Figure 13-1 illustrates the configuration in Seattle. Figure 13-2 shows the layout in Cleveland. To help you see how the basic design worked in different situations, no graphics are included in these illustrations.

Cost.   You will ask about that. Studies put the average cost for custom exhibits at over $100 per square foot of booth space rented for design and construction, with an expected life of at least four shows. Marriott's booth came in at about $70. This solution is not for everyone, but it cannot be discounted, especially when one adds what could be higher freight, drayage, and setup costs for traditional, wood-based exhibit structures and their crates.

It is not easy to provide specific advice in a book. Authors fear that readers might react all too quickly. However, for the big-booth exhibitor with but a few shows per year, the old-fashioned approach may be more cost-effective. (And one can save on freight and drayage by avoiding crates. See Chapter 16.) If there is lots of diversity, shows are many or close together in time, custom-designed already-manufactured systems can make very good sense. They are available through both traditional custom builders and newer-wave outfits such as Joan Carol.

Design Concepts for
Different Product Types

There are design concepts used that reflect the product type, or service, offered. We present a sampler so that you will not be completely surprised by what your designer might suggest.

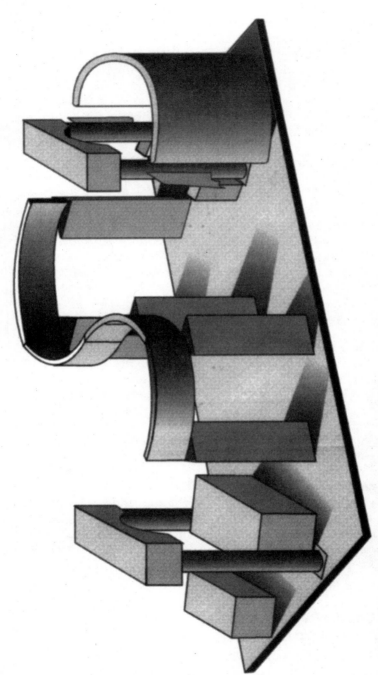

Figure 13-1. This drawing shows the Marriott booth as it was planned to aid in marketing food service concessions to airport managers. For the most part the booth was designed around already-manufactured systems. One was the "Exposure" line from Abex Display Systems. The other was a system from Nimlock. (*Sketch courtesy of the Joan Carol Exhibit & Design Group.*)

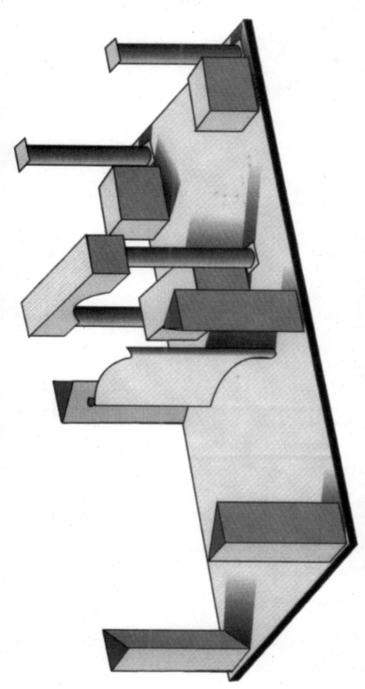

Figure 13-2. Two days after airport managers (in Seattle), the "same" booth opened in Cleveland at a Marriott shareowners meeting. Now it displayed a broad range of company services and products in a different space size. In addition to the two already-manufactured systems cited in Figure 13-1, the overall Marriott display strategy required some pure custom design and fabrication. Custom signs, both back- and front-lighted, were also prepared for the Marriott program. (*Sketch courtesy of the Joan Carol Exhibit & Design Group.*)

You will note that here, and throughout the book, we have asked display designers to prepare illustrations as one-color sketches. This is a management book. Color photographs of completed units could have been included. However, the displays are so beautiful that they mask the underlying design principles.

Floor-Standing Products

There are many types of floor-standing products displayed at trade shows. Machine tools, office machines, medical equipment, cars and trucks and tractors and boats—even aircraft are among them. Very large items, such as an airplane, military vehicle, or harvester are often displayed outdoors, not in a booth. We dwell on booth display.

Elsewhere in this book we mention a design created to allow a very large product to be demonstrated in a booth. It was a block-long color printing press. The working press was surrounded by 30-foot flower leaves that covered the gamut of colors the press would print. That kind of display does not emerge very often!

In the first edition of this book, floor-standing display design was illustrated (by Heritage Design in Dallas) with a concept that centered on a mirror angled over the top of a machine tool. Booth visitors could look at the side of the machine and by glancing up see a top view.

The Turntable Approach. Anyone who has visited a consumer auto show has seen cars placed on slowly revolving turntables. The product is on a pedestal, and the movement conveys motion. You see the whole car at eye level, and as it turns, you can visualize its appearance as it drives by.

Figure 13-3 illustrates the same idea used, in this case, to display an exercise machine. Jim Andersen, president of Displaycraft,[4] makes a point that cannot be illustrated properly. He says, "The turntable concept is not limited to circular motion. By placing springs or rollers under the table we can emulate up-and-down movement at the same time." He goes on to point out that for products of this type the turntable system is used to attract visitors. Other product samples are placed in the booth space for actual demonstration or "try me."

Desktop or Countertop Products

There are a large number of office and home products used on desks or counters. Display and demonstration for many of these products can be vexing, especially office products that are operated while sitting down—a computer terminal, for instance.

Figure 13-3. Turntables lift floor-standing products up to easy viewing range and provide a sense of motion. That motion is not necessarily limited to the horizontal. Adding springs or rollers to the turntable assembly can create a sense of up-and-down at the same time. In this case the turntable display is to attract visitors—another exercise product sample on the floor for actual demonstration. (*Sketch courtesy of Display-craft.*)

The High-Pedestal Display Concept. For the most part, booth visitors and staff people stand while examining or demonstrating products. Boston and Atlanta-based Access TCA,[5] an exhibit firm, illustrates the use of a desk product display placed on a pedestal a full 4 feet off the floor (see Figure 13-4).

The sketch was produced at the specific request of the author. Access TCA's director of computer-aided design, Richard M. Dugdale, pointed out that the illustration is an adaptation of an actual design. However, to his knowledge the company has never actually built to the 48-in height. Dugdale is probably correct. It seldom has been used, but we feel has great merit.

Though perhaps not 100 percent the case, we credit IBM for much of the initial research leading to high-pedestal display. IBM used this type of display when it introduced its first personal computers at trade shows. Some other high-technology companies have used the concept on occasion. Regardless, here is what we know.

The average height of a real desktop off the floor is about 30 inches. A kitchen counter at home is about 36 inches above the floor. There are variable heights for display counters, but rarely do we see one with a

Figure 13-4. A 48-in-high pedestal is suggested for desktop products. This sketch shows a pedestal in contrast to a lower top. Demonstrations are more user-friendly. Visitors deal with the product in much the same way as they would sitting down. The other advantage is that observers can see what is going on more easily. For that reason a high pedestal is also appropriate for home products used on counter tops. (*Sketch courtesy of Access TCA.*)

top more than 42 inches above the carpet. A 48-in height provides two distinct advantages:

1. *User-friendly.* It allows for a far more user-friendly demonstration. For most people it tends to replicate the feeling of working with desktop products from a seated position, the way they are designed to be used. They feel easier to use, and they *are* easier to use.

2. *Easy observation.* It is also more relaxed for observers to watch the demonstration. With products placed lower, onlookers must crane their necks to see around heads and shoulders.

There is a trade-off. A higher pedestal reduces the vertical space available to the top of a standard 8-foot-high booth for signs. That is true. However, after a show gets going, there are people in the booth. They can range in height from an average of a bit over 60 inches to 72 inches and more. That masks lower signs anyway.

Note: Where at all possible, we also suggest that a demonstration unit be placed on a roll-under counter at true desk height to help visitors in wheelchairs. Some may ask, "Why not put *all* demonstrations down low and let *everyone* sit down? Observers can see over shoulders." Lowered productivity is the answer. Ambulatory visitors get tired feet, and because of that alone they tend to stay seated far longer than those in wheelchairs. That prevents others from trying out the product.

A standard-height desktop product pedestal is illustrated in Chapter 20. In that case it was placed near the aisle, facing sideways. Visitors could still see the signs on the back wall.

Services Selling

Frequently exhibitors who sell services feel at a disadvantage. They look with envy at those with a product that moves, lights that flash, screens that change, printers that print, or items that can be handled. They should not. Exhibitors with those products often forget that the most essential part of exhibiting is discussion, a back-and-forth dialogue. When selling a service, discussion becomes mandatory. As a result, service sellers are many times the most effective exhibitors.

Signs As a Surrogate Seller.   Many without physical products substitute by putting up long-text signs, "Bullet Points Forever." We spotted and named one booth "The 30-foot Brochure." There were two fundamental errors. First, not one person in 500 will read all that. Second, the existence of heaps of text takes the breeze out of the sails of the booth staff. It signals a lack of trust.

Then there are service companies that spend extra dollars to tell their stories in some kind of animated fashion in hopes that it will attract an audience. That is okay if you have the money to spend and you are careful. However, nothing substitutes for conversation.

The Conversation Booth.   We do not illustrate the services-only design concept in this chapter. That is because custom builder Dottinger Design[6] prepared a classic illustration that appears in Chapter 3, Figure 3-1. That chapter is mainly for those starting out and who need a small booth. However, the Dottinger team went an extra step. They showed how the concept works in large areas as well. That includes how you can go above the standard 8-foot height limit for small booths on an aisle if you have a larger, "island" booth design.

One can add bells and whistles. The design allows for that. However, the concept meets criteria in exquisite fashion. There is plenty of room for person-to-person conversation. Signs, front or back lighted, are very large and simple. They invite conversation rather than tell.

The Multiaudience Booth

Many midsize and larger companies face situations in which more than one audience appears at a large show. Research at business trade shows, year after year, indicates that the most common visitor complaint is that they did not get to talk to an expert who could answer their questions. With proper guidance, exhibit builders can design booths to eliminate or reduce that problem.

The best way to explain the solution concept is with an illustration. An exhibitor asked Edward Jones, president of Executive Education and Management,[7] for help in sorting things out as a consultant. There are times when an outsider can see things more easily than someone sitting in the midst of the forest.

What Jones was able to isolate was that this company, which is midsize, has three different but related product streams. Within each of the three, there are two issues to resolve. One is related to application. The other is technical. Audiences at this company's shows are mixed between technical and general management.

As part of his consultant's role, Jones asked Al Niño Ticzon, a custom exhibit designer and builder,[8] for insight on how what had been learned could be applied. Figure 13-5 illustrates, in part, the concept that emerged and the booth that was fabricated and is now in use.

The Obvious and Obscure.   When you look at Figure 13-5 you will see three double-sided demonstration areas arranged in a circle. The booth space is a small island, a 20-by 20-foot space. Each product stream has its own two-sided display. One is for general management, the other for technical issues related to it. That is the obvious.

Because this book is printed in black and white, there is an obscurity. Its name is *color*. Ticzon said, "We had an advantage. The company had developed sales literature on the three products, each in its own color. Thus, we were able to color-code each of the displays so that what people saw related to product literature, a synergistic marketing approach."

Jones pointed out, "The color code also helped booth staff members." They were able to say, "That product is over here at our color-purple highlight display."

Of interest is that the sketch reflects the exhibit as it was first used in a 20- by 20-foot island space where one could build up to 16 feet. It has

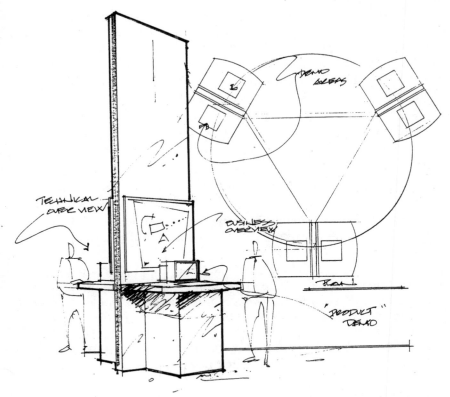

Figure 13-5. Technical and management answers are offered back to back at each display. In addition, product areas are color-coded. (*Design and sketch courtesy of Ideas, Atlanta, Georgia.*)

also been used, in pieces, for smaller appearances where the booth space is linear and only 8 feet high.

Committee-Think

Complications that get in the way of what should be a simple design were recited in Chapter 3. We repeat some of what is there and add a little here. The problem for big-company exhibit managers is committee-think. You need a clear eye and persuasion to end up with a good booth.

- *The video.* Somebody will come up with the idea of showing TV spots or the sales video at the booth. The TV spots are moving wallpaper; the video is too long and one-way-outbound. These devices are fine, but do not bet the company's ROI on return delivered at shows.

- *Interactive video.* Visitors trot through their own presentations on screen and provide some demographic information along the way. Less work and less return. Learn more.

- *Video wall.* Use it right, showing live booth action, and you may have something. If all you want is a moving billboard that flashes the logo, soda, or beer can, please send the money here.

- *Signs.* It seems that there is not a sales or product or tech manager around who trusts people. Sign copy should pose a question, illustrate a value. No answers without talking to a staff person.

- *Literature racks.* Everybody does it, and most everybody should not. If you want people to get literature, mail it. That is cheaper, and what you send is more often read.

- *Impress visitors.* Ultimately, big buyers prefer solid business purpose to flash. You can show both if you can afford it. If you cannot, go for the practical.

- *The "show" within the show.* Live acts, often supported with A/V and music, are great if well staged, though primarily for outbound-only communication. Unfortunately, many exhibitors think of them as something apart from the real business of the booth or as a substitute for doing real business. Exhibitors have to remember that they are not in "show business" for its own sake or just to create an image. It may be the wrong image these days.

Nontraditional Design and Fabrication

Readers of Part 4 know that large exhibits are often constructed for the first time right on site. They are used and then tossed away after the exposition.

The "Trooping" Show Tradition

The custom in the exhibition industry is that booths are designed and constructed so that they can be used at several events, even if signs are changed or different configurations required. For most exhibitors that makes a lot of sense. However, the construction methods needed are more costly than for a booth that is going to be used just once.

The Once-Only Option

Exhibit design, from the viewpoint of reaching objectives, is the same. However, that part of the design *that nobody sees* is radically different.

In fact, even the "skin" materials and painting differ. Costs for construction are far lower than for those that require movement and reuse.

The Designers and Producers. Some booth builders may not agree, but most traditional exhibit houses do not have much experience in once-only fabrication methods. There is more expertise in another design industry segment broadly represented in cities around the nation. These companies design and build sets for stage plays, television stations, and films—and sometimes once-only special events such as a product launch extravaganza.

What are the differences? There are many, but to provide you a feeling for what could happen, we offer a few examples:

- *Back wall.* A traditional back wall is faced with a surface that lasts a long time without repair. It is connected to a rugged frame. The design reflects the need for booth parts to be packed in crates. An identical "look" from a once-only set designer might be to stretch canvas on a simple, lightweight frame and then roller-paint a surface on the outside.

- *Flooring.* Many reuse exhibits include carpeting. In large booths carpet pathways in different colors are used to help direct traffic. A once-only set designer might substitute ordinary floor tiles from a local home center for more expensive pathway carpet and pad.

- *Roof and sidewall decor.* Dottinger Design,[9] a traditional custom builder, has used theatrical fabric, a loose-woven "scrim," to roof an exhibit. Chuck Price, from Charles Price Associates,[10] consistently uses fabrics intended for clothes or drapery making to accent highlights to bring attention to specific display elements. (Leading-edge versus old-fashioned fabric textures and designs and so on, depending on the product and message.)

Has the approach been employed in domestic exhibiting? Yes. Our own small company once employed a stretched-fabric back wall that we never used again. Chuck Price designed a booth for Colgate-Palmolive with little more than spray-painted Styrofoam blocks (spray paint in push-top cans from the hardware store). West Coast set designer George Parrish[11] has created this type of display design and fabrication approach for corporate entities, including the Amdahl Corporation.

Do-It-Yourself?

Inexperienced exhibit managers, reading this, may be thinking, "I can do all this by myself." If you are handy and want to invest sweat equity, we suppose that is true. But the answer is no.

Design Skill.   At the start of this chapter we pointed out that most exhibit managers are not professional designers. We may be able to design a room, office, or even a home to suit our own taste. That may not be appropriate for others, especially as we combine raw design with buyer expectation.

Materials Use.   Most of us are not aware of all the materials available and how they can be employed. Furthermore, we are not aware of safety rules, especially those related to fire retardation.

Marketing Focus.   Our jobs should be focused on how to use the booths, rather than on how to design, build, and install them. It may be fun to try building a booth. But we would do better by using the stage to make money.

14

Promotion Before and At the Show

The "winds of change" have been blowing hard. That is true everywhere, including the world of exhibiting. Forgive our cliché. However, the days are long gone when those attending an expo could afford the time or money for a relaxed voyage to nowhere.

Everyone arrives with an agenda. From an attendee viewpoint, there is learning, exhibit shopping, seeing old friends and associates—even exploring for that next job. Most have the specifics written down according to priority.

Once buyers arrive, time is squeezed. Two-end candle burning is the name of the game. Breakfast meetings, morning seminars, booth visits in the afternoon, postday receptions, and then dinner—plus late evening confabs. All of this is combined with cab or bus trips around town.

The Show Management Relationship

Associations and their show managers promote attendance. Using direct mail and advertising, they talk about the educational seminars and exhibits, the social events, and more. Some exhibitors feel that is enough. They are wrong. The show goal is to attract a total audience. It is up to the exhibitor to go after its own within the overall group.

Many shows offer assistance to exhibitors in their programs. For instance, reproduction-quality show emblems or logos may be supplied for your printing. At many events show tickets are provided to exhibitors to send on to their prospects and customers. Often, direct-mail lists are made available at low cost.

Show Size Differences.   The degree to which you get involved with preshow promotion often depends on the size of the event. If you are participating at the summer meeting of the Maryland Bar Association, there will only be two or three dozen exhibits and a few hundred attendees. The event will be low key, and there should be plenty of time for all visitors to take a look at all the booths. You should still do something—perhaps a quiet letter to all. The bigger the event, the greater the need. For instance, at a 300-booth show with 8000 attending, there won't be enough time for everyone to see every-thing! The goal of preshow promotion is to make sure that the right exhibitors connect with the right visitors.

Promotion Timing.   Except for ads that might run well in advance, your preshow promotion should hit just a couple of weeks in advance of the event. If mail goes bulk rate, you will have to send it well in advance, or course, but that decision can be made on the basis of how many pieces are to be mailed.

Preshow Promotion Problems

Preshow promotion has emerged as a fact-of-life need for most exhibitors. They fully understand the time competition that surfaces at shows and want to be on the must-see lists of as many attendees as possible.

Mistakes That Are Made with Direct Mail

The fact that companies, more and more, invest in preshow promotion is good. However, most of them don't do it very well.

Going after Everybody.   Here is a "war story." We were presenting an exhibitor education seminar at a large trade event. As a result, our name was in the show's database of those who would attend—the pre-registration list. During the month before the event we received over 400 "see-us" booth invitations of one sort or another! Our mailbox was overwhelmed. There were enough so that we put them into a small, plastic trash bag.

Clearly, exhibitors were not doing their homework. We talked to show management. The direct-mail list was being offered to exhibitors on a segmented basis. We were in "other," which is where we should have been placed since we were not a potential customer for anybody!

Nonbusiness Content.   The same war story illustrates a second problem. Because we were speaking to exhibitors, we decided to spend extra time to actually read all these invitations. With the exception of 20 or 30, every one of them was fun-only. "Bring this card to our booth and win a free TV set." The show took place in San Francisco, in October. Thus, there was the obligatory football-shaped invitation from an exhibitor to watch *Monday Night Football.* Who would want to spend that rare October evening in San Francisco plopped in a vendor suite watching the Rams and Steelers?

Saying Too Much.   Of the 30 invitations that were not fun-only, some went too far in the other direction. Several exhibitors sent very detailed descriptions of products that would be displayed. That's better, but so much information was provided that at least some delegates would be convinced that there was little else to learn from a booth visit. These fulsome mailings can actually reduce traffic. Less traffic can actually be better for you, but only if you want to reduce visiting to those who know they want to buy.

Mistakes That Are Made in Trade Advertising

Our war story illustrates mistakes in the use of direct mail. Large and midsize companies also run schedules of ads in trade periodicals. Many get lazy when it comes to promoting their booth. Typically, they pick an ad out of the current bank and slather a banner across the bottom, "See Us in Booth 232 at the Show." There are two problems: First, no reason for a booth visit is presented. Second, most trade ads are so heavily detailed that they can convince readers that the ad text is all they would learn anyway .

Preshow Promotion Solutions

There are a number of things we can do to make preshow promotion more effective and to reduce its cost simultaneously. That does not happen often, but this is one case where it works.

Define the Targets

In Parts 1 and 2, we devote attention to mission statements and goal setting. At any trade or even consumer event, you do not want to waste time trying to talk to everyone, if for no other reason than that you will not have enough space or personnel to meet everyone in the time provided.

To illustrate, let us say that you have a 20-foot booth that will be staffed by 5 people. The show will be open for a total of 12 hours over three days. Assume that each team member will talk to 10 people per hour—short contacts and long, sometimes in groups of 2 or 3. The outside limit is 600 contacts—probably fewer buyers from a company viewpoint, or family perspective at a consumer event.

The show estimates 3000 attendees who are buying delegates or consumers, but only about 16 percent of them are true targets for you—just under 500. The team and booth size are about right, but the preshow promotion must be aimed at the target, not at everyone. Good promotion can overwhelm you with traffic. If aimed at all, true potential buyers will get less attention at the booth.

The Four Targets.   There are really four target groups among those who will attend an exposition:

1. *Current customers.* These people are most important. They know you, and you know them. There may be some new things to discuss, and there may be new people to meet who have joined the customer's organization.

2. *The prospect target group.* That is that broader target within the overall show audience we outlined above. From a direct-mail viewpoint, even the most targeted list should be perused. For instance, a show organization may sell name labels by title—let's say purchasing manager. You may find that other exhibitors are part of that list or that purchasing managers are included on the other side of the country where you can't serve. You should edit the lists.

3. *The VIP prospect list.* For the most part you will know the names and addresses of key players you have not been able to reach on a personal basis. However, they offer the most potential for growth. This is a special target within a target.

4. *Last year's leads.* Your own company's customer and prospect database will be part of your mailing program, of course. Pay special attention to those who gave you leads at last year's event, even those that were not productive. Between 30 and 40 percent audience change is about standard, but some will be coming back. Those marginally interested before may be hot now.

Specific Programs for Each Target

Don't throw up your hands! It is easier to do than it reads. They all start from the same base point, providing a good business reason to visit the booth. You can add excitement and fun, but the central purpose must be related to serious business.

Don't Spill All the Beans.   All of your communications should stress that the booth is the place to learn. The information you provide should be applications and issue oriented, rather than feature specific. In all of your letters, ads or printed materials, *position your booth as an answer center!*

Current Customers.   There are a number of imaginative approaches, starting with a simple letter of invitation that includes a simple listing of subjects or issues of common interest. Booth meeting appointments are requested with a response card. Some companies do more. For instance:

- Diebold, the ATM and safe maker, has a program. It has involved salespeople calling key customers to see if they will attend an upcoming trade show. If a customer says yes, there is a follow-up question, "What in particular is of interest to you at this year's show?" The answers signal customer concerns at the time, which is valuable input from several viewpoints.

- Jansport, the outdoor clothing and gear company, introduced a new line at a ski dealer show in Las Vegas. Invitations to a private party were sent to selected dealers and distributors. After explaining the product introduction, the mailing pointed out that tickets for the party had to be picked up at its booth in advance. There is more about this, and the outcome, in Chapter 15.

The Prospect Target Group.   It can and should be a simple, low-cost approach. It is based on a letter citing issues of concern and how a booth visit can provide answers to help solve problems. This letter does not have to go to all those planning to attend. If you can only see 600 people at a show (see above), restrict the mailing to under 2000, even if your target market is more. Often you will find that your target is far larger. You then face a decision. We suggest mailing to only three times the number of people you can talk to in the time allocated at the event. Others, walking the show floor, will find you. You will have a busy booth!

With that decision made, and lists winnowed, what do you send? Be practical first, and then have some fun. Here are illustrations:

- Tote-Cart, Inc., a shopping cart manufacturer, invited buyers to its booth at a huge exhibition for food distributors and chain stores. Thousands attend, but Tote-Cart's letter was sent to just a few hundred, identified as buyers for capital equipment. Because of industry concerns about damage and destruction of equipment, the letter's focus was on seeing what Tote-Cart claimed was "the world's strongest shopping cart." There was an incentive. Those that brought the letter to the booth could participate in a contest, the winner of which would take home new luggage.

  Note: The contest? A shopping cart was loaded with zinc balls. It sat on a scale, and one could see the weight was 1000 pounds. Contestants guessed the number of balls. The product advantage, strength, was demonstrated in the contest.

- Our own company sent an envelope with "Live Fish Inside" rubber-stamped on the outside to 500 planning to attend an International Exhibitors Association convention. Enclosed was a plastic fish that curls up in your hand, along with a booth invitation. Those who arrived at the booth with the invitation card were offered a prize, a "hook" to help them land their next big customer. The letter cited issues of concern to people like you. The prize, in addition to information, was a fish hook, buried (for safety reasons) in a cork. Fun can be part of what you do. Margit Weisgal, who planned the promotion, is a national award winner for preshow marketing promotions.[1]

The VIP Prospect List.   Your salespeople may identify special people they have not been able to reach. Often that is because lower-level people in the same outfits are self-protective. However, it is polite to try and meet the VIPs if they attend a show. A letter to those people, signed by your company president or someone else of equal status, can do the trick without putting your salesperson into an uncomfortable position.

You can be creative at the same time. Some years ago a London firm sent VIP prospects a box. In the box was a letter and response sheet, *plus a live, trained carrier pigeon.* Obviously, those boxes were hand-delivered with loving care. Recipients were asked to prepare a response, place it in a capsule provided for the bird's leg, and release the flyer! The response was 100 percent, and the promotion was the talk of the industry.

There are other approaches, less work intensive. One of Weisgal's clients had identified 100 super VIP prospects they had never been able to meet. Virtually all were registered to go to an upcoming trade show. Each was sent a very nice leather portfolio. Inside was a letter of invitation to the booth, citing business reasons for visiting. At the bottom of the letter was a postscript: "You will note the small indented area on the outside of your portfolio. We have engraved your initials on a brass plate that we will affix during your visit." Over 90 of the executives showed up! The others were called later, and all accepted an appointment during which the plate was added.

AT&T was exhibiting at a convention for automobile dealers. It identified VIP dealers, typically those who own and operate several dealerships. The show mission was to introduce products and services designed to help auto dealers reduce overall costs. The company's retired employee organization was selling premiums to raise money for charitable causes. One of them was an early-century model of a telephone truck that doubled as a piggybank. The VIP auto dealers were sent one with a letter inviting them to the booth to learn how to save money.

The Advertising Solution. A special ad should be created aimed only at inviting show visitors to your booth. It can be done simply, in one color. It should outline learning reasons to visit. "You will learn about our solution to the XYZ problem." "You will see how our ABC can fit into your migration strategy." If you participate at several shows a year, a standard format can be created, with appropriate copy changes for each show.

A simple approach is appropriate for another reason. Often these ads appear in the "show issue" of the magazine. These tend to be extra thick and many times are delivered at the show site as well as via mail. The ad clutter can be massive. The chances of being seen are less. It is unlikely that the show issue copies delivered at the show itself will be read until well afterward. There is too much else to do.

We suggest running your come-to-our-booth ad in the month or months prior to the event, not just in the show issue.

At-Show Promotion

The message stays the same. Position your booth as the answer center. There are, however, different kinds of media opportunities.

The Show Program

The event's official program is the only must-read document visitors get. Your most valuable "ad" is in this book—and it is free. Your program listing is vitally important. All too frequently companies are satisfied with a simple listing of their products. Work a little harder. Relate the listing to learning messages sent out in the preshow promotion.

Media Opportunities

There are many different ways in which your message to see us at the show for the following reasons can be delivered.

In-Hall Media.   There are several ways in which you can get out the word. Among them are:

- *Show dailies.* Many events publish daily newspapers distributed in the convention hall and in key convention hotels. Readership? We don't know, but assume it differs by show.

- *Literature kiosks.* Positioned in the registration lobby, these are large displays containing literature from exhibiting companies. Exercise caution. A brochure that is too heavily detailed may convince readers that they have already learned what they want to learn.

- *Video locators.* There are times when ads can be placed in these programs. Scattered about the hall, the primary motive for these interactive displays is to aid visitors in finding what they want.

- *"Treasure hunt" promotions.* There are several forms, but the objective is to encourage booth visits to participating exhibitors. Visitors are given a card or some other device and can win prizes if they bring back evidence of booth visits—a stamp, punch, or something. We are not overly fond of that approach since all visitors are not necessarily your potential customers.

- *Flyers.* Produced privately by exhibitors, they are distributed outside the hall as people flow in.

In-Hotel and In-City Media

- *Cable TV.* Some shows sponsor TV programs that appear in hotel rooms. It is a video form of the show daily. In some cities and hotels, when a room TV is turned on, it starts with this channel.

- *Network TV.* Some large companies purchase TV commercial time in the local breaks to support their booths. Most often these run during morning shows. There is a good amount of wasted reach because the general public sees these spots as well, and stations are paid for total audience.

- *Taxi cards and outdoor media.* Again, these media outlets are for the corporate elephants. With that in mind, even these companies must understand the city. For instance, Las Vegas is a good place for taxi cards and billboards. At big shows visitors are staying all over town. Taxi cards do well in that situation. In addition, the routes to the Las Vegas Convention Center are well defined, and outdoor billboards are acceptable along them. In contrast, these media outlets are less cost-effective if the event is taking place at Chicago's McCormick Place. For instance, outdoor advertising is not permitted on the main route between the hotels and hall.

- *Transportation displays.* If the show city is served by a small or midsize airport and most visitors pass through one or two areas, you can consider placing a booth ad in one or two of the airport displays. If the route into town, or from hotels to the hall, is appropriate, you can fly corporate flags from lampposts. Colgate-Palmolive did both of these things for an international dental convention held in Singapore.

- *In-room delivery.* There are some shows at which virtually everyone is staying at a key convention hotel. Arrangements can be made to deliver your promotion, leaving it outside the doors in the middle of the night. One exhibit manager, at a banking show, arranged to have copies of *The Wall Street Journal* delivered to each room with a note attached inviting a booth visit. The exhibit manager knew that these delegates are readers of that paper.

A warning: At some events in-room delivery can be so extensive that it is overwhelming. We were at one show where so much arrived that we called housekeeping. The manager helped us weigh it all—over 9 pounds in two days, with one more day to go. The manager also said that extra staff was to be called in on the final day to help remove these mounds from vacated rooms.

At-Booth Promotions

There are a number of ways to promote at the booth itself. What you do and how you do it depends on your objectives.

Literature at the Booth

Booths are places for sharing conversations. They are not cost-effective simply as places for distributing company brochures or catalogs. It is far less expensive simply to mail everyone a copy! Different studies produce different results, but it is safe to say that between 60 and 80 percent of it is never read by anybody! Much of it doesn't get any farther than the hotel room, joining the mound of in-room delivery materials left behind. Most of the rest resides, for several months, on an office credenza top—then during cleanup, they are tossed. Here are some thoughts, based on our experience, on trade show literature.

It is far better to take the name of a person who wants literature and send it later. There are three reasons: One, it is more likely to be read when it arrives. Two, it traps a name for your database. Three, the mailing is a second contact between your company and the prospect. It can be the start of building a relationship.

Low-Cost Literature.   If you cannot avoid passing something out, prepare a low-cost brochure offering more if the taker makes a second contact. Restrict the piece to one or two colors, instead of passing out the fancy four-color materials that cost a lot per copy to print.

Restrict Quantities.   A rule of thumb is to bring only enough copies of your brochure, even that low-cost item, to cover 5 percent of the promised audience. If the show projects 8000 delegates, bring no more than 400 copies of your key brochure. It is great to run out! That signals popularity. You can mail it to those who ask after the cupboard is bare.

Literature Racks.   Try to avoid them. If you must have literature racks, place them back in the middle of the booth, rather than on the aisle. There are some visitors who simply like to pick up brochures, even if they may never read them. Make it too easy and you will get rid of a lot of brochures, but for what purpose?

Giveaways

Badly used, these items are little more than trash and trinkets, soon forgotten. They comfortably reside in right-hand desk drawers or pencil trays. We delve into the best uses of premiums or giveaways shortly, but for now, remember that the world is filled with little-used and soon-forgotten rulers, cheap pens, or fuzzy things pasted to badges. Give mementos away if you want, but don't expect much in practical return in an uncontrolled giveaway distribution program.

Product Samples.   Many companies use their own products as giveaways. Magazine publishers offer copies of their periodicals. Colgate-Palmolive's Oral Products organization gives away sample tubes of toothpaste. Food and beverage manufacturers provide samples of their products, from Budweiser beer to Ben & Jerry's ice cream.

Some of the best corn on the cob we've ever tasted was in the corn company's booth at a Produce Marketing Association convention.

Many companies hand out samples on a catch-as-catch-can basis, never bothering to use the occasion to get into serious business discussion. In fact, some companies measure booth performance on the number of samples that are handed out. The forest becomes more important than the trees.

To illustrate, we asked delegates at food shows about their concerns. Product quality and taste was one, so sampling is fine. However, bigger issues emerged such as inventory management, delivery schedules, package size options, and finance. Companies that fail to sort out the serious from the curious (or hungry) fail to learn from those attending and fail in opening up new business opportunities.

Some of these companies argue that the show goal is industry relations. Fine. But in a downsized business world, many of them have eliminated direct contacts with smaller distributors and outlets. The show is one place where they can keep that going at low cost.

Shopping Bags. Those who instinctively grab anything like to have shopping bags to haul home conquests. Invariably, one or two exhibitors provide the bags. The purpose is to help build booth traffic because others on the show floor see the bag. That can be a good idea, but there are a couple of provisos:

- The bag graphic has to be big and direct. "See What XYZ Is Offering at Booth 232." Too often the company logo is big, but nothing else, and the opportunity is lost.
- Bags often are hung from racks at the aisle edge. People can take them without meeting staff people. Since the goal is to build booth traffic, why not consider placing these bags back inside so that at least some conversation takes place? A bird in the hand...

Booth Shows

Several different types of booth events are staged. In some cases they are designed almost wholly to attract an audience. Others are staged with a greater emphasis on education.

Traffic-Building Booth Shows

There are all sorts of approaches in use. Among the most popular are magicians. The illusionist works from a counter near the aisle. To draw the crowd in close, most tricks are of the smaller sleight-of-hand type, using cards, coins, shells, or other small items. The magician combines tricks with patter that emphasizes product features or applications. There is always dialogue with people in the audience, but most often it has to do with the trick—not the product. There is outbound teaching, but little inbound learning from prospects and customers.

There are others. Fortune tellers, golf teachers, and even games are part of the picture, along with artists who do quick sketches of visitors. We have observed picture taking, that is, visitors having their picture taken with a celebrity or a celebrity look-alike. There are also autograph lines featuring well-known athletes or musicians. We have seen basketball shooting and even baseball pitching contests. There are several problems with these types of promotions:

- Based on observation, magic and games appeal more to men than women (with perhaps the exceptions of golf and tennis). More and more show delegates are women.
- The "show" is treated as something apart from the rest of the booth by staff people.
- There are times when a game or show can supplant business purpose as the primary goal. Company people start thinking the game is the end game! That is like the food merchant thinking product sampling is the whole reason for being at a show.

"Working the Show."   Instead of treating these traffic-building booth events as something apart from all else, a far better idea is to use them to meet at least a few customers or prospects. Here are three suggestions:

1. Ask one or two booth staff people to be "the audience" at the start of the show. Others, seeing watchers, are encouraged to stop and join in. As the crowd builds, the booth staff people drift back through the audience gathered, reading badges as they go. They select people to introduce themselves to at the end.

2. At the end of the show, the entertainer introduces the booth staff members at the back and suggests that if visitors have questions, these people are available to answer them.

3. Almost always one or two visitors will want to chat with entertainers after the show. Work out a procedure in advance allowing the entertainer to introduce a staff member as a takeover.

Educational Shows

These shows place more emphasis on presenting product knowledge, in a number of formats. From a staging viewpoint, there are two choices, based on objectives and content: combo aisle edge shows and booth center presentations.

Combo Aisle Edge Shows. These are designed both to attract an audience and deliver an in-depth message. Sticking with our food manufacturing illustrations, the best we've seen was produced by Checkrobot, a Florida-based company offering highly automated checkout systems for retail stores. The booth show worked at three levels, simultaneously:

1. *Show floor invitation.* A video wall was above the booth. It could be seen at long range. This video wall did not present canned graphics. It was obviously showing, silently, something "live."

2. *The Presentation.* As one walked to the booth, it was obvious that the live video was showing a system being demonstrated. The narrator, who one could hear close up, was illustrating system advantages from several viewpoints.

   Note: Products are placed on a moving belt. Items are automatically fed through a scanner and then right into waiting takehome bags. A video display shows each item and its price. At the end a slip is printed with the total owed. The customer pays a cashier.

3. *The payoff.* At show end the presenter asked those interested to stay and try the system for themselves. Those few were greeted by salespeople who explained more about how the system worked, which allowed them to obtain facts on potential buyer utilization.

Booth Center Presentations. Longer educational presentations are placed in the center areas of larger booths. Often there is a closed room. It is far easier to cover more in that kind of environment, with show floor hubbub eliminated.

Audiovisual Presentations. These should be restricted to booth center presentations. Plopping a video player out on the aisle edge is not all that effective. The shows are too long, the light is too bright, and there is far too much noise. These presentations become moving wallpaper. Fine, but that's about it.

Interactive video has emerged at booths. Delegates deal with the machine to get their answers. In most cases we are reluctant to suggest it. There is less learning opportunity for the exhibitor. Often visitors are asked for demographic information that is stored for future use, but the essential is *why* the interest. That takes talk, and exhibiting is a live medium, if done well.

Booth Prizes

Most trade show travelers have seen how these things work most of the time. Here are a couple of illustrations. First is what we call the "treasure chest," often done in a pirate motif. If the key you are given, or sent in advance, opens the chest, you win something. Another approach one sees frequently is a "Wheel of Fortune," similar to the TV show or casino game. Spin the wheel, and what you win depends on where it stops.

As traffic-building attractions, these entertainments are effective. If properly used by the booth staff, they provide an opportunity for business dialogue with visitors that can help in sorting out potential customers. (See Chapter 18 on the relative importance of dialogue to simple outbound message delivery.)

There is, however, a problem. Games can become more important than business. The objective is to attract your potential buyers, not everyone. You waste time, and so do visitors, if fun fully replaces true value. Margit Weisgal suggests a tougher approach to prize giving. She says, "Don't clutter your booth with those who just want to take a free flyer on winning a portable TV or whatever." The solution is to make your prizes business related. There are many ways that can work:

- Winners get 15 percent off on their first order.
- Winners don't pay shipping charges on orders for six months.
- Winners get up to three no-cost product display units for their stores.
- Winners get free service for themselves (or their customers) for six months after ordering.

The list can go on and on. You get the idea. Attract and reward those who do business with you. The booth may not be as busy, but it will be more productive. Weisgal offers one more hint on how this kind of promotion can make more money: "Do not put these attractions out on the aisle. Place them back in the booth." That dovetails with the prize structure suggested. Cut out some chaff to find the grains of wheat.

The ultimate goal for advance or at-show promotion should be to encourage one-on-one discussion. That is not to say that image building and education are not important. However, there are cheaper ways to reach those goals, if they are all you want to do, than sponsoring a booth.

15

Special Events, and Off-Site and Hospitality Management

Expo booths are not everything. There are off-site events tied to exhibit participation and even private trade shows to consider. How you handle these opportunities can save you money or help you achieve your objective.

Hospitality Management

The problem for professional event managers is that everybody, every client, is an expert. Anybody who has produced a big-league wedding or birthday party knows more. Many of these folks are part of a group called "unconscious incompetents." Partly because they are bright, they do not know they do not know. That is fine for a wedding or birthday. Return on investment is measured on how "the producer" senses the success of the event, plus the comments of friendly neighbors or family members. Supplier errors notwithstanding, these events are always great!

Professional Situations

If you have paid for that wedding, birthday party, or corporate hospitality event, you know what it costs. Now, in a professional sense, think about what it is costing your guests. If 20 professional guests earning $60,000 a year attend your event, the total cost is $1200 *an hour* for their *time*.[1]

Professional event planners these days project several hundred dollars per guest as their out-of-pocket cost for high-level private events—golf outings and such. Add to that the time and expense of those who elect to attend. Those at that kind of event may earn far more than our conservative $60,000 per year. There is a fun façade, but lots more is happening.

Event planners live in a world of no tolerance for mistakes. Do not spell a visitor's name wrong on an invitation or table card. Airport pickup must be seamless. VIP needs must be understood and accommodated. (A former President of the United States liked popcorn in his hotel room to nibble on before he went to the ballroom to "eat" and deliver a keynote speech. The "advance person," a political title for an event planner, had to make sure popcorn arrived fresh, hot, and on time. The Secret Service had to make sure nobody buried a bomb in the bowl! No mistakes are allowed.)

Exhibit Manager Involvements

More and more, large corporate downsizing has created combination jobs. Exhibit and event functions, once performed by two different people, now are two hats worn by the same person. Event planning involves many different kinds of tasks. There is a large body of literature on that subject. Professionals in the field go through educational programs to earn professional certification: Certified Meeting Planner (CMP) from Meeting Planners International, a professional association.

This book is mainly about exhibiting. However, because at certain levels exhibit managers get involved in events, we touch on the subject in this chapter. For the most part exhibit managers get involved in the following ways:

- Providing VIP food and beverage services, transportation, and tickets
- Creating off-site hospitality and seminars at shows
- Furnishing the site and support for news conferences and similar events

Hospitality Goals and Measurements

Earlier in the book we broke expo audiences into groups. Three were current customers, VIP prospects, and press. Off-site hospitality programs often are used to reach goals with these groups. We add a fourth: your employees, especially top-level managers.

Most exhibit managers do not know how to set specific goals and establish measurements to evaluate these programs. They live on the end of a diving board called "subjectivity." If the boss's boss likes what takes place, fine. If not—they get pushed off the end. One mistake is remembered more than 1000 seamless events.

Setting Goals and Budgets. Objectives must be agreed on in advance. Just as with exhibiting, they break into two parts. First, what is the mission of the event? What do you expect to accomplish, in real terms, as a result of producing the event? Second are numbers. How many people are to be involved? In context with the goals, how much money are you willing to budget?

There are no magic numbers. The cost for entertaining a large number of people can be as little as $25 each. If you are producing a fancy show, it can go up to $100 each or even more. VIP programs can be as high as several hundred dollars per person.

Measurements. Just as with exhibiting, there are cost-per indexes. In addition, there are results-oriented measurements similar to those used in exhibiting.

- *Cost-base measurements.* For the most part measurements compare the number of participants to the total cost. The exact process for doing that is detailed in Chapter 10. An index is created with ease. Similar to an exhibit measurement, the index means little for an individual event. It becomes useful only after a few similar events have been produced. Then comes one where the index result is out of the norm. You will ask yourself why. An exploration will provide some reasons, and you will be led to changes in future planning.

- *Results-based measurements.* If the goal for a hospitality suite is to sign orders, how many were signed? What was the dollar value? The dollar value can be compared to cost to create an expense-to-revenue ratio index. (That process is outlined in Chapter 10, too.) Are there any other ways that you can assign a dollar value? Again, the index becomes meaningful only after you have a few similar events under your belt. Look for the anomaly, and wonder why.

Check out the reason for the difference, and revise future plans accordingly.

These measurements never will completely replace the subjective. "The food was great." "Everybody loved it." "You blew it when the vice president saw her name badge." "The PR spin was great." "The service was crumby. We'll never go back there again." "Great! Everybody likes music from the fifties." "The sound system was terrible." You've heard it all. What these measurements do is provide a way to measure on a consistent basis, as well as the subjective.

The Hospitality Suite

Hospitality suites should be special, memorable. Those that don't break the mold are little more than expensive company club rooms. We hasten to say, however, that there are times when a company club room has merit. That is especially so when employees from different offices who do not know each other are gathered for a show. The goal can be providing an environment for them to get to know each other. For the most part, however, you should try to do more. Translate it into a venue for a special off-site event, and it takes on a life of its own, added to the booth.

Operations and Costs.   We combine what you do with how much it costs in the following series of hints. Figure 15-1 lists items that can be part of a hospitality suite or small event budget.

- *Rent.* Usually you will rent a suite or function room in a hotel. Often, the hotel rent is low, depending on the food and beverage service to be provided. Convention facilities add to the hotel's profits by selling their food and beverages to guests. Your choices often boil down to providing a multiple-use location. For instance:
  - Booth staff training room before show opening
  - Off-site office center during the convention
  - News conference or private customer presentation room
  - Secondary display center
  - Private meeting or "closing" room
  - Company club room

- *Food and beverage service.* It is rare that you will be allowed to bring your own food and drink into either a hotel or convention center room. Rent prices depend on the hotel's providing food and beverages. At convention centers, many operated under government sponsorship, catering outfits bid for the business in the facility. *High bidder wins.* They pay fees or a percentage. It will cost a lot.

	Estimate	Actual
1. Room charge		
Room		
Tax =	$_____	$_____
2. Food per person $_____		
Times number of people ×_____		
Base cost		
Times 15-percent gratuity × .15		
Total before tax		
Plus tax on base cost +_____ =	_____	_____
3. Liquor, wine, beer, soft drinks		
Bottle cost _____		
Mixers _____		
Condiments _____		
Supplies _____ =	_____	_____
4. Personnel (host, hostess, bartender, etc.)		
Hourly cost $_____		
Times hours open + 1½*		
and setup, cleanup ×_____		
Base personnel cost		
Plus 15 percent gratuity +_____ =	_____	_____
5. Leather-bound guest book and pens	_____	_____
6. Decorations—flowers, etc.	_____	_____
7. Entertainment		
Fees _____		
Production (sound, lights) _____		
Personal expense _____ =	_____	_____
8. Audiovisual equipment		
Slide projector _____		
Sound system _____		
VCR _____		
Easel _____ =	_____	_____
9. Miscellaneous gifts, delivery service, etc.	_____	_____
10. Total	_____	_____
11. Plus contingency (10 percent) +_____	_____
12. Total $_____	$_____

*Presume suite will be open longer than anticipated.

Figure 15-1. Hospitality budget checklist.

In a standard hospitality operation, excluding a dinner, there are five time periods a day that may require decision making. They are breakfast, midmorning, lunch, midafternoon, and evening—usually early evening. Each requires its own focus.

- *Service personnel.* Service is packaged with food. These people are critical:
  - One of those assigned to your event will be a supervisor. Know who is who.
  - One bartender will be allocated for up to 100 people. If there are more, a "bar back" will be added to the team to keep inventory up to snuff and help out with service during busy times.
  - The way food is presented dictates service personnel assignments. For instance, if guests select hors d'oeuvres from tables, service people restock and maintain presentation quality. In other cases, trays are carried throughout the room to serve. There is more consumption management!

- *Host or hostess service.* The best way to prevent a hospitality suite from becoming just a club room is by establishing ground rules, and enforcing them. For instance, "Employees must arrive with a customer they are escorting." (Outside, unescorted gate crashing must be stopped, too.) Have a formal sign-in book at the door. Hire an outside host or hostess to make sure everyone follows the rules. A company employee, assigned the gate-keeping role, will not be able to do so.

The Event Translation. There are several things you can do to make your hospitality more memorable, something special:

- *Theme approach.* In Boston, host a clambake! In Dallas, a barbecue. A smoked salmon tasting in Seattle. Crab feast in Baltimore. Add some display materials, and you have a theme party. Flowers and overall room decor can add that extra touch as well. For instance, have the hotel use a colored tablecloth, and make certain the flowers are the same color. All reds, for instance.

- *Entertainment.* The extra touch can be entertainment of one sort or another. Here are some ideas:
  - A small suite can be transformed into a piano bar, or a strolling violinist can add grace.
  - A magician can make an entrance or an artist can sketch guests, providing something to take home.
  - In larger-scale situations involving entertainment, make sure that clear contracts are signed.

  Your contact should become the contractor. There could be fees, production expenses, and travel to cover. There are legal and insurance coverage issues.

- *Gifts.* Imagination counts. The take-home sketch works. An apron at finger-food events. A city-logo cap is another. A magic trick, all packaged up. A CD from the musician. You don't need to overwhelm—just create a memory. Your own logo does not have to appear on these gifts.

- *Coat check and security.* When, where, and how big the event determines these needs.

- *Transportation.* An extra touch can be providing private car service for VIPs.

- *Invitation and response management.* Try to be exclusive. Invitations should be sent in advance, though some can be held back for the first show day. A response should be asked for. (The hotel or caterer will require a guarantee in advance.) The invitation should include directions to the venue if it is not familiar. Regardless of responses, follow-up telephone calls should be made to ensure that the invitation or event has not been forgotten.

Economizing on Hospitality

We don't work with the same catering managers, one on one, on a continuing basis. They do not know what we do not communicate clearly. Here is an illustration. You might say, "We need to entertain 100 for three hours." Do you really mean, "We need to entertain 100 *over* three hours"? That manager's plan, and your cost, depends on a subtle difference in language.[2]

Planning Hints for Food

- At a "stand-up," plan six one-or two-bite snacks for each guest. If 100 are to attend, 600 one- or two-bite snacks is the rule.

- Save leftovers. A "cheese round" may be offered at your event. Ask the catering manager to cut up what is left over into cubes that can be served the following evening.

- A "raw bar" is a special treat—clams, oysters, shrimp, crab legs. To reduce cost, simply change the ratio to provide more lower-cost coverage. Oysters are generally the most expensive. Reduce consumption by having service people "shuck" each one. The same gracious impression is created.

- Fresh vegetables (and fruits) are more and more popular as hors d'oeuvres. They are healthy. They can be less expensive than hot, baked snacks. You can also have vegetable dips that are regional and fit into a theme party as well. For instance, avocados are locally grown in California, so use them if you are exhibiting there. Mixed with a light blend of Mexican spices, an avocado dip ties in with a taco party event theme.

Planning Hints for Beverages.   How much do people drink? Alcoholic or not, our source[3] reports that two drinks are consumed in the first hour of attendance. The *maximum* is six in a three-hour period. If you anticipate 100 guests, each of whom will stay for one hour, allow for 200 drinks, regardless of content. If everyone stays forever, the maximum will be 600 drinks.

Moving ahead, most "hard" alcohol is served in 4-ounce servings that include 1.25 ounces of alcohol—21 drinks per "fifth." Wine is generally served in 6-ounce glasses. Soft drinks in 10-ounce glasses. Beer, 12 ounces per serving.

What is your audience profile? Is this a rough and tough group of good-old-boys that likes boilermakers? Or does your guest group belong more to the white wine and mineral water crowd? It truly makes a difference in what you order and how much you spend.

> *Note:* What follows is an illustration based on serving 600 drinks. If the crowd preference is completely "hard alcohol," you want the equivalent of 30 "fifths," each containing 25.4 fluid ounces, or from a metric viewpoint, 750 milliliters. If your guests are at the other end of the spectrum, mineral water with slice of lime lovers, order 188 quarts of mineral water, or 178 1-liter bottles. Make your judgments and get out your calculator!

- *Purchasing methods.* Hotel and catering company prices are high because they cover at least a portion of labor costs. Depending on your supplier, there are two ways to purchase:

  1. *By bottle.* The tradition is that one buys by the bottle. If the cork is popped, you own it. If so, keep it, or ask the supervisor to set "opens" aside for the next evening. (That includes mixers as well as alcoholic beverages.) Some catering managers will accept by-drink pricing, but that does not appear to be the norm.

  2. *Outside purchase.* After an initial order, in some places the caterer will allow you to bring additional bottles for a second or third evening, bought for less at a local retailer. There will be, however, what is called a "corkage charge," a fee for serving a product not purchased through the contractor. That is not unreasonable, given that room rent was priced low in anticipation of food and beverage supply and service sales.

- *Consumption management.* For budget and other reasons, you may want to lower consumption. Though it may cost extra as part of a service fee, provide a tray service, indicating concerns in advance to service people about guests who might overdo. They will "slow down" without having people notice. The hospitality industry is very sensitive to shortcutting potential guest problems. That should be your guideline as well.

Note: Bartenders are worth every penny. If total guest consumption exceeds minimum levels from a service viewpoint, bartending will be provided at "no extra charge." If not, an extra fee will be levied to cover service. Either way, professional bartenders do far more than mix drinks or pour beer. They keep an eagle eye on guests. They close the bar at a predetermined time without putting the hostess or host in an embarrassing position.

Ask and It Is Yours—The Extras

We do not point fingers, but catering people are not as professional at sales as some others! After the basic agreement is made, you might want to ask for some extras that your supplier simply did not think to offer, perhaps because much training has been in pure "food and beverage."

To stimulate thoughts, here are a couple of questions and possible answers:

- "Could you give us an ice sculpture reflecting our theme on the table?" The answer could be, "Certainly. The hotel has an ice carving artist on staff for that very reason. It is provided as part of service or at minimum added expense."

- "For our 'Mexican' reception, could you supply red tablecloths and candles?" The answer is probably yes, and it won't cost a fortune, if anything.

The Audience and Cost

Theme parties that provide narrowly focused food and beverages can save money in contrast to more general entertainments. At a typical hospitality suite a wide range of beverages are provided, and you will pay for every bottle opened, even if little is used from it. At $30 each or more in a hotel, that can become very costly. Even if you make a corkage agreement, it is still costly. The same is true for a broad selection of snacks.

A theme party—a state wine tasting, or perhaps a crab feast that provides only soft drinks and beer, or maybe a taco party serving only margaritas, beer, and soft drinks—can be far less expensive. Wine tastings are popular. You would be surprised at the number of states that produce excellent local wines, not just California, Washington, or New York. Even Florida has a wine industry! If the event is large enough, you might contact the state's wine board for a volunteer speaker. For the most part, snacks at these events are restricted to cheese and fruit.

Theme Party Illustration.   Jansport, the sportswear manufacturer, was introducing a new line of outerwear at a major ski industry dealer show in Las Vegas. The objective was to sign orders from key dealers. It decided on a theme party to aid in reaching that goal.[4]

Dealers were invited to a "mountain party" in advance. It was set for the second night of the show. A critical part of the plan was that dealers could not get in without their tickets, which had to be picked up at the booth beforehand. That ticket was a specially designed T-shirt that *had to be worn to get in.* No gate crashers at this event!

Dealers who came to the booth for their tickets were shown the new line in advance of the party. That was very important in reaching the goal.

The company had tested the new outerwear on a mountain climbing expedition and had taken photographs. The slides were shown at random on the walls of the party room. A small "mountain music" group provided background entertainment. With everyone in T-shirts, a degree of informality was produced. That allowed food and beverage services to be limited to picnic items. Beer, wine, and soft drinks were placed around an ice sculpture of a mountain.

The company signed orders right at the party. In addition, it upstaged larger competitors running far more expensive and formal hospitality suites. A Jansport party "ticket" became a hot property at the show during the two days before it took place.

Private Shows

A private show is an event operated under the aegis of one company not tied to a particular trade show. There are different types. In all cases, however, the ultimate sponsor's objective has been to enhance its position, even if it elects to take a backseat at the confab or exposition it is sponsoring.

Essentially, these boil down to user or dealer meetings. *Dealer meetings* are attended by franchise holders or otherwise independent dealers working with a large corporation—or divisions of a large company screening what is available from an approved supplier group. *User meetings* are for large customers who use products and services in-house supplied by the ultimate sponsor.

User Meetings

Big-time high-tech companies seem to have started these. They are run by a company itself or by a group of large customers with encouragement and support from the company. These private to-dos should not be confused with traditional trade expos that focus on a technology, such as the MAC-World series, or by an industry group—food, broadcasting, or travel.

IBM has long sponsored a series of private events for its customers. Amdahl Corporation has done the same. These tend to be one-exhibitor events. Frequently, they are operated by semiautonomous user groups, with background support from the corporation. The seminars are very important in this context. Subcontractors or related service suppliers are much involved.

Dealer Meetings

A number of big companies sponsor private meetings for dealers. Most of these are for locally owned franchise holders. Often these events are packaged to introduce new company products, the car, sandwich, or perfume emerging from stage-mist with marketing steam. Added to the main tent presentation is a lot of information, including what outside exhibitors offer to dealers.

Exhibitors are those approved by corporate—supplies and tools and resale inventory to finance. Ford and other auto manufacturers come to mind as corporate sponsors. Ace Hardware was a pioneer. Another is Century 21, the real estate outfit. There are many others. Some phone companies sponsor private events to showcase approved vendors to interested departments. The goal is to provide dealers (or departments) with access to prescreened suppliers, with seminars on management topics presented as well.

Betwixt and Between

There are hybrid private events. One of the most interesting is the U.S. Postal Forum, operated by a not-for-profit board representing companies involved with mail processing. It acts under the aegis of the United States Postal Service. Those attending are from outfits that do lots of mailing.

At one level the forum is a place for sharing views among the Postal Service and other experts and large-scale mailers: direct marketing, catalogs, magazine publishers, and others who do much mailing. At the exhibitor level, it is an opportunity for those with equipment, services, and technology for those mass mailers to offer what is needed to do the job. The Postal Service is one of the exhibitors, offering its own services.

The key to this kind of hybrid, and it is quite sophisticated, is that those attending are not captive "dealers" and exhibitor-suppliers are not wedded to the sponsor. However, the board does prohibit USPS-competing haulers and delivery services from exhibiting. Natural enough. Would Federal Express, at some kind of a corporate show, want Airborne, Emery, UPS, or USPS?

Media Events

Some large companies introduce new products to the public at the same time they are introduced to the dealers. For instance, Microsoft has done full Broadway spectaculars to introduce new products. In addition to "the trade," invited to the event, the consumer press is invited as well. The result is an extra splash of publicity aimed at end users in newspapers and magazines and on TV.

16
Exhibit Transportation and Setup at the Show

Logistics is what we call a "how-to" subject. The details of transportation and setup are very important, but our purpose in this book is to help improve overall exhibit process management. There is little of that in print, and far more on the how-to of getting the job done at an implementation level. We cannot, however, ignore the subject. In this chapter we provide detailed hints on how to do the job better, but we do not pretend to be expert in exhibit freight or setup at the show. Somebody has always helped us on that.

Freight Options

From a domestic viewpoint, there are three options: van line, general carrier, and airfreight. (For small exhibits a fourth is "lug-a-booth-yourself." We don't suggest that, in spite of portable exhibit claims. There's plenty of show work for you to do without engaging in small wrestling matches.) An exhibitor should elect the most economical and safe method—an obvious reality. However, there are some complications, and our goal is to help you figure out which method is best for you.

General Carriers. Interstate highway travelers see these trucks every day! Logos such as "Roadway," "Yellow," and "CF" drift by in the center lane as they make their way to the next city. These trucks carry much of the commerce of the USA. Each works with a depot system. Shipments are concentrated and driven, long range, to other depots where they are broken down for local delivery. Within the industry these companies are often called *common carriers,* tracing (we think) to old governmental regulatory terms. The term *general* would fit better than *common* since the service is far from ordinary.

Van Lines.   You see those emblems too. Among them are "Allied," "Atlas," "Beekman," "NorthAmerican," and "United." As consumers, we are more familiar with that part of the moving industry. These companies haul our possessions, home to home. We cover differences shortly, but the key is that van lines work point to point and do not use depots.

Airfreight.   This method is used less. Except for small packages or emergencies, it is considered more costly. This is true or not, depending on the situation. Airfreight uses a "depot system" like general carriers over-the-road. There are times when air has been a savior, and for small shipments more economical than one might imagine. The show exhibitor kit lists its airfreight contractor.

Choosing Is Easy—Up to a Point

Most companies use small exhibits. They come complete with good-quality packing crates made for a bit of banging around. Others, small and large, also ship delicate equipment more susceptible to damage. There are some very large exhibits shipped without any crates at all. The transport choice you make depends on your situation.

General Carrier Advantages.   Fred Buonacorsi, trade show director for CF MotorFreight[1] is a well-known expert. He helps us understand how the system works. He says, "For many exhibitors using exhibits that are crated, a general hauler can be the most cost-effective and convenient way to ship." Overall, use of general carrier service is less expensive than van service, though differences can be marginal sometimes.

Show organizers include the name and order forms for the exhibition's official general freight contractor in its exhibitor kit. The company picks up the crates and delivers to the show's warehouse in advance. They are concentrated with other show shipments and brought to the hall, then placed in the booth space at the start of setup. The process is reversed after the expo is over.

There are disadvantages as well, for some exhibitors. Your crates do not go directly from your exhibit company's warehouse to the show's warehouse. The depot system, which works a lot like the airline hub-and-spoke systems, requires your freight to be handled several times in transit. That should not pose a problem for well-crated materials. These companies, after all, carry a large percentage of the commercial freight hauled around the nation every day.

Buonacorsi points out that there are exceptions to the use of the depot system. "There are times when large exhibits fill up a trailer. In those cases it can save everyone time and cost to run direct to the show."

Van Line Service Advantages.   A well-regarded van line competitor is Edward J. Laub, president of Hoffman Moving & Storage, an agent for Allied Van Lines.[2] He makes the case for van line services by first pointing out, "High value product hauling—exhibits, electronics, and art—has become a highly specialized function within the household goods moving industry. We use specially built trailers to minimize any risks of damage." He goes on, "In contrast to the tradition in general freight, our drivers are given extraordinary training and own their own tractors, at least. Some own their trailers as well."

There is less handling involved using van line service. A full truckload goes directly from the exhibit house to the unloading dock at the exhibition hall. If your exhibit does not fill a trailer and another load is to be carried with it, a first-on–last-off delivery schedule is employed.

Another advantage is that exhibit materials do not have be crated. Laub points out, "Coming out of the household moving tradition, our people know how to pad-wrap, pack, and tie down delicate items so they arrive unharmed."

A disadvantage is that van line service can be more costly, though competition has forced pricing down to close to general freight levels. Laub, however, points out trade-offs. "Crates are costly to build, bulky, and weigh more. We have a customer with a very large booth used once a year. There are no crates and for a reason. The transport cost for pad-wrapped trailer service is higher, but only two trailers are needed. Were that exhibit to be crated, we would need three trucks. The transport cost would be higher than two pad-wrapped vans. As well, add more drayage cost at the show and for crate manufacturing."

Airfreight Service Advantages.   We explain this less than the two main competing hauling methods. Air advantages and disadvantages seem clear. Air is very fast. You can play "pick up sticks" to correct a late emerging problem with ease. However, air, like general freight, uses a depot system. Your materials will be handled several times. They must be well packed. The cost is higher than road.

There are exceptions to every rule. We have waited for luggage at airports in areas where trade shows take place for many years. It is rare that we have not spotted, on that rumbling runway of a conveyor belt, an exhibit shipping container or box enclosing something meant for an upcoming show. (Fortunately, knock-on-wood, we have never lost a bag. Occasionally, bags did not make it on the same flight, but they caught up with us quickly.)

This is a form of airfreight. Simply check the booth and materials when you fly with them. However, you do not have to do that. Your show's exhibitor kit lists its official airfreight contractor. If your booth is small, get an estimate. The cost may be such that you can avoid tug-a-booth through airports, endless taxicabs, hotel bell people, and so on, saving yourself and all those cash tips for what you *should* be doing, getting yourself ready and rested to *use* that booth.

Here is another hint: There are times when overnight mail is required. Have those small packets delivered to your hotel instead of directly to your booth. You can avoid a substantial minimum drayage service charge for in-hall delivery of small packets.

Transport Pricing

In the USA interstate transportation service costs were, until recently, strictly regulated. That is no longer the case. And because of governmental budget cuts, the regulations that still exist are not as well policed as in the past. As shippers, we are not as concerned about that as those who do the actual hauling—over the road, in the sky, or by ship. Laub points out, "A price and services schedule is just that. Our customers evaluate what it costs for what they feel they want or need."

Pricing Concepts

During the days of regulation, haulers competed pretty much on the basis of service. There were exceptions, all dutifully signed and sealed with government approval. Essentially, volume shippers could negotiate lower prices with their haulers.

The same is true today, but the burden falls more on the shipper and less on government to ensure equitable treatment by the hauler. The same is true in other USA industries that have gone through the pains of deregulation—passenger airlines, communications, and banking, for instance. Like it or not, the consumer has to take up the slack.

Because of this, it is wise to know a bit about pricing concepts that drive the cost and service schedules presented by haulers. Darlene Lane, a long-time exhibit specialist sales manager with a NorthAmerican Van Lines agency, helps explain these principles.[3]

The Dimensional Weight Mystery. Lane points out, "Managers start out by thinking that exhibit weight is what is crucial. Postage for envelopes is priced that way. Drayage, the movement of materials in a trade hall, is priced that way. But raw weight by itself, from the necessary viewpoint of any hauler, is only one factor."

Space use as well as true weight has to be taken into consideration. There are both true weight and space limits to contend with in any kind of container. As Lane points out, "A carton of feathers or potato chips does not weigh a lot, but it takes up more space than a bucket of water or bag of sand of the same raw weight." Regardless of true weight, a truck or plane or ship with built-in space limits must go from point to point, with all the costs included in the price.

The transport industry has created a pricing formula based on what is termed *dimensional weight*. It reflects both true weight and space requirements. It is calculated on the basis of 7 pounds per cubic foot. The base price is set by comparing actual weight and dimensional weight, calculated with the formula. The shipper pays the higher of the two.

An exhibitor we met said, "My booth is heavy but small. Why should I pay extra?" (This exhibitor wanted to display kitchen work centers with granite counter tops![4]) Added to space, haulers face practical and legal limits. Darlene Lane points out that the Interstate Commerce Commission levies hefty fines if the whichever-is-higher rule is broken. She goes on to say, "And they *will* find out. It is mandatory for trucks to stop at highway weigh stations and show complete documents while their vehicles are on the scales."

Service Differences

The cost of handling, and where these charges emerge, creates transport price differences. Air and general freight contractor price and service schedules are easier to understand than those from van line operators. The air and general freight companies carry crated goods. Van lines do that as well, but they also transport uncrated materials.

As a result, the van line schedules reflect different labor situations. Packing crated exhibits in a trailer costs less than pad wrapping and loading an uncrated exhibit. There are, as well, mixed loads—some crated materials and other items that must be pad-wrapped for shipment. Pricing shifts to meet those requirements.

As we've said, the general freight companies are somewhat less expensive. However, they do not include the costs for loading—

absorbed by the shipper's exhibit house and passed through, with commission added most of the time. In the case of van lines, the driver-owners pack the van. Those costs are part of the price paid to the transport company. Costs remain, however, for "picking" from storage and delivery to the loading dock by the exhibit houses.

If, by now, you start to think that shipping is a complex exercise, you are right! However, this book's purpose is not to force you into becoming an instant "freight expert." Considering the dynamics of change in that industry, it would be impossible anyway. A danger is that you think you know but do not. What you know now could be last year's newspaper. It is best, we believe, to understand just the basics and thus the kinds of logical and wise questions to ask.

Hints on Saving Transport Money

This list, in part, simply summarizes the above. There are, however, some added items:

- If your booth is small and crated, the most economical shipper is a general carrier.
- If your exhibit is used frequently, going from show to show, crate your materials.
- Airfreight is fast and economical for smaller shipments.
- If your booth is large and used infrequently, do not use crates except for delicate equipment.
- Ship early, always.
- Concentrate your shipments into as few crates or boxes as possible.
- Make sure that your shipping documents clearly include both true and dimensional weights. (Even if dimensional is used for pricing over the road, in-hall movement is priced on the basis of true weight.)
- Envelopes and overnight air packets should be delivered to your hotel, not the booth. There are minimum in-hall delivery charges added for deliveries to your booth.

Cost Trade-Offs

Transport costs billed by the hauler do not stand alone. There are questions to ask yourself, or your vendors, that do not directly relate to the price of the shipment. For instance:

- For a period of time there is no storage charge for putting your booth in your show contractor's warehouse. If your booth bounces from show to show, you can save money.
- Your exhibit house should bill "pick-and-load" cost if you go out on general freight. Van line drivers load. Does your exhibit house use a lower rate? (At shows hall labor unloads and loads.)
- Can you or your exhibit house negotiate a discount for volume shipments over the year? Yes. Exhibit production companies negotiate in the interest of all clients as a collective. Compare that cost, including exhibit house commission, with dealing directly. (If you are a large-scale exhibitor, you might be able to negotiate your own contact, dealing directly.)
- If you contemplate not crating a large exhibit, there are several comparisons to make:
  - The cost of design and crate building will be lower, but by how much?
  - The rates for shipping pad-wrapped items are higher, but they take less space. What's the balance?
  - The cost of storage in the exhibit house is lower because of less space, but it will cost more to move it to the loading dock.
  - The price for in-hall movement is reduced by weight, but premiums are paid to cover labor cost.

Services at the Show

One of life's adventures is first seeing a large exhibit hall in the midst of setup. "This show will *never* open!" It takes a while to sense that this visual chaos is actually very tightly controlled. It all comes together at the end. That does require cooperation, and everyone doing specific jobs, all working within the framework of a grand plan.

The Grand Planners

The show manager is ultimately responsible, but he or she works with others to create and implement. Key among these coworkers is the show's general contractor, often called a *decorating company*. It gathers together the subcontractors we see listed with their order forms in the show's exhibit kit. (See Chapter 3 for details.)

Our job, as exhibit managers, is to coordinate the activity. For small booths that is not a difficult chore. Just send orders in advance, and show up a day early. But many large exhibitors, with big booths, must hire outside service companies and "lead" people to administer the job. Exhibit design and production companies offer these services. There are, as well, specialist contractors.

The General Contractor

Working with the show's manager, the general contracting or decorating company provides many services. We experience working with that company when we see the exhibitor kit or go to its service desk area at the show. The company also serves the show itself. It will lay out the floor, making up the maps. It provides the registration areas, directional signs, carpeting, and much more. For instance, it, or a subcontractor, will provide the local warehouse and local transport service.

Drayage.   A common exhibitor complaint is about the cost of drayage, that is, the price for moving materials into and out of the hall. However, there is more to that job than meets the eye. Have you ever seen an exhibitor try to wrestle boxes up an escalator? First, it's illegal. Second, who has the insurance to pay the bills if a box tumbles back down and hits people?

Have you ever seen an exhibition hall loading dock in action? Ton after ton of freight has to be moved, quickly, to the right spot in the hall. At million-pound shows, and there are a lot of them, exhibit hauling trucks are scheduled to be at the unloading dock at certain times, based on the exhibitor's booth space position in the hall. Exhibits must be moved to the far side first!

If you want chaos and a show that never opens, eliminate drayage. The truck mob outside and cluttered aisles will create frustrations that you would never believe or accept.

Setup Labor.   Exhibitors express confusion about who does what. There are carpenters, decorators, riggers, electricians—the list goes on. The confusion emerges among experienced exhibitors because they work in many cities, and there are differences in what each union group can do based on the way contracts were negotiated in each city.

The solution is simple. It starts with, "When in Rome..." It continues by asking questions about what is appropriate in the venue. It concludes by avoiding show floor confrontations. The floor workers, and their stewards, have no choice other than to follow work rules. Management skills are required to blend work groups. Start with what must come first. It makes no sense to have skilled assembly workers standing around, waiting for carpet layers to complete their work, which must be done first.

An exhibitor complaint in the past has been worker skill. That was especially the case in smaller cities where the labor pool had to be supplemented with inexperienced people at big shows. Both problems have diminished in the last few years. Unions have instituted training programs for exhibit workers, and the pool sizes have increased, reflecting increased demand.

Mike Yorke, a Canadian union leader,[5] explains one of the more recently introduced programs: "Traditionally, unions in the exhibit industry have been relatively passive deliverers of labor." That is no longer the case. As in other craft industries, exhibit industry unions now create and sponsor member and apprentice training programs.

Yorke's union local is in Toronto, part of the United Brotherhood of Carpenters and Joiners. He writes that it "has embarked on an ambitious multidimensional strategy...."[6] It has joined forces with its city and Province to help build local and provincial business. That has been reflected in Local 27's 10-week training program, operated by its training and apprenticeship director, Cosmo Manella.

Added to technical skills, the program includes education about the exhibit industry, helping members understand the pressures on exhibit managers. It also includes general information on the area that may help exhibitor visitors who ask questions. Also part of the program are lifestyle modules—dress code, appearance, sexism, and more. In addition to the skills of exhibit setup, made ever more complex by the introduction of new construction and connection systems, members are expected to make exhibitors comfortable and help build repeat business for Toronto, the Province of Ontario, Canada, as a whole and, of course, themselves.

Tipping. Based on the above, it seems embarrassing to have to address cash gratuities. However, until a few years ago there were some venues where it was acknowledged that exhibitors paid extra cash for special favors. The answer then and now is no! These are professional people, well paid for what they do. Unions discourage the practice and discipline members who solicit or accept tips.

You can, however, reward those serving you. It is certainly acceptable for you to serve coffee and pastry or soft drinks to your team! If you have a company giveaway at the show, a T-shirt, for example, that can become an appropriate "thank you." Workers, or their kids, will appreciate it. Recognition for a job well done is always appreciated.

Electrical Service. Small exhibitors complain about the need and cost of having a union electrician connect their lights and appliances. "We only have three lights and one personal computer. Why should I pay for something that I can do myself?" You may know what you are doing. But does your exhibit neighbor? In part, a union electrician is your insurance policy. Proper electrical work prevents fires.

It may not appear that way during show time, but exhibit floors can be very dangerous industrial workplaces. What would happen if a wall were to fall or a sign were to fly from the rafters—or a fire break out? There have been few accidents to date and the industry wants it to stay that way.

Independent Labor Contractors. Larger-scale exhibitors often want to use an independent labor contractor, not the show's official service, for show setup. The supervisors who travel to the show site "know the booth" and how things should be organized in the most efficient fashion.

Most of the workers hired are from the local labor pool, people who have been prescreened by the contractor based, in part, on past experience with the customer's booth. Because of that, show management must be notified of the intention to use an outside contractor in advance. That need is practical because it helps the officials to know how many craftspeople they must call in to serve the show on a need basis.

Avoid Last-Minute Shock

It is a lot easier to prevent problems than to solve them:

- Read your exhibitor kit well before the show, when it first arrives. Send orders in early, and you may earn some discounts.

- Bring all your papers along when you travel to the site. These include copies of your space contract, service orders, freight papers, going-home shipping labels, clear setup drawings, and your insurance certificate. It is a lot easier to locate a lost order or crate if you can give service personnel the order number. Good setup drawings speed that process.

- Have some cash or travelers' checks tucked away for last-minute purchases. Credit cards are often accepted, but you never know. In a strange city it can be tough to find an ATM machine that accepts your bank card.

- Write shipping labels for both to and from the show in advance. Print, by hand if necessary, using very large type, and include your booth number. (Type the size of this text is hard to read in the dim interior of a truck!) Place labels on two sides of your crates.

- Make going-home freight arrangements in advance.

- Shows will require a certificate of insurance in advance. Your insurance agent will provide that. At the same time, check your coverages. Freight or service contractors may not have enough coverage to completely replace or repair damage.

- Many times empty crates stored during a show are not empty. Some unused materials may be inside. Alert the handler! Extra-gentle care will be the result. (Have you ever seen fast-working empty-crate handlers play "pitch the penny" with empty crates on a forklift?)

- Store cartons you will need at teardown inside crates. If you don't have any crates, ask an exhibit neighbor if you can tuck your cartons inside one of his or her crates.

- Make sure your shipping papers include both the dimensional and real weight of each item.

- Write exhibit damage notes before the unit is shipped, at setup, and then again at teardown. These notes help identify where damage took place.

- The word *Fragile* printed on the side of a crate has lost its meaning. One high-technology exhibitor has crates made with plastic windows so handlers can see what's inside. That attracts attention!

This random list is not intended to frighten you. In reality, the problems are few and far between. Still, precautions will reduce the odds even further that problems will occur.

17

Exhibit Staff Selection, Training, and Management

Chapter cruisers will have noted in several places that we suggest extra attention be given to the *next* chapter—18. It is all about floor performance by booth staff members. In addition to issues and answers, an outline is provided for a floor performance training meeting. People are the most important part of exhibiting. A good booth staff can make up for a lot of sins.

This chapter is its companion. If you can select and recruit the right mix of people, the booth performance training program will be all that more effective. Second, there is more to training than the nuts and bolts of booth contact. We cover that here and suggest an overall approach that can incorporate Chapter 18's nuts and bolts. In parallel with these subjects we suggest management approaches that can help you help your team.

Selecting a Staff

Many think of show audiences as one big mass of like-minded people. That is not so. There are shared interests, of course, but big differences as well. The better you understand those underlying differences, the better able you will be to match your staff to that profile. The "golden rule" is that likes attract. They already share something extra. That extra will be what you want to aim for.

Drawing Up the Profile

We discussed at some length the setting of exhibit goals in Chapter 5, and part of that process is analyzing the audience. We expand on that here in some respects. Fact gathering should be fairly easy. You may have some facts together already and included with the show prospectus. For more, you can call up the show's manager. Even if accurate data is not available, a calculated guess will help a lot.

Michael Muldoon, a well-known show executive,[1] points out that data provided is based on past shows. The audience anticipated is just that, an expectation. He goes on to say that even at the most stable events, there is up to a 40 percent audience shift each year. That is the case even if the overall audience size projection is quite accurate. Several factors, including show location, job changes, and shifts in industry interests, affect audience size and makeup.

We once talked to a show executive who manages one of the largest events in the world. We asked why the show prospectus did not include much detailed data on past events. He said, "We have a lot of information, but so few exhibitors have expressed interest that it is not cost-effective to send it all out. When somebody calls, we send an abstract and help interpret what it means." Call your show manager!

Location. Research over the years points up that even at national shows audiences are dominated by visitors from the region where the show is taking place. Up to half travel less than 500 miles to attend.

Most association-sponsored national conventions move from one venue to another each year. The uninitiated think that is simply to provide a fresh visiting opportunity for delegates. There is a bit of that, but of far greater importance for associations is to provide their overall membership an equal opportunity to participate at the national event, at least once every few years.

Connie Akin is an in-house show manager for a major association.[2] Her show moves from region to region—from New Orleans to Boston to Denver to Washington, D.C., to San Antonio and so on. She says that these relocations help both delegates from each area and exhibitors from those same regions as well.

The regional flavor is also present at worldwide, international events. Events in Europe will attract a far greater audience from Europe. Asian shows, from Asia.

To the extent possible, your booth staff should try to mirror the audience from a location viewpoint. That is no problem at a local expo. Most everybody, audience and booth staff, will be from the same city. All know where the doughnut shop is located. The same is true for a statewide event. At a national or international event, try to have half your staff come from the same region where the show takes place.

Special Interests.   At many larger shows the audience will break down by special interest, even if the event is for only one industry.

- Company CEOs and presidents have their own specific interests.
- Department heads, often the end users of products sold for in-house use, have other interests.
- Purchasing agents or product resale buyers are a third.
- Technical people are looking at other issues.

The most common complaint that emerges in audience research can be summarized by, "The booth person was not expert in what I wanted to learn about." Again, your team should try to mirror the anticipated audience profile. If, for instance, half the audience is technical, half your staff should be technical. (If one of your technical people is in conversation with a department head with other interests, a pass-along introduction can be accomplished.)

Female-Male Balance.   It has been a gradual and powerful trend and it will continue. More and more women have been accepted into what were at one time exclusive male camps of management, sales, purchasing, and technical development. To what extent has that happened so far in your industry? Can your show manager advise you on the degree to which female delegates participate at your events?

   If, for instance, about 40 percent of the buyer delegates are female, you must strive hard for female company people on your staff. A booth team entirely made up of men sends a not-so-subtle psychographic[3] signal that your company is behind the curve in its value system and culture. You are less likely to sell.

Personalities.   You will not be able to gather specific information on delegate personalities. We make assumptions that bankers or doctors are stuffy, truck stop operators "tough," movie producers gregarious. None of that is true! The best we can do is to provide a mix of personalities among those we know in the company. A shy person can be a very valuable resource at a booth. For example, shy people get along quite well with the back-slapping, outgoing types. They can be blended into a good team.

Age, Ethnic, Race, and Religious Balance.   If you have it, flaunt it! The signal you send is that you are professional, ahead of the curve. In terms of balance, see what you can learn about the ages reflected in the audience. If a major audience chunk is 30 to 45, try to have your team reflect that.

A warning on international shows: There remain some parts of the world in which custom makes it very difficult for women or members of specific religious groups to be effective or feel comfortable. But don't make fast assumptions. Do some homework.

Recruiting

There are two situations in which recruiting is really easy! One is a local or regional event at which salespeople will be seeing their own personal customers. They will sign up in a heartbeat and were probably asking for the show in the first place.

The second is a convention that offers very specific leading-edge seminars. Many of these are technical. Your more scientific people will jump at the chance. Frankly, however, they don't give a whistle about serving the company at the booth. That's just the way they pay tuition enabling them to build personal knowledge at one or two seminars.

There are other situations in which it is far more difficult. Starry-eyed younger employees with a thirst for travel paid for by somebody else will sign up. Those who are a bit older and have done this before realize there is far more work than play and that airports, hotels, and convention halls are pretty much alike, no matter where. They are tougher "sales" unless they see some personal professional benefit.

The Team Concept.   Booth selling is unselfish. You don't always pick whom you want to talk to. They pick you. In addition, you are responsible for picking out visitors to talk with who may or may not become your personal customers. Your booth team "prospects" know that already. Admit it up-front, and then point out the values in working as part of a team. The program can include a number of management steps that help everyone reach personal objectives:

- Pass-along introductions in the booth
- Appointment setting for times when a team member is not at the booth
- Third-party endorsements
- Corporate backing for individual salespeople
- Exposure to company VIPs

Learning and Image.   We once met a woman who paid her own way to a national convention after not being selected for her company's booth staff. She arrived unannounced and did some booth duty as a volunteer. However, she spent more time attending show-sponsored seminars.

We asked her why she was willing to spend $2000 of her own money for travel, registration, and hotel. "That's easy," she said. For the next year her participation became part of many customer presentations. In discussion, she would say, "Did you happen to go to the XYZ Seminar at last year's convention?" As it turned out, a good number of her customers had not attended the show or seminar, a typical situation. But her inquiry sent two instant signals. One was that she had a true interest in the customer's business problems. Second was that she was respected enough by her own company to be sent to the convention. (That was not true, of course, because she did it on her own. However, customers did not know that and were not told! *Many would have taken too much personal credit. She realized that part of her sales power came from a perception of the value of her company as a whole.*)

The greatest value she derived, however, came because she had taken good notes. She was able to position her company offerings in terms of industry applications and values that were hot and therefore covered in the seminars. Sales soared for that woman. Was she cut out of the company convention team again? Never. She helps herself, others, and the company as a whole.

The Presentation Package.   The biggest team-building mistake for an exhibit coordinator is making a simple phone call to another manager: "Can you supply two people to work at the trade show?" The answer will be yes. Only God knows who you will get—or the number of name changes that will be made as weeks go on.

In Chapter 18 we detail a preshow information packet that should be sent to staff members. That package can start life as a shorter recruiting document sent to managers or potential staff members you want to recruit for the team. That document can include:

- Show information—what, where, and when
- Company mission and goals
- Audience analysis
- Seminar summary
- Preshow promotional activity
- Company VIP participation
- Off-site event operations of interest

The packet can also include lists of advantages for signing on such as:

- Meeting current customers—your own advance appointments
- Looking for new prospects
- Attending seminars, learning what's hot
- Meeting company VIPs
- Gaining prestige
- Learning what competitors are offering and how they are doing it

Make that phone call. However, it should call attention to a packet in the in-box. The yes decision will be more emphatic, and you will experience far fewer changes in team members as time grows shorter.

Out-of-Pocket Cost Coverage

If it is possible, try to absorb travel and hotel expenses in a central corporate budget. For most companies that is against tradition. However, it all comes from the same "bottom line," and it produces two advantages for exhibit coordinators:

1. Fewer staff changes emerge in the last few days. These are very costly. Early travel reservations save a lot of money.
2. More ability to insist on cooperation. One big company uses the practice and sends people home midshow if they fail to follow participation ground rules.

Training Sessions

We have delivered exhibit marketing training programs at annual sales meetings. They are fine and work well, but they need to be supported by your own training at the site just before an event takes place. That is much more than a "briefing;" standing around in the booth 15 minutes before the opening bell to see what it looks like.

Staff members must take the situation seriously. A far more formal training meeting is needed just before an event. Even if for no other reason, they need it to sort each other out in what is a relatively infrequent environment. (See Chapter 18 on psychological issues and answers for staff.)

Meeting Agenda

No matter how large or small your group, formal or informal, a pre-event meeting requires an agenda. It is broken into modules. Figure on a couple of hours or even more, combined with breakfast or dinner. This social experience is important. Ask people to sit with others they don't know well.

- *Introductions.* Start it yourself. In 30 to 60 seconds, mention something personal and professional. State your exhibit experience and something you are proud of. Then ask everyone else to do the same, even if they know each other well.
- *Show summary.* Summarize why the company is exhibiting. Outline the overall program and include a reminder about the overall audience.
- *Company VIP.* Invite a company leader, other than yourself, to say something. It can be very short—perhaps how exhibiting fits in with other company activities.
- *Product summary.* Ask someone else to summarize, in a short moment or two, what is being offered at the show and the applications or benefits. (Most will know already, but they will know *too much!* The summary will be used to shorten contacts.)
- *Exhibit layout.* With perhaps the aid of a sketch, quickly point out what is where.
- *Floor performance.* This the heart of the meeting. An outline for this module is in Chapter 18. Edit that outline, and select the elements you find most important.
- *Administrative and housekeeping.* This information is what everyone has been waiting for, but wait until now to provide the information. These items include:
  - *The work schedule.* Booth hours, seminar and team assignments, postday meetings, hospitality suite assignments, and competitor observation and report duties.
  - *Paperwork handling.* Leads, orders, expense statements, seminar content reports, and competition analysis reports.
  - *Key account sharing.* List everyone's special visitors so it can be posted at the booth, along with the booth work schedule. Everyone then can be on the lookout and tell visitors when their key contact will be there.
- *Specific goals.* Outline numerical goals for the show as a whole and each day (see Chapter 5). If, possible, have the team elect a "most valuable player" before the show's end, or perhaps invoke an informal team competition if you split the staff into groups. Nondollar recognition works also. People are pleased when their names are

mentioned in a company newsletter. Perhaps a small cut that will be engraved. These small recognitions can be shown to family members and are really important. Winning-team prizes can be as simple as a bottle of wine for each person, given by each of the losers! Both sides go home with a memory, and friendships will be created. "I'll never forget when I had to give you that bottle of cheap wine!"

- *Booth visit.* Save this until the end. Provide time for team members to practice their presentations with each other before the show starts. If your company provides divergent products or services, an expert on each can present a summary at the booth where that product or service is to be shown.

- *Team gift.* There are times when you should inspire teamwork. A memento of training can help to do that. One we find effective is a carabineer, the snap-link used in mountain climbing (and by riggers). In the closed position they look like links of a chain. Link them and then ask team members to break the chain. They can't. Then give each a link with the message that everyone is strong, but they will be more powerful working together.[4]

Training Room and Layout

We have been part of these meetings when only 4 or 5 people are attending. That can become an informal sit-around in a hotel bedroom or small suite. When the group is somewhat larger, say, 10 or 12, rent a hotel function room, and combine the meeting with food service for the team. Provide a long rectangular conference table with seats on either side for those attending. Save one end for yourself, and put some books or handouts at the other end so nobody sits there. That arrangement establishes you as the leader, without a "competitor" at the other end.

If your team is large, a larger room can be set up with six- or eight-person tables on either side of a center aisle. Have them angled, chevron style, so all participants can see the speakers easily. The center aisle can be used by speakers who want to move about during a presentation.

In all cases use handouts and visual support—even if just a few photocopy sheets and an easel pad! That would be appropriate for a very small group meeting in your own hotel room. More bells and whistles are needed if the meeting is any larger. Content is just part of the reason why. The serious-business message is being sent simultaneously.

Management to Help Staff Performance

There is much you can do to help people work smarter, doing more for themselves and the company as a whole.

Booth Team Schedule

Some events open their trade shows only four hours a day, others far longer. Booth work is not easy. Four hours is about the maximum you can expect from anyone. After that the body may be seen, but mental exhaustion will have taken its toll. It is far better to have two teams working two on and two off.

Off-hours will also allow staff people to do other jobs:

- One is simply walking the show floor to see what else is being presented. As part of that, you can ask team members to make notes and then compile reports on what competitors are showing.

- Second is providing quiet time for salespeople to meet with their own clients. The hubbub of a busy booth is not really the place for those longer confabs. (They may wish to *visit* the booth for a short time to look at a product, but it is better for them to find a private spot for their discussion.)

  Note: If you are in or close to your hotel and have rented a company suite for the show, the suite can be ideal for those meetings.

- A third can be attending seminars of interest. A booth staff person may have a particular interest in one or more subjects. However, you should ask that notes be taken so that a summary can be passed on to others.

Postday Critique

It is a very good idea to schedule, well in advance, a postday meeting to compare notes. It should be short so that it does not interfere with evening dinner plans with customers or event-sponsored evening activities. There are times when these meetings take place right in the booth. It can be far more relaxing, however, to hold them back in somebody's hotel room or in a company suite. We suggest no more than a half hour or 45 minutes. The agenda can include:

- Reports from staff members on exciting prospect or customer meetings

- Quick reports summarizing what competitors are showing

- Summaries of seminars attended that day
- Special requests from staff members—"Be on the lookout for XYZ on Tuesday."

Arrival and Departure Schedules

The entire team should arrive the day before the show opening. That will provide everyone time to adjust, to get the lay of the land. It will also provide time for some training and getting used to each other before the team has to "go on."

Departure scheduling can be more sophisticated. For instance, if you know that the last afternoon at the show will offer light traffic, plan earlier flights for the morning group. Where the show takes place can influence team or shift makeup. In Las Vegas, for instance, there are more east-bound flights in the morning than afternoon. Eastbound staff members may have to stay over the extra night anyway. Those flying west will find far more flights out in the afternoon. You can schedule people with those thoughts in mind.

Local Show Schedules. A common mistake emerges when companies are exhibiting at home. There is a tendency to split the work equally among all in the office. For instance, assume there are 18 people there, and 3 are needed at one time at the booth. Team A works the first half day and leaves, never to return; Team B, the afternoon of that day, leaving never to return; and so on.

This is fundamentally flawed thinking. It takes time to get used to exhibiting, and at just about the moment people get into the groove, their one shift is over. We find that overall results are about half of what they should be with that approach.

A far better approach is to assign only six people, rotating shifts each day. The others can be encouraged to escort their own customers to the show and booth. At the next local event another group of six can become the booth team itself. Over time, everyone will have an opportunity at booth work.

Say Thank You

Many get so lost in doing the job that they forget that another show will come along just like it and that they will need the help and cooperation of others in the company again. Part of the coordination job is thanking those, both inside the company and outside, who have helped out. These activities can include the following:

- Thank-you notes, handwritten, to key participants

- A congratulatory dinner for the team
- Postshow results reports to all
- MVP award presentation and an article in the company newsletter
- A team gift, perhaps a T-shirt from the city to take home to the kids

What to Do with Your CEO

Except for very small companies, the president or CEO should not be part of the booth staff that searches out people to talk to or fields initial requests. Your VIP should serve in other special roles:

- This person should be introduced to a prospect after a lead is taken, to provide assurance that there is top-level interest in doing business with the prospect.
- Your VIP can be of great help in solving current customer complaints. If a particular problem has been generated by an overall company policy, at the very least the customer will know that the top-level person is aware of the situation.
- Meetings with VIP customers or press representatives can be organized in advance.
- There are large companies that try to organize top management feedback methods to provide a sense of what employees are thinking. An exhibit show can be of great value to a CEO in that it enables him or her to spend time with lower-level managers in an informal and unusual environment. Things are said that never surface in formal programs.

Large-company chief executives often elect to spend one day at a major show and then disappear. Sometimes they leave because they do not know what they can do to help. These folks can feel like a fifth wheel, just getting in the way. So feel free to suggest roles that are productive.

The Exhibit Manager's Role

First in and last out, plus plenty to do in advance and after the show. This chapter covers only the people part of the job. If you take the job seriously, especially the people-end of the function, your company will prosper.

18
Exhibit Floor Selling

"The person in the booth was so intent on product pushing that finally I had to say, 'You do not want to listen and learn about my needs or market. I am leaving.' I could not waste any more time, even though there might have been a fit. It hurt to be rude, but there was no other choice. I guess being pushy is necessary up to a point, but there is a limit."

Catherine Audi was inventory shopping for her Detroit area store[1] at the Chicago Gift Show. She was placing orders—spending money. The exhibitor who would not listen got not one thin dime and never will.

Do you think Audi's vision is vastly different than your customers' or prospects'? Think again. Your customers may not be hunting for inventory. In many industries the emphasis is more on lead giving and taking. In others the goal is information so that visitors will suggest or specify what you offer—medicines or travel destinations, for instance. However, there are great similarities in visitor outlook.

Catherine went on, "Meeting the pushy type was unusual. More often just the reverse happens. People do seem to listen. But there are times when I feel that what I say goes in one ear and out the other." Exhibit sellers should never bulldoze. However, there has to be good back-and-forth. Most of the time it must be encouraged by the exhibitor.

The Show-and-Tell Mistake

Most big-league exhibitors have seen all sorts of studies that signal why visitors attend. There are several reasons, but key among them is learning. "I want to see what's new." That seems to dovetail with an exhibitor's selfish motives, presenting the product and information.

However, this masks reality. Catherine Audi did not spend the money to fly to Chicago and spring for several hotel nights to learn what could be gleaned by reading a trade ad or catalog. She did need to see the products, but there is more involved that required two-way communication. That is true for most of your visitors as well.

There are some exceptions. For instance, the travel industry sponsors many events that bring agents together with hotels, resorts, and transportation company exhibitors. Less information is traded face to face than should be the case. Too much time is spent simply picking up literature for the file. (Agents must have bulging file cabinets.) The same is true at shows where manufacturers offer promotional products or advertising specialties to brokers. Having visited some of these events, we smile and wonder why nobody is exhibiting filing systems!

The Two-Way Street

Here are illustrations that signal the way the medium is supposed to work, one from a buyer viewpoint and one from a seller viewpoint.

Buyer Goals. Elsewhere in the book we mention the story of a supervising nurse from a large hospital in Jackson, Mississippi. It is worth summarizing here. She attended a medical equipment expo to winnow down a list of potential bidders for a large machine. Over a dozen companies produced them. They were all fairly similar and in the same, seven-figure price range.

She wanted to see the machines, of course. However, the big issues were service and training, plus an evaluation as to how well the manufacturers' people would get along with hospital personnel. That required two-way learning. One of the three companies she selected at the event sold its machine.

Seller Goals. We stick with the medical field. Seattle-based Practice Development, Inc. (PDI), wants to expand the sales of its expectant-mother educational program, provided by ob/gyn doctors to patients. An evaluation of competing programs signaled that the PDI offering was cost-effective only when sold to physician groups, not so for individual practitioners.

When it exhibited, PDI had to do more than show and tell. It had to learn which booth visitors were part of groups and the role each played in the group. When an appropriate group wanted more information later, PDI also had to learn the name of the group's supervising nurse or office manager. Once back in their offices, doctors are difficult to reach.

The Razzamatazz Approach

We saw an exhibitor attracting traffic with a basketball shooting contest. Another offered a baseball pitching game. A third, miniature golf. In all three cases things got out of hand. The games became something unto themselves. There was plenty of booth dialogue, but almost all of it centered on the contests.

There are, of course, exceptions. John Woolsey, from Mannington Mills, handled a putting game quite well. The miniature course was made with a variety of Mannington floor coverings. Visitors were escorted by representatives. They traded information as they played.

At another show an exhibitor offered fashion shows to build a crowd, including *Sports Illustrated* swim suit models. Again, very little business discussion. (These people did not sell swim suits or magazines.) And, frankly, we feel this bit of razzamatazz cost them dearly. Female exploitation does not sit well in the 1990s. What's more, half the buyers were women!

The Answer Center Approach

Another exhibitor at the same event where we saw the fashion show did far better. A sign said, "Produce plastic ID cards in-house on a laser printer." Visitors who were interested in this application stopped and learned how the system worked. The booth staff people, at the same time, learned a lot from these visitors.

Floor Performance Issues

This chapter is about training people to do a better job. It concludes with a training program you can do yourself (see Figure 18-5). However, for the training to be effective, you should have an understanding of underlying issues.

Psychological Implications

Though much of what is presented here is "how to," there are two academic issues that will signal *why* we present what we present. This is the first of them.

Booth selling is unique. Properly done, a great deal can be accomplished very quickly, a true need. Booth staff training to help people do the job well has been around a long time. It started with some really basic "housekeeping": dress, posture, badge on the right, and all that. Those things are still important, but training programs have become more sophisticated.

We began to notice, more and more, that those we trained did not accept what they were being taught. The people were hardworking back home and well educated. Many had masters degrees. Why did these people resist training that would help them?

A university psychology department[2] studied the issue and provided sensible answers.

Fear of Rejection.   Most people find meeting new people, without introduction, somewhat difficult. That is less a problem in business. We are used to business rejection—linger time in reception rooms, calls not returned, emergency reports unread, watching the boss take phone calls during a meeting.

Shows are different. Conventions are convivial. We see happy delegates wandering the aisles talking with each other. There are social events. What emerges is a subtle sense that any rejection is more personal. That is not true, of course, but the feeling is there.

New Interpersonal Roles in a Group.   We tend to behave in expected fashion, depending on where we are and what's going on. Your behavior with a boss or coworkers in the office is different than what is expected at a picnic or even at lunch. We are used to that and shift gears easily.

Even if you work at a booth three or four times a year, the experience is infrequent. A whole new set of ground rules has to be worked out among people who are working together. It is tougher to make the shift. The "office mouse" may want to be more outgoing at a show. The gregarious salesperson may hate the whole thing and want to hide behind the ferns. Who will you turn to if you have a problem? It may not be the boss.

When you see coworkers clustered together in the booth talking, especially on the first show day, they are telling each other office war stories or trading travel adventures. What's really happening is that they are trying to figure each other out. Each wants to know what to expect from the others in this unfamiliar environment. (One of the reasons booth teams meet privately before a show is to get through that stage before the opening bell.) Of all of the psychological factors, this one is the most important.

The Retail Expectation.   Show visitors go through their own changes, and this affects booth staff people. Business and professional people operate on pretty much the same wavelength when it comes to meetings, letters, phone calls, and such. The game changes on the show floor.

Delegates find themselves in what amounts to a high-quality shopping mall or department store. For them, too, this is an infrequent business experience. What happens is that there is a subtle shift in what visitors expect from booth staff people. The expectation is far closer to what one wants in a store than in an office or factory, or on the phone.

Ask yourself what you expect in a quality store. Do you like to see the store people clustered in the back, drinking coffee? Do you want to see merchandise splattered about, or a pile of papers helter-skelter on a counter? Do you like being ignored—or ganged up on? Do you want the salesperson to be overly friendly? Or cold?

Think about what you like, and aim yourself in that direction when you work at a booth. Interestingly, our staff training programs owe a debt to retailing. Several of the methods come from management and staff training given to personnel by high-quality stores.

Deepening Current Relationships. Ask managers why shows are important, and sooner rather than later they will say, "We want to meet with our customers." They mean it—people they know already.

In all life's aspects we prefer to strengthen current links, in contrast to starting new relationships. Sales managers talk about prospecting, and a booth is great for it. However, that is not as comfortable a task as meeting with an old and valued customer.

Combine this natural desire with that subtle fear of personal rejection and you face a pretty powerful influence that slows down booth effort.

The Self-Fulfilling Prophecy

What are our attitudes toward success or failure? Those who arrive at an event all excited about the chance to meet people and make progress will do just that. Others first think failure: "This is something to get through as painlessly as possible." They must be coached to take a more positive view. There are failure-first symptoms. Often, they can be seen in what people say:

- "Prospecting is okay, but our most important customers are those we have already."
- "I have to go back to the hotel. I left the spec sheets in my room, and we need them."
- "I can't ask my customers to come to the booth at a special time."
- "This 'no smoking' drives me nuts. I'm stepping outside for a few moments."

- "When the demonstration unit broke down, it killed the day."
- "I had to spend a lot of time with that person, but it solidified our relationship."
- "I'll be late arriving at the booth. A special client meeting came up."
- "I have to take a break. My feet are killing me."

There is nothing wrong with any of these statements. However, if you see a pattern, it can signal a lack of positive outlook. Some kidding back and forth can help inspire an attitude shift.

Psychographic Implications

This is our second and last academic intrusion. We touched on psychographics from a goal-setting and strategy viewpoint in Chapter 2. We summarize the subject here to help booth teams do a better job.

Booth staff folks probe for a number of answers: applications, time frames, budget, visitor buying influence, and more. Boil it down, and you end up with a "why buy from us" (or not) answer. Add learning what researchers and academics call *psychographics*.

This is the study of value systems as they apply to purchasing motives. Baylor University's Jeff Tanner[3] points out, "Business buying decisions are most often based on applications value, or ability to resell from inventory, or of value as part of a combined final product. However, selling *your* particular product can depend, in part, on understanding the buyer's corporate culture and value system."

Is the potential buyer defensive, with something to protect? Or is the buyer more the risk-taking type? Is the buyer self-satisfied or struggling? Is the company downsizing, striking fear in the hearts of managers? Or is it expanding, "on top?" Are its products for limo-riders or those who clip grocery coupons? Learn a bit about these things at the booth, and you can better position your products.

Simplification: security blanket or next step up? Here are some more specifics:

- Do you do it in small steps, a migration strategy, or as one big leap?
- Does postsale service matter? How much?
- Do features matter more than price? Or less?
- Does the customer want to buy in small lots, at higher unit cost, or large lots for less?
- Does the customer want to bargain more than normal, or less?

- To what extent are committees involved with purchasing decisions? More or less than you are used to?
- To what extent does the booth visitor try to impress you with what he or she is doing today?
- How much "hand-holding" will be needed to service the account?

The answers to these questions will be logical in themselves. Taken as a collective, they also flag a corporate value system and culture. Compare it to your own culture. If there is a match, regardless of the relative sizes of the two companies, there is likely to be a greater potential that you can work together. (In the USA size seems to matter less. Overseas, company sizes can come into play as part of value systems and culture. Corporate elephants like to do business with each other, regardless of extra cost at times: smaller companies with each other.)

Psychographic is a fancy term. Fancy terms are often created by those trying to sell an idea that is tough to explain in simple words. (Their creators may be defensive, protective.) However, some "have more legs" than others. This one has merit and will stick with us, help us grow.

Professor Tanner points out that you have to read between the lines but you can also ask some direct questions at some place in the discussion:

- "What is your company like to work for?"
- "What does your company value more than anything else?"
- "Where do you see the company headed?"

Tanner says, "Do the answers reflect an aggressive or protective philosophy?" The answers will provide clues on what to do or not to do, or whether to do anything at all. A thoughtful evaluation? You bet! Exhibiting is not rocket science, but...

Before the Show

Planning for performance is half the battle. A good advance plan almost always produces better staff performance.

Mission and Goals

Clarity is critical. If your mission and goals are clear, and doable, the staff responds. We covered that process in detail in Chapter 5. In summary, avoid wishy-washy statements. Don't be vague. The more specific you are, the easier it is for the staff to understand what is expected.

Advance Staff Information

We've hinted at staff advisory kits elsewhere. A complete kit prepares the staff with specifics. It also signals serious purpose. Figure 18-1 is a list of potential items to include.

Developing this kind of staff advisory binder sounds like a lot of work. It is the first time around. However, your format can be set up

---

Staff Advisory Kit Contents

- Cover letter from a company VIP who welcomes participation and cites importance
- Statement of mission and goals
- Information about the show: Audience breakdown, other exhibitors, and education program
- Map of the show floor showing booth space
- Product information including brochures to be available
- Overall activity schedule: Training, special events, booth
- Booth work schedule: Times and assignments
- Hotel information including name list and check-in, check-out dates
- Dress suggestions: Booth, evening, social events
- Weather summary for the city
- Reminder lists: Business cards (lots), stationery, and stamps
- Local transport: Airport, around town
- City restaurant and entertainment guide
- Registration information: When and where to pick up badge and show packet*
- Comments sheet to fill out after the event: Booth, show

*If you arrive early, pick up credentials for everyone. Have the hotel hold the papers and give them to people at check-in.

Figure 18-1. Advance advisory packages help booth staff people do a better job and signal serious purpose.

as a computer file. A standard binder with tabs can be specified. From then on it becomes a matter of filling in the blanks and getting appropriate printed matter for insertion.

A number of exhibit managers have adopted the approach. Mary Jo Mendel, from Nielsen Market Research, says, "It turns out to be easy, especially if you have an in-house printing department—and not too tough even if you have to use the local quick-printing shop."

Floor Performance Training: The Core

A short program was presented in Chapter 3. It includes things like a hints list you can reproduce for your own program. Here we embellish, expand, and add information plus exercises.

Staff Qualifications

Exhibit managers we have worked with express concerns. "My staff members are not pro salespeople." "The people who work at our booths have territories and don't care about much else."

It is easier for non-sales professionals to learn booth contact than it is for the pros. Engineers, technical, financial, and marketing trained people start with a blank canvas. They learn easily and do well, especially after they understand that exhibit selling is not confrontational.

The sales professionals, though, have to do some unlearning because the methods are different. They also need more encouragement so they can work better as a team. Booth contact work must be unselfish. "I'll help you, and you'll help me." There are ways to achieve that.

Information Exchange

This is a how-to for developing and managing a dialogue presentation in a short time period.

Some delegates walk into booths with question list in hand! Others are less specific. A good number do not know they want to talk with you until they see your booth and you introduce yourself. In all cases learning must be two-way and must be encouraged by you.

Some companies provide employees with presentation skills training, often with videotapes so participants can track their progress. They tend to focus most of their attention on the outbound communication. They are less strong on encouraging and managing the inbound. This program provides more attention to that.

Contact Breakdown

Each contact has three parts: introduction and evaluation, presentation; and "What's next?"—the conclusion.

Introduction and Evaluation.   We cover this from the viewpoint of what you do to start the conversation. Visitors who barge right in, questions in hand, are a different kettle of fish. As you go through this instruction, you will see where these folks join in:

- *Search.* Stand alone near the booth edge, observing traffic. Visitors are identified by color codes on their badges. You are looking for the color worn by delegates, buyers. Here comes one!
- *Identify interest.* Keep your eyes moving, but check to see if your badge wearer glances at your booth once, and then twice. (Some will stride right by, eyes front.) Do not try to stare down the aisle walker, forcing eye contact. That is uncomfortable for both of you.
- *Greet.* Step out and introduce yourself to the person who has glanced, more than once. Start with a question. "I see you noticed our booth. What is it that attracted your attention?"
- *Evaluate.* After the icebreaker, ask a few more questions to help the visitor start talking. (People like to do that.) A sampler of questions follows:
    - "What's your main goal at this year's show?"
    - "Which seminars are you attending?"
    - "How is the show so far?"
    - "What's your responsibility, back at the company?"
    - "How long have you been there?"
    - "How many folks from your company are at the show this year?"
    - "What are you shopping for this year?"

There will be some byplay along the way, but by asking these types of questions, you will be able to make a judgment in short order as to whether or not to continue. If not, shake hands and say good-bye. "It was pleasant meeting you. Have a good show."

All these questions are open-ended. None can be answered with a simple yes or no. The idea is to encourage visitors to talk about themselves and what they are doing. The other idea is for you to listen. That is not as easy as it seems. Most of us spend more time thinking up what we are going to say next than truly listening to what we are being told.

It has taken you far longer to read this than it takes to do it. Figure on about one minute or perhaps a bit more—often less if there is no potential.

Two-Way Presentation. It makes sense to continue! That happens about half the time. Invite your visitor into the booth, even if it is just a step or two, so "I can show you some things that might be of interest."

Note: It is at this stage we catch up with that visitor barging in, question list in hand. Slow things down a little. Ask a few of the questions from the list above. Learn a little before plunging ahead. You must manage the contact, not the visitor. When people ask, they often anticipate. Ask the wrong question, get a wrong answer. Probe and you will know.

- *Your summary.* You know far too much about your products, the features, prices, services, and all the rest. There is a terrible tendency to ramble on at length. That is because you enjoy telling!

Note: This is the one place where technical experts have to back off. Ask one question, and the poor visitor is off on a 28-minute voyage of information delivery. An observer can see the glazed eyes betraying what's being thought. "This is more than I ever wanted to know about the Phase III Kolactoskammer. Please just tell me what it does for me."

- *Buyer summary.* You know your product, but buyers have strengths as well. They know more about how your product might work for them, which could differ from your vision.

Note: Every so often you will meet a visitor there to show off. You get an earful of what they are doing now and how wonderful! Worse yet, some start telling you about your own product. Back off. They are not buyers. Exhibit contacts are not wrestling matches. In addition, booths are not the place for graduate students writing their next papers.

- *The Method.* At each step in your presentation you should insert a question that involves the visitor. The answers will signal interests and guide you on how to adjust. (This is where some "presentation skills" training can be weaker. It is easy to get on a roll and do a great job. What happens when the audience wants to toss you off the track?)

You will have to write your own questions in advance. A later section entitled "The Learning Program," includes a work process for doing this. To help when you get to that, here are some generic questions that can be folded in with your presentation:

- "Why are you looking for another approach?"
- "What is your long-term goal on this?"

- "How are you handling this now?"
- "Who has been supplying you up to now?"
- "What's most important from the viewpoint of your customers?"
- "What kind of a Stock Keeping Unit profit ratio are you looking for?"
- "How do you see your company position on this issue?"
- "Who else at your company should we be talking to?"
- "When do you want to get going on this?"
- "How much do you anticipate spending on what we are talking about?"

Again, these are all open-ended questions. No yes or no answers. While you are presenting your product or service, teaching, you are also learning a great deal.

There are questions to avoid. The most important no-no goes something like, "What will it take for you to buy from us?" Even if asked with a grin, a booth visitor with spine might reply, "Based on that question, you will never know." Avoid confrontation unless you are willing to face very fast rejection.

- *Listening.* You will gather all kinds of information following this approach. Do not hesitate to make notes along the way. If your visitor is at all serious, he or she will appreciate your taking notes. (If not, it signals less potential.) Added to good listening and note taking on specifics, be sensitive to answers that provide psychographic clues about company values and culture. Here are answer illustrations and what they might mean:
  - "We've been working with the same supplier for years, but we are always open." It will be a tough battle. The company is protective, somewhat defensive.
  - "We're doing fine, but we have lost some market share." The company is in a bit of a struggle, and there may be a chance for you, but be prepared to join the battle.
  - "There are 10 on our purchasing committee." The company is bureaucratic, and your contact does not chair the purchasing committee.
  - "The market keeps changing, and we need to stay ahead of it." This company is more of a risk taker and probably cares more about features than lowest cost.
  - "What do we do if our initial order does not work out?" They bargain a lot and will need quite a bit of hand-holding.
  - "We've been working on this but must make a decision this

year." The value system is such that they wait until the last possible moment—perhaps a dictatorial top management.

- "Things have been go-go. We have to move fast." You will have to be able to respond very quickly, complete with late-night phone calls.

You get the idea. Make up your mind. Evaluate the company culture, match it with yours. If there is a fit, go for it. If not, pause to see if you can work with their company culture.

"What's Next?"—the Conclusion. There are only three ways out of a booth contact. *First:* You can't help at all. These are the short contacts at the aisle edge, plus those that might have produced something of mutual value but don't work out. *Second:* There is a reason to stay in contact but no immediate business. These are people to be added to your mailing list. *Third:* There is near term business likely, and booth dialogue must be followed up by subsequent contacts—personal, phone, and mail.

Your booth responsibility is to sort out which is what. A few visitors will ask for what they want next. Most will not. That is your job.

- *The next step.* What is your next step? After only about five minutes into the contact, you should probe to see if that is possible. Use a leading question, one that does require a yes or no response. For instance:
- "Is this something we should be talking about after the show at your office?"
- "Are we aiming at something that is of interest to you?"

The answer will be accompanied by a reason or an indication of relative enthusiasm. In some cases it might lead you to stop and fill out a lead form with the visitor while talk continues. Then a polite thank you and good-bye. Resist the temptation to continue. There is only so much you can do during an initial booth contact. Leave well enough alone unless you can gather more information that would be important later.

In other cases the visitor will surface an objection or question that has not been discussed before, and it will provide a new direction for the meeting.

How to Develop and Manage Dialogue

Our mental computers leap ahead faster than we can talk or listen. As our minds race ahead, we can make wrong assumptions. Going

Dialogue Development Work Form

- *Step 1: What to learn.* What are your fact needs? Write down what is important to you. Just a few words for each will do.

- *Step 2: Open-ended questions.* For each fact need write an open-ended question. These always include one of the following words: *who, what, when, where, how.*

- *Step 3: Features.* Write down product features, just a couple of words for each.

- *Step 4: Open-ended questions; features to applications.* For each feature write (or select) an open-ended question that starts with a simple explanation. "We provide XYZ with the program; what are you doing about that now?"

- *Step 5: Question ranking.* Select the questions you want to use in the introductory and preliminary evaluation phases of your contact. Next, run through your applications or feature presentation, and slide in the question you want to use in conclusion for each.

- *Step 6: Role-play.* Most of us are not particularly fond of role-playing exercises. Yet, at least in this case it is very important. If you don't practice, you will find you don't use the process at the booth.

  Note: Groups of three work well. Rotate roles—customer, representative, and observer. When it is your turn to play the customer, take a moment to figure out what situation you will present to the representative.

Figure 18-2. This form guides training to develop booth dialogue. For instruction on its use, see Chapter 18, the section called "How to Develop and Manage Dialogue: The Learning Program."

.through the contact process outlined above requires a disciplined approach. It is not as easy to do as it appears.

The Learning Program.   In order to manage a contact, you simply must work things out in advance. Figure 18-2 is a work form to follow in doing that. There are six parts, summarized here. This is a good group exercise.

- *Step 1: What to learn.* What are your fact needs? Write down what is important to you. Just a few words for each will do.

- *Step 2: Open-ended questions.* For each fact need, write an open-ended question. These always include one of the following words: *who, what, when, where,* or *how.*

  Note: Some readers may say, "I don't need that." Yes, you do. At training meeting after meeting, we have watched very smart people backslide into leading questions. We wake them up by answering, "No," followed by silence.

- *Step 3: Features.* Write down product features, just a couple of words for each.

  Note: The purpose of step 3 is to isolate essentials from a more detailed approach. That will help you shorten explanations.

- *Step 4: Open-ended questions; features to applications.* For each feature write (or select) an open-ended question that starts with a simple explanation. "We provide XYZ with the program; what are you doing about that now?"

- *Step 5: Question ranking.* Select the questions you want to use in the introductory and preliminary evaluation phases of your contact. Next, run through your applications or feature presentation, and slide in the question you want to use in conclusion for each.

- *Step 6: Role-play.* Most of us are not particularly fond of role-playing exercises. Yet, at least in this case, they are very important. If you don't practice, you will find you don't use the process at the booth.

  Note: Groups of three work well. Rotate roles—customer, representative, and observer. When it is your turn to play the customer, take a moment to figure out what situation you will present to the representative.

Dressing for the Booth

People are the most important part of exhibiting. The back-and-forth communication is critical. However, visual appearance counts in that connection. Every booth staff person is, at the same time, a walking advertisement for the company. Here are some dress guidelines.

Standard Business Dress.   The safest approach is to wear the standard business dress that is appropriate for the industry, region, and venue. Bankers have one standard. Golf course superintendents have another. A formal meeting at an in-town hotel presents one situation. A meeting held at a resort is another.

In any situation in which delegates dress down from the formal suite level, you should try to dress up one notch. If visitors are dressing in fancy casual clothes, a somewhat more formal skirt or slacks approach makes sense. By overdressing one notch, you signal respect for customers and convey a professional appearance.

There are exceptions. We were presenting a seminar in Tel Aviv during the summer. The summer dress code for business people and government officials during that time of year is open shirt and slacks or simple skirt. As a person from another country, it would be presumptuous to emulate that dress code. The USA Commercial Attaché advised wearing the standard business dress that we would use at home. We were told that we would be invited to take off our jackets and remove our ties. That happened, but the signal of respect had been given first.

A note about briefcases. Avoid lugging these leather security blankets to the booth. A smaller portfolio should suffice. Women should try to bring small pocketbooks. Storage space is always limited, and luggage clutter is quite unattractive.

Booth Uniforms.   There are times when booth staff people resist the idea of wearing a uniform. However, more and more companies are doing it, and there is general acceptance by visitors, except at the most formal events.

An approach that works even at formal events is to provide each staff member with a tie or scarf in the same color. An alternate is providing a lapel flower each day.

- *Applications selling.* IBM was demonstrating grocery chain applications at a large food show. The show is a coat-and-tie event. However, booth staff people removed their jackets and wore old-fashioned appearing grocery aprons. The look was excellent.

- *Metaphor selling.* Our small firm's name, Sextant Communications, is a nautical metaphor for guidance. We wear boat shoes, slacks, polo shirts, and cotton sweaters in the company color.

Body Language

Many books and articles have been written on the importance of body language. It's important.

Observing Visitors.   What body language signals are being sent? What do they mean? What do we do about them?

- Does the visitor appear intense, perhaps walking with small, quick steps? Or does that person walk more slowly, looking more relaxed? Try to mirror what you see during the contact.

- When your visitor glances at a watch during discussion, it may signal limited time or that what is under discussion is of limited importance. Ask.

- If a visitor moves to the side to allow another group member to see better, it may signal that you have not been as inclusive as you should have been.

Your Own Body Language Appearance.   You send signals as well. Here are some illustrations.

- You stand with hands folded across your chest. That signals a defensive or challenging attitude.
- You are standing with hands clasped behind, at military parade rest. You are castle guarding.
- You stand with hands in your pockets. It signifies a don't-care outlook.

The best message is sent if you stand with your hands hanging at your sides, feet about 12 inches apart. The signal is ready-to-help with a slight degree of vulnerability, a good thing. Many find it difficult to simply let their hands hang down for an extended time. Those people could clasp their hands together in front.

Contact Control Body Language.   We have already said that you should not stare to make eye contact. Visitors think of that as intrusive, too intense. Glance back and forth. Here are some more hints:

- When you invite someone into the booth, take the lead by turning and starting to walk.
- Stand beside your visitor during conversation without a counter between you. More friendly.
- Signal the end of a demonstration by standing up straight and turning to face your visitor.
- When talking to two or three people, you will address one, but use eye contacts to make sure others feel they are involved. That signals inclusiveness.
- When you accept a business card from a visitor, take a brief moment and read it. That practice is standard procedure in other parts of the world and should be adopted in the USA. It sends a signal that you care.

Voice and Language Management

The next time you enter a busy trade hall, take a moment, stand still, and just listen. Even close your eyes. You will realize that these are very noisy places, as much as a factory floor.

The hubbub is the underlying reason that experienced booth staff people wear their name badges up high on the right. Visitors can see your name as you speak it during a hand-shaking introduction. When we shake hands, we almost always angle our upper bodies to a degree. A name badge on the left side faces away.

One of the more annoying practices we see are people who wear name badges on a necklace or attached to a belt around the waist. It is embarrassing to try to read them. Badge holders, these days, are designed so they can be attached without piercing fabrics.

The difficulties caused by the high ambient sound level are exacerbated because many people do not hear well. About 1 person in 10 suffers some degree of hearing loss, though most of them do not know it. We suspect the percentage is somewhat higher among younger people who grew up listening to music played very loud—the "boom box" generation.

Added to all this is that people want to be polite. It is rare that anyone says, "I didn't hear you." Instead, some inconsequential response is delivered. We rumble on, not knowing that something important may have been missed.

We focus extra attention on this subject because research over the years, much of it done by Exhibit Surveys, Incorporated, tells us that visitor recall of information is more dependent on what they hear than on any other thing; demonstration, booth signs, or printed matter.

Is there anything we can do other than asking people to speak louder, slower, and more distinctly? Yes there is. We can help them learn how to do it.

Speaking with a Round Mouth.   We grow up speaking with a flat mouth, lips pretty close together except when shouting. That produces a fairly "thin" sound with something of a nasal quality. In addition, most of us also learn to say things as fast as a machine gun spits bullets. There is another way and it is very easy to learn, very easy to get used to.

Performers—actors, actresses, singers, speakers, and TV and radio news people—speak with what is called a *round mouth*. For the most part this is not natural but instead is taught at the early stages in acting or speaking courses. Trial lawyers and professional presenters have also learned the method. There are several approaches to learning.

We offer one that is quite simple. Figure 18-3*a* is a short voice exercise. It works well as part of a group training program. More important, if you practice it for three days in the shower, it will become instinctive. There are four results:

Voice Exercises

Voice Management. The objective is to make each word easier to hear: to produce a somewhat slower speech rate, to project better without increasing volume, and to slightly deepen your voice register.

Ground Rule. Think of your mouth as a megaphone, with the small end your lips and the open end at the back. Purse lips slightly, open up the back and top inside. Feel it. Performers call this a "round mouth."

Practice speaking with a round mouth:

1. Recite the alphabet normally.
2. Recite the alphabet with a round mouth. Be radical. Sound funny.
3. Create a short sentence. Say it normally and then with round mouth. Be radical. Sound funny.
4. Recite alphabet again with a round mouth. Not radical. Sound normal.
5. Recite sentence again with a round mouth. Not radical. Sound normal.

Do one set morning and night for three days. Don't be self-conscious. You don't look different. Just "think megaphone," and it will happen by itself.

Figure 18-3a. These voice exercises can become part of your staff training program.

1. You will automatically slow down a bit.
2. You will pronounce each word more distinctly.
3. Your voice register will deepen slightly.
4. You will project better without raising your voice level.

- *Think megaphone.* When you read the exercise, you will see that its goal is for you to think of your mouth as a megaphone, with the small end your lips and the open end at the back of your mouth cavity. You will learn to purse your lips slightly when speaking.

Some worry that they may look strange doing this. That is not so. Turn on the evening news. Do the TV reporters look strange? They all use the method, one way or another. We found as an added plus after doing the exercise ourselves, that we gradually adopted the round

mouth approach for normal conversation as well as at booths or during speeches. It works there too.

Language Management.   We dwell less on this but do want to issue
a warning or two.

- *Use plain words.* Every industry has its own language. There are
  terms and acronyms. We assume that everybody in the business
  knows them. We assume that their meaning is universally understood by all in the same way. A term that floats up and down the
  halls at your company means the same thing at other companies in
  your industry.

  That is not always the case. An "SKU" to you may not mean the
  same thing as an "SKU" to somebody else. The booth is not a place for
  industry or company shorthand. A major problem is that your visitor
  will do one of two things. One is to assume that how you define the
  term is exactly as they define the term. The second is that the visitor
  does not want to indicate his or her lack of understanding. "Is this
  something I'm supposed to know but don't?"
  There are also phrases that "everyone knows." What does "Catch-
  22" mean to you? Does it convey the same meaning to everyone else?
  Maybe so, maybe not. Sports idioms are the same.

- *Stick to business.* Don't let conversations drift off to subjects that are
  not appropriate. Public issues, politics, and religion can lead to big
  trouble, fast.

Physical Warm-Up

Every so often we see booth teams going through light exercise as a
group before the show day starts. "What is this, some form of Japanese
management?" Yes, but mainly it comes from the methods used everywhere to help performers perform better.

Athletes, dancers—all performers warm-up before they "go on."
Warm-ups depend on what will be needed to do a good job. Athletes
and dancers stretch and warm muscles up to the point of starting to
perspire. Others warm up simply to increase blood flow to the brain,
making it easier to react quickly to input from others during performance—other actors or actresses, the audience, whatever. The exercise
program offered here is of the second type. It is Figure 18-3*b*.

You can do this as a group or alone. It is perfectly appropriate in a
hotel hall or public bathroom. Those observing seem to know exactly
what you are doing and why.

Physical Exercises

Physical Warm-up before Going on and at Breaks. The objective is to increase blood flow to the brain, to make you sharper. This concept is employed by professionals on stage or TV, and athletes, before "going on."

1. Side stretches: A set of 10, alternating 5 on each side.
2. Arm swings: A set of 10, alternating 5 on each side.
3. Wall leans: A set of 5. Start by leaning, beyond balance point, arms stretched out. Bend elbows and straighten. (Better than a wall, do this exercise with a team member, hands clasped and leaning on each other.)
4. Midcalf touches (like touching toes, but not so far down): A set of 10.
5. Repeat arm swings: A set of 6, alternating 3 on each side.

For foot comfort and blood flow: Every 10 minutes during the show, if standing, wiggle toes, a set of 10, alternating 5 on a side. Make a conscious effort to walk a few steps every 5 minutes. The objective is to reduce blood pooling in the feet. Don't wait until your feet start hurting to start. Do it from the beginning.

Figure 18-3b. These physical exercises can become part of your staff training program.

Personal Well-Being

Two-end candle burning is traditional. Breakfast meeting—morning seminars—afternoon on the show floor—reception—dinner—late-evening confab; and it all starts again the next day. The only way to stay alert with that kind of schedule is to eat lightly (except for breakfast), get good sleep, and stay away from indulgences. A quick swim in the hotel pool, a morning run, or a few moments in the health club can help a lot, too. Here are some hints.

- Be late for cocktails. Don't "join the gang" right away. Take an extra 45 minutes for a fast swim or workout. The gang will be there.
- Go to bed early. Leave that gang after dinner during the confab. We have gone so far as to "go to the restroom" and never return—saying the next day that we met someone in the corridor.
- Restrict evening client meetings to dinner. Avoid after-dinner entertainments.

The goal is to be alert at the end of each day, right through the final hours on the last day. Time after time we hear about that most serious lead that arrives right at the end. The visitor has been shopping all week. Now is decision time for that person.

Foot Care.   Everyone complains about aching feet. Days of walking on concrete thinly masked by industrial carpet will produce that feeling. We talked to three podiatrists about the problem. Here is what they offer:

- *Dr. Thomas Fatone.*[4] He makes two points. First is that Native Americans walked our forests and meadows with no more on their feet than leather moccasins. There were no foot problems. These emerged only after we created hard-surface streets, from cobblestones on. Second is that we spend large amounts of energy dealing with low-level pain, reducing our effectiveness.

- *Dr. M. David Price.*[5] Dr. Price offers some practical advice:
  - Anticipate. Don't wait for pain.
  - Use a good foot cream and powder every day.
  - Back in the hotel use a foot soak before going out for the evening.
  - Wear older, more comfortable shoes.
  - New shoes? Buy breathing leather such as calf. Leave a $\frac{1}{8}$-inch space above the big toe. Leather bottoms, rubber heels. Rubber soles "stick" too much. You want to slide.
  - A 1-inch heel is plenty. Stay away from higher heels.

  Dr. Price also suggests a preventive exercise to be done on the show floor. It is at the bottom of the exercise program presented in Figure 18-3.

- *Dr. Eugene J. Carr, Jr.*[6] Dr. Carr points out that there are now well-advertised dress shoe brands on the market that convey a professional appearance and are healthy to wear. He also suggests wearing a sport walking shoe to the hall and carrying dress shoes to change into when the bell rings.

We asked all three doctors about the use of support hose. The answer was a ringing "No, not without your doctor's okay." There can be heart problems that argue against that approach.

Team Signals

Work together and you can correct contact problems quickly and easily.

- *Complaints.* Every so often a visitor arrives with a complaint. The rule: Move that person out into the aisle to discuss the problem.

Don't hold forth in the booth with others listening. However, there are times when the complainer is rooted to the spot and won't move. In that case call over and introduce another staff member who is an "expert." However, work out a verbal signal in advance. Here is an illustration. Most of the time we introduce people using first and last names. In this case make the introduction using last names only. "Mr. Jones, I'd like you to meet Mr. Smith." Jones knows that Smith has a complaint, that he is the "expert," and that his job is to move the customer out to the aisle and take good notes on why the complaint came up.

- *Clingers.* Sometimes lead givers are so happy they don't want to leave. There are other times when a student just won't let go. In that case use a subtle body language signal to get help. For instance, pulling on an ear lobe during conversation. Another team member, spotting the signal, breaks in to say, "Pardon me, Jane, but you have a call on the booth phone." Thank your team member, saying, "Tell them I'll be right there, we are just saying good-bye."

Working with Outside Talent

Chapter 15 includes booth shows presented by outsiders. One of the key points is that these shows too often are considered something apart from the rest of what is happening.

Include entertainers in your booth staff training. Make them part of the team. There are several advantages:

- Team members can help build a show audience by being the start-up audience.

- Postshow introductions from the entertainer to a booth member can be worked out.

- Entertainers can be given a list of VIPs to memorize. When they spot one, they will escort the VIP over to meet a booth staff person.

Lead Forms

An exhibit's currency is paper—orders or lead forms. They are quite valuable assets. We focus on discussing leads because orders are more self-explanatory.

Exhibitors gather names in several ways, from the ridiculous to the sublime. The ridiculous is what we call "cards in a fishbowl." You get names, people who attended the event. Why did they stop at your booth? What is their product interest? Are they serious buyers? It's cheaper to buy a mailing list. The sublime is a neatly written lead card packed with information, complete with why the lead was taken.

Automated Registration Systems.   These started with credit card–type registration systems. The visitor's plastic name card impression was registered on a form in a machine rented from the company. Now we can swipe or insert those cards in slots, and paper printouts are prepared. (After the show is over, you can even buy a disk with all of the names trapped in computer-readable form.)

The newer approach is far better, but we do have some concerns that must be expressed:

- *Poor input.* Accuracy is an issue. That is not always the fault of the registration company. However, here are the places where errors emerge:
  - Many larger companies send several delegates. However, the registration forms are prepared in one place. Often those typists use a corporate address and phone number. Your lead may be from the San Francisco office, but the address and phone on the registration: Boston!
  - Software writers tend to restrict space to what can appear on the plastic card. That is not always the case, but information is often edited. For instance, if the title is too long to fit in a prescribed computer space, reduce it.
  - Many visitors have badges made at the show, after waiting in line. Rare is the visitor who asks for a correction whenever there is a typing error. Spending extra time in the lobby is not what anybody wants.
- *Form space.* The printed forms produced are not spacious. There will be demographic information printed out, and some programs allow exhibitors to customize what they want to see. The small size presents two problems, even if product interest check blocks are included:
  - Outside of an accurate address and phone number, perhaps the most important section of a lead form is "remarks." That is where the booth staff member should write why the lead was taken as well as any other subtleties of importance.
  - Handwriting is a problem. Lead notes are written standing up, often in the midst of the hubbub on a counter top. "Scrunch" writing is needed because the forms are small. Those notes can become a puzzle later.

- *Data use.* The newer systems trap information in registration company computers. Though these outfits and show managers are honorable, one wonders. For what other use can your lead list be used? Think about it.

New Options. Interestingly, new automated systems are emerging that can be employed by exhibitors alone. As of this writing, computer scanners are coming down in price and becoming more sophisticated. There are even small machines that read business cards.

There is a lot to be done before these systems become practical for exhibitors, in addition to cost reduction. We asked Edward Jones, from Executive Education & Management in Atlanta, about programs that read handwriting. He said, "There are several years ahead of us before they are really practical on a show floor. Today, you must write neatly, and each user's handwriting must be programmed individually into the software."

The Old-Fashioned Lead Card. We love it. Staple a business card to the top and you have an accurate name, title, address, and phone number. There is room for "check blocks" that can include demographics and product interest information. There is room for a good-sized "remarks" area. The lead taker has room to add his or her name and phone number for more input.

A sample lead form is included as Figure 18-4 that you can revise for your company. Based on that form, here are some hints on sheet design and use:

- Make it big, not an envelope-size card that fits in a jacket pocket. Provide double-spaced lines for writing in information that is not checked off.

- Provide a clipboard for writing. That is another aid in making sure handwriting is readable.

- Don't hurry when filling out a lead. Observers will know that you will give them the same concern when it is their turn. (Often a lead giver will help. We have had several ask to write out the lead themselves to assure we got everything!)

- Review leads at the day's end. Clean up your notes.

Thank-You Notes

Some leads require special attention. Some companies make phone calls from the show to those who will follow up on hot leads. A few

---

Lead Form Prototype

Information/Consultation Request

Name: _____

Title: _____

Address: _____

Phone and fax: _____

Show name: _____

Product interests

_____Product name   _____Product name   _____Product name
_____Product name   _____Product name   _____Product name

Other _____

Remarks _____

_____

_____

_____

Lead taker_____ Phone_____ Date_____

Figure 18-4. Allow plenty of room for clear writing or printing.

have worked out compensation splits between lead takers and those who follow up. For everyone, there is value in sending a handwritten note from the lead taker at the event that will be in the prospects in-box upon return. It says, "We care." The note does not have to be long. For instance:

> *Thanks for visiting with us at the booth today. We look forward to working with you. We will be in touch shortly, but I've enclosed another copy of my card if you want to call me even sooner. Again, thank you for today's meeting.*

**Prototype Staff Training
Program Outline**

Booth Contact: How to Do It

A.   Exhibit fit in communications
     1. Ads are one-way—exhibits are venue for two-way.

B.   Performance at the show
     1. Focus less on story.
     2. Focus more on what you can learn.
     3. Trap information for later.

C.   Psychological barriers to overcome
     1. Feelings of personal rejection
     2. New interpersonal relationships
     3. Subtle "retail" expectations emerge in visitors
     4. Natural tendency to focus on those we know already

D.   Symptoms to look for
     1. Avoiding the exhibit
     2. Avoiding the goals
     3. Avoiding the use of training

E.   The basics of floor selling
     1. Maintain professionalism.
     2. Respond to retail expectations.
     3. Be polite but control the contact.
     4. Use dialogue selling and qualification techniques.
     5. Write down results clearly and quickly.

F.   Dialogue selling essentials
     1. One-minute prequalification.
     2. Back-and-forth sales presentation.
     3. Use open-ended questions except at close.

G.   Open-ended dialogue questions and answers
     1. What to learn: a list of facts.
     2. Now write an open-ended question for each fact need.
     3. Rank list, and use top 2 or 3 in prequalification minute.
     4. Write benefit feature summary.
     5. Use with other questions.
     6. Close with a yes/no question.

Figure 18-5. You can add or subtract subjects from those covered in Chapter 18. Substance content is presented for each. A basic hints list appears with Chapter 3. We have used modifications of this type of program in recent years. It works.

H.   Body language issues and answers
1. Posture—ready and professional.
2. Mirror visual attitude of visitor.
3. Watch for signals during contact.
4. Use body language to help control the contact.

I.   Voice management issues and answers
1. Expo halls are relatively noisy.
2. One in 10 suffers hearing problems.
3. What's heard is what's remembered.
4. People don't say, "what?"
5. Wear badge high on right.
6. Speak more slowly, distinctly.
7. Avoid phrases with double meanings.
8. Speak with a round mouth. Practice.

J.   Team selling methods
1. Introducing an expert
2. Using the boss
3. Employing "point" people to prequalify and pass along

K.   Team problem solving
1. Verbal "takeover" signals
2. Body language "help" request

L.   Leads and orders issues and answers
1. Write twice, initial and clean.
2. Split leads, follow-up/info only.
3. Get business card or print phone number.
4. "Remarks" very important: Why the lead.
5. Goal: trap information for later.

XYZ. Personal well-being
1. Good rest
2. Foot comfort
3. Warm-up exercise

Figure 18-5. (*Continued*) You can add or subtract subjects from those covered in Chapter 18. Substance content is presented for each. A basic hints list appears with Chapter 3. We have used modifications of this type of program in recent years. It works.

19
Postshow
Pandemonium

Chapter 8 started with the story of the lonely booth, casting shadows under a security lamp on an empty convention hall floor the night after the show had closed. Because of pass-along responsibility, nobody remembered to make arrangements for teardown and shipping. The most important part of that story was that even the sales leads and orders had been left behind, scattered about. Chapter 8 was about processing paper, the currency of exhibit success.

We refer to that here because people do not read books like this one cover to cover. However, in this chapter we take a closer look at logistic management issues, that is, what you must do to get the physical property, the booth, taken care of properly.

Dismantling and Shipping

When the public address announcement closes the show, it will be less than one minute before labor teams emerge from behind the floor-edge drapes. Last on, first off is the rule. Aisle carpet is rolled up and placed on forklift trucks and moved out. At the same time electricians are moving through the hall, disconnecting electrical systems and packing up what the hall supplied. The plant people emerge to pick up their rented floral contributions. So do the audiovisual people and others. Labor teams arrive at booths to start taking down. The forklift drivers, after dropping off their carpet loads, start picking up and delivering empty crates back to exhibit spaces for packing. This is the same chaos one sees before an event, but in reverse. It takes less time than setup.

Exhibit Manager Roles

There are a number of jobs that should be done or supervised, and some hints along the way.

- *Orders in Advance.* To avoid joining ranks with our lonely exhibit sentinel, *somebody* has to show up at the decorating company's service desk during the show and fill out takedown orders! You do not have to worry about rentals; plants, audiovisual, electrical, furniture, or whatever. They will be Johnny-on-the-spot to collect what is theirs. The issue is what belongs to you.

- *Dismantle operations.* You or a professional supervisor has to be at the booth to guide. Except for the very smallest booths, display parts are packed in special places inside each crate. The setup drawing is used in reverse!

  Note: You will remember that during setup a plastic sheet was placed over the carpet to help keep it clean during assembly. At the end it was cut away from standing units. If you own your own carpet and pad, have a plastic sheet spread before take-down. It saves money later.

  Damage notes must also be taken during dismantling. There will always be little nicks and scratches that emerge during a show. They must be touched up or repaired before the next event. Take thorough notes to save time and money later, rather than making an overall review in the exhibit house. An advantage to making notes before shipping is that you have a record of the physical condition of the booth before it was loaded onto a truck and transported.

- *Outbound transport.* You must fill out transport instructions as well, and make very sure that your freight supplier's shipping labels have been placed on outbound crates. We will not embarrass anyone by naming names, but one freight company forgot to do that *for its own exhibit* at a show where it was selling itself! (A shoemaker's child problem.) The freight outfit exhibit supervisor left the booth during take-down. Another freight hauler, the show's official contractor, ended up with the crates, delivered, and correctly submitted its bill. Blush face on that one!

Paperwork

Sales lead administration, sales orders, competition and seminar reports, even thank-you notes, are covered in Chapters 8, 9, 17, and 18.

From a tactical as well as strategic management viewpoint, there are some additions:

- *Service orders.* Copies of take-down orders and transport documents must be held for bill comparison later.

- *Damage reports.* These must be photocopied for the file and sent on to the exhibit house for action before the next event.

- *Preliminary management report.* A flash-report on what happened should be prepared for top management, even though all the results are not known.

- *Budget-actual update.* It may not be final, but you should be able to put together a fairly close cost summary shortly after the event.

Postshow Research

If you have contracted for postshow research by outside professionals, now is the moment for you to review and revise the product and service list from what was provided before the event. There were probably changes, in spite of good planning.

The Short Chapter

You may wonder why the material here deserves a chapter. The answer is emphasis. We have observed far too many experiences, and been part of some ugly situations ourselves, that trace to thinking that the show is over at the closing bell. That is never the case.

20

A Real-Life Case History

Throughout this book you see snippets of real-company exhibit experiences. We illustrate targeting with Tote-Cart and Practice Development, global village marketing with Colgate-Palmolive, computer-based exhibit marketing management with Nielsen Market Research, and more. In this chapter we trace the entire process. Our own computer expert, Mitchell Fink, was developing and introducing a new product, using a trade show approach.

The Exhibitor

Mitchell A. Fink Associates[1] (MFA) is a small computer consulting and software company based in New York City. For the most part it specializes in developing local area networks, communications programs, and management software. Much of that has been for investment advisory companies. The best known of several segments in that industry are mutual funds.

With encouragement from a trade association for advisors, The Investment Company Institute, MFA embarked on designing an integrated, off-the-shelf software product for smaller investment advisory firms that cannot afford big-time, custom computer systems.

The Situation

The team had been working for a year. They were fine-tuning and testing. Fink knew that marketing and sales operations were only six months away. Fink did not have an advertising agency. MFA did not have much more than letterhead and business cards. In its line of work, services were sold by word of mouth and meeting people at Wall Street lunch clubs!

One thing Fink did know: A big-league, six-figure investment had been made in product development. He knew the product, but he had no idea as to how to introduce it to the larger world of small investment advisors. His decision was a New York City–based trade show for 1500 investment advisors, about 250 of them purported to be potential customers.

Show Evaluation.   The exposition offered two long days, a total of 16 hours of selling time. Most of the 8- by 10-foot booth spaces were rented for $800. A few, in what were felt to be premium places, were priced at $1200. Fink opted for the premium. *If you have invested a lot of money in product development, do not try to sell it from a couple of camp chairs parked behind a white-top table in the corner.*

Booth Objectives and Results

There were goals and results that could be anticipated, based on what is presented in this book.

Sales Contacts and Leads

- There would be 2 people on duty at the booth. Based on show hours (16) and people (2), we anticipated 320 sales contacts at the booth.

  Result: There were quiet hours, offering no traffic. The overall audience was much smaller than anticipated, as well. There were only 200 booth contacts.

- Based on the norm, we had estimated 32 qualified sales leads for personal follow-up from the projected 320 contacts.

  Result: 48 leads were generated, much more than the estimate, in spite of lower traffic.

Suite Operation

MFA decided that it needed to be able to present private product demonstrations to invited guests or booth-screened visitors. A suite was rented for that purpose. It also served as home base for team members, preshow training, and postday critique meetings.

Result: Ten private demonstrations were conducted, and 12 VIP customers, who were not actually prospects for this product, were entertained in the suite. The suite goal was 15 private demonstrations to potential product customers.

What It Took

The firm started at "ground zero" from a marketing perspective. You visualize direct mail or advertising to support the operation. Fink needed more.

Requirements

- *Product logo.* That had to be approved by government authorities.
- *Packaging.* Computer software is packaged in a slip-in box. Inside is a binder and packet of disks for installation. These support materials had to be designed and produced.
- *Advertising and direct mail.* An introductory advertisement and mailing had to be created.
- *Booth and signs.* A 10-foot back-wall exhibit was rented and custom graphics prepared. The booth system was later purchased for use at other events (see Figure 20-1).
- *Pedestal.* A specially designed pedestal was built as the booth demonstration stand.

An exhibit production company provided related designs for all properties, including preparation of the ad mechanical and printing the direct-mail piece.[2] From product logo and package to booth, design and color management were consistent and presented a coherent image.

Costs

By large-company standards this product launch was small potatoes. Done several years ago, the total out-of-pocket expenses for the launch was $14,000, soup to nuts. Added to out-of-pocket cost was $3000 in *time cost* for Fink and his team, directly attributed to the program. Total: $17,000. A similar program today would cost over $20,000. That is no small investment for a small outfit.

Figure 20-1. The back-wall surface was custom-made, placed on an already-manu-factured system. In this case it was a frame manufactured by Exponents in San Diego. A custom counter, carpet, and lights completed the exhibit. (*Sketch courtesy of Cindy Spuria, Carrboro, N.C.—Alan Sitzer Associates.*)

Out-of-Pocket Cost Breakdown

- Booth space: $1200
- Design and production costs (for *everything*): $7900
- Booth rental (including carpet and pedestal): $1800
- Show services: $1000
- Mailing and advertising space: $1100
- Travel and hotel: $1000

To some extent, the MFA launch costs were reduced because its opening show was at a local hotel. In-city travel costs were relatively low, and only one suite was rented in the hotel. Later on MFA partici-pated at industry events in other cities. There were no development costs, so out-of-pocket expenses were reduced in that area. However, travel and hotel were higher, which ate up some of the savings.

Profitability

Our purpose has been to tell a real-life exhibit marketing story. Readers, knowing that it took place several years ago, may wonder what happened, long range. Sadly, we must report that MFA's product never earned back enough to cover its high cost of development. It was and is very good software. The marketing was professional. However, this highly specific market of small investment advisory companies was not deep enough to provide sufficient sales.

We will never be sure, but a fundamental error might have been made at the very start. Many in the investment management business waxed enthusiastic about the idea. Perhaps a greater effort in preliminary market research would have provided more exact guidance. Maybe a less expensive off-the-shelf program, without so many bells and whistles, would have fared better.

There is, however, a happy ending. Mitchell A. Fink remains in business, working with mid- and larger-size companies in the investment industry, and others. His interest in exhibiting has not waned. He has written extensively on the application of personal computer technology in exhibit management.[3]

As an exhibit marketing story, this is a good one. It also illustrates that exhibiting does not stand on its own. It is but part of the process toward profit.

PART 4

The International Scene

21
International
Exhibits Planning

We had harbored the thought that readers from other nations would learn more about exhibiting in the USA and Canada than the reverse. Then we read a 112-page paperback book entitled *Successful Participation in Trade Fairs Made in Germany.*[1] It is quite good. Our book addresses more subjects in greater detail, but there are striking similarities in the selection of fundamental issues. That is especially pleasing to us when you put things into historical perspective.

The Hanseatic League was a trading network linking northern European cities that started early in the fourteenth century and ultimately brought together traders from England to Russia. The league's birth was in towns such as Lübeck, now part of northern Germany.[2] With that as a backdrop, we felt that these pioneers could have created far different or more sophisticated management standards than what we offer. No. *For many reasons there are almost universal exhibit marketing principles.*

There are differences, of course. However, from an exhibiting perspective, if you can create a good marketing experience at home or in the U.S.'s Birmingham, Alabama, you can do well in Bangkok, Barcelona, Beijing, Bombay, Boston, Brisbane, Budapest, or Buenos Aires.

We explore some differences here, but the fundamental management principles are the same worldwide as they would be if you were to exhibit right down the street.

About Part 4

Go to the public library. Tell a staff professional that you want a bibliography of articles or books written on doing business in the European

Economic Community. Most libraries, even those in smaller cities, are computer-linked to databases that provide sources. Faced with a request like this, a wise librarian might ask, "Can we define your need more closely?" The reason? Ask computers the question as first phrased, and you might end up with a 6-inch paper pile weighing 5 pounds. And that would be just a book or periodical source list! No facts you can use.

The same situation would arise were you to ask about what is available on any region or country. We were honored with a tour of the international commercial information library maintained as a customer service by Bureau of the Census in Maryland.[3] Hundreds of nations around the world share information, and this is the USA's official repository. To provide a sense of magnitude, one floor-to-ceiling bookshelf "stack" well over 50 feet long is required to file information from Mexico alone! The librarian points out that new materials arrive each day, and it is a chore just keeping up with entering information in the computer database catalog.

The Five-Year Book

Books such as this one are used by readers as reference for several years. Management principles remain much the same. However, the ways in which they are employed are dynamic. That is especially so on the international scene. Trade fairs are one of our most important vehicles for starting and developing trade around the world. As a result, we have made an effort to restrict this book to essentials, avoiding answers so specific that they may be out of date when you read. The advice is to use our essentials but check out specifics.

Logistical War Stories.   The USA–based International Exhibitors Association[4] has presented international exhibiting seminars at its annual convention for several years. For the most part these sessions have focused on logistical how-to questions and answers. We have heard horror story after horror story. We provide advice on how to avoid horrors, but problems emerge most often for two reasons:

1. *Failure to read.* The information provided by international show producers is quite thorough. The exhibitor kits are comprehensive, including rules and order forms, and timing. Read the kit.

2. *Failure to respond.* There are times, as well, when exhibitors do not like some of the rules or guidelines. They want to do things their own way. It does not work as a guest in another's home.

Essentials Everywhere

Far more important than worrying about booth transport, setup, and other logistics, there are some issues that become very important to discuss at shows, other than your product and its features. A private-sector expert, Leslie Stroh[5] provides input. He points out three subjects that come up in exhibit discussions that rarely emerge in domestic booth conversations. On a domestic level they can come up later and can be resolved without a lot of back-and-forth.

1. *Service or training after the sale.* If you do not bring it up, your prospect will certainly do so. The question is obvious enough. It becomes a bigger consideration when goods are shipped a half world away. In some cases parts availability and delivery is very important as well.

2. *Who pays for what, when, and how.* Complications are created by import fees and the ever-shifting relative values of different currencies. The buyer may cover import fees, but must they in part be reflected in pricing? More importantly, perhaps, is the price firm, or will it change based on the currency exchange rate at the time of product delivery?

3. *Product transport arrangements, costs, and timing.* Stroh points out that an initial order can involve a sea freight container filled with several products from the supplier. Cost and delivery timing can be estimated closely. What will come up in booth discussion is how subsequent orders are handled and related costs. For instance, one item might sell better than another, yet a full container reorder might not be appropriate. The same is true for parts supply. Be prepared to discuss these questions right at the booth.

The Decision Process

There are some basic questions to ask yourself if you are just starting out:

- Has product distribution been established already? Do you have an in-country partner? Or are you exhibiting to seek an in-country partner?

  Note: If you are just starting, it might be wise to visit the exposition first, before exhibiting. That is especially so if your first search is for an in-country partner or distributor. Frequently these are found among other exhibitors, not delegates. You will have to ask the show's manager. There are other methods to start dialogue that recruits partners. For instance, in the USA, the Department of Commerce organizes trade missions to assist.[6]

- How long can you wait to get those first orders processed, billed, and paid? Things take longer on an international basis, so you must have "deeper pockets" than might be the case at home.

- What do you know about your product's suitability in the region? For instance, you might want to sell window screening in Europe. In southern Europe that makes sense. In Holland and the rest of northern Europe, there is less need and thus a smaller market.

- What have you learned about your potential direct customers? Who are they, and where are they located? If you don't know, can you find out?

- What is the history of the show you are contemplating? To what extent can it provide audience demographic information that allows you to isolate your particular prospect base? Be warned that in some nations, including many in Europe, there are stringent privacy laws. As a result, there may be limits on the degree to which show managers can ask delegates for information.

Information Sources

We have already mentioned some sources in the text or chapter endnotes. There are both public and private origins. Since the majority of our readers are from the USA, we illustrate with USA sources. However, most nations offer similar services on a governmental or private-sector basis.

Your Chamber of Commerce

It is just down the block. The United States Chamber of Commerce operates as the tip of a private-sector iceberg that includes hundreds of local chapters, or chambers, throughout the nation. What few realize is that the U.S. Chamber also has offices in well over 50 international cities around the world. Because it is privately, rather than publicly, funded, the Chamber is a friendly "competitor" for publicly funded sources such as the U.S. Department of Commerce. (Chamber of Commerce organizations sponsored in other nations are as active, with their own local chapters and national outreach offices. When it comes to trade, everyone works together!)

It is easy to understand the potential ripple effect of a call to your own Chamber of Commerce. You will get into what we call "the loop" and ultimately may get back far more than you asked for! (If your company is not a Chamber member, you may be solicited. That is not harsh, and the benefits, on a domestic or international basis, can be quite valuable.)[7]

Industry Associations

You probably belong to an industry association or two. One might serve the industry of which you are part. Another could be an association serving your customers. Call both to see what information or overseas contacts they might have in the geographic area that is of interest to you. Again, you are entering a potentially productive loop. Some of these organizations are truly international in character. Even if not, it is a good bet these days that they have forged some links with sibling groups in other nations. For instance, the USA's International Exhibitors Association is mainly composed of USA companies. However, it has made overseas contacts with others interested in exhibiting as a work process. The same might be true in your industry.

Government-Sponsored Programs

Many governments have created excellent programs to help their business export. Quite often they are also good at preparing explanations of how these programs work. Where most fail is letting their business communities know about them. After an initial press release announcing a program, little is done to inform potential users except through word of mouth and group meetings. Earlier we mentioned an international library maintained by the U.S. government that contains information of potential value to USA exporters. Before reading this chapter, had you ever heard of it? Some know because it is busy. However, we suspect most requests come from those already involved with international trade, "in the know."

Smaller companies interested in export but not already involved do not know about assistance programs and do not know to search them out. It is like asking someone to find a needle in a haystack when that person does not know there is a haystack.

U.S. Department of Commerce Programs. The U.S. Department of Commerce operates a wide diversity of programs, and the costs are reasonable. Among them are:

- *Comparison shopping service.* This provides a quick and accurate assessment of how your product might sell in a given market. In addition, it provides information of competing products, pricing, and any import quotas or other impediments as well as information on who might be interested in becoming an in-country partner of one sort or another.

- *Foreign market research.* This service provides broader statistical data on selected products and industries in countries that offer the best opportunities for U.S. exporters.

- *Matchmakers.* After background work that is quite detailed, you would participate in a Matchmaker Trade Delegation trip during which you would meet with qualified potential clients or possible in-country partners.

- *Trade missions.* This is a higher-profile version of the Matchmaker program. Included are meetings with high level government officials as well as with key business people.

- *Foreign buyer program.* The Commerce Department works with USA trade show organizers in selected industries. Overseas attendance promotion programs are mounted by the show and by Commerce Department representatives in the target nations. The buyers will attend the event in the USA. An International Business Center is established at each expo. Introductions are made, and private meeting rooms plus other services are provided.

- *Agent/distributor service.* The ADS program is well suited for small business. The Commerce Department locates, screens, and assesses agents, distributors, representatives, and other types of foreign partners.

This is only a partial listing. The Commerce Department operates district offices in cities throughout the United States. When you call, indicate special interest in programs administered by the Commerce Department's International Trade Administration and U.S. and Foreign Commercial Service.

Exporting Reference Guide.   When you call your district office, also ask about obtaining a copy of an excellent book published by the U.S. Department of Commerce in cooperation with the Federal Express Corporation. The title is *A Basic Guide to Exporting.* There is a small charge levied to partially cover costs. Though not all about exhibiting, it is a wonderful reference tool. The name, address, and telephone number lists cover the United States and the rest of the world as well! They include all sorts of government agencies, at all levels, plus private-sector operations such as the Chamber of Commerce and other associations. Even those already experienced in export and international exhibiting will find room for this publication on their 5-foot shelves.

Foreign Nation Services at Home.   Many nations have embassies, consulates, and their own permanent trade offices in the USA. Mexico, for instance, operates offices in a large number of USA cities. Regardless of office type, one of the reasons these countries are here is to help stimulate bilateral trade. By contacting one, you may be able to learn even more.

The Trade Show Relationship

You may be wondering why we spend these pages on subjects that may seem not to be closely allied to exhibiting. Certainly many of those we talked to while gathering information asked why we were interested in what they had to offer when our book is about exposition participation. Most of them, like many others, think of shows in context with physical presence.

Book readers, and especially those who have perused Chapter 2 and the chapters in Part 2, know differently. The how-to of booths, signs, transport, and setup is certainly important. However, our focus is on process management. That starts with creating practical mission statements and establishing specific objectives and related measurements. Many companies have trouble doing that at even domestic events. Certainly it is not any easier for overseas participation.

When you make that "go" decision, know why, what you expect, and what you want in return. We hope the information provided here allows you to do a better job of that.

Government-Sponsored Trade Show Programs

Most governments are interested in developing trade. Participating at international trade shows is part of the effort they make. We say "governments" because more than just nations are involved. For instance, in the USA states and cities have also exhibited to attract trade for key industries. New York State has exhibited, as an example. The city of Miami has participated at international travel industry events to attract tourism. Even trade associations gather members together for exhibitions. Among many, the Washington State Apple Growers Association has exhibited.

The degree of government support differs considerably, depending on the situation or tradition. For instance, in Germany a degree of financial support is provided by a subsidy covering part of the cost of freight.

U.S. Government Trade Show Support.   Financial realities have decreased the degree to which the U.S. Department of Commerce can support or subsidize USA exhibiting at overseas shows in dollar terms. However, it still mounts a powerful program for USA companies that want to participate.

- *Special exhibitions.* The Commerce Department organizes special exhibitions of USA products for "solo" shows, often taking place at world trade centers in various nations. The department also organizes USA pavilions at the largest international exhibitions. Virtually all logistical concerns are covered, booth to transport. Marketing and promotional support are provided.

- *Certified trade fairs.* The department identifies other international fairs offering the most opportunity. It also identifies and certifies private-sector "packagers" who provide the same services as one would get from the department itself from a logistics viewpoint. One of the advantages is that basic homework has been done. You are exhibiting at a reliable expo with credible support.

As is the case with other Commerce Department programs, you can find out more about the trade show support program by contacting your district commerce office.

We were, for some years, reluctant dragons when it came to participating in pavilions, and especially those offering diverse products. Our notion was that visitors are not especially interested in visiting booths that simply offer "The Products of " Argentina, Australia, Brazil, Canada, Chile, China, England, France, Germany, Ireland, Israel, Japan, Mexico, Peru, Singapore, Spain, South Africa, Sweden, the USA, and so on. Instead, we felt delegates would search out products of interest regardless of country of origin. We have bowed to reality. International show delegates are indeed interested in visiting national pavilions.

International corporate behemoths have names that are well known on a global basis. They put up the monster booths in the center of the floor. They can afford the luxury of standing alone, in their appropriate product sector, at a large international exposition. As for the rest of us, the pavilion can be a good solution. Added to promotion of the pavilion as a whole, you may be able to send preshow letters of invitation to prospects of special interest who will be attending.

Pavilion Booths.   They come in many shapes and sizes. Some include private meeting centers. However, there is a common dominator. A large space is rented, and individual exhibitors participate by renting one or more spaces within. A concept is illustrated in Figure 21-1.

Figure 21-1. This design, prepared for Unilink Canada, illustrates the fundamentals of how pavilions are organized. Each participant rents one or more spaces within the pavilion. It also illustrates what is called the *shell scheme* provided to small, independent exhibitors in most nations. In contrast to the "pipe and drape" concept seen most often in the USA, the shell scheme rims each booth with a high hard walls out to the aisle. Exhibitors decorate the interiors. (*Design and sketch courtesy of Pico Art Industries, Singapore.*)

Advice from an International Show Expert: Bowie Bits

Private citizens often comment, "Government employees don't really *do* anything. They push paper from pillar to post and tell you to go to the next office." That has never been our experience except for battling against a parking ticket in Manhattan. (We could do a book on that!) Almost universally we find public servants, elected, appointed, or permanent, to be just that: They truly want to serve constituents.

In this chapter's endnotes we have mentioned the names of three people, both current and former U.S. government employees, who have helped us with this book, and we hope you too. The content of Chapter 23 is owed, in substantial part, to a government employee in the People's Republic of China.

We met a very special person during interviews with officials at the U.S. Commerce Department in Washington, D.C. His name is David Bowie.[8] What makes his contribution unique is that in addition to traditional government service, he has served on the front lines of international exhibiting for many years. He has been there and has done it himself.

Some of what he told us we knew already, and those comments validated our own long-held beliefs. Other thoughts were new to us. The same may be true for you. By the way, if you are an expert as well and have a difference of opinion about what is important, don't blame Bowie. What you are reading is our interpretation of his advice.

Combined in what follows are notes taken during an exhaustive meeting, far too short, and a multipage letter sent later. We have made an attempt to break down the hints by category.

Information Sources.   Bowie says, "The U.S. government, particularly commerce, has tons of information to help a company do market research that may lead to an exhibit decision. Our industry and country experts can help a lot." He agrees with the programs cited earlier and offers more.

Companies can subscribe to the National Trade Data Bank or the Electronic Bulletin Board or call the Trade Information Center (800-USA-TRADE). One also can call local U.S. Export Assistance Centers for help. Earlier we suggested calling your district office of the Commerce Department. You may find that the Export Assistance Center is located there, or at another place to which you might be referred. And, over time, terms change. The names and organizational setups may mutate, but the services will remain and be improved. He also points out that subscribers to Internet will find they can get at commerce and other government department information through that source.

There are, as well, state (as we have pointed out) and private organizations that provide information. Those include such services as AT&T's 800-US-Export phone and fax system. Bowie's concern is that *there may be too much information available.* Do not get scared off. The topic is very hot, and everybody wants to get into the act.

The First Suggestion: Your Freight Forwarder.   After the show itself, it can be that your best decision is on an experienced freight forwarder. These folks know more than trucks, planes, and ships. For instance, they will know how many other USA exhibitors are participating.

> *Note:* In Chapter 23's section entitled "Dealing with Experts—A Value Story," we focus on the "extras" that a good forwarder provides. We will not spill the story here, but the forwarder, TWI,[9] was sensitive to political changes going on during the time it was hauling an exhibit country to country. It prepared paperwork in different formats to suite each nation's boarder checking teams, depending on how things stood at the time.

Exhibit Security.   Be sure to lock up anything of value at night. The shows provide security, but sometimes the security personnel are the culprits. (Other exhibitors are guilty, as well.) You might want to have your own lock-up area and bring your own lock and key.

- *Public days.* Many overseas shows invite the general public in for a day to satisfy curiosity. Smaller exhibitors often simply abandon their booths on that day. If you do, don't leave anything other than literature you don't want to toss out after the show. Even on trade-only days do not leave your booth unattended for even a moment.

Measurement Conversion. Bowie points out that USA exhibitors should be aware that the metric system is used in most other nations. Booth sizes to weights to even literature sizes are involved. We provide a simplified conversion chart as part of Chapter 23. The conversions provided are those more appropriate to exhibiting. (For instance, we do not feel it useful to ask that you observe that 1 teaspoon, $\frac{1}{6}$ fluid ounce, is the equivalent of 4.9 milliliters.)

Electrical Service. New exhibitors at overseas shows often fail to remember that electrical equipment must operate on the electric standard used in the nation where the show takes place. Bowie says, "I have seen companies bring in computers,...then find they need a frequency converter plus transformer to make them work." Problems get solved. It is easier and less costly to read the show kit up-front and bring what's needed along with you, or advance-order what can be rented on-site.

Preshow, At-Event, and Postshow Promotion. David Bowie's position on this subject mirrors our own, whether the event be domestic or international. Among his hints are:

- Obtain the program from the last event. Sort out the names of customers or prospects that attended. Invite them to meet with you at the upcoming show. Suggest a specific appointment for a business reason, such as learning about what is new.

- Send press releases and editorial matter to trade magazines for use in their preshow, *not necessarily at-show,* issues. Invite press representatives to your booth to see what is going on, and have something special, such as a prewritten release, to give them for use after the event.

- Invite local TV stations to visit your booth if you are showing something that moves, grinds, makes smoke, or does something else that is quite interesting from a general public viewpoint.

- Spend extra dollars on having good-quality photographs taken of your booth "in action." They can be used internally or for press releases to domestic trade magazines.

VIP Management. Again, Bowie and I agree. If the big boss must visit the show, give that person something to do that is productive. Do not force a director to stand around in a booth just getting in the way.

- Seek out government ministers that might have some interest in what your company offers and set up appointments. The Commerce Department representatives in the nation can assist.

- Create private appointments for your VIP to meet with appropriate VIPs in current customer companies. The objective is to bring to the surface gnawing problems or discuss new initiatives.

- *Schedule* your VIP at the booth in advance for two purposes. First, the staff can invite big customers or prospects back to meet your leader during those times. It may be just for a handshake, or maybe something more. Second, VIP delegations—including government ministers—are often escorted through major trade events. Find out when that will happen from the show organizer. Ask that the delegation stop at your booth. Promise at least a "photo opportunity" with your executive, and then make sure that your VIP is standing by at that time.

  Note: Bowie and Zhao Weiping (in China) both point out that VIP meetings with government ministers do not realize signed orders. However, both say they talk with other important people who *are* buyers, with amazing results. See Chapter 23 for an extensive examination of trade with and exhibiting in the People's Republic of China. Bowie suggests a snappy demo, if your product lends itself to that, and a small but useful gift, one that does not expire with time such as a calendar. It will serve as a reminder.

We had not thought of it, but Bowie points out that major international trade events sometimes attract senior USA officials as well. If, by chance, one or more of your congressional representatives will be in attendance, invite them to stop by. It is a good photo opportunity for them and useful in your own publicity. High-level appointed officials can and do help, too. For instance, Bowie observed, at an air show, the FAA administrator going from booth to booth, really trying to help out exhibitors.

Look Before You Leap. Before investing in your first exhibit experience, it can be a good idea to attend the show yourself. Talk with some potential customers, and observe what competitors are displaying. If it is a major show on the Commerce list, you might want to dip your toe in the water by participating in the U.S. Commerce Department Literature Center. The cost is very low.

During your first visit to the nation of interest, drop by the Commercial Office in the embassy. Explain what you are doing, or contemplating, and you can get some good tips. It can be of special value to chat with the full-time locals who work there. Top managers come from the USA and are rotated every few years. The staff is local, and they are long-service employees.

Pavilion or Not.   Bowie agrees with us that pavilion participation is far better for most than going it alone. He adds another reason to what we pointed out earlier: The national pavilion concept is ingrained around the world. Visitors instinctively go to them. He also points out that because many of these shows are quite large, it may be very difficult for your potential buyers to find you, exhibiting alone.

Networking.   Bring lots of business cards, and take every chance you can to network—on a bus or train, in a restaurant or cafeteria.

Promotional Products.   Readers know that we suggest caution on the indiscriminate distribution of giveaways. However, small logo item trading is very much a tradition at international events. Small pins are appropriate and, in Europe or Asia, a cigarette lighter with your logo works well. And do not use them just at the booth. Bowie has even given pins to air crews on flights over. In your hotel, for instance, in addition to tipping the luggage carrier, give a lapel pin for that person's collection.

Get to Know Show Management.   This is good advice for domestic as well as international events. It is likely that you will have never met the show manager, face-to-face, before you arrive. Take a few moments, drop by the show office, and introduce yourself as a courtesy. You are a customer, but there are a lot of them. That introduction could become valuable down the line for both of you.

The Must-Do Show.   You might find that there are some exhibitions where exhibiting becomes something of a right of passage. It is not true everywhere or in all industries, but there are situations in which you must exhibit to show support for the national government.

Book Content Suggestions.   In addition to his lengthy and helpful list of hints, David Bowie offered a couple of suggestions that are not specifically related to international exhibiting. He advised mentioning the emergence of college-level exhibit marketing courses in the United

States. (We do that as part of Chapter 24.) In addition, Bowie feels strongly that there is a great need for booth staff training and that we should present both content and method. Chapter 18 is totally devoted to that cause, and there is coverage in part of Chapter 3 as well.

There are two more chapters in Part 4. This one has been devoted to fact gathering so that sensible decisions and plans can be made. In addition, basic participation suggestions are presented. The next chapter is short. For the most part it is a case history that shows how a major corporation used much of what is presented here in Part 4 in planning and implementing a large exhibit at a global event. The last chapter in "The International Scene" provides a wide diversity of specific information not covered here. Cultural and language issues and answers are addressed. International freight is covered, complete with a case history. Legal pitfalls are addressed. We even present a special section on one nation that will be a very important trading partner for the world in a very few years. Read on! It's good stuff, and much of it is quite interesting.

22
The "Global Village" Show

Our goal in this chapter is to provide some thoughts on show types and an insight into how one company applied much of what is presented in the three chapters of this book part at a global event.

Domestic Show Types

When industry professionals talk about show types in the USA, they are referring to two general classifications: business-to-business and consumer, or public shows.

Business to Business

Within that frame of reference, there are special areas, depending on the industries and their objectives and traditions. There are some combination show types as well:

- *Purchasing for their own use.* From computers to machine tools to medical equipment to printing presses and more, there are many events where the primary objective is easing the purchasing process for companies that need something to be used internally.

- *Purchasing for inventory.* There are large numbers of dealer expositions where the main objective is buying for resale. Home electronics, fashion, fishing tackle, furniture, gifts, and hardware right down the alphabet to toys are among them.

- *Learning what to recommend.* In several industries practitioners are asked to specify or recommend products and services to others. A number of medical events pop to mind at which doctors learn about new ethical drugs being offered. There are others, including events for travel agents and brokers such as those who sell promotional products or specialty advertising items.

Consumer or Public

We devote an entire chapter to just this type of event. There is wide diversity: from antiques, autos, and business to sports equipment and stamps. In all cases the shows serve consumers who are comparison shopping for items of special interest.

We mention "business" as part of this group. That requires explanation. These events offer local small businesses a chance to see a wide diversity of products and services that are of interest. These companies do not attend national or regional trade shows. Thus, we classify the events in the "public" or consumer category.

The sponsor might be a local Chamber of Commerce. Many are professionally mounted. For instance, Maryland-based Industrial Shows of America manages a large number of local business shows around the country.

Many of these consumer shows have trade-only days as well. Recreational marine industry boat shows are among them.

International Exhibitions

These events tend to break into three large categories: in-country shows, special-interest global shows, and broader-interest trade fairs.

In-Country Shows

These are events primarily for domestic consumption within the nation where the show takes place. They tend to mirror the profile of special-interest events presented in the USA for domestic audiences.

Special-Interest Global Shows

Regardless of where they take place, these events attract an audience from several countries. The well-known Paris Air Show is an example. The International Dental Federation is another, and we address that event later in this chapter. The communications industries gather for a global event every four years in Geneva. There are large printing equipment events that are global.

USA readers automatically think that global shows always take place in other nations, not in their home country! That is not the case. For instance, the World Travel Congress meets every second year in the United States, in alternate years shifting from country to country. The Food Marketing Institute's annual event in Chicago is considered "domestic" but in fact is a global show. The Consumer Electronics show, an annual event in Las Vegas, has global as well as domestic implications. There are many others.

Broader-Interest Trade Fairs

The term trade *fair* is often used to describe a large exposition that attracts visitors and exhibitors with widely divergent interests. On a consumer level, this is what a "World's Fair" is all about. Of interest in this context is that there is now a permanent, though ever-changing, privately sponsored World's Fair. It is Disney's EPCOT[1] Center, located in Orlando, Florida.

Wide-interest, business-to-business fairs are held far more often in Europe than they are in the USA or elsewhere. That tradition may trace back to the operations among Hanseatic League cities about 500 years ago. Among the best-known fairs today are those mounted in Hanover, Germany.

Audience Draw

In-country events draw a domestic audience. In the USA, for example, even "national" shows tend to attract more delegates from areas near where the show is taking place. For instance, a medical event taking place in Shenzen will attract more delegates from southern China. The same event, taking place in Beijing or Dallian, will attract a bigger audience from northern provinces. That situation is less a factor in countries that are smaller from a geographic viewpoint. An in-country industrial event in Sweden, Belgium, or Israel, for instance, may not "regionalize" quite so much.

The same is true for global events. Except for extremely narrow interest shows, there is more attendance from the global region where the show takes place. When the International Dental Federation meets in Europe, there is a larger European audience. In Asia? More Asian.

Participating at an In-Country Event

There are some situations in which that is your best choice. Very large nations such as Russia or China come to mind. Mexico is another. There are, however, some implications.

If you are exhibiting for a nation's domestic audience only, there is an assumption that you are well versed in that nation's business and cultural practices. There is also an assumption that you are more fluent in the country's language. (That is less the case in the large countries.)

For the most part, in-country shows are best if you already have established a presence in the nation. Large companies may have country-teams that include managers from the nation. Others may have created dealerships with nationals, or a group of representatives. In those cases exhibiting is easy. Provide corporate goals and support, but let the nation-team take the lead.

Small companies often think that participating at a show can be a good way to find local partners. That is true, partners often being found among other exhibitors. However, Chapter 21 readers will realize that there are other methods. An alternate to exhibiting might be simple attendance at the conference, visiting the booths, and networking among delegates.

Participating As Part of a Global Village

There are some underlying characteristics that favor participating at a global event, characteristics that make such events advantageous to many exhibitors, including smaller-company, start-up exporters.

There is always a host nation. However, once you emerge at the exposition, you will have entered a late-century version of what futurists predicted decades ago. It is a global village.

Global Village Advantages

You may ask why that is important. The answer is that the global village is a place where it becomes apparent that our similarities are more important than our differences—culture, boundary, and so on. In contrast to an in-country event, there is a lowered expectation that you are an expert on the delegate's nation: its language, culture, business practices, and regulations. Of course, the more you know, the easier things become. However, there is an unwritten acknowledgement that both you and your buyer have more to learn—and that you are on neutral ground.

Your Booth As a Home

Small or large, your booth is like a home in the village. You are its host. As you would be at your own home, you will be courteous to your neighbors, and that is appreciated. Your neighbors will be courteous to you, as expected. You and your neighbor may not share exactly the same values, education, or other things. However, differences are less vital than what brings you together.

- *Mutual respect.* Just as would be the case in your own home, neither you or your guests should try to impose your values on others. At the same time, however, each is somewhat sensitive to the values of others, even if that moderates behavior.

- *Language.* The international language of commerce is English. However, the form of English spoken, or read, is not that used in any nation where it is native. Instead, "international English" is best described as how it is used in nations where it is learned as a second or third language.

In Chapter 23 we delve into specifics on these issues and more, including tactical issues surrounding booth and transport. This chapter has more to do with planning and goal setting, though in our story we outline implementation.

The Colgate-Palmolive Planning Story

Colgate-Palmolive is a global leader in the provision of oral care products. Quite literally, the sun never sets on Colgate. We were involved as a consultant to the company's advertising agency[2] in planning a large-scale exhibit marketing operation at a global show.

The Show

The International Dental Federation produces a large event each year. It brings together oral care professionals from around the world. These include dentists, educators, trade press, and the companies that offer products in the field, both those used professionally and those suggested or given to patients. Professional papers are presented, along with seminars. There is an extensive exhibition. There are networking social events.

The event hopscotches the globe. That is done so that all members can more easily participate over time. An event may be worldwide, but a greater portion of the audience comes from the region where the show is taking place. During the year we were involved, the convention was mounted in Singapore. Thus, there were more delegates from Asian and Pacific Rim nations.

No Ego Trip

An error we've observed at times inside other large companies doing this kind of work is that "New York" or "Chicago" or "Detroit"— wherever the head offices are located—descends on the project like an all-knowing elephant wearing blinders. They do not do as well as they would were they to sit back and listen and build a true team.

The Internal Team. Colgate was cooperative within itself. There appeared to be a team-building culture. The team was created by its Global Marketing Group in New York. However, this division was careful to include others within the company.

Perhaps best known of the company's products is Colgate Toothpaste. There are, however, other products, including products for dentists to use in their offices. The planning group was careful to include product management. The company's global activity runs through a series of country-teams and distributors that include managers from each of the nations. Professional direction was provided by Colgate country-team leadership based in Europe and from the host country's manager group.

The External Team. Elsewhere in the book we point out that large international companies like to deal with other large international companies. Colgate is a case in point.

- *The advertising agency.* Colgate's long-time advertising agency has been Young & Rubicam. It, too, operates on a global basis. It, too, operates on a team basis. Though basic principles and creative concepts are developed at a corporate level, it listens with great care to Y&R family members who come from and work and live in other nations.

- *The exhibit builder.* The exhibit builder is global as well. Its name is Pico Art Industries. It operates 23 offices and facilities around the world. Though especially strong in Asia and in the Pacific, it also has its own offices in eight locations serving North America, Europe, and the Middle East. Just as with Colgate and Y&R, the sun never sets on Pico.[3]

- *Key local vendors.* Both Colgate and Y&R know that it is important to do as much business as possible with local sources. It makes you more a part of the local community and assures high quality because the local partners will continue to do business there.

As it turns out, though global, the head office for Pico is located in Singapore. There was an added plus. In addition to creating exhibits, the company also serves the decorating company for shows themselves. It had been hired as the decorating company for the event as a whole by the International Dental Federation.

You may ask how I, hardly a global corporate elephant, managed to become part of the team and thus able to write this story. We were employed as a consultant for Colgate by its ad agency. Y&R, to its credit, did not feel "strong" on exhibit marketing. Most large agencies, and especially those who work heavily in consumer advertising, are not experts in trade show marketing and related creative development. Y&R knew what it did not know and did something about it.

In addition to work on helping to set clear objectives and preparing internal training programs, we were asked to suggest exhibit designers and builders and evaluate designs. In this case we suggested Pico. Without knowing it, we were suggesting the same company that was being recommended by both the Y&R and Colgate teams on-site.

Colgate-Palmolive Strategy and Goals

One of the beauties of exhibiting is that you can do several things at once. In fact, the more the better from a return-on-investment perspective. Fundamentally, however, Colgate wanted to protect its global leadership position while at the same time striving for new growth opportunities.

"Owning" Singapore. Without in any way seeming arrogant, Colgate wanted to be seen as a global leader in several respects, in part because it is a leader in the place where the show was taking place.

Professional Competence. The company also wanted to continue enhancing its reputation in the oral care field by presenting and publishing professional papers.

Deepening Current Relationships. Because of its presence in the field, the company had created relationships with key practitioners who would attend. It wanted to deepen these relationships with meetings and some entertainment.

Informing Practitioners and Creating New Relationships. A key objective was informing dental practitioners about all that the company is doing. In addition, it wanted to identify more VIPs who would influence attitudes among other professionals in the oral care fields.

Local Consumer Confidence.   The show was for professionals. Yet Colgate sells to consumers in Singapore as well. To the extent possible, the show presence was also to be used to create more consumer awareness locally.

Implementation Objectives

You may be thinking, "All this is well and good for a big-time outfit with scads of people and money, but it is too big a bite to chew for us smaller players." In terms of magnitude, you are right. In terms of scope, you are wrong. Colgate became a big-time operation after it was smaller. The company dealt with scope first, then magnitude.

Colgate marched in with platoon-strength troops, but it worked with only five basic premises that fit just about anybody:

1. Keep it simple. No matter how much you do, boil everything down to the essentials.
2. Make it graphic. Visual impressions are important. Keep them simple and make them strong.
3. Create excitement. Do things that inspire interest.
4. Be informative, but learn too. Provide good information, but keep your ears open as well.
5. Dentists are human too. This is a face-to-face medium. Visitors are people, not computers.

The Execution

You may not be able to do all that Colgate did at this exposition. However, even if you have just a 3- or 6-meter booth, try to see how you can apply the concepts.

"Owning Singapore" and Local Consumer Confidence

When delegates arrived at baggage claim at the airport, they were greeted by a special advertising sign that welcomed them to the convention. Along the route into town, Colgate hung banners of welcome on each light standard. It keyed in on the conference itself, but Colgate as the banner sponsor was readily seen. (Its consumer advertising art, "The Colgate Smile," was being used so that artwork was part of the banner.)

The banner program was aimed at both delegates and local consumers. There was another aspect of the program that did double duty.

The convention center with its expo hall and meeting rooms is linked to a consumer shopping mall. As a result, and because Colgate used knowledge from local teams, the main exhibit space selected "backed" onto the consumer mall!

The booth design was, in effect, two-sided. On one side, and in the booth interior, professional visitors were invited and did their work. On the back, outside, consumer messages were presented to mall walkers. TV monitors ran loops of local on-air commercials. Colgate tries to make a consumer effort, regardless of where it exhibits, to a professional audience. That is sensible.

Informing Practitioners and Creating New Relationships

The design of the main booth (there was a second) followed the international tradition for large exhibits. Those who wished to visit, or were invited, went first to a place where they signed in, a greeting area. They were then escorted through the booth, sometimes with the aid of a translator, and were shown specific products and demonstrations.

During this process Colgate was learning as well. Questions on the sign-in form, as well as conversations with Colgate representatives, provided the company with information. You will remember, from the objectives section of this story, that the company wanted to expand its list of practitioners who might influence others in the oral care fields. These would be people with whom the company would want to encourage continuing contact. Generally speaking, these new VIPs would be educators, government ministers, trade press representatives, leaders of local dental societies, and those who managed practices that involved several dentists in a group.

Note: Of interest is that this custom booth was designed and built using the relatively new concepts outlined in Chapters 3 and 13. First of all, the never-seen frame was made of aluminum, an already-manufactured system. In this case that was from Octonorm, deigned and patented in Germany. Second, the "skin" and graphics were produced for one use only, not to troop from nation to nation in crates. Octonorm, by the way, is another global company in the exhibit industry.

Another Double-Duty Program

There was another and much smaller Colgate booth. It was an information center for delegates. That booth served two goals. First, delegates could pick up information about Singapore in general. Second, published papers prepared by Colgate speakers at the conference were made available. The objectives were "owning Singapore" and also demonstrating "professional competence."

There were, as well, involvements with VIP entertainment and trade press representatives. In addition, Colgate experts wrote technical papers to help practitioners without sales in mind, thereby enhancing corporate reputation. Regardless, you can see that Colgate operated in focused fashion and gave itself a chance to earn back as much return on investment as possible. Maybe that is why it is a world leader in its industry in the first place.

Can you do this? Yes. Your scale may be smaller and the opportunities less broad, but you can make an exhibit marketing program work very hard for you.

23

International Business Culture, Language, and Practices

This chapter arrows in on four subjects.

1. Cultural and language issues and answers
2. Booths and freight
3. Possible impacts of commercial laws in host countries
4. Exhibiting (and doing business) in the People's Republic of China

Cultural and Language Issues and Answers

People talk about the USA as a melting pot. That implies an amalgam, a homogeneous blend. Though less dramatic, it is more accurate to describe the nation as a mixing bowl filled with wheat, rice, corn, and spices. There is a strong flavor of shared ideals and values. However, each group retains its own, too.

The Global Show Reflection

A global show is a smaller-scale version of the mixing bowl. Delegates and exhibitors come from different nations, religions, languages, traditions—there are many differences. However, there are also those underlying threads of shared knowledge, interests, and ambitions.

A pleasant plus is that one is not expected to be an expert on all the nuances of culture, language, and even business practice within all the nations represented. You should know perhaps a little, especially about what is proper in the host country. (That has to do with getting around town more than booth behavior.) However, there are two guidelines that will see you through, regardless of what you know or do not know.

Be Polite and Formal.   A bit of restraint is always wise when meeting new people. That is especially the case at global shows. Do not assume you know the traditions of the country. In the USA, for instance, people start using first names with each other quickly. Chinese culture is much more formal.

Do Not Impose.   People from the United States are getting better about not imposing their own values on others. However, there is a long history of "the Ugly American" to overcome. It is a global reputation, and when cited, it means only people from the USA, not those from other American nations.

Perhaps fueled by vastly improved global communications, the Ugly Americans have been learning, rapidly, how to be better guests in other lands and how to be better hosts as well.

Each booth in the global village is a home. Be polite, stick to business, and do not try to impose your ways on others. Guests and visitors will be flexible, too.

Names

At USA domestic shows, where a relatively higher degree of informality is acceptable, business cards are exchanged with hardly a glance. Worse than that, little effort is made by either delegates or booth staff people to remember more than each other's first names. This practice, too, is changing as booth staff people awaken to the reality that they do better after they focus more on the person they are talking to.

Business Cards.   At international events, or in-country shows outside the USA and Canada, considerably more attention is paid to the names and titles of those meeting each other. Each person spends a moment *actually reading the card* before tucking it away.

- *Title confusion.* Frequently, executives use an acronym to describe their title. They save space on the card, and think they appear less self-important. However, these titles can mean very little in other nations. For instance, in the USA one sees cards with titles such as CEO, CFO, GM or Ph.D. (chief executive officer, chief financial officer, general manager, doctor of...). Many people have no idea as to what the acronyms mean.

- *Art confusion.* Many companies use fancy logos as part of their marketing communications program. These emblems are used on company business cards. They are fine on a domestic basis, but they can be confusing in other nations. The same is true for cards that feature small type or fancy colors. They can be very hard to learn from by people from other nations.

- *In-country language.* Make a judgment as to whether it is needed at your global show, but if you attend an in-country event for its domestic community, it can be a good idea to have cards printed with your own language on one side, the host country language on the other. The degree of difficulty in having this done differs considerably, depending on where you are going. The service may be offered in the exhibitor kit. Or, for instance, if you are going to China through Hong Kong, your hotel will send out a copy of your standard card, and they will return a box of dual language cards within a few hours.

Use of Names. Though not as critical at worldwide events, it is wise to have a basic understanding of how names are used in different cultures. Here are some illustrations:

- *USA.* Mary Ann Knauss Fish would be addressed as Ms. Fish, her husband's last name, which appears at the end of the name string on her card. Mr. Edward Chapman, Jr., would be addressed as Mr. Chapman.

- *Parts of Europe.* In Holland, for instance, Ms. Fish's card would be printed, Ms. Mary Ann Fish Knauss. Her husband's name appears first. You would still address her as Ms. Fish. Mr. Chapman remains Mr. Chapman.

- *Latin America.* A formal name includes the last names of both parents. However, the name string is printed differently depending on culture. For instance, much of Latin America is based on Spanish tradition. Were Edward Chapman to come from one of those nations, his name would be Edward Chapman Moore. He would be addressed Mr. Chapman again, his father's name, printed first in the name string. However, were Chapman to have been born in Brazil, which uses Portuguese as its language and follows that culture, his name would be Edward Moore Chapman. You still address him as Mr. Chapman, looking at the end of the name string.

- *China.* There are two standards, depending on family religious traditions. Mr. Zhao Weiping is from the Buddhist tradition. His last name is printed first. Thus, upon reading his card, you would address him as Mr. Zhao, not Mr. Weiping. On the other hand, Mr. James Lau comes from a Christian tradition. His last name is printed last. You would address him as Mr. Lau, not Mr. James. As you read a business card, you will know because those from a Christian tradition have first names that reflect it.

Body Language

Take the lead from your visitor. However, be restrained. When you are just getting started with a new person, err on the side of conservatism, even if the delegate seems gregarious—perhaps a Russian, Italian, or Australian.

Avoid gestures that convey specific meanings as they may not convey the same meaning in other lands. For instance, in the USA a specific gesture used occasionally is a circle made by touching the tips of the thumb and first finger together. Its meaning: Everything is okay, all correct. In some other cultures the same gesture is an obscenity. In Japan it signifies money.

- *Bowing.* In a large number of nations bowing is used frequently as a sign of respect, especially at the start and conclusion of conversations or meetings. However, there are many different types. At a global show can you remember that when meeting with a person from Thailand, it is best to bow with fingers of both hands pressed together in a small "prayer" gesture? Probably not.

The author's late mother offered good advice: "On all things observe your hostess (or host) and follow suit." If that is not possible, you can bow your own way, without exaggerating things—perhaps with just a formal nod of the head and slight lean. The idea, a signal of respect, is what counts.

Business Dress

Again, unless asked, be yourself as you would be at home, but err on the side of conservatism. It may be that you are exhibiting in a hot climate and most delegates will be wearing open neck clothing. That's fine for you to do as well if you come from a hot climate and business dress is the same. However, if you wear a coat and tie at home, or more formal suit and jacket or dress for women, continue with the practice until invited by others to shift. You signal respect.

Women in Business

On a worldwide basis, more and more women are surfacing in positions of responsibility and are accorded the same respect that was traditional only for men a generation ago. However, there remain nations, cultures, and religious practices that specify roles based on gender.

At a global event that should be less a problem than at some in-country shows. However, the last hurdles are yet to be crossed. Women should take extra care to be conservative in appearance and behavior. (If you are a movie star attending a film festival, that advice may not be valid. However, for the most of us...)

There is a second hint. Correctly, many female executives feel a responsibility to aid in the cause of cultural change. However, we observed one situation in which that became more important than the business being done. There are places to encourage new value systems. In our view a global or in-country trade event is not one of them. Making money is the name of that game!

Language

The international language of business is English. However, as we point out in more than one place in this reference book, the English used is not that spoken with ease where it is the birth language. (Even among those nations, there are vast differences.) Instead, the international commercial English that should be employed most of the time is that taught and used in nations where it is a second or third language.

Vocabulary and Speech.   For the most part, native English speakers will find those who learned the language later in life have a limited vocabulary. Often it is restricted to about 3000 words, though this can depend on the educational system in the nation. Here are some guidelines:

- *Use simple words.* That is obvious, but use simple words that have a clear meaning. For instance, the English word *get* can mean several things such as buy, rent, borrow, obtain, and so on. The word *right* can mean correct or a direction—and in spoken form could be mixed up with *write.* Try to be exact in your selection of words.

- *Avoid idiomatic expressions.* An American might say, "This is a Catch-22," tracing back to the book. Few will know what you are talking about. Sports idioms are confusing. For instance, few will know what "a ballpark figure" means. There are, as well, idioms or acronyms in an industry that the speaker might feel are used universally, but that might not be the case. For instance, a manufacturer of goods sold in stores may use the term *SKU* (stock keeping units) without realizing that his visitor does not use the term, or has a somewhat different understanding of it.

- *Stay clear of contractions.* Native English speakers use them constantly. However, they are actually idiomatic uses of the language. Instead of the contraction "Don't you agree?" say "Do you not agree?" It may sound stilted to the speaker, but the meaning is clearer, more appreciated.

- *Do not repeat the same words.* Frequently we observe an English speaker repeat a sentence, using the same words, but LOUDER. The listener can hear perfectly well. Pause, and that is appreciated by the way, think again about what you want to communicate, and use different words.

- *Slow down and enunciate clearly.* That is easy for us to write but very tough for many to do. Many English speakers rattle on at a blistering pace, leaving listeners in the dust. This is a serious problem even at domestic shows in the USA where most people grew up on English, though Spanish has emerged as widely spoken as a first language in some regions.

In Chapter 18 we present a very short voice exercise that is easy to complete. This type of program has its roots in the training given to performers—stage, screen, TV, and radio. It is based on learning what amounts to a trick, speaking with what is called "a round mouth." The result of practice for three days while taking your shower is fourfold. First, somewhat slower talking. Second, clearer word-by-word enunciation. Third, better projection without raising your voice. Fourth, a slightly deeper voice register. We suggest it. We use it.

Special warning: Native English speakers from the southern part of the USA speak more slowly than others, as do people from northern New England. However, the accents are more difficult to understand on an international basis. In addition, there are regional idioms that pop up frequently. They are fun if you can figure them out. That is difficult for those who have learned English as a second or third language. (As a writer born in the USA, I hesitate to cite vocabulary, accent, and idiom problems in other nations where English is the first language. That would not be polite. However, if you come from one of them, we suggest thinking things through a bit.)

- *Using a translator.* You may be from Sweden doing business with someone from Argentina. You might be Canadian, or from the USA, and doing business at HungExpo in Budapest with a Russian. Everyone is using international English. However, it may be that you are getting very serious about making a sales deal. Then, at least, it is wise to have a translator involved so that there are no mistakes made on specifics, such as exact product features required, pricing, or shipping. There are three guidelines:

  - *Hire in advance.* Translation services are available in most major centers. However, that does not mean your translator, no matter how fluent, instantly understands all aspects of your business, its products, and pricing. Provide advance information so that the translator gathers an understanding. (You are not looking for a translator of words but instead *an interpreter* of facts and ideas in another language and culture. There is a big difference.)
  - *Speak in short chunks.* During a back-and-forth dialogue, cite facts or opinions in short paragraphs, not long-winded monologues. Your translator will be far more accurate, and you will get an appropriate response in similar fashion.
  - *Speeches and seminars.* Less frequently, perhaps, you will present a paper or make a speech. Simultaneous translation services will be provided for delegates wearing ear phones. You will not "speak in short chunks." Written speech copies are given to the interpreters in advance. If you have not done that, slow down to the chunks! In this case it is not to wait for specific responses, but instead to allow time for an unfamiliar translator to think more about what you mean before putting words in your mouth.

Do's and Taboos Around the World

This is the title of a book compiled and sold, at low cost, by the Parker Pen Company.[1] The editor and compiler was Roger E. Axtell, a Parker vice president who spent about 20 years traveling the world. The company has offices in over 150 countries. (Axtell's job had to be fun and a learning experience, as well as productive for his company.) We think the book is unique.

- It is not self-important. Easy reading, and it does not try to do too much.
- It covers the basics without creating fear that you do not know enough.

We write with a view toward evenhanded explanations and offering readers supplier options. Not so now. We think there is no comparison with Parker Pen's book for anyone just getting started, unless you can afford large education costs. It covers the essentials of protocol, customs, etiquette, body language, gift giving (and receiving), language jargon and idioms—broken down by world region and nation. It's also fun to read. The compiler's purpose was to create *sensitivity* to customs and provide basic instruction on how to deal with them. It works.

Stands and Graphics

Here are a few words about three terms. In the USA the terms *exhibit* and *booth* are used to describe physical display structures. (The term *booth* is also used by some people to describe the space rented. We heard an exhibitor say, "We rented a booth." Since that is possible, we did not at first understand that what the exhibitor meant was that a *booth space* had been rented.)

In other parts of the world the term *stand* is used to describe physical display structures. Since this book was written in the USA, it uses the terms *exhibit* or *booth* throughout, except for this short section entirely devoted to booths or exhibits in other nations.

As you plan your stand and products for display, there are some things to keep in mind. One, interestingly enough, can be your product name. That is a strategic issue not related to exhibiting but one that certainly can have an impact.

Product Name

A number of years ago Coca-Cola was introduced in the People's Republic of China. Their soft drink had to be renamed slightly because the spoken translation in some parts of China was something akin to an animal fluid. In a similar situation, during the same time period, Sikorsky Helicopter introduced a model named "The Spirit of The United States" to international markets. It rapidly learned that in some nations the word *spirit* is reserved for religious purposes. The name was revised. There can be, as well, legal complications regarding names. The Pelican Products story is told later in this chapter. We do not dwell at length on this, but the essentials of company strategy have great impact on exhibiting's power to produce return.

Stand Design

There are similarities and differences between domestic and international exhibiting design practices, when one compares the USA with most other nations. We look at differences.

The Metric and English Measurement Systems. Figure 23-1 is a selective comparison and conversion chart, comparing the English-created measurement system (inches, feet, and pounds) with the more universally accepted metric system (centimeters, meters, and kilograms). It is selective because we include only measurements we think are of most interest to exhibitors.

In the USA a small company might say, "We rented a 10 by 10." In Europe it might be a "3-meter." The terms differ technically. But it is just about the same space. Of marginal interest, but perhaps something to tuck away, is that there will come a time when everyone will settle on the metric system. It is simple. All is based on manipulations of the mathematical symbol 10.

Design Systems

The subject of international design standards has been touched on in Chapters 13 and 21. In summary there were three main points to consider, as follows.

The Shell Scheme. USA domestic exhibitors, and some others, are provided what is called "pipe and drape" to outline their space. The shell scheme is one in which show management substitutes hard walls for the drapery. It is nicely illustrated as a design element in a national pavilion sketch that is part of Chapter 21. It is a design that was prepared for Unilink Canada (see Figure 21-1).

Already-Manufactured Systems. These are lightweight frame systems that allow for the application of custom graphics and other parts. They are used inside both pipe and drape and shell scheme rimmed stand spaces. In fact, some of these frame systems are used to create the shell rims themselves. For more information, see Chapters 3 and 13.

**Metric-English Measurement
System Conversions**

Booth Space.   In the USA booth space is rented in feet. In most cases linear booth spaces are offered in increments that are 10 feet long by 10 feet in depth.

The Metric-English Relationship.   One linear foot equals 0.3048 meters (m). A "10-foot space" in the USA is the close equivalent of a standard "3-meter space" in other nations.

Conversion Guide

Feet to meters: Multiply feet by 0.3 for meters.

Meters to feet: Multiply meters by 3.3 for feet.

Sign or Panels.   Assuming a booth built on metric measurements, USA exhibitors bringing their own signs should know that there can be "fit problems" unless suppliers are notified. The same is true for exhibitors in other nations having booths built in the USA following English measurements.

The Metric-English Relationship.   One linear inch equals 2.54 centimeters (cm). A standard sign size in the USA is 30 by 40 inches. The metric equivalent is 76.2 cm by 101.6 cm.

Note: Frequently panels or signs are slipped into booth frame slots. The width of the slot will depend on whether it was built to English or metric measurement. If your signs are too thin, they rattle. If too thick, they bind. Know your frame, and apply the conversion guide.

Conversion Guide

Inches to centimeters: Multiply inches by 2.5 for centimeters.

Centimeters to inches: Multiply centimeters by 0.4 for inches.

Weight.   Exhibit transport and drayage costs are most often quoted on the basis of weight, actual or "dimensional." See Chapter 16 for what that is all about.

The Metric-English Relationship.   One pound equals 0.4536 kilograms (kg). A "hundredweight" (100 pounds) equals 45.36 kg. Thus if a USA exhibitor sends a crate that weighs 800 pounds, its equivalent is 362.88 kg.

Figure 23-1. The information source is the U.S. Department of Commerce, National Bureau of Standards.

Conversion Guide

Pounds to kilograms: Multiply pounds by 0.45 for kilograms.

Kilograms to pounds: Multiply kilograms by 2.2 for pounds.

Temperature.   People count too! Most shows provide weather information including temperature ranges. If the show says the average temperature at the time of the event is 10°C, what does that mean to those used to the Fahrenheit system? It means 50°F, so bring a light coat. On the other hand, if the average is 85°F, those who use Celsius daily should know that the equivalent is over 29°C, pretty warm!

Conversion Guide

Celsius to Fahrenheit: Multiply by 9, divide by 5, and then add 32.

Fahrenheit to Celsius: Subtract 32, multiply by 5, and then divide by 9.

Figure 23-1. (*Continued*) The information source is the U.S. Department of Commerce, National Bureau of Standards.

Large Custom Stand Designs.   Exhibit mission and objectives should always drive the design process. The more specific the goals, the better the design. However, there are some traditions that have to be addressed.

- *Controlled environment.* In the USA, big booths tend to be open, with access provided to visitors on all sides. Traffic flow is somewhat controlled, and an effort is made to help guide visitors to what might be of most interest, but it remains very much a sort-it-out-yourself process.

In other parts of the world more big stands are designed for far more control of a visitor's experience. The fundamental design is focused on encouraging delegates down a defined path to a reception or greeting center where they sign in. Figure 23-2 is a sketch that illustrates entry pathway design. Often people are escorted through the stand. There will likely be private meeting rooms plus food and beverage service. A good number of appointments are set up before the opening of the show.

Fabrication and Setup.   There are different methods employed depending on stand size, as described below:

Figure 23-2. This sketch shows how visitors are directed to the greeting area of very large stand. It was prepared for Motorola at Communic *Asia* in 1994. (*Design and sketch courtesy of Pico Art Industries, Singapore.*)

- *Small stand spaces.* Smaller exhibitors own or rent structures that are placed in the space. Many are based on using the already-manufactured systems that come complete with shipping containers. This is something of a global standard.

  However, there is an excellent option for smaller exhibitors participating at an event where the hard wall shell scheme is employed. The walls are always freshly painted in a very plain color, often white or just off-white. Display items or graphic signs, plus other items to create decor—fabric, banners or whatever—can be affixed to the walls. Counters or pedestals can be rented and decorated as well.

- *Big stand fabrication and construction.* Large-scale exhibitors in the USA tend to have their big booths built for reuse. They are packed in specially designed crates and assembled in the space. Often the design allows small booths to be "carved" from the big for smaller events.

In other nations most of the monster stands are fabricated near to or at the trade hall itself. With perhaps some small units within the stand as exceptions, they are built for only one use. They will be torn down and tossed out after the show.

Big-time USA exhibitors get very nervous about this until they have experienced it. They worry about cost and quality control. They worry about what the whole thing will look like, and wonder if it will really happen.

There is always room for a disaster in the exhibit business, but experiences are generally quite good. The Colgate stand (see Chapter 22) was fabricated on-site. Here are some thoughts:

- Fabrication and construction costs are far lower than those associated with booths designed for reuse. The materials are different, and so are construction methods. The "look" can be the same.
- Frequently the actual builder will also be the decorating contractor for the show as a whole. You, or your USA exhibit house, can hire extra supervision to provide an extra level of comfort, but most times the jobs are well done and on time.
- Finally, and a good rule, is to allow the fabricator to complete the design, based on a concept, rather than to specify everything at home. USA exhibit designers have less experience in materials selection and fabrication methods used for one-use stands. (A stage set designer in the USA is far better in that context.)

The International Freight Forwarder

In Chapter 21 we touched on a lot of international expo planning issues and answers. That chapter also included some solid advice from David Bowie, a senior official at the U.S. Department of Commerce who has long experience with international exhibiting. He feels that if there is any one part of the process that can discourage new companies most, it is transportation. As a result, we spend extra time and space on the topic.

Strange Terms

If you do all of it yourself, you will be buffaloed by strange terms. They include such things as:

- Shipper's export declaration
- Commercial invoice
- Certificate of registration
- Certificate of origin
- Bill of lading
- Carnet
- Export license
- Master airway bill
- Shipper's letter of instructions

Have you had enough? It is a paper blizzard. Even with expert help, it takes extra time to ship your materials into another nation. An international freight forwarder will pull all of this together for you and provide explanations. However, there are some things that we need to point out about transport, as follows.

Items of Special Interest

- *Export license.* A very accurate and detailed explanation of what is being sent will be needed, and it can take some time to obtain the license.

- *Carnet.* This is a blessing. It is a passport for samples that are carried from country to country.

- *Export declaration.* This form helps the government track the value of goods leaving and entering the USA. It helps to produce all those billion-dollar in-and-out reports we read.

- *Shipper's letter of instruction.* This letter sets the value of the shipment for insurance and customs purposes.

The Exhibiting Specialty

Leslie Stroh, publisher of *Exporter Magazine,* is also cited in Chapter 21. He hints at complications when he points out that an important subject in booth discussions will be how orders for goods will be shipped—especially when they are for less than a container load. There are other complexities, of course, and many of them are logistical. Stroh agrees that international freight forwarders wear many hats and are great problem solvers. David Bowie adds that within the family of freight forwarders one should seek out an exhibit specialist. There are many little wrinkles that differ from the issues faced daily in the ordinary flow of goods around the world.

Stephen J. Barry, Jr.,[2] is one of the specialists and he makes a crucial point for exhibiting companies. In an article for the International Exhibitors Association journal, *IdEAs,* he wrote, "Not all forwarders are familiar with the *temporary* import regulations in their own country....The market [exhibits] is not big enough for them to employ people familiar with their temporary import regulations." He points out, "Every day, millions of entries [border crossings] are made around the world for the permanent importation of material(s)."[3] In that context exhibiting is small cheese.

International Exhibit Freight Forwarders. Barry's company (TWI) is large, but there are other forwarding outfits that specialize in handling exhibit freight. What differences are there between exhibit freight specialists and normal import commerce? Among them:

- Some nations may require a bond to be paid when exhibit materials and product samples are sent in, to be paid back when the materials and product samples leave. Others no. As we said before, there are little wrinkles. As Zhao Weiping points out later in this chapter, in the People's Republic of China samples can be brought in without paying an import fee and can be stored in a bonded warehouse after the event for a time—pending a potential sale in China. If sold, the import fee would be paid. If not, it could be shipped back home with no harm done except for the transport bill.

- There are countries in which different kinds of exhibit materials must be sent in separate boxes so they can be treated differently. For instance, it is possible that "consumables" such as product literature or gifts to be given out at the event should be shipped by themselves with duty owed—not so for product samples or exhibit structures that will leave the nation after the exposition. (In the case of consumables a supplier bill helps to establish value.)

- "The forwarder or customs broker taking on temporary importation services takes on a potentially large liability," says Barry. If materials brought in just for the show are not exported later, there could be import duties—fines and other penalties owed by the forwarder or broker within the country. They are careful!

Selecting a Forwarder

Barry points out that the receiving end is the most important. That is where the war stories emerge about exhibit freight held forever, unknown legal restrictions, and resultant costs. It is easy to avoid all of that.

The Show's Contractor. The organizer's exhibitor kit will include information about the show's official freight-forwarding contractor. That contractor was selected, as Barry points out, because "the organizer wants to know as little about freight as possible." The official contractor can and does provide the name of its partners in the USA or any other country so you can work through them.

Some organizers produce international trade shows outside the boundaries of their own country. One purpose is to encourage export for their own companies, though anybody can participate. Barry points out, "German organizers have done that, for instance, with government support. What is important is that support includes covering part of the freight cost for exhibitors, regardless of the exhibitor's home nation." When you find that situation, you can save money by letting the show management's freight-forwarding contractor handle the whole thing.

An alternate is working through a well-known domestic company such as Barry's that has well-established worldwide contacts.

Timing and Cost.   There are two factors that create consternation at the other end. By far the most important is time. It simply takes a lot longer to ship worldwide than it does on a domestic basis. (First-class airmail letters between little-town USA and Beijing, for instance, take about 10 calendar days.) The second is cost. Leave things until late and you will face a lot more cost in shipping.

Dealing with Experts: A Value Story

Most international exhibit transport involves relatively small shipments but such is not always the case. The story of Gulfstream Aerospace Corporation's "Gulfstream V" illustrates the big and, importantly, focuses on problems that international freight forwarders avoid. Barry provides this information. He summarizes a feature story written for the magazine, *Tradeshow & Exhibit Manager*.[4]

The Product.   The Gulfstream V was designed as the longest-range executive aircraft ever to fly. It had to be marketed before prototypes were in the air! At a 30-plus million-dollar cost per plane, the need for preproduction marketing is easy to fathom. Even deep-pocket manufacturers avoid building finished big-ticket units without orders in hand.

The Marketing Program.   Gulfstream built a model. It was not childs' play. The mockup value was over $2.5 million itself. Though it did not fly, the "model" included full cockpit, with operating instruments, and a sample passenger interior, air-conditioned. Included, as well, was one engine covering affixed to the side of the mockup and a somewhat smaller, walk-around model of the whole machine. Altogether, two trailer loads!

The goal was to introduce the Gulfstream V to potential buyers in England, Spain, Italy, Switzerland, Germany and, finally, at the Paris Air Show, with many nations represented. Then home to the USA for more of the same!

The Freight Project.   The two trailers moved from the Gulfstream facility in Savannah, Georgia, to Norfolk, Virginia, to a "roll-on, roll-off" sea freighter bound for England. Experienced international drivers were on the other end. Two more sea-segments were involved—from England to Spain and then back to the USA. The other border crossings were on land.

Forwarder Added Value.   What makes this case of value is that the program took place at the time the European Economic Community agreement was signed. The rules for shipping across boundaries were changing. The forwarder knew that each signatory nation would have to create new instructions and training for its border entry people. Cabinet ministers sign treaties, but nothing happens until the people "below" have instructions on how to implement a new policy.

Because the freight forwarder understood these realities, the drivers were supplied with extra copies of both the old and the new required documents. The result: seamless border crossings and no problems at "show time."

Time Is Almost Everything.   Treating domestic exhibiting as a casual exercise, like nipping over to the shopping mall to purchase just in advance of need, creates problems. On an international level that failure can spell disaster. Start far enough in advance, six months or more, and there is time to sort out any problems that may emerge along the way.

Obey the Law!

Most exhibitor frustrations are created because of belated planning and inadequate attention to the show's exhibitor kit. Other problems can emerge because of late shipping. There are, as well, a few situations where *commercial law* in the host nation can create problems. It does not happen frequently, but it is worth asking about.

The Pelican Adventure

We summarize a story written by the author for *Exhibit Builder Magazine*.[5] It traced the quest of Pelican Products, a small business based in Torrance, California.[6] Started in a garage in the late 1970s, Pelican Products grew and included export marketing almost from its opening days.

The company started with a line of high-quality submersible flashlights that are used by sport scuba divers and in commercial underwater activities. Later the technology was used to create a line of reusable crates for delicate equipment. (Some have been used by exhibitors for repeat shipments of fragile electronic equipment.)

The Situation.   Pelican knew that its line of crates had never been properly introduced to the European photo equipment market. It sent a 30-foot booth, product samples, and all the rest to Photokina, an every-two-year photo event in Cologne, Germany.

In spite of exporting to Europe, including Germany, for a decade, the company did not know it was breaking German law. It found out at Photokina. Partway through the show German authorities closed and confiscated the booth and samples. Pelican's sales manager was threatened with jail! As a wake-up call, this was a beauty.

The Law.   There is a German law that prohibits foreign companies from using the same name or one that is similar to that of a German company or brand. Pelikan AG (different spelling but in translation the same) is a very large multinational. It is a worldwide company that sells office supplies, pens, pencils, computer printer ribbons, and related products.

The reality that the two "pelicans" did not compete on products made no difference. The law was written without that specification. To illustrate the point, we stay with birds. A similar law in the USA, for instance, might protect the makers of "Dove" soap from others using that name, including the company that sells Dove Chocolates. (In fact, in the USA there is more likelihood that the two would get together. After all, some chocolate eaters may need soap!)

The First Fix.   The sales manager was not thrown behind bars. However, there were meetings among lawyers representing both companies. An agreement was reached that the USA's Pelican could market in Germany with a name change to "Peli." At considerable cost for a small outfit, the changes were made in product packaging and all the rest. It had to make the changes. Exports to old German customers had been stopped, costing the company several hundred thousand dollars a year.

Two years later Pelican was back at Photokina. And, of course, the booth again was visited by German authorities. And again it was closed, and everything confiscated. Pelican had failed to make the name change in two places in product literature. One was a list that retained "Pelican" identifying its Australian dealer.

The Resolution.   More adventures later, Pelikan AG and Pelican Products top managers met and settled things in quite friendly fashion without police and lawyers. There is a great deal of mutual respect. Pelican is back in Germany doing better than ever. But it was not accomplished without great cost to a David fighting its Goliath!

The Lesson.   Ask! The show manager, your freight forwarder, or another exhibitor might know if there are any unusual commercial laws to be evaluated. The U.S. Department of Commerce representative at the U.S. embassy is another source, along with representatives of the Chamber of Commerce in the nation. A Pelican situation does not emerge often, but when it does, it can be very costly.

Exhibiting in China

We have elected to pay special attention to the People's Republic of China (PRC), even though that might seem inappropriate in a general exhibit management book. There are many nations, from Argentina to Mexico to Russia to the USA, about which it might be appropriate to write an essay.

In the mid-1990s there have been barrels of ink spilled in books and periodicals about international trade to and within the European Economic Community and North American Free Trade Agreement partners; plus other multinational and bilateral treaty signers.

Because of that, and book life, we look to the future and select China for special attention. You can opt not to read this chapter section now if you are not at all thinking about trading in China. However, please remember that it exists and come back to it at the right time. We say that because it seems inevitable that trade with the PRC will surface in your life. If you elect to read now, it may encourage you to start thinking about the subject sooner rather than later.

Note: There are some items included in this section that are redundant. They appear in our general treatment of what is expected and done in other countries. That is intentional. Exhibiting in the PRC differs in some respects. However, you should also know that the process is global. Some things you do down the street are the same in China.

Russell Berrie, chairman and CEO of RUSS Berrie and Company, and executive-in-residence at Baylor University's Hankamer School of Business in 1994, said then, "I predict that by the year 2000, China will be the powerhouse in the marketplace,...a really good US trading partner....If we don't work together China will dance with somebody else."[7] Berrie is correct.

There are four reasons for special interest. First is the sheer size of China (see Figure 23-3). Second is its economic growth pattern. As we enter the twenty-first century, the PRC will be one of the strongest economic powers on earth. Many businesspeople in the USA and all over the globe know that. Third, and importantly, there are unique business practice differences that all must understand. Fourth, though there are many ways to initiate trade, for smaller and midsize compa-

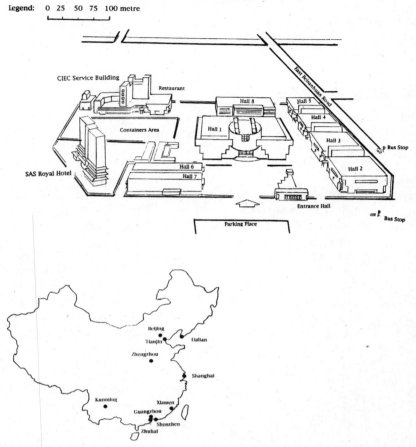

Figure 23-3. Everyone knows something about Beijing, and many have heard about its Exhibition Centre. That extensive facility is in the top part of this sketch. However, China is a very large nation. The lower sketch shows cities where other big exhibition facilities are located and filled with expositions. (*Sketches courtesy of Zhao Yuan, Beijing, China.*)

nies there may be no better way to start than with in-country trade fair participation.

To illustrate the increasing influence of foreign trade in China, at the end of 1993, 167,500 foreign-invested enterprises had registered to do business in the People's Republic. That was up a remarkable 83,100 from the end of 1992.[8] That year reflects the start of the free-market economy. What amounts to a doubling of the number of foreign businesses starting in China won't happen every year. However, there is little doubt that we will see continued substantial increases for years to come. If you are starting to think China-trade, you are not alone!

This chapter, its author, and readers, owe a special debt. For several years we have been communicating with Mr. Zhao Weiping in China. As of this writing, he is an economist and General Manager of Exhibition Department at the China International Exhibition Centre in Beijing. He has provided much of the information included and has shared his viewpoints generously.[9]

An Overview

Until the early 1990s China's economy was almost entirely centrally planned. China has now changed to a free-market economy. The transition itself has been planned with care, especially as it impacts on the use of foreign exchange. As a result, there remain some unique issues to be understood. More and more latitude is being given, but China's end-using businesses and government departments prepare international purchasing plans in advance for approval.

Though not yet convertible, there is an exchange rate. As of this writing, it is about 8 RMB (the Chinese currency) for 1 U.S. dollar. Purchasers have to come up with the RMB equivalent as part of the approval process. Sellers are paid in Swiss francs or U.S. dollars.

The international purchasing process also involves the use of specialist foreign trading companies. You will deal first with the end-using customer, making the sale. However, at the end both you and your customer will deal with the trading company. That company handles all the details. Your contract will be made with the trading company instead of the end user. Payment will be made by the foreign trading company.

Exhibiting Implications

There are a number of ways in which the overall purchasing process affects exhibiting. Key among them is that exhibitions are often used to close sales and sign contracts, instead of simply starting the process with a lead for follow-up later.

Timing.   It should be obvious that just starting will require extra time before a first sale. Your end-using prospects have to know you, your products, and pricing well in advance if they plan to buy.

There can be situations in which what you offer competes with other, similar products. In those cases some prospects may have already gained their approvals for purchase. However, they still have to get to know you and will want to address service issues. It may be realistic to assume that your first show could be one purely for introductions: gathering leads for follow-up and potential sales later, even the following year. Zhao says, "Please be patient."

Preshow Promotion.   Providing information in advance and inviting prospects to visit with you can be very important, whether or not this is your first show. The show's producer will help you organize that.

Trade fair organizers routinely prepare exhibitor product books sent to those who will attend. Product descriptions are detailed and include pricing information. Readers use them to help prepare their final purchasing plans.

Show Length.   Trade events in China last longer than is the experience in the USA. But most run for no more six days. (The sixth-day need is created because of the formalities required to finalize purchasing with the trading company.)

The end user's advance approval process normally takes about 10 days. The value in preshow promotion is that this work can be done in advance. There is another option if that was not done. Most exhibitors bring product samples. In some cases at least an initial purchase can be made from the samples. The samples can be stored in a Chinese bonded facility. If the paperwork is completed, after the show is over the importer, not the seller, will pay whatever duties are required and take delivery from the bonded warehouse.

Of necessity, our explanation is brief. There are some intricacies involved. Zhao Weiping suggests that you might want to involve a reliable agent in the process. He says, "Usually the Hong Kong people know both the western trade and Chinese systems. They are well qualified."

The Chinese Show Industry

The exposition industry is not as fully developed as it is in the USA or Europe. However, as you might imagine, it is quite substantial and growing rapidly. Most automatically think of the China International Exhibition Centre in Beijing. It is the nation's largest hall. It provides 170,000 square meters of exhibit space, over 180,000 square feet. China is very large, and there are 14 other facilities, with planning and construction for more (see Figure 23-3). The centers are busy. As of this writing, there are just under 50 medical events a year alone. And the numbers are growing.

Show Selection.   The show picking process can be puzzling, especially for those just beginning. There are, however, some things you can do to reduce risk. Zhao passes on some thoughts expressed first to us by the U.S. Department of Commerce.

- Find out if the exposition suggested to you is sponsored by Chinese governmental organizations and the degree to which these organizations really support it. Usually, exhibitions organized by the China Council for the Promotion of International Trade (CCPIT) are reliable.[10]

- The U.S. Department of Commerce runs a certification process for expositions. If the show of interest has also been certified by the DOC, it is even more an indication of reliability. (See Chapter 21 for more information and sources in this regard.)

- Regardless, you will be making initial contact with the show organizer. What you can learn from that source can be the most valuable. Find out about the show's background. If it has been held before, you should be given its history. And, from a list of its prior exhibitors, you should be able make some calls and get advice. However, because China's exposition industry is growing, there are many first-year events. These may not be appropriate for first-time exhibitors, unless you find that the event is well backed in China.

Implementation Issues

After making a decision to participate, you will be sent what is called an "exhibitor kit" in the USA. Most often it is quite a thick binder. They are thoroughly produced, difficult to go through, but quite important. That is especially so for international events, and especially for China since there are so many differences in practices and procedures to explain.

In addition to show rules and information, the kit provides order forms for services. There are many additions to what one might see in a kit produced for a domestic event, including such things as translation services.

Hints from Zhao Weiping

Earlier in his career Zhao sold space for and then produced trade shows in China. The hints that follow are not a complete checklist, as one might find in an exhibitor kit. But important issues that many seem to ignore are included.

Select Space Promptly.   Order early. First come, first served. There is research that points out that space position matters less than one might think, at least in the USA. But Mr. Zhao feels it can help in China if you book space close to the main show entrance. Large exhibitors should select an island space early, too, for the same reason.

Send Service Orders and Payments Early.   Some required costs are far more expensive if left late. These include such things as transportation for samples and exhibit properties, visa application fees, air fares, and hotel reservations.

Ask Show Management about Costs.   Plan early, and if you have a question, contact the show organizer. For instance, if you think that charges from any service contractors are unreasonable, show management will check it out and let you know. If a contractor offers a "free" service, be suspicious. Zhao says, "There is no free lunch, anywhere in the world."

Plan for Contingencies.   For the inexperienced, plan the budget with a good set-aside to cover the unexpected. There will be things you have not thought about!

Forwarders and Contractors.   It is especially important to select a reliable freight forwarder, on-site booth contractor, and good travel agent. Your goal should be to concentrate on business at the show, not to worry about samples that do not arrive on time, the booth setup, hotel, in-city transport, and other logistical matters.

Cultural Guidelines

Long before he became Vice President and then President of the United States, George Bush made his first visit to China. During that trip he made a mistake that is natural but instructive. He brought a gift to the Chinese Premier. It was a pair of custom-designed "cowboy boots" that included artwork of the American and Chinese flags, intertwined. The Premier said, in effect, "We are not used to putting our flag or another country's flag on our boots or shoes, since flags are Holy to us."

Be Conservative in Gift Giving

Token gifts, given away at the stand, are acceptable. Included can be such things as a plastic bag with the company imprint. Do not, however, try to overwhelm people. That will simply embarrass them.

Avoid Politics

Stick to business. (That advice is good anywhere in the world.) Discussions, literature, or any other form of comment on a nation's political system or situation is not welcomed, even if the person you are talking with agrees with you.

Artwork that depicts the map of the People's Republic of China should include Taiwan and Hong Kong but not Mongolia. If the text in a brochure refers to Hong Kong, do not imply that Hong Kong is a nation. Nations should be represented as equals, and Hong Kong is a region, not a nation. For instance, assume you are giving out a list of dealers:

The Wrong Way

Our distributors include the following:

Australia: The XYZ company in Sydney at...

Hong Kong: The XYZ company at...

A More Appropriate Way

Our distributors include the following:

In Australia: The XYZ company in Sydney at...

In the Hong Kong region: The XYZ company at...

Avoid Sexual Implications

China is very much family oriented. From a male, as well as a female, viewpoint, photographs of nude models are considered to be in poor taste, except for medical situations in which those depictions are necessary, both male and female. (Conservative bathing suits are fine. Just don't go too far.)

Business Entertainment

Chinese hospitality is well known. That extends to business. Cocktail and dinner parties, and more formal banquets, are very much part of doing business in China. As an exhibitor, you will most likely be invited to one or more events.

Depending upon the situation, it may be appropriate for you to *host* a dinner or banquet. (The U.S. Department of Commerce can provide more advice. However, even without that, if orders are signed at the event, it is a good idea to host a thank-you dinner for your end-customer and trading company representatives.) That dinner or cocktail hour can be arranged with ease.

If Invited, Go. You may be surprised at the number of social invitations you may receive. The Chinese are very hospitable. There is no direct business involved in these, except for a congratulatory dinner that might follow a contract signing. There are three basic types: A *banquet* is a formal dinner or lunch with people seated around a table. A *reception* implies that while lots of food will be served, it is a "stand-up" situation. A *cocktail party*, typically lasting a relatively short time, will feature wine and drinks but less food, perhaps just light snacks.

Interestingly, if you find yourself hosting an affair—perhaps after contract signing—the host usually pays a tip to the drivers of Chinese officials attending. The tip runs from 30 to 50 Yuan for each, from $3.00 to $6.00 in U.S. dollars. Chinese officials rarely drive. Their drivers, whether company, or government employed, often wait two hours or more through long banquets and get their own meals during that period. The tip pays for that. (Tipping is not necessary for shorter events because the drivers will not miss their own dinner hour. Normally, in China, cash tips for taxi drivers and such are not acceptable from foreigners.) The host can also give tips to the interpreters who may accompany main guests at banquets. That is considered appropriate for the same reasons. They *work* during the banquet!

The social schedule, added to long days in the trade hall, can be exhausting. However, even if no direct business is done, they are valuable. As Zhao Weiping says, "Often, Chinese ministers attend, and these people are technical experts. Many speak English well. They might mention you to end users of your products."

Chinese show organizers often invite Chinese officials for a private visit to the trade hall, generally in the evening after formal show hours. Plan on keeping your booth open. Again, they can be influential is suggesting you to buyers. Whether or not, Zhao counsels, "Well begun, half done."

Language Problems

The advice provided by Zhao is similar to general advice we cover elsewhere. Many Chinese do speak English, but they prefer the English spoken in other countries where it is taught as a second language, such as in Germany or France. English vocabularies are relatively small, and sentence structures are kept simple.

Those who come from the USA or Britain, for instance, use far too many long words and slip into complex sentence structures that are hard to follow. The advice: Speak slowly, clearly, using simple words. For instance, it is better to say "I knew him three years ago" than "I *made his acquaintance* three years ago."

Using Translators

There are two situations where translators are very important. One is during the detailed technical and financial discussions leading up to a contract. The other emerges if you are to present a paper at a seminar.

Business and Technical Discussions. Provide your translator with as much information as you can in advance. Often there are terms unique to an industry to be learned and applied appropriately. When working through your translator, break what you want to say into small parts. Avoid long statements. There is less chance for error.

Presenting at a Seminar. If you are making a presentation, it should be written in advance. A copy should be given to the interpreter with enough time provided so that your ideas are thoroughly understood. When you speak you can be assured of accuracy in simultaneous translation.

Do It!

Most of what we have seen that discusses international trade and exhibiting makes the process seem as though it is loaded with time bombs. There are some differences, of course, but sometimes writers and speakers focus so much on problems that they lose track of the positive. If we have done that, we apologize. Thousands of companies sell and exhibit far away from home, and there are few problems.

PART 5

The Industry and Management

24

The Exhibit Industry: Who Does What and Where to Learn More

Even experienced managers can become confused about who does what in this industry. It may not matter. They know who they have to know. But there are frustrations, some of which trace back to that lack of understanding, and the natural alliances that emerge. For instance, exhibitors know their exhibit builder; show management executives know their decorating company and facility managers.

This chapter also includes lists of information sources and publications. More and more periodicals have been created specifically for exhibitors. That reflects a perception of increased importance, as well as higher cost and return potential.

Six Fingers and a Thumb

Industry experts differ as to how its segments break down. We view it as six fingers and a thumb.

Exhibitors and Visitors

Taken together, this is the thumb. The reason is that these two groups end up paying the bills. For most events the larger share is paid by exhibitors to help the show's producer reduce visitor costs, which encourages more participation. That is not to say that it costs visitors next to nothing! Their registration cost may be low, but everyone spends money on travel and hotels. Exhibitor costs do not stop with at-show out-of-pocket expenses. Their costs are wide ranging and include the booth, graphics, transport, and promotion.

Exhibit Designers and Producers

These individuals or firms are primarily the suppliers of custom booths and graphics to exhibitors. They design, build, crate, store, refurbish; and they can provide management services that involve transport and the provision of services on-site. For the most part, design service costs are absorbed in the billing for fabrication, lights, carpet, and graphics production. In addition, these organizations are funded by markups on the other services provided. For instance, the exhibit house must charge for managing external services such as those for on-site services and transport.

This cluster of design, product, and services has long been referred to as what a "full-service" exhibit house provides. This industry was an outgrowth of the furniture industry in the early part of the century. Until recently most fabrication was based on wood framing, with graphic panels added. Today, a variety of construction materials are used to create modular parts that are bolted together at expositions.

Already-Manufactured Units.   Competition for the wood-based framing systems emerged a number of years ago. There are quite a number of them, for the most part based on the use of aluminum extrusions. Each system, patented, features slots for graphics and specialized connectors. The manufacturers developed local dealer networks. Dealers would offer standard units and add graphics and other touches.

At the start traditional exhibit builders were hesitant to move in the direction of using the metal-based framing systems. They did not have the equipment or trained people to cut and otherwise manipulate metal to form their custom designs.

Today, the two sides have started blending. Classic exhibit houses have gained in their capabilities. Already-manufactured dealers have done so as well, now designing and building custom designs with their systems.

Independent Designers.   This is a small industry segment, designers who are not staff members at an exhibit company. Some exhibitors prefer to use them for initial design development, then bidding the result to several exhibit houses for competitive quotes.

New "Full-Service" Definition.   Some larger exhibit builders have started offering things that expand the envelope of classic full service. These include such things as staff training and the development of promotional programs such as direct mail and advertising, and even lead management. In some cases these services are provided in-house. In others, they are supplied from the outside, much as an advertising agency gathers appropriate supplies and suppliers.

We offer more on this industry segment in Chapters 3 and especially 13.

Ad Agencies and Sales Promotion Firms, Consultants, and Trainers

Advertising agencies, and especially those that work with business-to-business sellers, have started taking greater interest in exhibiting. They will act as a one-stop shopping resource for their clients.

There are, as well, consultants and trainers. (Our firm is one of many.) They can provide a wide diversity of services within their special areas. Trainers work directly with exhibitors, through exhibit builders and through show managers. Consultants offer specialized services—from management analysis, preshow promotion development, on-site setup supervision and lead tracking, to full outsource of the exhibit marketing management function.

Transportation Companies

Haulers—land, sea, or air—are an important part of the industry. The largest segment: over-the-road trucking companies. There are both general haulers and van line services. They work directly with exhibitors or through their exhibit houses and their show managers. We pay considerable attention to them in Chapter 16.

Facility Managers

For the most part exhibitors do not have direct contact with those who manage the facility where an event takes place. Most contacts with the exhibitor are through show management.

Facility Types

- Best known are large convention halls built and operated by governmental authorities. There is hardly a large or midsize city in America without its own hall. The objective is to help attract visitors, building business for the community.

- There are hundreds of privately owned exhibition facilities as well, many of them tied to hotels. The Hilton in Las Vegas, for instance, offers over 100,000 square feet of exhibit space that is located less than 100 feet away from the Las Vegas Convention Center! The twin towers of the Hyatt Regency on Wacker Drive in Chicago are perched on top of over 100,000 square feet of exhibit space, three floors below the front desk.

- Meeting and exhibit spaces are also provided by many resorts. For instance, in Orlando, Florida, just across the main road from the Disney theme parks, sits a large Marriott-owned resort. It includes meeting and exhibit hall space.

- A new industry has emerged in the last decade and a half—the suburban conference center. The focus is on providing meeting facilities, but most also provide at least limited exhibit hall space. For more on facilities, see Chapter 25.

Show Managers

Every so often an exhibit manager calls, and along the way in the conversation mentions the acronym for a favorite trade show, assuming we know all about the event. If only that were true! People are familiar with *their* shows. They do not know that there are thousands of business-to-business trade events each year—and thousands more consumer shows. One of the USA's largest associations is the American Society of Association Executives. Smaller, but influential, is the International Association of Exposition Managers.

Association-Sponsored Events.   The majority of our business-to-business events are sponsored by not-for-profit trade associations. They combine educational opportunities with an exhibition of products and services of special interest to the industry.

In some cases exposition management is provided by association staff people. In others the function is managed by an outside, professional show management company. Either way, a trade show can be a key association funding source.

For-Profit Business Expositions.   There are a large number of trade and general business events that are independently sponsored by the promoter. Some of these offer educational programs to help attract an audience, others do not. (Of those who do not provide a parallel learning experience, most are events designed exclusively for retail inventory ordering.) For more on show managers, see Chapter 25.

Private Shows.   As mentioned in Chapter 15, there are expositions created by large companies providing head-office–approved vendors to show their wares to dealers, franchise holders, and corporate divisions.

Show Services Contractors

These companies work for both the show itself and exhibitors on site. We see them listed, with order forms, in our exhibitor kits. A short cruise through one of these binders signals that there are a wide range of services and rentals. See Chapter 15 for details.

There is always a key general contractor. The term used: *Decorating Company*. That company recruits subcontractors and also provides some services in-house. There are some services, however, that the facility itself provides, through contractors it works with. For example, electrical service is often provided through a facility, and in some instances food services are provided in the hall.

Exhibit Industry Associations

The exhibit industry is far larger and more complex than many realize. In fact, it has its own alphabet soup of associations that serve one or more parts of the industry—show managers and exhibit builders, for instance.

Exhibitor-Interest Associations

This book is primarily intended for exhibitors. Thus, we provide extra attention to the associations that directly serve them.

The International Exhibitors' Association (IEA) is perhaps best known. Midsize and large exhibitors from different industries are members. Though the word *international* appears as part of its name, most members are from the USA. It has over 1300 members, combining corporate exhibitors and companies that supply products and services to exhibit managers.

There are other exhibitor associations. The largest is the Healthcare Convention & Exhibitors Association (HCEA), with over 600 members. There, is, as well, a smaller association especially for technology companies, the Computer Event Marketing Association (CEMA). Another is for those who supply educational materials in the Roman Catholic Church market.

There is, as well, an umbrella organization that serves the industry as a whole and that provides direct services to exhibitors. It is the

---

**Associations of Direct Interest
to Exhibitors**

The International Exhibitors Association (IEA)
5501 Backlick Road
Suite 100
Springfield, VA 22151
T: 703-941-3725   F: 703-941-8275

The Healthcare Convention & Exhibitors Association (HCEA)
5775 Peachtree-Dunwoody Road
Suite 500-G
Atlanta, GA 30342
T: 404-252-3663   F: 404-252-0774

The Computer Event Marketing Association (CEMA)
C/O Dinieli & O'Keefe Associates, Inc.
Association Management
490 Boston Post Road
Sudbury, MA 01776
T: 508-443-3300

Center for Exhibition Industry Research (CEIR)
4350 East-West Highway, Suite 401
Bethesda, MD 20814
T: 301-907-7626
Former name was The Trade Show Bureau (TSB)

Figure 24-1. These are broad-based associations and information sources of direct interest to exhibitors. There are many other associations serving the industry as a whole.

Center for Exhibition Industry Research (CEIR). Many are familiar with its former name, the Trade Show Bureau (TSB), the industry research arm.

A list of the four organizations with the broadest appeal to exhibitors appears, with addresses and telephone numbers, as Figure 24-1.

Information Sources

By some estimates, over a half million USA companies exhibit, someplace and somehow, at least once every year. Membership in exhibitor associations represents a very small tip on top of a very large iceberg.

For the most part these exhibitors get their information, all they think they need, from their show's exhibitor kits. But these kits cover only essentially tactical subjects. There is, however, increasing awareness that there is a lot more to exhibit marketing than meets the eye when one drifts through kit-presented rules and suppliers.

For instance, our first book on this subject was written with McGraw-Hill in the late 1980s. It sold 15 times more copies than the combined exhibitor membership of all exhibitor associations. Most readers of this book are not members, though it could be of value for many to join one.

Periodicals and Directories

Another signal of increasing interest is the degree to which exhibiting coverage has expanded over the past few years, in both specialist and general business publications.

Figure 24-2 is a lengthy list of publications that covers the industry or present occasional editorial matter of interest. It is not in any particular order. We suggest you scan it for publications you already read so that you can keep an eagle eye out for exhibit marketing material. You also might want to subscribe to one or two of the specialist exhibit periodicals.

You will also see that a number of directories are marketed by these publishers. In addition, at the very end of Figure 24-2 is a short list of periodicals and references that cover international subjects.

You might also be alert for exhibit marketing coverage in your own trade magazine. A number of these highly specialized periodicals have started to carry occasional articles on exhibiting within their industry. For instance, we have written on exhibiting for the recreational marine, floral, steel, produce, food manufacturing, and travel industries. There are others who have done the same.

Academic Opportunities

Over the past few years the increasing awareness of exhibiting importance has been reflected in the academic world. At one college-level symposium sponsored by the University of Nevada in Las Vegas (UNLV), professors from over 30 campuses, nationwide, attended.

Degree Programs

Two universities now offer programs leading to degrees in exhibit marketing. Georgia State University in Atlanta offers a degree-earning

---

Publications and Other Information Sources

IdEAs Journal
The International Exhibitors' Association (IEA)
5501 Backlick Road
Suite 100
Springfield, VA 22151
T: 703-941-3725
Note: This journal leads a long list of educational materials available from the association. The IEA also produces an annual conference and exposition for exhibitors.

Center for Exhibition Industry Research (CEIR)
4350 East-West Highway, Suite 401
Bethesda, MD 20814
T: 301-907-7626
Former name was The Trade Show Bureau (TSB)
Note: This industry research center funds and publishes research studies of interest to the exposition industry, including exhibit managers. Its current publications catalog is 16 pages thick with descriptions. The studies are available to both members and nonmembers. (Costs are higher for nonmembers.)

Tradeshow Week, Inc.
12233 West Olympic Blvd.
Suite 236
Los Angeles, CA 90064
T: 213-826-5696
Note: In addition to its weekly newsletter, this publisher provides several well-regarded annual directories. Included is the *Tradeshow Week Data Book* (USA/Canada and a separate international edition) covering shows broken down by group. Added to that are the *Tradeshow Week Services Directory,* the *Tradeshow Week 200,* an analysis of the largest 200 shows in the USA and a smaller group in Canada, and the *Tradeshow Week Major Facilities Hall Directory.*

Tradeshows & Exhibits Schedule
Successful Meetings Data Bank
633 Third Avenue
New York, NY 10017
T: 212-973-4890

Figure 24-2. The publications serving primarily the USA market that tend to include more exhibit marketing material appear first. These include show list publications. The publishing world is dynamic. Addresses are correct as of this writing.

The SRDS Tradeshow Catalog
Standard Rate and Data Service
3004 Glenview Road
Wilmette, Il 60091
T: 800-323-4601

The Exhibit Review (Show List Book)
Phoenix Communications
4620 Southwest Beaverton Hillsdale Highway, Suite B1
Portland, OR 97221
T: 503-244-8677

Exhibitor Times: Virgo Publishing
4141 North Scottsdale Road
Suite 316
Scottsdale, AZ 85251
T: 602-990-1101
Note: This is a four-color, well-rated publication intended for exhibitors.

Exhibitor Magazine
Exhibitor Publications
745 Marquette Bank Building
Rochester, MN 55903
T: 507-289-6556
Note: This is a high-quality monthly, four-color publication for exhibit managers. The company also publishes an annual directory of sources. It publishes a show schedule in its pages. In addition, it sponsors an annual convention for exhibitors.

The Healthcare Convention & Exhibitors Association (HCEA)
5775 Peachtree-Dunwoody Road
Suite 500-G
Atlanta, GA 30342
T: 404-252-3663
Note: Among other educational materials, the association produces a comprehensive list of conventions that serve the health care fields.

Figure 24-2. (*Continued*) The publications serving primarily the USA market that tend to include more exhibit marketing material appear first. These include show list publications. The publishing world is dynamic. Addresses are correct as of this writing.

Exhibit Surveys Incorporated
7 Hendrickson Ave.
Red Bank, NJ 07701
T: 908-741-3170
F: 908-741-5704
Note: This is not a publishing company but may be able to provide sample research papers for your review.

Exhibit Builder Magazine
Exhibit Builder, Inc.
PO Box 4144
Woodland Hills, CA 91365
T: 800-356-4451
Note: This magazine is intended for exhibit designers and producers but is of value to exhibit managers as well. It publishes an annual source directory and produces an annual convention.

Exhibit Marketing Magazine
256 Columbia Turnpike
Florham Park, NJ 07932
T: 201-514-5900   **F:** 201-514-5977

TradeShow & Exhibit Manager
1150 Yale, Suite 12
Santa Monica, CA 90403
T: 310-828-1309
Note: Also published is an annual buyers' guide.

Marketing News
American Marketing Association
250 South Wacker Drive
Suite 200
Chicago, IL 60606-5819
T: 312-993-9517   **F:** 312-993-7542
Note: This is the journal of the American Marketing Association. It includes material on specific exhibit topics on a sporadic basis.

EXPO Magazine
8016 Pennsylvania
Kansas City, MO 64114
T: 816-523-5693
Note: This magazine is the official publication of the International Association of Exposition Managers.

Figure 24-2. (*Continued*) The publications serving primarily the USA market that tend to include more exhibit marketing material appear first. These include show list publications. The publishing world is dynamic. Addresses are correct as of this writing.

Successful Meetings
Bill Publications
355 Park Avenue South
New York, NY 10010-1789
T: 212-592-6400
Note: Though primarily for meeting planners, exhibit manager material is included.

Sales & Marketing Management
355 Park Avenue South: Bill Publications
New York, NY 10010-1789
T: 212-592-6300
Note: Exhibit-specific material is included on an occasional basis.

Meeting News
1515 Broadway
New York, NY 10036
T: 212-869-1300
Note: This book is for meeting planners, but exhibiting is included.

Business Marketing Magazine
740 N. Rush Street
Chicago, IL 60611
T: 312-649-5260
Note: This is an *Advertising Age* publication that pays attention to exhibiting.

Sales & Marketing Strategies & News
Hughes Communications
211 West State
PO Box 197
Rockford, Il 61105
T: 800-435-2937
Note: The magazine includes special articles on exhibit marketing. It also produces a convention that includes exhibit-related seminars.

Creative Magazine
37 West 39th Street
New York, NY 10018
T: 212-840-0160
Note: The design and materials used in exhibiting are emphasized with other subjects.

Figure 24-2. (*Continued*) The publications serving primarily the USA market that tend to include more exhibit marketing material appear first. These include show list publications. The publishing world is dynamic. Addresses are correct as of this writing.

Business Week
1221 Avenue of the Americas
New York, NY 10020
Note: This general-interest business magazine includes exhibiting material.

Crain's Chicago Business
740 Rush Street
Chicago, IL 60611

Crain's New York Business
220 East 42nd Street
New York, NY 10017-5806
Note: These two publications include exhibit marketing coverage.

Meetings & Conventions
500 Plaza Drive
Secaucus, NJ 07096
T: 201-902-1760
Note: This publication, primarily for meeting planners, includes exhibiting editorial.

Agent & Manager
650 First Avenue
New York, NY 10016
T: 212-532-4150
Note: This magazine serves mainly the facilities management industry, but it includes exhibiting topics as they relate to that.

Amusement Business
PO Box 24970
Nashville, TN 37202
Note: This serves an important industry segment.

Association Meetings
63 Great Neck Road
Maynard, MA 01754
T: 508-897-5552
Note: The content is mainly for association managers.

Figure 24-2. (*Continued*) The publications serving primarily the USA market that tend to include more exhibit marketing material appear first. These include show list publications. The publishing world is dynamic. Addresses are correct as of this writing.

Association Trends
7910 Woodmont Avenue
Suite 1150
Bethesda, MD 20814
T: 301-652-8666
Note: The content is mainly for association managers.

Convene
PO Box 663
Ardsley, NY 10502
T: 914-693-6246

Marketing Communications
50 South 9th Street
Minneapolis, MN 55402-3118

Potentials in Marketing
50 South 9th Street
Minneapolis, MN 55402
Note: Both of these publications include material of interest to
exhibit managers.

Meetings & Conference Executives Alert
PO Box 24
Prudential Center
Boston, MA 02199-0001
T: 617-267-7151
Note: Meeting planners get more attention, but exhibiting plays a
part.

Nation's Business
1615 H Street, NW
Washington, DC 20062
Note: This is the U.S. Chamber publication, and it does include
references to exhibiting.

USAE
4341 Montgomery Avenue
Bethesda, MD 20814
T: 301-951-1881
Note: The primary audience is made up of association executives.

Figure 24-2. (*Continued*) The publications serving primarily the USA market that
tend to include more exhibit marketing material appear first. These include show
list publications. The publishing world is dynamic. Addresses are correct as of this
writing.

International Focus

Business America Magazine
U.S. Department of Commerce
14th and Constitution
Washington, DC 20230
Note: The focus is on export, with exhibiting included.

M + A Verlac GMBH
Postfach 10 15 28
Frankfurt, Germany 6000
Note: This is a key European exhibiting publisher, international in character. It works with the USA's *Tradeshow Week* on publication of the international edition of *The Tradeshow Week Data Book,* listing and describing shows around the world.

Shows & Exhibitions
54-70 Sunnyside Drive
Louden, ON N5X 3W5 Canada
Note: Content covers issues of interest with a special Canadian focus.

TWI
3190 Clearview Way
San Mateo, CA 94402

- *The TWI Calendar of International Tradeshows and Exhibitions.* It lists over 1000 exhibitions outside the USA.
- *The TWI Management Guide to Information Technology and Related Industries.* It includes exhibiting opportunities in over 60 nations, not including the USA.
- *The TWI Management Guide for International Aerospace, Defense and Space Industries.*
- *The TWI North American Calendar of Technology Tradeshows.* Listed are over 350 trade shows, broken down into almost 30 industry groups.

Note: TWI is a global leader in managing international exhibit transportation. For international readers the TWI telephone is USA 415-573-6900. Fax: USA 415-573-1727. Telex: 184841.

Figure 24-2. (*Continued*) The publications serving primarily the USA market that tend to include more exhibit marketing material appear first. These include show list publications. The publishing world is dynamic. Addresses are correct as of this writing.

Trade Shows Worldwide
Gale Research, Inc.
835 Penobscot Building
Detroit, MI 48226
Note: Over 6000 shows are listed in the current edition, of which over 3000 take place in 75 countries outside the USA. Industry breakdowns are provided, along with lists of facilities and service providers. Directories are available in printed form with options for online and computer-readable formats. Call 1-800-877-4253.

Overall Guidance Service

Dial 1-800-GoShows, Just Ask! (1-800-467-4697)
Note: This source acts as in information repository. There is no cost to get basic facts and source information. This book's author is among a group of experts who answer the questions.

Figure 24-2. (*Continued*) The publications serving primarily the USA market that tend to include more exhibit marketing material appear first. These include show list publications. The publishing world is dynamic. Addresses are correct as of this writing.

program for those interested in show management. Philadelphia's Drexel University has a degree-level program for those interested in corporate exhibit management. It also runs a continuing education program for today's corporate managers.

Courses and Course Inclusion

We risk missing campuses in what follows because there are so many and the number grows. There are both special courses and exhibit marketing inclusions in other courses. UNLV offers full course coverage. Cornell, the University of Massachusetts at Dartmouth, Washington State University, Emery, Auburn, the University of Central Florida, Perdue, and Baylor University are among those involved at one level or another. The list builds.

Academic leaders have recognized the changing face of our world. They are trying to prepare the next generation to be effective in that context. In Chapter 25 we summarize what just one futurist, Alvin Toffler, signals. There are many other signs of the times. The global village is already here. A lot of its success will depend on the trading of information and goods among those with communities of interest that have little to do with political boundaries. "Show business" is important today—and will be even more so in the next century.

Trade Union Education

College-level programs are not the only sign. Chapter 16 outlines an educational program being provided to apprentices and members of an Ontario, Canada, craft union. We point out that this program takes a step ahead of just teaching craft skills related to the proper installation of exhibits. It covers communication skills, teaches the "why" of exhibiting, and provides information allowing members to better "sell" their province and its major city, Toronto, for future shows.

Though leading edge, this is not the only craft training program.[1] What was an on-and-off second-job for many has become a highly professional activity. Just as with college-level education, exhibit-related union managers recognize the future and are preparing their people.

25

The Exhibit Medium: A Hidden Giant

There is no CNN, NBC, CBS, ABC, FOX, CBC, BBC, SKY, or another big-name network in exhibiting that is a household word in one part of the world or another. Trade shows are like individual TV or radio stations. We know about "our" shows. We know little about the rest. This is a massive "iceberg" industry but with each participant's seeing a different peak.

Because trade events and consumer expositions are tailored for people with special interests, there is little broad public knowledge about any of them. There are many presenters instead of a few meganetworks. The largest single North American producer is the Canadian-based Southtex Exhibitions. As of this writing, it creates 57 shows a year, in several different industries. Second is Reed Exhibition Companies. It is based near Boston but has offices in 16 countries plus today's region of Hong Kong. It produces 55 events a year at the moment. These are big-time operations, but few exhibitors know even the names of the managing companies.

The medium is so big, yet so segmented, that we will not attempt to list all the economic impact studies and statements. However, taken as a collective, we are into multibillions, so many that it staggers the imagination and dwarfs other media. Thus: "The Hidden Giant." You may not really care. It can be enough to know about "your" shows. However, here is background that can help you understand the *whys*, followed by instruction on picking the right shows in the maze.

A Historical Perspective

In one way or another exhibiting has been around for a while, 2000 years or more. Some older businesses have settled down to one place, not moving about any more. In old Jerusalem there is an Armenian bazaar that finally settled there at about the time of Christ. The display work is still excellent, in fact better than what many of us do today. South of that city sits a small handblown-glass company. The family owners got off the road. That was 800 years ago.

For more than 1500 years temporary trade fairs were the primary mechanism for trading goods into money and money into goods. These events were the world's banking system. It took very little time to balance currency values over thousands of miles.

Marco Polo opened the Great Silk Route from Europe to China in the early fourteenth century. Here-today, gone-tomorrow trade events popped up everywhere as the caravans passed back and forth. *Just as today, trading information was just as important as selling product.* For instance, it did not take long before Chinese oriental rug makers figured out how to design pieces attractive to European customers, based on designs they saw woven in France, Persia, and Mogul, India. That was long-distance information, and it traveled far faster than one might think.

Leslie Stroh, publisher of a trade periodical titled *Rug News,* reported an interesting aside. Hand-woven carpets and wall dividers became a common medium of exchange themselves! Design notwithstanding, traders, sitting in their tents, were able to count the handmade knots on the back of a rug, thus approximating the amount of labor required. However, everyone knew how long it took to produce whatever it was they were trading and compared to the rugs. It was an equitable system. Brass cups for spices? "Fine, but for that quantity you have to add those two rugs to even things out."

Some like to trace the start of our own trade show tradition to the fairs that emerged in Germanic Europe three centuries ago. Others argue for 1851, the first World's Fair. It was a seven-month affair that took place in London's Crystal Palace, a huge glass structure built for the show and torn down when it was over. Then came the great Paris exposition with a far more permanent reminder—the Eiffel Tower.

In the USA and Canada people point to the fur traders and medicine shows that crisscrossed by byways, trading information and goods in the eighteenth and nineteenth centuries. The medium continued to develop in the early part of the twentieth century. In the 1920s and 1930s the author's grandfather went on the road with his bedspring samples. Where to? Chicago's original Merchandise Mart for the furniture industry meetings.

Alvin Toffler's World

Fifteen years ago futurist and author Alvin Toffler wrote a classic book, *The Third Wave.*[1] He pointed out that the "first wave," encompassing all of human history up until about 200 years ago, was based on agriculture and handmade products. The "second wave" emerged because there were machines to do our work for us, helping us open whole new frontiers. The steam and gasoline engines were part of that, as well as the mechanical elevator, printing presses, telegraph and then telephone—and sewing machines. The second wave profoundly shifted the way life was lived in developed parts of the world.

The "third wave" arrived, almost unannounced, after World War II. People talked about the information explosion without realizing that we were already well embarked into an information-based age. The computer and communications sciences, and the jet engine, would change us forever again. Most people recognized that things were indeed in flux. Very few understood that these technologies were accelerating the *rate of change,* the speed of transformation. They did not see the technical, economic, manufacturing, social, and political impacts that so quickly resulted from the proliferation of information-based technologies.

People sighed about the passing of national magazines, printed in color, as that media monster, television, became prominent in the 1940s and 1950s. The next time you pass a newsstand, pause and look. You will see *scores or even hundreds* of beautifully printed periodicals. How did that happen? The technological base that allowed inventive people to create television was also there for those interested in lowering development and printing production costs.

There were product changes. Newer magazines are aimed at very specific reader interests. Even the surviving long-run magazines—*Time* comes to mind,—are not so old. They are produced in regional editions; from an advertiser viewpoint—and even with editorial changes reflecting reader interests. In *Time,* for instance, mail subscribers in the USA find special reports on how their own congressional representatives have voted printed in their copies. Editions in other nations focus on issues of interest there.

There are literally hundreds of illustrations. They all point to the reality that there is so much that is new to learn, all the time, that we simply can't do it! We are forced to pick and choose what is of most interest to us.

A parallel exists in product development. Technology has allowed even consumer products to be offered on a semicustom basis. Cars have so many options that we order what we want and the machine is assembled individually for us at the factory. Deodorant is offered in more than one scent, and in different package sizes, all under the same brand name. The same is true in business-to-business purchasing. There are highly specialized products and services now available, serving specific needs. This is a mixed blessing. Never has there been more choice. Never has it been more difficult to sort out all the options in purchasing.

Toffler pointed out, in 1980, another illustration that has yet to be introduced in any massive way, but when it does will impact on retailing—and exhibiting. During the first-wave era, clothing was custom-made by the seamstress or tailor in town. We were measured, we selected the cloth, and the garment we wanted was cut, sewn together, fitted, and adjusted.

The second wave, featuring mass-production factories, changed that. A critical cost step in clothing manufacture was the time it took to hand-cut material to measure. Machines could cut thick piles of cloth very precisely. The result: "sizes." Final adjustments could be made by the store tailor, but it was far less costly to mass-produce suits and dresses.

Here comes the third wave! Lasers can cut more single layers of fabric faster than the machine age cutters can cut thick piles to size. Computer software exists today, far more sophisticated than 15 years ago, that will allow our own measurements to become part of a database instructing the cutter. Toffler postulated on a resurgence of our first-wave neighborhood seamstress or tailor—custom-made clothing again! Pick the style and fabric and get measured. Your measurements are scanned into a computer and off "you" go to the factory via modem. The fabric, cut exactly, will be in the hands of your tailor or seamstress 24 to 48 hours later. (In 1994 this service was introduced by Levi Strauss, for its tight-fitting jeans line. In this case final sewing is also done in the factory.)

We have added a few details to Toffler's vision because we are writing 15 years later. But he is right. It will happen and save money. Several steps in the process will have been supplanted.

Why tell this story? Different industries are involved along with technologies used by each. As this application of the third wave emerges, there will be changes in manufacturing, wholesale distribution, and retailing. They will be reflected in trade shows serving those industries. This is just one application. Keep your eyes open, and, as they say, "your powder dry."

The Show Response

Alvin Toffler's fast-moving world requires specific continuing education. It also demands isolating increasingly specialized products and services. These two factors have resulted in a steady growth pattern in both the number of facilities required and the expositions mounted. Some readers may think that Toffler presented a world as he wanted it. It was, instead, a portrait of the world as he saw it and a prediction as to where it is heading. So far he is on target.

Facilities Development

In the USA and Canada alone there are over 350 exhibition facilities offering over 25,000 square feet of exhibit space.[2] The median is over 160,000 square feet. The average number of meeting rooms provided— 21. In addition, over 50 facilities in this size range are in the planning and construction phases, counting new halls, expansions, and remodeling.

Exposition Development

The provision of facilities reflects long-term growth in their use. At last count there were almost 4000 good-sized shows in the USA and Canada alone, each year.[3] By "good-sized" we mean an average of 300 exhibitors. The average space rented is about 300 square feet. There are, as well, many smaller exhibitions and facilities offering under 25,000 square feet of space.

The Show Breakdown. The more information-intensive the industry, the more it subdivides, requiring more shows. The health care fields, with over 500 shows, and computer fields, with 300, are the largest users of conventions and trade shows.

Chapter 24 readers will remember our discussion of audience shifts, especially as national shows move from one area to another. *The Tradeshow Week Data Book*,[4] points out that only about 15 percent of the 4000 larger events listed actually do move. There are three reasons:

1. A few events are so large that they cannot move! *COMDEX/fall* serves as an illustration. Too much exposition space, and in particular too many hotel rooms, would have to be set aside well in advance in any city other than where that show is now—Las Vegas.

2. Of far greater importance, however, is that a substantial number of our large events are regional and local! The gift industry, for instance, operates with over 125 large-scale buying events. The *Data Book* points to other show types as well. For instance, the *Michigan Dental Show* is on the list. Other industries, such as insurance and travel, offer regional and statewide events as well as national meetings.

3. Consumer shows that attract dominantly local or regional audiences are also on the list. The *Data Book* points out the *Vancouver
   Boat Show* as one. There are over 150 good-sized boat shows a year
   in the USA and Canada!

Exhibitor Participation.   Elsewhere in the book we estimate that
over a half million businesses participate in at least one event a year.
Another Tradeshow Week, Inc., publication examines, in detail, the
largest 200 shows taking place each year in the USA, and the largest 50
Canadian gatherings.[5] The latest data reveals that over 150,000
exhibitors participated at just these 250 events! There were almost 4
million professional visitors.

We cannot accurately measure the total impact of exhibiting on
product sales. However, the economic advantage for host cities (hotels,
restaurants, services, and so on) *is* calculated. These 250 events alone
produce an economic impact of $3.5 billion U.S. dollars in the host
cities. And, don't forget, there are thousands of smaller events as well.
It takes little genius to figure out why public and private facilities are
built for meetings, conventions, and expositions.

Knowledge Specialization Influences.   The thirst and need for
learning has influenced development of regional events. That is not all
of it. Specialized fields have emerged in many industries. Here are a
few examples:

- The "grandfather" show in the banking industry is the American
  Bankers Association meeting. Smaller, specialist meetings are now
  prevalent as well. For instance, banking professional meetings for
  those involved with communications and computers have been created.

- Retailing management serves as another illustration. The National
  Retail Merchants Association serves, primarily, those who operate
  department stores and chain specialty shops. A subgroup meeting is
  for those involved with computers and communications in that
  field. Another group and expo serves those who operate discount
  stores. There are many others, including associations and meetings
  for groups such as truck stop operators, tire retailers, and shopping
  mall managers.

- The broadcasting industry has shifted gears as well. The National
  Association of Broadcasters meeting and convention was the primary technical and management event. It grew until there were two
  parts—television and radio. A smaller event was spawned for
  broadcast executives involved with industry accounting procedures.

Then came the cable industry with its own unique problems. National and regional cable meetings are now well entrenched.

- Until the early 1980s the primary exposition and educational convention in the computer industry was *The National Computer Conference* (NCC). This huge event held annually in Chicago no longer exists! Technical specialization entered the picture. The industry as a whole was and is so fast moving that separate, specialist events were created, each nipping a chunk off of the old NCC audience and its exhibitor support. One of our large events today, New York's PC Expo, did not exist then. IBM's pioneering personal computers were just going into production. The same was true for AT&T's Unix operating system, now the focus for big shows. Apple? Just a seed then, now the focus for several shows. In that overall industry one wonders what will happen in the next few years as we tread down the broadening path of the information superhighway.

Picking the Right Show

You may be tossing up your hands thinking, "With all that's going on, how in the world do I pick the right shows to go into?" Here are some guidelines.

Your Own Company Category

Most companies fall into one of two categories. One offers products or services used in relatively few industries. The other offers products and services that are of potential value in many industries.

Special Industry Sales and Support.   From a trade marketing perspective, companies such as Miller Brewing serve narrow sectors. In the brewing company's case, we *guess* at the following:

- Large grocery store chains
- Smaller, mainly independent, grocery store operators
- Convenience stores
- Liquor store outlets in some states
- Restaurants and bars, both chain and independent
- Travel outlets—hotels, motels, train, airline, and cruise ship companies
- Resorts and private clubs of various types

Miller, like many companies, works at the franchise holder and dealer levels as well as at the corporate level. To some extent trade exhibiting aimed at these industries may be a responsibility for franchise holders or dealers. Regardless, Miller should find it easy to determine where industry trade shows work and where they do not. They know the shows or can find out easily.

There are many outfits, large and small, in the Miller category. Fishing tackle manufacturers look to sporting goods dealers of various types, chain and independent, and wholesalers or industry reps. Hotels, motels, and transportation companies know to try and reach travel tour operators and travel agencies. Gillette knows it needs to focus on trade events attracting general merchandise, and health and beauty care buyers in grocery, convenience, and drug stores. Prescription drug manufacturers want to participate at drug store meetings and medical events attended by doctors who can prescribe their products. Show picking is not a large problem.

For some, even though the product line is used in relatively few industries, there can be some head scratching. For instance, assume you market a line of commercial cleaning solvents. Who are the end users? Probably building owners, shopping mall operators, and plant maintenance organizations. There may be others, but that is a good start. You can support corporate sales or dealers by exhibiting at the shows for those end users.

General Industry Sales and Support.   For companies that produce products or offer services of value in many industries, the show selection process can appear more vexing. For instance, if you work in the computer or communications fields, the idea of drifting through *The Tradeshow Week Data Book,* perusing the descriptions of over 300 technical trade events, is daunting. However, if you decide to begin the show selection process this way and buy this 2000-page epistle and go through the entire exercise, there are ways to make it easier, as follows.

Homework and Its Applications.   Establish priorities. These should include an analysis of past sales and performance. Which industries seem to offer more near term potential than others? Another judgment is how much can you supply? If you are a midsize or small company, you may not really want to sign up a corporate elephant that will chew up your entire capability before you can "ramp up" for more production and service.

Show Type Choices.   With homework in hand, there are two fundamental types of shows to look at:

1. *Specific industry events.* If you sell to industries that have their own trade events, you will want to gather information on those shows.

See if a portion of the audience is specially interested in what you are offering. (Technology companies should be on the lookout for events that offer an audience combination: both technical staff and end-using department heads in prospect companies. At one time large-company computer and communications managers made all the technology purchase decisions. Now they work in partnership with end-using departments.)

There are no shows specifically designed for some industries. A number of manufacturing enterprises fall into this category. For instance, there are no general-purpose shows for auto, tractor, and truck manufacturers. None for tire makers or printing press builders. However, that does not mean you cannot reach these industries and companies at trade events.

2. *Cross-industry expositions.* Some of our most successful conventions are those appealing to specialists within a number of industries. For instance, let us say that you make something that is related to the use of robotic machines in manufacturing. There are shows devoted to robotics and major machine tool events. The audiences are liberally spiced with experts you can't reach at specific industry events that do not exist. Robotics experts from auto, tire, meat packing equipment, and other manufacturing industries go to these specialist events to learn and shop.

Selling to Other Exhibitors.   In industries without their own conventions, there is a logical avenue: exhibiting where your prospects exhibit to sell their wares. For instance, while there is no show specifically for tire *manufacturers*, there is an expo for tire dealers. Manufacturers are major exhibitors. There is no convention for farm equipment makers, but they exhibit at big farm shows to help sell their tractors and harvesters to end users.

Use some caution, however. Do some homework on who will be there from the manufacturer side. Frequently the exhibits are staffed by dealers and corporate marketing people, not buyers or specifiers of equipment and services used inside.

The Regional Show Solution.   The "glamour" of a national show sometimes can lead to making a mistake if your company is regional. It is all well and good to participate if that national event is taking place in home territory. Your customers and prospects will be there. However, if the venue is a half nation away or on the other coast, the audience from your area will be smaller. It can be far more cost-effective, productive, and less hectic to participate at events closer to your head office.

The First-Year-Show Warning

Elsewhere we have pointed out that the audience estimate for an upcoming convention is always an expectation, not reality. You are buying something that does not exist. However, older, more stable events are able to anticipate at least an overall audience with some degree of accuracy.

First-year events are riskier. They require more homework even if they seem attractive on the surface. What is the experience level of the producer? Has it done a lot of this sort of thing in the past and learned how to get shows off the ground? Or is the event a first-year pipe dream created by inexperienced management? What is the financial backing? It can take two years or even more for a new show to break even. What other support has emerged to help?

There is no magic bullet. However, some show production companies offer a lot of experience and have good track records. For reference, Figure 25-1 lists the top 10 trade and consumer show producers based in the USA and Canada. Some of their events are actually international, taking place in other parts of the World. Some events are pro-

---

The Top 10 Expo Management Companies

- Southtex Exhibitions   57 shows
- Reed Exhibition Companies   55 shows
- Advanstar Expositions   45 shows
- Atlanta Market Center Trade Shows   36 shows
- Conference Management Company   32 shows
- Expo Group   31 shows
- Industrial Shows of America   26 shows
- Industrial Trade and Consumer Shows   26 shows
- George Little Management   24 shows
- Society of Manufacturing Engineers   17 shows

Figure 25-1. This information was published in the *Tradeshow Week Data Book*. It reflects 1994. There are changes each year, but these companies have substantial experience. However, there are many other veteran show management companies and in-house association management groups. As noted in Chapter 25, there are almost 4000 larger events described in this publication. Within the mix of shows managed by these companies are industrial, consumer, and international events in North America and elsewhere.

duced as contractors to associations, others as entrepreneurial ventures. We point out in the legend for Figure 25-1 that there are many other experienced producers, not quite as large. You will have to ask about the experience of the show manager or association sponsoring the first-year event of interest.

We do not say, "Don't!" Just be thorough in exploration before making the choice. For instance, we were involved with a first-year event on environmental technology mounted in Vancouver, Canada. It was not produced by a company with vast experience in business-to-business trade events. It did have experience with consumer shows. The Canadian government backed the event to the extent of helping provide the educational symposium that would be presented in parallel with the expo. The producer had deep enough financial pockets to fund attendance promotion without waiting for the next check from an exhibitor. *Globe 90* worked.

It would be easier and perhaps safer for us to say, "Never participate at a first-year event." That would not be fair to you. It would not be fair to show producers. Most important, it would not be fair to potential audiences.

Our underlying message is that the medium as a whole has not changed in thousands of years. However, it is very dynamic. New knowledge, products, and whole industries emerge. Others fade away. There will always be first-year shows and those that diminish from view after a long run. You have to work hard to know when to hold or fold your playing cards. You also have to work hard to know when to gamble on what is new.

26
Retail Exhibiting to Consumers

Few readers of business books start at the beginning and work through to the end. Their purpose is not to learn everything but to use book parts to make their jobs easier in specific ways. However, the few who read this book front to back know we make constant reference to retail consumer exhibiting along with business-to-business trade shows. There is good reason for that. There is less difference and more that is alike between the two.

Jerry Lowery[1] was, without knowing it, both a futurist and a "today person." A keen participant in and observer of exhibit marketing, he said, "We worry a lot about how business-to-business sellers and their buyers respond to each other. There's nothing wrong with that. But exhibitors who need help most are those at shows for consumers." Lowery went on to present a doubled-edge sword. First, many do not know how to display and sell in the situation. Second, some do not readily accept the ground rules for participation and lose out as a result.

Consumer Show Power

In Chapter 25 we mentioned the fact that there are almost 4000 good-sized shows mounted each year in the United States and Canada. These events average 300 exhibitors each, and the average amount of space rented is 300 square feet for each exhibitor. But that is not the whole picture as there are many more smaller events as well.

Half the 4000 are "trade-only" events. The other half are at least partially for consumers, and about 400 shows are purely for retailing! There is additional data that wigwag how important these events have become over the years. The average large-scale consumer show is much larger than its trade-only sibling. Overall exhibit space at consumer shows is 21 percent higher than at a trade show, even though there are fewer exhibitors on the average. The average booth space rented is 450 square feet! And, as one might expect, the ratio of visitors to exhibitors is far higher—205 visitors for each exhibitor, compared to 26 to 1 for trade-only expos.[2]

Purchasing Impacts

The Trade Show Bureau (TSB) is the exhibit industry's not-for-profit research and education organization. It has sponsored several studies covering consumer events. One of them was of particular interest to us from a demographics viewpoint.[3] On the average just over one-half of our consumer show visitors fall into an age range of between 30 and 50 years old, with the 40 to 50 age group just a bit more than the 30 to 40 age group. That signals more buying power. In fact, one-half of the visitors have a family income of $50,000 or more. Not surprisingly, two-thirds of the average visitor audience has a least some college education, over one-third a bachelor's degree or more.

Another TSB study signals the degree to which consumer purchasing can be anticipated.[4] Seven consumer expositions were part of this study. Some 37 percent of the visitors made purchases at the events. The exit interviews showed that 59 percent had made buying plans for within one year at the shows.

The study pointed out that the average purchase was $8000. However, it went on to say that this figure was influenced by some boat sales. Thus, the study also presented a purchase range of from $70 to over $23,000. It also pointed out the *median* purchase per visitor: $66 with a range of $15 to $179.

Show Types

All shows appeal to those with special interests, both buyers and sellers. However, some are for more general interests, some for those with very highly specialized preoccupations.

More General Interest Events.   There are several categories—such areas as home, garden, computer, auto, and sports shows. These shows tend to be larger in both number of exhibitors and the visitor audiences. Big "flea markets" or "swap meets" fall into this grouping because of product diversity.

More Specialized Interest Areas. Specialist antique, art, stamp, card, jewelry, and recreational vehicle shows that appeal to smaller audiences and fewer exhibitors are very much part of the scene. The sales and exhibiting cost impacts are, however, similar to their larger-scale cousins.

Within our 2000 larger events a year, and many more smaller-scale shows, less than one-quarter are purely for consumers. Most include trade-only days or mix consumers and trade at the same time. We will address what to do about combination shows later, but this mix increases the degree of difficulty for exhibitors.

The Show Advantages

Exhibit marketing grows, a response to increasing product specialization and the requirement for both buyers and sellers to gain ever more sophisticated information. Even the most mundane of consumer products on supermarket shelves offer confusing choices—sizes, special ingredients for special uses, and so on, all under the same brand name. (Do you want the regular, "Healthy Choice," or pine forest version? Can you store the "giant size?")

Those choices are not too difficult for buyers to make. However, for virtually every other product or service offered to consumers, the confusions mount. There is simply too much choice! Some cry for the simple days when Henry Ford said something to the effect that purchasers could have any car they liked as long as it was black. Those times are long gone, and that is why shows have become increasingly important—*not for sellers as much as for buyers.*

It is at shows that consumers can learn quickly about a large number of choices within the same product family. They can winnow down options far more easily.

Business-to-Business Shows Came First

Specialization emerged first in the business-to-business community. Machine tools, computers, and all sorts of products and services that were at least semicustom became available. Business buyers had to decrease the confusion and time spent and thus costs related to making choices. Our late-century growth in trade shows started in that arena.

The second shoe followed. Companies were able to use new technologies and materials to create more highly specialized products for consumers on a very cost-effective basis. In spite of Henry Ford's early-century dictum, most new cars are now built on a semicustom basis. There are so many options that many are ordered from the factory individually. Thirty years ago one would never have thought that we would ever see the wide diversity of recreational vehicles or boats that are now available, each designed for specific uses and family situations. Home-use products from faucets to framing materials to refrigerators. Seeds and soil compounds—the list goes on forever. Arts and collectibles have become more specialized as well. Stamp aficionados do not simply collect stamps—they also look for offerings in their special-interest areas. That has always been the case among the serious, but even new collectors are well focused now.

Retail Exhibitor Problems and Solutions

The business-to-business sellers led the charge. In many cases they had no choice. Trade events were about the only cost-effective way for them to introduce their offerings! They were, in fact, reacting to buyer confusions that emerged in parallel with specialization.

Retail operations lagged behind. That is quite understandable. *Their* customers did not face the confusions until after manufacturers had begun presenting goods that were designed for specific subgroups based on new capabilities. Cars do not have to be black and don't cost any more even if pink. However, many manufacturers remain ahead in exhibiting, compared to their dealers who, in turn, exhibit to end-using customers. Here are some issues and solutions.

Audience Analysis

Many local consumer shows come along that have a good-sounding name but not much else. "The Collier County Marine Trades Association is sponsoring the show and everybody will be there." Ask yourself who and how many before plunking down dollars. Will it be a club meeting among suppliers, or will there be an aggressive attendance promotion program? We illustrate with a local association that does a whole lot better than that. However, you get the idea.

Past Performance. Show producers are likely to have information on audience in prior years. A projection of the anticipated audiences should be based on that. For first-time shows it can be more prayer than promise. You need to do extra exploration before taking the plunge.

Audience Breakdown. To what extent can the exposition producer estimate how the visitor audience breaks down? For instance, registration information in the past may provide demographic or interest information:

- *Income.* Data can include audience percent at various income levels.
- *Age.* You might also be able to learn about percents in age bands.
- *Family makeup.* Couples, single people, children—how old?—are among the questions.
- *Education.* What percents fall into which educational-level bands?
- *Housing.* To what extent do visitors live in apartments, houses—own or rent?
- *Item ownership.* Car ownership? How many and how old? The same for other big-ticket items such as computers or boats.
- *Special interests.* Data may have been gathered that signal particular audience interest percentages.

Psychographic Profile. This is a relatively new addition to the traditional types of demographic information assembled. It is unlikely that many show management organizations have gotten into it as yet. However, if you work with a major consumer product manufacturer, there may be information available there, or at the company's advertising agency.

Psychographic studies are done to reveal value systems that influence purchasing. Some people are strugglers, others are strivers. Some people are self-satisfied. There are those who are protective and don't like risk. (They are more inclined to worry about postpurchase service and warrantee.) Another group is more attracted by features than by cost or service. It is an oversimplification, but some like to ride in a limo. Others in the same income band instinctively cut grocery store coupons out of the paper. Old money or new? New clothes or 10-year-old sweaters? White wine or Kentucky whiskey? Chapters 2 and 18 discuss psychographics in context with business-to-business selling.

Audience Counting. You should find out how the audience is counted. For instance, the overall estimate may include exhibitors as well as visitors. You will have to deduct to get a clearer look at the buyer segments. Are there trade-only days? You should isolate that figure separately.

Some events use a turnstile counting system. Each time through the turnstile, click! The show uses the grand total to help promote the event the next time around. One very large business-to-business show that takes place in Europe follows that approach. Read the prospectus casually and you would think that the audience is 300,000 people; and this for a *business show?*

In this case, we probed a little deeper, and this is what we learned: First, a turnstile count was being used. Each time anybody enters the hall, no matter how many times, click! That includes delegates, exhibitors, the mayor. In this case there is a second show. For educational and public relations reasons, one show day is opened to the public for free—families, school groups, the entire city! Not a delegate is in sight. They know not to come then. Minus duplications, exhibitors, and the "public day" figure and you remain with a huge buyer audience, between 70,000 and 80,000. But that is hardly 300,000!

Many expo managers, and especially those operating larger events, have more information than they publish. We know a number of them and asked one why detailed information from the last show was not published. We knew this person's event was audited by a very reputable independent research company. There simply had to be more data than the broad-brush pap sent out! This manager's viewpoint made sense. There was no intent to deceive. However, it cost big money to print up lots of copies of the report. *Since so few exhibitors seemed to care about having the information, it was not worth it!* This executive went on to say that some exhibitors did call. They were given verbal advice, and, if desired, a photocopy of the report was sent out.

Ticket Management. The tougher the ticket, the better. That is a personal view shared by few. Take your choice:

> ME: I'd rather greet a small audience of serious buyers. Make visitors pay dearly to get in the door! As an exhibitor, that makes my work easier. There is far less sifting out grains of wheat from stacks of chaff. Business buyers attending out-of-town trade events have to spend up to $2000 or more just to be there! That creates a serious audience.

> THEM: Our "them," consumer show producers, have a lot more going on their side of the discussion. Many expos include products used by families. Visitors must come during their off-hours. Many have to bring their children along. In part, the show is also a social opportunity—an afternoon or evening out for the family at which all learn more about something that interests them. Thus, make it an "easy" ticket.

Our only true concern is what happens when too many tickets become absolutely free. Old-fashioned promoters did that simply to build numbers they could use next year to sell exhibitors. You can be overwhelmed by tire kickers who have nothing better to do on a

Saturday or Sunday afternoon. We try to help you sort out the serious later in this chapter and in Chapter 18.

Using Audience Information

Those who sell to consumers at events make a mistake by not looking closely at the anticipated audience, and making plans in light of what they learn. The best way to describe the situation is with a few illustrations. Put yourself into different sets of shoes for a moment:

- You sell remodeling services or products to home owners. You decide to participate at a local home show. That makes a lot of sense. However, the entire audience is not yours! To what extent does the anticipated assemblage include those who own older homes? Get that data, and you will improve your planning to reach those people, without bothering apartment dwellers and renters.

- You are a boat dealer. What type do you sell? Who buys *or should* buy? Is it a fishing or sail line for families with small children? Is it boats for water skiers, people slightly older with teenagers? Are your buyers among those who now have time for extended cruising? Only part of that boat show audience is for you. Plan for them. In subtle fashion discourage spending too much time with curiosity seekers. Start with learning the size of *your* audience within the total.

- You are a local office products or services company, perhaps competing against big-chain operations. Or you could be a local radio station or newspaper selling time or ad space. The Chamber of Commerce or perhaps a big-time producer such as Business Shows of America or Southex is sponsoring a "consumer" event at which end users are other local businesses, as well as that emerging market of those who have home offices. What allows you to compete effectively? Which business segments do the best for you? From a psychographic viewpoint, what kind of value system or company culture creates your best markets? How does the audience data match? Compare your profile to audience breakdown information. Planning will improve.

- You are an auto dealer, perhaps part of an area group. You will be exhibiting at an auto show, possibly with display support from your manufacturer. Two issues emerge: Most manufacturers provide products covering market segments, but there are differences. What are they? Demographics, including psychographics, are important. There is competition, as well, within a group. Can audience data tell you about who comes from where?

Four illustrations suffice. The concepts count for many others. Are you an art or antiques dealer? Are you a floral or garden supplier? Are you a catering or restaurant operator? Stamps? An aquarium and tropical fish store doing business with people at home and other businesses who use fish tanks as display? The same ground rules apply. Enough said.

Space to Rent. We've heard both expo space salespeople and exhibitors use the term *rent a booth*. What they both mean is "rent a space." Space is rented in increments—10 feet in width by 10 feet in depth (or sometimes, because of the hall, 8 feet in depth). In other nations that use the metric system, people talk about a "3-meter booth space."

The assumption is that a single space unit is expected. You are, after all, not the corporate gorilla spending megadollars on those big spaces in the center of the floor that seem to reach to the sky. But one "space" may not be enough, and that does not depend on product.

Audience analysis may signal that you need a larger space, and more booth staff members, to cover your potential. There is a time limit. For instance, let us say the anticipated audience includes 800 visitors who are potential buyers, out of, say, a total audience of 6000. The show will be open for three days, 6 hours a day, 18 open hours. If you want to reach 100 percent of your potential, you desire personal contact with 44 real prospects per hour, plus others who are not really prospects. That is pretty tough in 10 feet with just a couple of folks! For more on space needs and goal setting, see Chapter 5. *You can elect not to reach 100 percent of the possible market. Even corporate elephants back off. Just know you are doing that.*

Audience Promotion before the Show

Many retail exhibitors say, "The audience promotion? That's the show's job." We have a vision of the exhibitor sitting on a camp chair, feet propped up on a table, waiting for mobs of clamoring buyers charging down the aisles carrying sacks of money, all hand-delivered by the expo manager. Of course, that is not reality. The show has a responsibility to attract an audience, but you have a responsibility as well, mainly to help yourself.

The Exposition Program. Show executives work hard at building attendance. However, within the bounds of the interest area, it is their job to aim at everybody. Different media are used, depending upon the breadth and potential audience size.

- *Mass media.* Radio, TV, newspaper, and outdoor advertising are for broader-interest events, such as home, garden, boat, business, vehicle, and sports shows. Press releases are used too.

- *Targeted media.* For narrow-interest events, it is more frequent to use direct mail. An art, antique, or stamp show might fit that profile. There will be press releases as well.

- *Ticket promotions.* Many expo managers build attendance by distributing tickets that allow people to enter at a discounted cost or for free. We have seen discount ticket stacks on the counters of convenience stores and gas stations, for instance. We have heard of ticket distribution by high school students in their schools.

The question to surface is demographic. Are these tickets being distributed all over town or only in selected neighborhoods? What neighborhoods or malls? To what extent do people living in there match the profile of your best customers?

- *Store window signs.* This is another commonly used promotional tool. The question about demographics surfaces again.

- *Art service.* Many events have their own logo or emblem. Those with exhibitors who themselves advertise distribute reproduction-quality copies of the artwork. Exhibitors are encouraged to support the event by incorporating the logo in their own ads and promotion.

You should discuss the attendance program with your show manager in advance, and get as much detail as possible. In addition to media use, you should ask about message content. The answers to both of these questions can influence what you do yourself.

The Exhibitor Program.   Your job is *not* to help build the overall audience. Instead, your focus must be on building the audience of greatest interest to you. Your show may or may not reach the average of 205 visitors for each exhibitor we cited at the start of this chapter. Regardless, you may be overwhelmed at the show—with the wrong people.

Exhibit Surveys, Inc., based in Red Bank, New Jersey, is the nation's oldest research company that specializes in show audience and exhibitor performance analysis. Some years ago it engaged in exhaustive studies to define show types. Though these studies focused on trade-only business shows, the results are generally applicable to consumer events.

We will not take you through all of it, because it is quite an academic exercise. In summary, what Exhibit Surveys found was that there are very narrow interest events that feature both visitors and exhibitors who are specialists. Thus, there is a greater need for attendees to visit more booths. To illustrate, there is a very professional convention for operating room nurses. Most of the exhibitors provide products used only in operating rooms. The nurses visit lots of booths and do so for serious purpose. Assume, for purposes of illustration, that there is a consumer show for dealers and collectors of only nineteenth-century European stamps. Same thing.

At the other end of the spectrum are what Exhibit Surveys called "horizontal-horizontal" shows. While buyers and sellers share a general interest, there is wide diversity on both sides. New York's PC Expo comes to mind as an illustration. It is both a consumer and trade show. Because of diversity there will be a lower percentage of visitors who want to visit each booth. Home and boat shows fall into that category. The rule of thumb that emerged for participants at a horizontal-horizontal business event was that 16 percent of the show audience was interested in a single product type offered. That is pretty hefty all by itself, but it does signal that work has to be done in getting the right buyers and sellers together.

Enough of the academic! What kind of program should you put together to increase your chances for success at your show? What media and message? Here are some hints:

- *The message.* It is not enough to say, "See us at the show in booth 301." You should, as well, provide a reason to see you. For instance:

  - Learn about our new line of...
  - Compare our XYZ with the competition.

    Note: Sales come faster at shows because it takes less time for visitors to comparison shop. That is good. Get your yes or no quicker. They will comparison shop anyway.

  - Take advantage of our show-special discount on...
  - Win our extended service package without paying extra.
  - Attend our seminar on...

There is one warning. The message should be related to doing business with you. Things like "Win a Free Balloon Ride for Your Kids" (or whatever) attracts everyone, not just your prospects and good customers. The goal is to attract your own.

- *The media.* That choice is easy. Do what you are doing and include the show message.

  - *Advertising.* If you advertise anyway, include your show message.
  - *Direct mail.* If you have a customer or prospect list, send everyone a letter.

- *In-store promotion.* Place a sign on a counter that includes your message. (A sign in the window invites others as well as your own prospects.)
- *Ticket promotion.* If your event is offering tickets for distribution, take advantage of it. Ads can say, "Drop by and pick up your advance tickets." They can be enclosed with direct-mail letters. They can be placed on a counter next to a sign announcing the show and including your message.

The beauty of your own promotion is that those who respond are part of your profile of good customers or prospects. Cigar-chomping-old-time-big-time-advertising-men said, "Pick berries from a thick bush." Today's professionals come from both genders and are more likely to drink wine or sparkling water with a slash of lime. But they say about the same.

Your Program Listing. It costs you nothing extra. Yet the show program is very well perused by visitors who are serious shoppers. This "advertisement" should be far more than a list of products offered. Use the few words allowed to cite what visitors can *learn* as a result of a booth visit.

About Space, Booth, and Graphics

An area where consumer show exhibitors frequently fall down is booth—space, design, graphics, and display.

Space Location

It matters less than you think. Studies show that you can do as well in the back corner as you can just inside the front door. And there is an advantage to that back corner location. Booth clutter will decrease. The only time you want that front door space is when you are using the event mainly as an advertising opportunity. However, using an exhibit for just advertising is expensive. Visitor behavior is the reason. Here is the pattern:

- Before the show visitors will have noted down exhibits they want to visit. However, they also know there may be some surprises they do not want to miss.
- Typically, with program and floor show map in hand, attendees mark an X on the space spot of those they already know they want to visit.

- Then comes the initial cruise. They confirm the locations of those on their must-see lists and look for other exhibits that should be added to the visit list.

- From that point on, the second and even third time around, visitors will focus on exhibits that have attracted interest in the first place, before the show and on that first walk-about.

The Booth

Chapters 3 and 13 provide information on booth design and use. Featured are booth designs that focus on selling services, desktop and floor-standing designs, and small-product display designs. It would waste paper to repeat all that here. From an exhibiting perspective, the problems and solutions are the same—whether you are IBM at a computer show or Neighborhood Cleaning at a home show. With that as backdrop, here are some thoughts that may help at least some local retail exhibitors.

Visual Impression. Big companies at consumer shows set a high standard for appearance. These include auto manufacturers at those shows or large seed or flower growers at home and garden shows. However, some smaller, local exhibitors seem to lower their visual standards, in contrast to their permanent store locations.

It is surprising when retailers who make their stores and offices attractive to customers fall off the wagon at shows. We do not know why. Perhaps there may be a money-saving motive, which is natural enough. After all, the show is open only a few days. Some will say, "I want to support the Chamber, but enough is enough." That signals that they do not understand the money-making potential. Another reason could be that the space is small in contrast to the store and exhibitors do not know how to scale back their presentations.

We provide some display hints below, but as to cost and overall visual appeal, it is likely that more new people will see the booth in three days than the store in three months. Appearance creates part of image. Second, you do not have to spend a fortune to look attractive. Neat, tidy, welcoming, open. Good thinking can substitute for pouring dollars on the problem.

Display Dos and Don'ts. Keep retail display thinking in mind when you plan, but with subtle differences.

- *Be open.* Good stores use open interior display. Stay with that idea. Your booth may be only 8 or 10 feet deep, but put most of your display toward the back, leaving an open path.

- Avoid placing a counter across the front and then standing behind it. If you want a counter and would like a few items out on the aisle for display, place that counter along the side of your booth space, going into the back wall. Don't place an artificial barrier between you and visitors. An alternate is a pedestal counter, perhaps 30 inches square.
- Traditional glasstop and face counters are heavy and cumbersome. They increase drayage cost at move-in and move-out. Open shelving is better. If you display valuable items, place them on trays that can be stored at night. Most shows provide a secure area for that purpose, or excellent floor security. You can even hire your own security guard for the night, and you might even break even on cost in contrast to bringing in the big glass case.

- *Use vertical display.* Shows allow a booth back wall to be 8 feet high. Check show rules, but most often that 8-foot height can be carried out 3 feet from the back-wall line as well. (Displays closer to the aisle must be kept lower to allow visitors to see several booths at once while walking down the aisle.) Use this vertical display concept: back wall with wings in a 10-foot-wide space. If you have rented 20 feet, you can also place a wing in the middle.
- *Stay high with horizontal display.* Many exhibitors fall for the free table and chairs provided by show management. These tables are meant to be sat at, not crouched over by visitors getting a backache. The top surface should be in the range of 40 inches off the floor. Companies that offer products tested by visitors go even higher, up to 48 inches. Doing that makes it feel the same for those testing as it would if they were sitting down. In addition, it allows observers a chance to see without craning their necks around backs.

  - A few words about chairs: We do not suggest them at all, unless the space is large enough for a true conference area and there is a legitimate need for some extended discussions with visitors. There are two problems: First is that the people who will sit down will be yourself and the others who staff the booth, which will create an unwelcoming appearance. Second is that if visitors sit down, they will stay plopped far longer than you want. An alternative is a high bar stool or two, around a pedestal. You don't look as lazy.

- *Carpet.* You want it. If you own a booth, you probably purchased carpet to go with it. If not, the decorating companies that serve shows in convention halls rent carpet in several colors. Be sure to rent a pad as well. Expos that take place in hotel meeting or ballrooms may have carpet placed already. If so, take a look at it beforehand. These facilities select designs with maintenance in mind. They are multicolor and have complex designs. If your booth and display does not match, you should consider bringing your own carpet to put on top. It will wrinkle a bit as people walk on it, but your overall appearance will be far better.

- *Lights.* Lighting in all exhibition halls—hotels or arenas—is high and flat. It is designed to provide an even lighting over the entire room. Good retailers know that spots provide peak and valley lighting, a more interesting appearance that can highlight some things without detracting from others. Two or three pin lights in a 10-foot space can make you look special. It will cost extra for the electrical connection, but it is worth it.

- *Product massing.* Certain types of retailers use product massing as a display technique in their stores. It is also a method for storing inventory, saving back-store space. Booths are too small for that. Use the booth for samples only! Some retailers have gone so far as keeping inventory in a truck outside. Booth buyers, sales slip in hand, are directed to the parking lot. They swing their cars over and place purchases right in the trunk, thereby avoiding having to lug the purchase through the hall.

  - There is another viewpoint. We once met a pro who sold a home appliance on the state fair circuit in those "commerce and industry" pavilions. We asked why anyone would purchase the product, knowing it would have to be carried around all day. "It is psychological," he said. People feel the need to celebrate their attendance. Your choice!

- *Focus on what is hot.* Retailers offering diverse products are inclined to bring too much to the show. The result can be something of a confused mess. Take time to think. Bring samples of what seems to be going best plus high-markup items. You can print a handout flyer listing the rest. The booth will be far neater and more attractive to visitors.

Booth Sources. You can rent booth properties from show decorators. However, if you are going to appear at three or four events over a couple of years, it might be more sensible to purchase a new option, offered by a few custom builders, such as Custom Exhibit Systems, in Cerritos, California, that design large customer exhibits that are rented. If you want to consider purchase, read Chapters 3 and 13 and learn more about booth types. In Chapter 24 you will see a list of publications (Figure 24-2). Several industry publications also offer directories of services. Prominent in all of them are those who offer exhibits.

However, a good starting place might be the classified section of your own telephone directory. We live in the small town of Naples, Florida. Our directory, even here, lists four companies under "Display Designers and Producers."

Then there is the do-it-yourself route. You can save a few dollars if you are willing to take the time and have the talent and energy to cobble it together yourself. Our little-town telephone directory lists three companies under "Display Fixtures and Materials." There are some duplicates, but five companies are listed under "Store Fixtures." Added to that are furniture outlets and home and office discount centers that offer low-cost put-it-together systems. Exhibiting is the world of the imaginative!

Graphics Guide.   Good signs, nicely produced, help a lot. Here are some thoughts:

- Your company name may not be as important as what you offer, unless you are very well known and your name alone will attract prospects (Ford, AT&T, IBM, GE, Black & Decker).

- Higher, bigger signs are seen from farther away. Smaller signs, seen close up, should be in smaller type. Keep in mind that smaller signs can actually provide more information.

- Sign copy should pose questions, the answers to which can be obtained by visiting. "Learn about the latest in boating for young families." "Find out about new advances in framing artworks." The idea is to encourage prospects, not everybody, to stop.

- Write your copy, and then cut it by at least 50 percent! Do not try to replace conversation by putting your final messages on a sign. The goal of exhibiting is personal contact.

- Spend extra for one or two beautifully done signs that you can use for several shows. Do not make what we call "the supermarket mistake," a plethora of signs that become wallpaper not read by anybody—even those that make them.

Logistics Management

A number of consumer show exhibitors do not take time to read the rules before showing up. That is one of the concerns expressed by Mr. Lowery at the start of this chapter. Consumer show exhibitors, and especially those who are local, assume things are casual.

In most cases that is not so. You have rules for running your business. The facility has rules for running its hall. In many cases unions and insurance coverage are involved. You are not going to fight battles on the show floor and win many of them. Here are some examples:

- You object to not being able to bring your own booth into the loading dock and taking it to your space yourself, avoiding labor cost, called *drayage*. But consider the management view: even at a small event the result would be absolute chaos. The show would never open. (We watched an exhibitor trying to avoid the loading dock, hauling booth and samples up an escalator. All went well until a pile of boxes tumbled.)

- You say, "Why should I pay a union electrician to plug in a four-way box and my lights?" First, it is the law, and who is permitted to do any kind of electrical work affects insurance coverage. Second, a union electrician is an insurance policy in itself. You may know what you are doing, but what about your next-door exhibitor?

- You put a high display right out on the aisle. You are visited by the show manager who must say, "Take that down." Show rules require an easy line of sight for visitors so they can view several booths at once. Your high display would be unfair to neighbors.

There is more on this subject in Chapter 16. Business and consumer shows work alike. Our advice to both groups is to spend what you have to spend, and focus more on what you can return on that investment.

Selling at the Show

Booth visiting is different than store visiting. Because booths are small, and open, there is often a lower degree of buyer purpose when they stop. Retailers who operate shops in enclosed malls realize that "Saturday afternoon at the mall" is partly a social experience. However, they also know that when visitors actually walk into their enterprises, something has piqued their interest.

Some show visitors arrive with specific goals in mind, even lists of exhibitors to see. They are able to comparison shop far faster than nipping around town or up and down the highway. For others, the show may be more an opportunity to look at things they cannot buy, like little children with noses pressed against the glass of the candy counter. At some events, part of the audience can be made up of people who are just looking for an excuse to be out and about.

As an exhibitor, your job is to sort out the serious from curious in polite fashion, quickly. That is done by asking open-ended questions, encouraging your visitors to talk. Well-trained retail salespeople never ask, "Can I help you?" Except for those with something really specific in mind, the answer will be, "No, I'm just looking." Now what do you do? You can learn more by asking an open-ended question. "What can I help you with today?" "Why did you decide to stop at our booth?" The answers will send signals.

The conversation should continue in similar fashion, even as you show a product or two. "How is your home decorated now?" "Which type of car are you driving today?" "When did you decide to start learning more about...?" "Why have you decided to start looking for a new...? " "How long ago did you start...? "What are the most important factors in making your decision?" "Who suggested that you talk to us?"

You get the idea. These questions always include the words *when, where, why, how,* or *who* or *what.* Don't be reluctant to use them. The answers will guide your presentation. People love to talk about themselves. There is a point, however, when you should ask a "closed-end" question, answered yes or no. "Is this something you want to decide during the show?" "Should we arrange a visit after the show is over?" The answer will signal your next steps. Our own ground rule is to ask this closed-end question within five minutes.

There is much more on unique booth contact methods in this book. They appear in a training program we present in Chapter 18, and there are some hints provided in Chapter 3. However, it all boils down to developing and managing dialogue—rather than simply an outbound sales pitch from you or others on your booth team.

Literature and Giveaways

Seldom read and little remembered is the guideline about limiting literature and product handouts. Many exhibitors like to hand out brochures, instead of taking names and mailing later, which is a far better idea. The brochures land in a shopping bag and are carried home. Small giveaways land in the bag as well—refrigerator magnets and all the rest. Do these things if you wish, but do not count on much return. Studies indicate that of the literature handed out at booths, between 65 and 80 percent is not read. Little gewgaws land in a desk drawer or that "junk drawer" in the kitchen.

Solutions? If you feel compelled to give out literature, make up an inexpensive flyer for the booth. If you want to use an incentive or premium, send it later or make it related to sales follow-up—perhaps a more expensive item but perhaps of greater value to you in marketing.

Trapping Names

Shows offer a great chance to build your name list. In addition, there are hot prospects that emerge when you cannot complete the purchase process on the spot.

Large-show organizers now offer automated services to aid in this process. Visitors are provided with plastic name badges. Exhibitors are rented credit-card–type imprinters or swipe machines that produce paper copies. In the latter case, data are stored and a computer disk can be purchased later.

We are not altogether happy with these approaches at this point. If all you are doing is building a mailing list, this automated approach is fine. However, there are some accuracy problems, and booth workers tend to not make full notes at the booth for serious follow-up contacts.

At business shows, where most people carry cards, we suggest asking for one if a lead is being taken, either for mailing-list additions or personal follow-up. We advise these folks to bring a small stapler to the show. The card is then stapled to a form. (See Chapter 18 for a prototype.) Notes on what was learned and product interests are recorded.

Most consumer show visitors do not come equipped with personal cards. However, those that are serious potential buyers are perfectly happy to spend an extra moment to make sure your follow-up form is filled out correctly. If invited, some will even fill it out for you.

Some exhibitors worry about others waiting for attention during this process. Don't worry. They know what is happening and realize that at their turn you will give them full, exclusive attention as well. The visual signal sent is one of service, that you care for your customers.

After the Event Is Over

You will gasp after the closing bell and say, with delight, "We are out of here!" If only that were true. First comes packing and transporting samples, booth, and so on; the logistics. That is tough enough, but it really is the easy part.

Far more difficult, and time-consuming, will be dealing with the currency of exhibiting, those bits of paper that are orders, leads, or mailing-list additions. It would seem as though this would be pure pleasure! For one of several reasons, it is necessary to follow up on show results very quickly. If a prospect gave you a lead, it may be that this same visitor gave a competitor a lead! Don't be shocked. Many use shows to winnow down a long list of potential suppliers to one or two, but they have not made a final choice. Regardless, you want to take advantage of fresh contacts while they are fresh. This avoids backtracking, that is, going back to where you started.

Guess what has been happening while you were off at the show, even if it is in town? A pile of emergencies or "to-dos" have heaped up on your desk. Because you are now back in your more familiar environment, those jobs will become top priority. About all we can say is, "No." Your first day back at your desk should be allocated as your last "show day." Clear it out, get it going. The leads and orders are the currencies of exhibiting, representing the profit or opportunity created by several days of work and out-of-pocket expense up-front.

27

How to *Attend* a Show

"We just *have* to go to the show again this year. Maybe Bubba will get out on the diving board again, revving up his Harley." Those good old days are long gone. Bubba won't be there, or if he is, he did not ship in the Hog. In a sense that is sad. But we are part of a new, and in many ways, better world. In spite of constant gloom-and-doom news, the sun comes up brighter all the time.

This book is for exhibitors. However, you also *attend* shows to shop and learn. Thus this chapter. A more subtle reason for touching on this subject is that more and more people who visit expos where you exhibit are going through the type of exercise reported here. That is especially so for serious buyers. As a result, attending shows will encourage you to give even greater care to your own exhibit planning process—your mission, goals, preshow promotion, booth and signs, staff, training, and follow-up.

Late-Century Realities

There are several factors that influence whether people attend a particular show or stay home. They include learning, shopping, networking, looking for that next job, and gaining industry recognition. Most influential are learning and shopping. There is a price. And money, time, and what else you can do with that time are part of the price tag.

The Dollar Price. Dollar costs start, for most trade associations, with annual membership dues. There is no way to avoid that. Of course, association membership does other things for you, as well as sponsoring conventions and expos. However, for the sake of argument, let's say that membership costs you $500 a year and that the single most important reason you join is to participate in their exposition. Then there are many other expo expenses.

- *Registration cost.* Some kind of fee will be levied. The range is broad, depending on how the event is run. Does registration include "no-extra-cost" social events, or do you pay by event? Does registration allow participation at all educational seminars, or do you pay separately for each seminar you attend? The list goes on. Somehow, figure another $500.

- *Moving your body.* If the convention or show is nearby, you will drive. At today's costs, figure about 30 cents per mile, plus parking. Most times, however, you will fly. We have no way to estimate what that might require, so figure another $500.

- *Bed and breakfast.* You have to sleep and eat and move yourself around, even if a bus service is provided. Figure four nights at an out-of-town domestic show—at the *least* another $500.

We cannot be specific, but right now we are up to a minimum of $2000 out-of-pocket expense simply to attend a convention that is out of town. Less in town, of course, but there is still a high outlay. You get the idea: Whether the show is in town, in the nation, or a half world away, participating is expensive.

The Time Price.   In today's increasingly fast-paced world, there is far less time for lollygagging. Not many years ago the notion of nipping off for a week to attend a convention—on the company, of course—was easy to conjure up. The boss would say fine and maybe come along as well. Not so these days.

The event may last three days. You may get one day in the office, but for all intents and purposes, you will have invested one week of your work life. You must ask yourself what it is you want to accomplish that makes that investment worthwhile. You must also ask yourself what you would accomplish during that week were you not to attend.

You can look at the decision process from the viewpoint of the raw cost of your time. We offered a formula to do that in the budget chapter of this book. In summary, what do you earn before taxes? Add about 40 percent to that to cover typical benefits and office cost. Divide by an average of 220 workdays per year. That is your raw cost per day.

Evaluation

What kinds of problems or challenges exist in your company that might be solved, in part, as a result of attending the event? To what extent are there discussions about purchasing something new, or perhaps adding a product line? What personal, professional objectives do you have that can be reached by attending?

Review the materials sent to you by show management. Look at the educational program to see what might be of either general or specific interest. Do the same with the list of exhibitors who will be at the show.

If it does not appear in the materials sent, call the show management and find out when seminars of particular interest will be presented. You might find them clustered on one day. If so, you might be able to shorten your trip by a day. If you have a special interest in a particular product, call the exhibitor you know who might have it. Ask what they plan to display.

One of the great values in attending a show is reducing the time, confusion, and thus the cost of comparison shopping for the company, or yourself. You can see more, and meet more people in a day or two than you can over several weeks in the office. (Interestingly, exhibitors who are experienced in an industry can sometimes sense when something major is being contemplated. Normally the XYZ company sends three people. This year they are sending six. Why?)

Figure 27-1 offers a specific list of questions to ask yourself as you make a decision about whether to attend or not. It is not all-encompassing, but it can serve as a guide. The second value in answering these questions is that you can use your answers to plan your show time more effectively.

Your Show Plan

Going through the go-or-no-go decision process makes it easy to complete your actual plan of attack if the decision is "go." There are just a few added factors, as discussed below.

The Must-Do List

Seminar attendance and exhibitor must-see lists must first be placed on your planning document. There may be other items as well. For instance, you might want to schedule a private meeting, perhaps at breakfast, with a colleague or supplier. You might need to plug in a social event. You should also set aside time for a more general tour of the exhibit hall.

Decision Guide

- What are my general learning goals?

- What are my specific learning goals?

- What are my general shopping goals?

- What are my specific shopping goals?

- What are my other goals, general and specific?

- What specific seminars must I attend? (Include dates and times.)

- What specific exhibits must I see?

- What are the "next-step" requirements for exhibited products that I am interested in.

- What is the time required to attend? Be specific on dates out of the office.

- What will I miss by being away?

- What can I do while away to take care of situations back home at the same time?

- What is the cost estimate for attending the event?

- Are there other out-of-town visits that can be combined with a trip to the show? What?

Figure 27-1. Answering these questions will make your choice easier and start you toward developing your actual time plan at the show so that you obtain the best results with minimum stress and time spent.

Targets of Opportunity.   Most of those who go to a show want to take some time just to find what is new to them, things they did not plan on in advance. For instance, your first visit to the show floor should be a "cruise," with two goals in mind:

- You should locate your must-see exhibits and make an X on the show floor map. Later you can plan tours to save back-and-forth.
- During your cruise you are likely to spot a few exhibits offering products that may be of interest as well as those on the must-see list. Or companies might be offering something competitive to what you are looking for in the must-see list. Place a checkmark beside the booth position, different than your X, for must-see. Make a note, as well.

Before you cruise the floor, glance through the program listings. You might find some exhibits to evaluate by doing so, and make sure to at least glance and write notes. Be disciplined in that first walk-around cruise. For instance, if you are right-handed, start to the right and snake through the hall that way.

Which Is Where.   Your first visit to the facility should also be used to figure out where everything else is located. For instance, you may want to attend a seminar on the second day. The room number will be listed. Find the room in advance, or at least the area in which all seminar rooms are located. Conventions are pretty good about placing directional signs out front, but they can be confusing. These days, many facilities provide business centers, complete with fax machines and other services. One of your chores will be to find that location before you need it.

Personal Logistics

It takes more time to move yourself around than you think. There are large time differences, depending on where the show takes place. The sublime is a smaller show taking place at a large complex, such as the Marriott Center in Orlando. Everything is pretty much under one roof. The ridiculous is a huge show taking place in a convention center where the hotels are distant. We have waited in the bus and taxi line for over 45 minutes at Chicago's McCormick Place. Depending on the show and your situation, even registration can take extra time. If you have your badge in advance, all well and good. If not, you will spend extra time in the lobby!

Travel Planning.   Know your airports. How long will it take to get out to the airport in New York? Which airport and what time of day? If you are leaving late in the day, plan extra time to get there because of commuter crunch—rush hour slowdowns are universal occurrences in major cities in the USA and around the world. There are other issues. For instance, you may find fewer flights coming out of Las Vegas, eastbound, late in the day. If so, you might plan an extra hotel night and fly out in the morning.

We mention travel arrangements because they can impact on your show plan. For instance, assume you are attending a show at the convention center in Washington, D.C. Your hotel is fairly close and sort of "on the way to the airport." You can check out of the hotel in the morning and give your bag to the bell captain. You can spend extra time at the show and then have your taxi driver swing past the hotel so you can pick up the bag. But given the distance between the airport and the convention centers in Chicago, it is more efficient to bring your bag to the hall that morning and check it there.

You may say, "My show is nearby. I will drive." Fine, but even at an in-town event you will have to plan for commuting time, figuring out where to park, and then walking time. If you are driving to another city and are not familiar with the venue, you will spend extra time finding it, even if you have good directions!

Plan of the Day

Figure 27-2 is a prototype form for planning each day. We can almost guarantee that you will not follow it completely. However, if you fill it out in advance you will be far more likely to touch all the bases during the course of the event, ending up with a far greater sense of accomplishment.

You will find it easy to list what is mandatory from your decision list. What will be more difficult is planning time between for things like in-town travel, changing clothes, and so on. Most of us think, "That will take only a half an hour." Give yourself more. You will need it.

Plan of the Day

Date _____

- Breakfast meeting (time and location)

_____

- Seminars to attend (time and location)

_____

- Must-see exhibits (time and location)

_____

- Other daytime activities (time and location)

_____

- Evening meetings and events (time and location)

_____

Note: Allow time for around-town movement, changing clothes as required.

Time Plan

7–8 A.M. _____

8–9 A.M. _____

9–10 A.M. _____

10–11 A.M. _____

11–12 A.M. _____

12–1 P.M. _____

1–2 P.M. _____

2–3 P.M. _____

3–4 P.M. _____

4–5 P.M. _____

5–6 P.M. _____

6–7 P.M. _____

Later _____

At-Show Hotel Room and Phone Numbers

_____

_____

Figure 27-2. If you attend several shows a year, you may want to key into your computer this type of form.

Expenses

Travel related _____

Food and entertainment _____

Incidentals and tips _____

Notes

_____

Figure 27-2. (*Continued*) If you attend several shows a year, you may want to key into your computer this type of form.

28

The New Exhibit Manager

Exhibit managers come in a couple of different varieties: hat changers (the majority) and full-time professionals (either coordinators or managers).

Hat Changers

The vast majority wear lots of hats. The exhibit manager at Mitchell A. Fink Associates, the story we told in Chapter 20, has another job: He also owns the company. California's Pelican Products is larger, with perhaps 10 or so management people among 200 in the total force. We mention Pelican in Part 4. It does several shows a year, and exhibit management is a part-time job. There are "household-name" companies that do not employ a full-time professional. We know of one major hotel chain, an active exhibitor, that as of this writing, does not have one.

Hat-Changing Problems.   Perhaps the biggest problems emerge when a company does several shows during a year. The experiences remain infrequent. The management of a complex process must be accomplished with six other things going on at once. If, however, you participate at but one event a year, it is more likely that greater attention will be paid to it by all involved. Regardless, there are likely to be some knowledge gaps. We hope this book at least partially fills them.

The Corporate Exhibit Elephants

These are household-name companies that do enough exhibiting to require the services of a professional on a full-time basis, and several of them at some companies. Coca-Cola and Nabisco come to mind as illustrations. Corporate exhibit elephants are not always corporate giants. Many midsize companies do enough exhibiting to warrant a specialist manager.

More trade shows take place in industries that are very information intensive. Medicine, computers, and communications lead the way. On balance, the companies that serve these industries are more likely to employ either an exhibit manager or coordinator.

Where They Come From

Until quite recently companies grew their own:

- *Up from the ranks.* The exhibit manager at one of the USA's largest companies started in the typing pool inside of one of its divisions. This person rose through the secretarial chain and, as something of a reward for performance, was then offered a coordinator's role in the exhibit department. She continued to grow and manages the entire thing.

- *What to do with George?* A number of professionals, including your author, meandered into the medium because it was an answer to that question. Young and smart, or older and at the end of a developmental career, they landed in the exhibit function. Some did not quite fit the corporate mold for those climbing the ladder, but were quite able. For others, exhibit management has been a career reward.

- *The training ground.* A number of large companies slot their exhibit manager as a staff member in the advertising department. When that department recruited a young graduate, typically a communications major, the exhibiting was seen as a good place to start. From an internal viewpoint the incumbent simply has to get to know a lot about the company itself, that is, its products, people, and culture. At the same time, these companies work through experienced outside exhibit design and production firms. They protect the company from blunders and teach the trainee.

The ground is starting to shift. We pointed out, at the end of Chapter 25, that college-level marketing and communications courses are now being enriched with exhibit marketing coverage. There are presently even some degree-level programs offered.

What They Did and What They Do

There are also a couple of groundswells in terms of what is expected from exhibit managers. That is being driven by three complementary factors:

1. The raw costs for exhibiting have risen, along with everything else. Top-level managers know they can't stop inflation, but are more and more concerned about obtaining measurable return.

2. A few years back exhibit managers were responsible for only physical presence—booth, graphics, transport, and show setup and teardown. Other people, in other departments, were responsible for strategic and tactical roles. Exhibit managers are now starting to absorb more of those functions, in part as a result of staff downsizing in all the work groups in the company.

3. Consolidation has had an effect on exhibit departments themselves. At one time an exhibit manager worried only about shows where the company participated with a booth. These companies also employed special events managers who worried only about company-sponsored conferences for employees and customers. Even though there are distinct differences in the functions, there is enough similarity so that companies feel it is best to combine exhibiting with meeting planning.

There is no reason to think that these trends will not continue. These approaches work when skilled people are in place.

The Newer Responsibilities

What follows is a list of areas that have emerged as newer exhibit manager responsibilities:

- They provide more input on show selection, audience analysis, establishing corporate missions and goals, and determining the degree of involvement at individual events.

- They are far more involved in the development and administration of preshow promotions.

- Exhibit managers are far more likely to become actively involved with staff recruiting.

- There is more involvement with making hotel and travel arrangements for staff people.

- They also get more involved in staff training programs before and at events.

- More and more exhibit professionals get directly involved with lead and order administration after shows are over. More and more they are creating measurement systems to evaluate performance at shows.

- Frequently, corporate exhibit departments operate on "zero-based" budgets. They must at least self-liquidate costs that are spread among departments served. As a result, budget and cost management has become a far more sophisticated exercise.

- In addition, for those with events management responsibilities, there are all sorts of other jobs to be done—from meeting venue selection and negotiation to all the details involved.

The Road Warrior Stays Home

During one five-month period in the eighties, we supervised the physical planning for 18 good-sized exhibits in five months. We had to be at each and every one of them for setup and at least through the first day of the show. The show-a-week pace was tiring and confusing. At the same time one was involved with the current effort, phone calls were flying about next week and four weeks away and so on.

Exhibit managers still spend immense amounts of time walking through airports, but not nearly so much today. The reasons for that should be obvious, from the list above. A good bit of the work requires extensive internal contacts. Even though many do carry portable computers as an extension of the right hand, there is simply more need for them to stay closer to home.

Outsource Partnerships

Both companies that have exhibit managers and those that do not are moving in the direction of creating long-range relationships with outsiders. Outfits that have never had an exhibit manager realize the increasing complexity, yet do not want to add full-time staff. The already-downsized exhibit departments, adding more work, see outsource partners as cost-effective solutions.

The Exhibit Design and Production Company.   One reason that exhibit mangers, full-time or part-time, find it psychologically easy to explore this avenue is that there is already a history. Many companies have worked with "our exhibit house" for a long period. Booths built and refurbished. Signs designed and made. Storage and inventory maintained. In many cases the exhibit house has also managed transport of display materials to and from events. Frequently they have done at least the preliminary orders for show services on site, and many times have sent supervisors to the site.

With those positive experiences as a backdrop, it is no great shock that exhibit managers find it easier to think about adding functions. In some cases they ask their exhibit producer to take on new roles, even if the work is farmed out to specialists. In that context the exhibit house is acting in the same fashion as an advertising agency.

About the only difficulty we spot in doing that is that quite frequently the mark-up or commission rate for other services is about the same as that levied on shop work to cover capital and labor-intensive overhead. Rates should be negotiated.

Specialist Outsource Partners. An increasing number of outsource partnerships are being developed or are already in place. Training, transport, field service management, lead administration—even internal management and coordination services—are available from outsiders. Some companies have even hired back retired exhibit managers on a spot basis to fill holes. (There are some legal implications involved with that, however.)

- Companies that do a lot of exhibit shipping can find it cost-effective to make arrangements with a hauler, working directly without extra in-house time spent.

- Others deal on a consistent basis with outside specialists involved with the provision of on-site services. There is a good number of independent labor contracting companies that do this. For instance, one of the larger outfits of this type is I&D, based outside Atlanta. Others work through outsource managers providing a somewhat broader range of outside services. For instance, Thomas Claydon Associates, based on Long Island, will also work with exhibit builders on booth design and provision.

- Internal management help is also available. There are two levels. In one case the outsider serves in an assistant capacity internally and acts as the on-site supervisor as well. One of them, northern California–based Paddy Batchelder, has ended up with a desk and phone for occasional use within client offices and attends meetings and so on and prepares reports like an employee. At another level Akron-based Exhibit Program Management (EPM) will step in and run an entire operation. Companies such as EPM are often hired by good-sized companies that never have an internal manager.

- Lead administration is yet another area where specialist services have emerged. To provide one example, Atlanta's Executive Education & Management offers a comprehensive service. They enter leads in a database, send thank-you letters to lead givers, distribute leads to appropriate local offices, and provide tracking reports. They even offer a telemarketing follow-up service in situations in which additional qualification is required.

- Training and general consulting services are also available. For instance, our own firm has worked with one corporate client for over five years. Training runs the gamut from booth staff performance to cross-department management education. There are several others including Incomm in Chicago. From a general consulting viewpoint, show selection and audience evaluation are frequent demands.

Partner Selection and Management

Selecting an outside resource is not as difficult as hiring an employee or transferring in someone from another department who could become a stone to carry with little way out. However, it is hardly a casual exercise. You are not searching for a here-today, gone-tomorrow supplier.

Partner Selection.   There are some guidelines that help:

- To what extent can the outsource understand and work with your company culture? It is good when outside sources bring an extra, or difference, to the table. But there are limitations.

- What is the main strength of the potential partner? Because of increasing sophistication, the industry is quite segmented. But some know what they know and think they know everything else.

- How frequently will the partner have to recruit others to provide services and expertise? That is not necessarily bad. In fact, it can signal that your partner wants the best for you.

- Fee billing is negotiable up to a point. That kind of pricing can be reduced if an agreement is made for services over time. Client stability is of value. Fee billing is necessarily higher for short-term assignments since it must reflect start-up learning needs.

- Pass-through pricing must be discussed. Some expenses may be passed through to you "as is." However, your partner may face out-of-pocket expenditures for you that should be marked up. One reason is to cover the cost of administration not reflected in fees. Another is the cost of borrowing money to cover vendor bills before your bill payment schedule can catch up. If a major and costly project is in the mix, an advance payment schedule should be contemplated.

- Last, in financial management, the partner should know the level of detail required in support of bills. For many large companies the cost of processing a single invoice is high. They pass from pillar to post. The provision of a master bill, combining many small items, is of value. However, and anticipating potential audits, it may be that your company requires extensive invoice-by-invoice backup for their files. Make sure your partner knows those ground rules.

Partners Management.   At the start there is a need to sort each other out. Even a detailed letter of agreement will not accomplish that. "How do you like to work?" "How do I like to work?" "What are your expectations?" "What are my expectations?" Set aside a day or so, perhaps on a weekend, just to get to know each other better. When several people will be involved on both sides, a weekend retreat handled in very informal fashion can help. The idea is to open up lines of communication that involve a lot of mutual trust.

That type of gathering should be repeated every so often, at least once a year. Call it what you want, perhaps an "annual review." The meeting should encourage an honest expression of views and concerns *on both sides.* Both have to think of the relationship as a partnership, not a standard client-vendor yes-no, change-that, add-this kind of association. The objective is to avoid one group's taking advantage of the other, perhaps without realizing it. Sharing works far better than challenging.

- *Providing information.* To make partnerships work, there has to be a fulsome sharing of information. If you are the outsource, you must be willing to share with your client a lot about what else you are doing, and even include a bit of your own profit picture. We know of many times when a big corporate client is very willing to help out a smaller but valued outsource during tough times. The small outfit has to be willing to admit what is going on.

  It works in reverse. There are moments at which the outsource should know confidential information. It will aid in the production of better work at lower cost with less wheelspin. It can also lead to less discouragement. "Why do they want us to do that? It makes no sense." It may make perfect sense if the outsource knows more background. In some cases, for instance, we have signed nondisclosure agreements, happily, enabling contacts to tell us more.

- *Job process reporting.* This shoe is one worn by the outsource. Clear communication is the goal. *Very* short, easy-to-read reports are needed—some just a quarter-page long. For instance, we use a "meeting report" or "call report" system. These are the first-done jobs, right after the meeting or call, regardless of task emergencies. They cite subject, decision, or direction in telegraphic form. In the event of missed communication, the correction will be quick and painless.

- *Job results reporting.* This is the other shoe, and it falls to the client. Outcomes should be reported to the outsource quickly. When all has gone well, that happens in fast fashion, or should. However, there are times when things don't go quite as planned. Some clients will tend to hold back, letting wounds fester. If the partnership is a good one, the first call should be to the outsource. "Wow, have we got a problem!" In some cases the outsider can create a fast fix, if given the chance. In all cases future work will be better.

The New Manager

Exhibiting is not really rocket science. However, there are complexities for those who want the most return on their investment.

Whether you are a part-time exhibit manager or a full-time professional exhibits and events manager, you are not managing "an exhibit" or "an event." It may seem that way because each of these seems to have a beginning, middle, and end. However, that is not the case. What you are managing is a work process, very much like a plant or sales manager or any other professional who is responsible for a part of a company's success. We hope we have helped you do this one better.

Notes

Note: Readers will find a number of references to Trade Show Bureau (TSB) studies in book text and chapter notes. Just prior to publication that key organization changed its name to the Center for Exhibition Industry Research (CEIR). Its new address appears on pages 334 and 336.

Chapter 1

1. The *Harvard Business Review* article was researched and written by Thomas V. Bonano and appeared in the 1983 January-February issue.
2. Trade Show Bureau Study Number MC26. Two waves of research were conducted in 1985 and 1991 by Dr. Gary Young, professor of marketing at the University of Massachusetts at Dartmouth, Mass.
3. The late Jerry Lowery, a renowned exhibit, show, and arena manager, expressed the conviction that retailers exhibiting at their hometown shows need more help than anyone.
4. Over a half dozen Trade Show Bureau–sponsored studies include evidence that booth visitor memories consist largely of their conversation with exhibit staff people. Several of the studies were done for TSB by Exhibit Surveys Incorporated, the industry's oldest independent research organization.

Chapter 2

1. Jeff Tanner, research director and associate professor of marketing, Hankamer School of Business, PO Box 98007, Center for Professional Selling, Baylor University, Waco, TX 76798-8007. Tanner cites research industry value system indicators for consumers in clusters that range from "strugglers" to "strivers," eight in all. The application of psychographics to business selling lags behind, but the same concepts are being applied more and more.
2. Our estimate is based on research projects implemented by Exhibit Surveys Incorporated that cover a quarter century of experience. It is the nation's oldest commercial firm specializing in exhibit research. Its address appears as part of a list of selected exhibit industry associations, publications, and reference sources on page 338.
3. Ibid. This is our analysis of many Exhibit Surveys Incorporated studies.
4. The Center for Exhibition Industry Research (formerly The Trade Show Bureau) is the industry's not-for-profit research and education arm, supported by industry associations and corporations. A continuing study (TSB SM20 is most recent) identifies the cost of an exhibit contact. The cost per

visitor reached at a show is compared to the cost of an office call as calculated by the Cahners Advertising Research Reports organization. Over the years costs increased for any type of person-to-person sales contact, but exhibit contacts remained less costly, by about $100 each, for over a decade.

5. Sandra Smith, president of Seattle-based Practice Development, Inc., illustrates what can happen during those last few hours of a show. Her company, offering physician groups educational and marketing services, stayed "open and ready to go" right to the end of an event. She said, "Many other exhibitors had already started taking down their booths when two different prospects we had seen briefly early in the show came back to the booth and gave us our best sales leads." Smith reported that in both cases the prospects had taken extra time to think and had come back when they were sure of their interest.

6. Among the companies that have used this procedure is Diebold, Inc., the ATM and bank safe manufacturer. Their long-time events manager, Jerry Bryan, said, "When our sales folks do this, and it's something of a 'free' sales call, they ask *why* the customer will attend. The answers give us clues as to what is of interest in the industry."

7. International Exhibitors' Association meeting, August 1–4, 1994, held in Chicago.

8. Ms. Connie Akin, CEM (certified exposition manager), trade show manager, Produce Marketing Association, 1500 Casho Mill Road, Newark, DE 19714.

9. Michael Muldoon, president, Convention Management Group, 3918 Prosperity Avenue, Suite 102, Fairfax, VA 22031.

Chapter 3

1. Cost ranges were prepared with input from industry suppliers and in particular the Joan Carol Design & Exhibit Group. With its head office located at 7363 Old Alexandria Road, Clinton, MD 20735, near Washington, D.C., it is one of the USA's largest designers and distributors of portable and near-custom displays. That company also has provided pen-and-ink art illustrations for this book, both for this chapter and Chapter 13.

2. The addresses of the publishers are among those cited in publications listed in Chapter 24, Figure 24-2.

3. Dottinger Design is located at 20 Passaic Avenue, Pompton Lakes, NJ 07442. It is a leader among a number of custom exhibit builders that have added design capabilities based on the use of already-manufactured frames to traditional wood-based fabrication methods.

Chapter 4

1. Trade Show Bureau Study Number MC-20.

2. The industry pioneer is Exhibit Surveys, Inc., based in Red Bank, New Jersey. Another is Executive Education & Management, from Atlanta, Georgia.

3. There are specialist training companies that focus on team building. We suggest and use Rick and Theresa Torseth's Triad Partnership, based on Vashon Island, outside of Seattle, Washington.

4. The *Tradeshow 200,* published by Tradeshow Week Publications.

5. Trade Show Bureau Study Number SM-22.

6. Show directories differ in the extent to which they provide information about each show, ranging from a name and address list with show dates shown, to far more comprehensive descriptions. *The Tradeshow Week Data Book,* about 2000 pages long, makes an effort to provide fulsome information about shows listed.

7. Trade Show Bureau Study Number AC-23.

8. Exhibit Surveys, Inc., based in Red Bank, New Jersey.

Chapter 5

1. The seminar was led by Ms. Connie Akin, CMP, exhibits manager at the Produce Marketing Association, Newark, Delaware; Mr. Michael Muldoon, president of the Convention Management Group, Fairfax, Virginia; and this writer.

Chapter 6

1. A study reported in 1994 by the Institute for the Study of Business Markets at Penn State's Smeal College of Business Administration makes the following points. Over $\frac{1}{3}$ of the businesses surveyed (36 percent) said they participate at shows primarily to develop new prospects. The second largest group, 15 percent, exhibit primarily to sell new products or open up new markets. General support of selling activities and the enhancement of current customer relationships were cited as primary goals by 14 and 13 percent, respectively. The authors were Valerie Kijewski and Eunsang Yoon from the University of Massachusetts, Lowell and Gary Young, University of Massachusetts, Dartmouth.

2. "Education" or "public days" are sometimes part of an audience count. That is especially true for some very large international shows based in the USA or in other nations. For instance, an every-four-years telecommunications show in Geneva, Switzerland, invites the community in for one day, for public relations reasons, as an educational experience. The count for that audience should be deducted for purposes of projecting space and staff needed for prospecting.

3. Margit Weisgal, from the Sextant Communications exhibit training and consulting group, conducted an experiment. She placed an empty bowl at

the far end of a counter with nothing at all nearby, not even a sign promoting some sort of prize drawing. Two days later there were almost 100 business cards in the bowl. None of the names matched with any of the actual leads taken.

4. The Trade Show Bureau studied relative sales efficiencies. On the average a salesperson working in the field will contact four to five potential customers in a day. At a booth those numbers are reached in one hour (TSB Study Number MC14).

5. The close ratio for show leads was studied by the Trade Show Bureau (TSB Study Number SMRR 18). Companion research (TSB Study Number SM20) provides data comparing the number of calls required to close sales using traditional methods and methods that start with a booth lead.

6. Audience agenda information appears in composite data released by the Trade Show Bureau, compiled by Dr. Alan Konopacki at Incomm International.

Chapter 7

1. One Fortune 100 company runs its exhibit freight as part of a huge product delivery operation. It is difficult to sort out what exhibit costs are in contrast to the rest. This company runs several hundred shows a year, serving all from a midnation warehouse. We suggested storing exhibit properties on a regional basis, in exhibit houses, where they could be refurbished and changed as needed. The transport costs, for the company, would be reduced. The exhibit budget? Up.

2. You may have a "feeling" about average compensation, benefits, and office backup expense for the kind of people involved with exhibits. If not, talk to a responsible person in your personnel department. Explain your motive, and most times an estimate can be provided without violating what otherwise might be considered personal employee or corporate privacy. The figures will be used as a guide, not something more specific.

Chapter 8

1. For those not familiar, many trade magazines operate a reader service. Ads in the periodicals are numbered. At the end of the magazine, a card is inserted. Readers circle the numbers of the ads that have attracted their interest. The names are passed on to the advertisers so that additional information can be provided. The term *bingo card* has emerged covering this activity.

When we get these advisories, we call the periodical and ask, "How many advertisers did this person circle on the card?" If the answer is five or more, we still respond but with a note to ourselves that nothing will likely emerge. Those who circle but one or two, perhaps competitors, illustrate specific product interest. For the others, do a little and sit back!

2. One we have worked with is Executive Education & Management, 1140 Hammond Drive, Suite A-1295, Atlanta, GA 30328. In addition to telemarketing itself, it provides exhibit-related direct-mail fulfillment services, research, and sophisticated management reporting. It even offers an off-the-shelf exhibit marketing management computer software package.

Chapter 9

1. One failure in this regard is that ad agencies do not have a handle on "ratings" for shows. It is not hard to do, but nobody has done it in broad scale. That is probably a reflection of a lack of demand. As much or more money is spent for exhibiting as in any other medium, however, the costs are diffused and less apparent.

2. Here is a real-world illustration. One company, offering construction and teardown services, used a baseball-pitching contest at its booth to attract visitors—complete with a "speed gun." Over half of the buyers were female, not as much interested in how fast they could throw the ball as they were in learning about services and costs. Unfortunately, the booth became the "boys night out."

Chapter 11

1. Thomas E. Fitzgerald is controller, operations and engineering, marketing communications, for the Amdahl Corporation. This company provides large-scale computer systems on a worldwide basis. Fitzgerald is the firm's exhibits and special events manager, and he uses PC technology every day in his job.

2. Mary Jo Mendell is exhibits and events manager for A.C. Nielsen, the research giant and a company of The Dun & Bradstreet Corporation. With just one assistant, she plans and implements between 25 and 30 events per year.

3. Mitchell A. Fink, president, Mitchell A. Fink Associates, 375 South End Avenue, Suite 35E, New York, NY 10280. The firm provides consulting, implementation, and continuation services on the use of automation.

4. The program was created by Executive Education & Management, based in Atlanta.

Chapter 13

1. See Chapters 2, 18, and 26 for more on psychographic implications, that is, value systems that impact purchasing decisions.

2. In this case the exhibit design selected was from Gallo Displays, 1260 East 38th Street, Cleveland, OH 44114.

3. The Joan Carol Design & Exhibit Group head office is located at 7363 Old Alexandria Road, Clinton, MD 20735.

4. Displaycraft is located at 5060 27th Avenue, Post Office Box 5663, Rockford, IL 61125-0663.

5. The Access TCA head office is located at One Main Street, Whitinsville, MA 01586. It also operates an office and production facility in Atlanta, Georgia.

6. The Dottinger Design Corporation is located at 20 Passaic Avenue, Pompton Lakes, NJ 07442.

7. Edward Jones, president, Executive Education & Management, 1140 Hammond Drive, Suite A-1295, Atlanta, GA 30328.

8. Al Niño L. Ticzon, Ideas, 2375 Button Gwinnett Drive, Suite 300, Atlanta, GA 30340.

9. The Dottinger Design Corporation.

10. Charles Price Associates, 200 West 58th Street, Suite 10E, New York, NY 10019. There is a second office and studio in Wainscott, New York.

11. George Parrish, Nova Productions, 240-B South Whisman Road, Mountain View, CA 94041.

Chapter 14

1. Margit Weisgal, president, Sextant Communications, 14354 Rosetree Court, Silver Spring, MD 20906.

Chapter 15

1. The figure is based on a 3M study done in the 1980s. Most would agree that today's reality is more than was the case at that time.

2. We are not events experts. Much of the information in this chapter was provided by Theresa Bellinghausen-Torseth, from Vashon Island, Washington—a Seattle suburb. She is a graduate of the School of Hotel Administration at the University of Washington. She worked in various capacities at major chain hotels. Later she ran her own events management company working with Fortune 500 companies.

3. Bellinghausen-Torseth.

4. Ibid. Bellinghausen-Torseth produced the event for Jansport.

Chapter 16

1. Fred Buonacorsi, director, Trade Show Division, CF MotorFreight, 4723 West Hacienda Street, Las Vegas, NV 89102.

2. Edward J. Laub, president, Hoffman-Allied, 465 State Highway 17, Ramsey, NJ 07446.

3. Darlene Lane, Midwest and East Coast Sales Manager, Relocation Systems (NorthAmerican), 500 South Hacienda Boulevard, City of Industry, CA 91747.

4. We suggested a display concept change to this exhibitor: Reduce the number of actual granite kitchen centers displayed to one, showing the others with photographs. Over-the-road hauling was not the only place where sticker-shock would surface. Since in-hall drayage is billed on real weight, this exhibitor was facing a husky show service bill as well.

5. Michael Yorke, business representative, Carpenters and Allied Workers Union Local 27, 64 Signet Drive, Toronto, Ontario M9L 1T1 Canada.

6. *TradeShow & Exhibit Manager,* vol. 9, no. 4, August/September 1994.

Chapter 17

1. Muldoon is president of Convention Management Group, based in Fairfax, Virginia. It manages conventions and trade shows for a number of associations.

2. Akin is the national show manager for the Produce Marketing Association, based in Newark, Delaware.

3. Briefly, psychographics is the study of the impact of value systems and company culture on purchasing. For more on psychographic implications, see Chapters 2 and Chapter 18.

4. For this type of item, check your local sporting goods store. If you get a blank-stare response, and you should not, companies such as Recreational Equipment, Inc. (REI), based in Sumner, Washington, can serve you on a mail-order basis. REI is an international seller of sports equipment.

Chapter 18

1. Catherine Audi's store is Too Too Oh 37, 22037 Michigan Avenue, Dearborn, MI 48124.

2. New Jersey's Fairleigh Dickinson.

3. See Chapter 2, endnote 1. Professor Tanner is very interested in exhibit marketing. In part, that results from the fact that his father was long involved in exhibit management with the Amdahl Corporation.

4. Dr. Fatone's practice is located in upstate New York, in the city of Troy.

5. Dr. Price's practice is based in New York City, in the Wall Street area. He treats people who spend much time on their feet, including stock exchange floor brokers.

6. Dr. Carr's practice is located in Naples, Florida. Patients also include younger, healthy people who spend lots of time on their feet such as bank, real estate, and restaurant employees.

Chapter 20

1. Mitchell A. Fink Associates, 375 South End Avenue, 35E, New York, NY 10280.

2. The exhibit company was Alan Sitzer Associates, then based in New York City, and Research Triangle Park, Carrboro, North Carolina. Subsequently, the New York office was closed. The designer and producer was Cindy Spuria, based in North Carolina.

3. Fink, Amdahl Corporation's Thomas Fitzgerald and this writer coauthored a two-year series of columns, "The Computer Corner," for the International Exhibitors Association journal, *IdEAs*. Fink is expert at developing local area networks and custom lead distribution systems.

Chapter 21

1. The publisher was The Confederation of German Trade and Exhibition Industries (AUMA). Write to Ausstellungs-und-Messe-Ausschuss der Deutchen Wirtschaft e.V. (AUMA), Lindenstraße 8, D-50674 Köln, Deutchland. It was edited by Dr. Peter Neven and Mathias Wüstfeld. Telephone (in Germany): 0221-20907-0.

2. An interesting general interest article on the Hanseatic League appeared in the USA's *National Geographic* magazine in October 1994 (vol. 186, no. 4). It was written by Edward Von Der Porten and included photographs by Sisse Brimberg. Map by the NGS Cartographic Division.

3. The librarian is Eugene Vandrovec, Coordinator, International Visitors Program, International Statistical Programs Center, the Department of Commerce, U.S. Bureau of the Census, Washington, DC 20233. At this writing the library is being moved to a new location. We are unable to provide its new customer service telephone number. However, you can contact the library through the U.S. Department of Commerce in Washington.

4. See Chapter 24, Figure 24-1, for address information.

5. Stroh is the publisher of *Exporter Magazine*, 34 West 37th Street, New York, NY 10018. Telephone 212-563-2722. He has long experience in trade and exhibiting internationally.

6. The U.S. and Foreign Commercial Service, U.S. Department of Commerce, International Trade Administration. Our source is Ann H. Watts, Director, Corporate Events Division, U.S. Department of Commerce, Export Promotion Services, Room H2114, Washington, DC 20234. At this writing the office telephone is 212-482-6029.

7. Our primary information source on Chamber of Commerce services was Lonnie P. Taylor, Director of Senate Liaison, Office of Congressional and Political Affairs, U.S. Chamber of Commerce, 1615 H Street, NW, Washington, DC 20062-2000. Mr. Taylor served at a high level in the U.S. Commerce Department before joining the Chamber.

8. David C. Bowie, Deputy Director, Office of Export Promotion Coordination, U.S. Department of Commerce, International Trade Administration, Room 2003, Washington, DC 20230.

9. Stephen J. Berry, President, Logistics Management Incorporated (TWI), San Mateo, CA 94402. Telephone 415-573-6900.

Chapter 22

1. The acronym EPCOT means "Experimental Prototype Community of Tomorrow." Though this and government-sponsored World's Fair developments around the world are mainly aimed at consumer audiences, there are always behind-the-scenes programs for business leaders who want to share and trade.

2. The advertising agency was Young & Rubicam. Its primary manager for Colgate International at the time was David M. Sable, Executive Vice President, Y&R, 285 Madison Avenue, New York, NY 10017-6486.

3. Our information source was Ms. Sylvia Phua, Director, Corporate Affairs and Business Development, Pico Art International PTE Ltd., Pico Creative Centre, 20 Kallang Avenue, Singapore 12233. Telephone (65) 290-0100 and Fax (65) 290-5771. The company offers a broad range of exhibitor services.

Chapter 23

1. *Do's and Taboos Around the World,* the Parker Pen Company, 1985, can be obtained by contacting the Parker Pen Company, Public Relations Department, PO Box 1616, Janesville, WI, 53547 USA. It can also be obtained through Parker Pen's offices in Newhaven, East Sussex, England; Don Mills, Ontario, Canada; Miami, Florida, USA; and Chippindale, New South Wales, Australia. The book may be ordered through your book shop. The publisher: The Benjamin Company, One Westchester Plaza, Elmsford, NY, 10523. The order code is ISBN 0-87502-164-6 for the softcover. The hardcover edition is ISBN 0-87502-163-8.

2. Mr. Barry's company is TWI, 3190 Clearview Way, San Mateo, CA, 94402 USA. (Tel: USA 415-573-6900. Fax: USA 415-573-1785) It has other offices in New York, Los Angeles, Dallas, Ottawa, Canada, and London, England. It has decades of experience in shipment of exhibit freight to virtually all countries in the world, and for shipment of exhibit freight from those countries to exhibitions in the USA.

3. *IdEAs,* July 1994.

4. *Tradeshow & Exhibit Manager,* vol. 8, no. 5, October/November 1993.

5. *Exhibit Builder Magazine,* vol 10, no. 6, July/August 1993.

6. Pelican Products is located at 2255 Jefferson Street, Torrance, CA 90501. The telephone number is USA 310-328-9910.

7. Mr. Berrie's company was started in 1963 with an investment of $500 in a garage in New Jersey. In 1984 it went "public."At that moment its sales were $100 million a year, and it continues to grow today, worldwide. It creates and markets *impulse gift* items, including "the Trolls" and products licensed by professional sports organizations, including Major League Baseball and the National Football League in the USA.

   Mr. Berrie's remarks were first printed in the newsletter of The Center for Professional Selling, Hankamer School of Business, Baylor University, Waco, TX, vol. 2, no. 4. It was published in 1994. The review board was composed of Larry Chonko, Ph.D. and Jeff Tanner, Ph.D.

8. *Beijing Review,* vol. 37, no. 11, March 14–20, 1994.

9. Mr. Zhao Weiping, Exhibitions General Manager and economist, China International Exposition Centre, 6 East Beisanhuan Road, Chaoyang District, Beijing 100028, People's Republic of China. Telephone: 8614664433. Fax: 8614676811.

10. Ibid: Contact the China Council for the Promotion of International Trade (CCPIT) for information or a list of expositions they organize. The organization's address is the China International Exhibition Centre, 6 East Beisanhuan Road, Chaoyang District, Beijing 100028, People's Republic of China. Telephone: 8614664433. Fax: 8614676811.

Chapter 24

1. The program described in Chapter 16 was created by the Carpenters and Allied Workers Union Local 27, 64 Signet Drive, Toronto, Ontario M9L 1T1 Canada. We point out that while leading edge, this program does not stand alone. One of the pioneering programs for craft workers was developed in Detroit. Among others, the USA–based Teamsters Union, and especially its Chicago Local, has been involved with development programs of various types for a number of years.

Chapter 25

1. *The Third Wave* was first published by William Morrow & Co., New York, in 1980.

2. Information comes from the latest edition of the *Major Exhibit Hall Directory,* published by Tradeshow Week, Inc. It reflects data in 1994.

3. Tradeshow Week's latest *Tradeshow Week Data Book* is our source. It reflects 1994 information.

4. Ibid.

5. This publication is Tradeshow Week's *Tradeshow 200*. The most recent edition reflects 1993 data. There are changes each year, but the fundamentals remain the same.

Chapter 26

1. Mr. Lowery was a highly regarded exhibition industry expert. He was first a product manager, then a corporate exhibit manager. He went on to become a show manager. Finally, he was a big-league executive in the management of facilities in which shows take place, all of this before his untimely passing while still in his fifties. He was president of the Albert Thomas Hall in Houston. Then he was the first president of what was later named the Javits Convention Center in New York City. He went on to become the first president of Washington State Center in Seattle. His last assignment was as the first president of the new convention center in Hong Kong.

2. *The Tradeshow Week Data Book.* The information presented reflects 1994 data. There is a long-term slow growth pattern, but the relationship between business-to-business events and consumer shows is pretty stable.

3. Trade Show Bureau Study Number AC27A. For the address and telephone number of the bureau, see Chapter 24, Figure 24-1.

4. Trade Show Bureau Study Number AC27B.

Index

About the Author

Edward A. Chapman, Jr. founded Sextant Communications, an exhibit marketing, training and consulting firm. A former Exhibits Manager for AT&T, he created its Exhibits Management System. He is a frequent contributor to trade journals and is a recipient of the International Exhibitors Association's Chairman's Award for distinguished service to the industry.